METS
JOURNAL

D1560445

Year by Year & Day by Day with
the New York Mets Since 1962

Mets
JOURNAL

JOHN SNYDER

For further information, contact the publisher at:

Clerisy Press
PO Box 8874
Cincinnati, OH 45208-0874

www.clerisypress.com

Library of Congress Cataloging-in-Publication Data

Snyder, John, 1951–
    Mets journal : year by year & day by day with the New York Mets since 1960 /
        by John Snyder.
            p. cm.
        ISBN-13: 978-1-57860-473-9
        ISBN-10: 1-57860-473-7
        1. New York Mets (Baseball team)—History—Juvenile literature. I. Title.

    GV875.N45.S63 2011
    796.357'64097471--dc22

                              2010051445

Distributed by Publishers Group West
Edited by Donna Poehner
Cover designed by Steven Sullivan and Scott McGrew
Interior designed by Mary Barnes Clark

Front cover photo courtesy of WikiCommons. Photo by Metsfan84 (Citi Field during
    the first regular season game at the ballpark. 4/13/09.)
Back cover photo of David Wright courtesy of Aaron Doster

About the Author

John Snyder has a master's degree in history from the University of Cincinnati and a passion for baseball. He has authored more than fifteen books on baseball, soccer, hockey, tennis, football, basketball, and travel and lives in Cincinnati.

Acknowledgments

This book is part of a series that takes a look at Major League Baseball teams. The first was *Redleg Journal: Year by Year and Day by Day with the Cincinnati Reds Since 1866*, the winner of the 2001 Baseball Research Award issued by *The Sporting News* and SABR. That work was followed by *Cubs Journal: Year by Year and Day by Day with the Chicago Cubs Since 1876*, *Red Sox Journal: Year by Year and Day by Day with the Boston Red Sox Since 1901*, *Cardinals Journal: Year by Year and Day by Day with the St. Louis Cardinals since 1882*, *Indians Journal: Year by Year and Day by Day with the Cleveland Indians Since 1901*, *Dodgers Journal: Year by Year and Day by Day with the Brooklyn and Los Angeles Dodgers Since 1884*, *White Sox Journal: Year by Year and Day by Day with the Chicago White Sox Since 1901*, *Angels Journal: Year by Year and Day by Day with the Los Angeles Angels Since 1961*, and *Twins Journal: Year by Year and Day by Day with the Minnesota Twins Since 1961*. Each of these books is filled with little-known items that have never been published in book form.

Greg Rhodes was my co-author on *Redleg Journal*, in addition to publishing the book under his company's name Road West Publishing. While Greg did not actively participate in the books about the Cubs, Red Sox, Cardinals, Indians, Dodgers, White Sox, Twins, or Angels he deserves considerable credit for the success of these books because they benefited from many of the creative concepts he initiated in *Redleg Journal*.

The idea for turning *Redleg Journal* into a series of books goes to Richard Hunt, president and publisher of Emmis Books and its successor company Clerisy Press, and editorial director Jeff Heffron.

And finally, although they should be first, thanks to my wife, Judy, and sons Derek and Kevin, whose encouragement and support helped me through another book.

Contents

NEW YORK METS DAY BY DAY

The National League's Abandonment of New York and the Birth of the Mets

The Mets have become a New York institution, but the franchise would never have come into existence had two other New York institutions not abandoned the city for California. In 1957, the unthinkable occurred as the Brooklyn Dodgers left for Los Angeles and the New York Giants for San Francisco. The Giants had been a National League franchise since 1883. The Dodgers were formed the same year with a team in the minor league Interstate League. A year later, the Dodgers joined the American Association, an organization that existed from 1882 through 1891 as a major league to compete with the NL. The Dodgers moved to the more prestigious National League at the end of the 1889 season. The league had a monopoly as the only major league in baseball from 1892 through 1900. That situation changed with the creation of the American League in 1901. The Yankees became New York's third major league in 1903 by joining the AL.

From 1947 through 1957, New York's three major league teams dominated baseball. During those 11 seasons, there were 66 World Series games played. Of those, 53 were played within the confines of New York City. Of those 53, 45 involved two New York teams. The Dodgers and Yankees met in the Fall Classic in 1947, 1949, 1952, 1953, 1955 and 1956 and the Giants and Yankees in 1951. In addition, the Dodgers and Giants had formed one of the greatest rivalries in all of sports, and there were certainty the best in baseball.

However, fans were not attending the games of the two National League clubs in numbers sufficient to satisfy Dodgers owner Walter O'Malley and his Giants counterpart, Horace Stoneham. The 1951 season was an early warning sign. The Dodgers held a comfortable 13½-game lead over the Giants in August, but by the end of the 154-game season, the two clubs were tied for first place to force a three-game playoff to decide the NL pennant-winner. The Giants won the first game and the Dodgers the second to create a winner-take-all third game. Trailing 4–1, the Giants scored four runs in the bottom of the ninth, the last three on a home run by Bobby Thomson, to win 5–4. Despite the presence of two New York rivals, the game drew only 34,320 to the Polo Grounds, which held 56,000. With the Yankees as their opponents, none of the three World Series games at the Polo Grounds were sellouts.

The Dodgers and Giants were involved in another tight pennant race in 1952, with the Dodgers winning by 4½ games. Yet the home attendance figure for Dodgers games was 1,088,704, a sharp drop from 1,807,526 just five years earlier in 1947. The Giants attendance had declined from 1,600,793 in 1947 to 984,940 in 1952.

As Dwight Eisenhower took the oath of office as the 34th President on January 20, 1953, Major League Baseball had 16 teams in the same 16 locations they'd occupied since 1903. The National League lineup included Boston, Brooklyn, Chicago, Cincinnati, New York, Philadelphia, Pittsburgh and St. Louis. The American League had teams in Boston, Chicago, Cleveland, Detroit, New York, Philadelphia, St. Louis and Washington. It was obvious to nearly everyone that Boston, Philadelphia and St. Louis could support only one baseball team. It was also becoming increasingly apparent that three teams in New York was one too many.

Aging ballparks were also a problem. The Indians played in the "newest" stadium in the majors. Municipal Stadium in Cleveland opened in 1931 as a multi-purpose facility with 80,000 seats and wasn't conducive to watching baseball. Yankee Stadium opened in 1923. Every other major league team played in a facility built between 1909 and 1915. The Polo Grounds in Manhattan had served as the home of the Giants since 1911. Ebbets Field in Brooklyn opened in 1913.

The first franchise shift in 50 years took place in March 1953 when the Boston Braves moved to Milwaukee. Attendance in Milwaukee exceeded everyone's wildest imaginations. After attracting only 281,278 in Boston in 1952, the club attracted 1,826,397 in 1953, which was then a National League record. Attendance in Milwaukee topped two million in 1954. The St. Louis Browns moved to Baltimore in 1954 and were renamed the Orioles. The Philadelphia Athletics transferred to Kansas City in 1955.

The Orioles drew 1,060,910 in 1954—not bad for a club that lost 100 games. The Dodgers drew 1,020,531 to watch a team with a 92–62 record. The Athletics attracted 1,393,054 in their first season in Kansas City. The Dodgers started the 1955 season with a 23–2 record and were in first place all year, yet were able to draw only 1,033,589 into Ebbets Field. It is the smallest attendance figure for a World Series participant from 1945 to the present. After winning the World Series in 1954, the Giants had an attendance of 824,112 for an 80–74 team in 1955. The Dodgers drew 10,546 fans per victory in 1955, which ranked 12th in the majors. The Giants, at 10,301 fans per win, were 13th among the 16 teams. The only three teams with a worse figure were the Reds, Pirates and Senators, all clubs with losing records. Both O'Malley and Stoneham shuddered to think what would happen if their club sank out of pennant contention. Stoneham received got an inkling in 1956 when the Giants were 67–87 and drew 629,179.

O'Malley and Stoneham blamed Ebbets Field and the Polo Grounds for their problems in bringing fans through the turnstiles. Parking at both ballparks was available for fewer than 1,000 cars, and traffic snarls were common. The neighborhoods surrounding the Polo Grounds and Ebbets Field were turning into slums and were considered to be increasingly dangerous, particularly at bight. The public transportation system was in decline, and more and more Dodgers and Giants fans were moving out of the city to the suburbs in Westchester and Nassau Counties, and they preferred the safety and comfort of watching their clubs on television rather than endure the hassle of going to the games in person.

O'Malley wanted to build a new stadium for the Dodgers at the junction of Atlantic and Flatbush Avenues in Brooklyn next to the Long Island Railroad Terminal. Included in the plans was a large parking garage and a dome over the ballpark. O'Malley wanted the city to condemn the land in what was a deteriorating section of the borough and turn it over to him. The Dodger owner would then build a stadium with his own money. New York City officials dragged their feet on the project, however, and O'Malley began courting Los Angeles as an alternative. By 1956, Los Angeles had given O'Malley what he wanted. The Dodgers received 300 acres in Chavez Ravine about a mile from downtown Los Angeles. On the site, O'Malley would build a ballpark with private funds. At the end of the 1957 season, he announced that the Dodgers were moving to California.

Stoneham wanted the city to build him a new stadium in Manhattan. Several plans were floated, but none got past the talking stage and were rejected by the city as too expensive. The Giants owner talked to officials in Minneapolis and St. Paul about moving his club there, but O'Malley suggested San Francisco. Stoneham was persuaded and moved his club. The Giants-Dodgers rivalry was now based on the West Coast instead of in New York. And instead of three major league teams, New York now had only one.

Mayor Robert Wagner set up a committee of four "prominent citizens" to find a replacement for the Dodgers and Giants. Heading the committee was 50-year-old William Shea, an energetic attorney and sports fan. He tried to convince the owners of the Pittsburgh Pirates, Philadelphia Phillies and

Cincinnati Reds to move to New York. All were willing to listen but refused his overtures. Shea also requested that the National League expand from eight teams to ten, but the plan was rejected.

Shea then began to explore another avenue to bring a team to New York by spearheading a third major league: the Continental League. It was formally announced to the media on July 27, 1959 that the league would consist of teams from New York, Atlanta, Buffalo, Dallas-Fort Worth, Denver, Houston, Minneapolis-St. Paul and Toronto. Branch Rickey was named as president, which gave the organization some credibility.

Major league owners were hostile to the Continental League and threw every roadblock they could into the path of the organization without incurring the wrath of Congress, which had the power to revoke Organized Baseball's antitrust exemption. A compromise was worked out in August 1960 in which the Continental League would dissolve with the promise that four of its members, including New York, would become expansion teams as the National and American League grew from eight teams to ten. Our story begins with the meeting that created the franchise that became known as the New York Mets.

THE STATE OF THE METS

It would be an understatement to say that the Mets experienced growing pains during the early days as an expansion franchise. The team became a laughingstock in the first season of 1962 by losing 120 teams. The 1962 Mets are still the standard by which bad teams are measured. Seasons of 100 or more losses followed in 1963, 1964, 1965 and 1967. But at the end of the decade, the Mets stunned the world by winning the World Series in 1969 in one of the greatest Cinderella stories in American sports history. Overall, the Mets were 494–799 during the decade, a winning percentage of .382, which was the worst in the majors. National League champions outside of New York during the 1960s were the Pirates (1960), Reds (1961), Giants (1962), Dodgers (1963, 1965 and 1966) and Cardinals (1964, 1967 and 1968).

THE BEST TEAM

Is there any doubt? The 1969 Mets went 101–61 during the regular season and dispatched the heavily favored Orioles in five games in the World Series.

THE WORST TEAM

Is there any doubt? The 1962 Mets set a modern major league record for losses in a season with 120.

THE BEST MOMENT

The best moment was on October 16, 1969 when the final out of the World Series settled into the glove of Cleon Jones, clinching the world championship.

THE WORST MOMENT

The worst moment may have been October 10, 1961 when the Mets were saddled in the expansion draft with a group of "has-beens" and "never-will-bes," setting the stage for years of inept play on the field.

THE ALL-DECADE TEAM • YEARS W/METS

Jerry Grote, c	1966–77
Ed Kranepool, 1b	1962–79
Ron Hunt, 2b	1963–66
Ed Charles, 3b	1967–69
Bud Harrelson, ss	1965–77
Cleon Jones, lf	1963, 1965–75
Jim Hickman, cf	1962–66
Ron Swoboda, rf	1965–70
Tom Seaver, p	1967–77, 1983
Jerry Koosman, p	1967–78
Al Jackson, p	1962–65, 1968
Jack Fisher, p	1964–67

Seaver is in the Hall of Fame. Third base was an almost constant problem during the first 25 years of Mets baseball. Charles was the best of a bad lot. The pitching was awful for most of the decade, which accounts for the inclusion of Jackson and Fisher as two of the four pitchers.

THE DECADE LEADERS

Batting Avg:	Cleon Jones	.284
On-Base Pct:	Ron Hunt	.344
Slugging Pct:	Cleon Jones	.403
Home Runs:	Ed Kranepool	62
RBI:	Ed Kranepool	292
Runs:	Cleon Jones	278
Stolen Bases:	Cleon Jones	68
Wins:	Tom Seaver	57
Strikeouts:	Tom Seaver	583
ERA:	Tom Seaver	2.38
Saves:	Ron Taylor	34

THE HOME FIELD

The Mets played at the Polo Grounds in 1962 and 1963. The aging facility was the home of the New York Giants baseball team from 1911 through 1957. The Mets moved into Shea Stadium in 1964. Considering the product on the field, the attendance figures were surprising, and the largely young and enthusiastic fans were dubbed "The New Breed." The Mets were sixth in the NL in attendance in 1962, fourth in 1963 and second in 1964. In 1969, the franchise led the majors in attendance. The Mets also outdrew the Yankees every year from 1964 through 1975.

THE GAME YOU WISHED YOU HAD SEEN

Game five of the 1969 World Series would have been the place to be as the Mets overcame a 3–0 deficit to win 5–3 and take the world championship.

THE WAY THE GAME WAS PLAYED

Baseball was played in several new cities and ballparks during the 1960s. Shea Stadium, Candlestick Park, Dodger Stadium, the Astrodome, Atlanta-Fulton County Stadium and Busch Memorial Stadium were among those to open. Expansion and franchise shifts brought National League baseball back to New York and major league ball to Minneapolis, Houston, Atlanta, Anaheim, Oakland, Montreal, San Diego and Seattle. Expansion to 12 teams in 1969 inaugurated divisional play and a playoff between the division champions to determine who would go to the World Series. The Astrodome, opened in 1965, brought more innovations: indoor baseball and artificial turf. In the wake of a strike zone expansion in 1963, offense declined during the 1960s until the owners lowered the mound for the 1969 season. The league ERA dipped to 2.99 in 1968, the only time it has been below 3.00 since 1919.

THE MANAGEMENT

The majority owner throughout the decade was Joan Payson. M. Donald Grant headed the organization chart as chairman of the board. General managers were George Weiss (1961–66), Bing Devine (1966–67) and Johnny Murphy (1967–70). Field managers were Casey Stengel (1962–65), Wes Westrum (1965–67), Salty Parker (interim in 1967) and Gil Hodges (1968–71).

THE BEST PLAYER MOVE

The best move was partially the luck of the draw. After the Braves lost Tom Seaver by signing him to an illegal contract in 1966, the Mets were one of three teams to bid for his services. The names of the three clubs were placed in a hat, and the Mets' slip was selected. The best transaction with another club was the purchase of Ron Hunt from the Braves in October 1962.

THE WORST PLAYER MOVE

The best two best prospects in the 1966 amateur draft were considered to be Steve Chilcott and Reggie Jackson. The Mets picked Chilcott, who never played a game in the majors. The worst trade sent Amos Otis and Bob Johnson to the Royals for Joe Foy in December 1969.

The Expansion Draft

The following is a list of the 22 players chosen by the Mets in the expansion draft, held on October 10, 1961. After the name of each player is their previous team, their age and position.

Craig Anderson (St. Louis, 23, p)
A rookie in 1961, Anderson had a 3–17 record with the Mets in 1962 and was 3–20 in three seasons in New York.

Gus Bell (Cincinnati, 33, of)
Bell played in four All-Star Games for the Reds, but was in sharp decline by 1961 and was a platoon player when drafted by the Mets. He played in only 30 games with the Mets, and hit .149, before being dealt to the Braves.

Ed Bouchee (Chicago, 28, 1b)
Bouchee looked like an upcoming star as a rookie with the Phillies in 1957 but never developed. As a Met, he played in 50 games and batted an abysmal .161.

Chris Cannizzaro (St. Louis, 23, c)
Cannizzaro spent four seasons with the Mets as a back-up catcher.

Elio Chacon (Cincinnati, 24, inf)
Chacon earned a job as the Mets starting shortstop in 1962 but hit .236 and wasn't asked to come back in 1963.

Joe Christopher (Pittsburgh 25, of)
A native of the Virgin Islands, Christopher played four seasons with the Mets. He batted .300 in 1964, but in the other three years his production was far below the league average.

Choo-Choo Coleman (Philadelphia 24, c)
Coleman played two seasons as a Met and hit .205 with nine homers in 415 at-bats.

Roger Craig (Los Angeles, 31, p)
Craig pitched on three World Series teams for the Dodgers, including two in Brooklyn, and had a 49–38 lifetime record when acquired by the Mets. Craig was the "ace" of the Mets staff in 1962 and

1963, leading the club in innings pitched, but without a supporting cast had a record of 10–24 in 1962 and 5–22 in 1963 before being traded to the Cardinals. In St. Louis, Craig pitched in another Fall Classic in 1964.

Ray Daviault (San Francisco, 26, p)
Daviault had yet to pitch in a major league game when drafted by the Mets. The club soon found the reason. He had a 1–5 record and a 6.22 ERA in 1962.

John DeMerit (Milwaukee, 25, of)
DeMerit lasted only 14 games with the Mets and batted .188.

Sammy Drake (Chicago, 27, inf)
Drake played in just 27 games as a Met and batted only .192.

Jim Hickman (St. Louis 24, of)
Hickman made his major league debut in 1962 and played in 634 games with the Mets over five seasons before being traded to the Dodgers. While in New York, Hickman batted .241 with 60 home runs.

Gil Hodges (Los Angeles, 37, 1b)
Hodges was an eight-time All-Star with the Dodgers from 1949 through 1957, but by 1961 was a part-time player. He appeared in 62 games with the Mets over two seasons. Hodges would return to the organization as a manager in 1968 and led the club to a world championship in 1969. He was still the manager when he died of a heart attack in April 1972.

Jay Hook (Cincinnati, 24, p)
Hook had a 17–28 record with the Reds over five seasons but was considered to be a tremendous prospect. He had an engineering degree from Northwestern University, but failed to master the dynamics of pitching. Hook was 12–34 in three years with the Mets.

Al Jackson (Pittsburgh, 25, p)
Jackson was in the Mets starting rotation for four seasons on clubs that never finished a season with fewer than 100 losses. Jackson took his lumps with

two years (1962 and 1965) of 20 defeats and was 43–80 overall in New York.

Sherman Jones (Cincinnati 26, p)
Nicknamed "Roadblock," Jones was 0–4 with a 7.71 ERA in a Mets uniform.

Hobie Landrith (San Francisco, 31, c)
Landrith was the first player selected by the Mets, and it was hoped he would provide some veteran leadership for a young pitching staff. He played in only 23 games for the club, however, before a trade to the Orioles.

Felix Mantilla (Milwaukee 27, inf)
Mantilla won a position as the starting third baseman in 1962 and gave the club decent production with a .275 average and 11 homers. He was traded to the Red Sox the following offseason.

Bob L. Miller (St. Louis 23, p)
There were two individuals named Bob Miller who pitched for the Mets in 1962. The other is identified in this book as Bob G. Miller to differentiate between the two. The one chosen in the expansion made his major league debut at the age of 18 with the Cardinals in 1957. Miller had a record of 1–12 with the Mets in 1962, and was traded to the Dodgers and played on three World Series teams in Los Angeles. He played for ten teams during his big-league career and had another stint with the Mets again in 1973 and 1974.

Bobby Gene Smith (Philadelphia 27, of)
Smith played in only eight games for the Mets, and hit .136, before being traded to the Cubs.

Lee Walls (Philadelphia, 27, of)
Walls was the only player taken in the expansion draft who failed to play in a game for the Mets. He was traded to the Dodgers in December 1961.

Don Zimmer (Chicago, 30, inf)
Zimmer played for the Dodgers from 1954 through 1959. As a Met, he appeared in 14 games and batted just .077, which included an 0-for-34 slump, before a trade to the Reds.

The original 28-man roster on Opening Day in 1962 included pitchers Craig Anderson, Roger Craig, Ray Daviault, Jay Hook, Al Jackson, Sheldon Jones, Clem Labine, Ken MacKenzie, Bob L. Miller, Bob Moorhead and Bob Moford; catchers Chris Cannizzaro, Joe Ginsberg and Hobie Landrith; infielders Ed Bouchee, Elio Chacon, Gil Hodges, Rod Kanehl, Felix Mantilla, Jim Marshall, Charlie Neal and Don Zimmer; and outfielders Richie Ashburn, Gus Bell, Johnny DeMerit, Jim Hickman, Bobby Gene Smith and Frank Thomas.

1960

AUGUST 2   At an historic meeting at Chicago's Conrad-Hilton Hotel, the American and National Leagues agree to expand from four teams in each league to ten. The two leagues had consisted of eight teams since 1901. The Continental League, which had hoped to become a third major league with eight franchises, agreed to dissolve with the promise that four of its members would become the expansion teams. New York City was given the additional promise that it would be one of the two new National League teams. It was hoped that the expansion teams would begin playing by 1962.

OCTOBER 17   At a meeting in the Sheraton-Blackstone Hotel in Chicago, the National League votes unanimously to grant expansion franchises to New York and Houston, beginning with the 1962 season. New York mayor Robert Walker assured NL president Warren Giles that the new stadium to be constructed in Flushing Meadows would be ready by 1962.

The principal stockholders in the New York club were Dwight Davis, Jr., Joan Payson, G. Herbert Walker, Jr. and William Simpson. Before the Mets played their first game, Davis sold most of his stock to Payson, making her the majority owner with about 80 percent of the stock. She was 49 years old and was born into the prominent Whitney family, and on her father's passing in 1927, inherited much of the family fortune. Joan married attorney Charles Payson, and the couple was known for their philanthropy and art collection, much of which was donated to New York's Metropolitan Museum of Art. She had previously been a minority stockholder in the New York Giants baseball team. M. Donald Grant, a close ally of Payson, was named president of the club. Grant was the only one of the nine members of the board of the New York Giants to vote against the transfer of the franchise to San Francisco in 1957. Grant became chairman of the board after George Weiss was named president (see March 14, 1961).

OCTOBER 26   The American League agrees to expand to ten teams beginning with the 1961 season. After allowing Washington Senators owner Calvin Griffith to move his club to Minneapolis-St. Paul, the AL voted to place a new expansion franchise in Washington and another in Los Angeles.

1961

MARCH 14   Two months after John Kennedy is inaugurated as the 35th President of the United States, New York's new National League baseball team formally introduces George Weiss as team president and general manager.

A graduate of Yale, Weiss was 66 and had been active in the administrative side of baseball since 1919 when he took over the New Haven franchise in the Eastern League. In 1929, he became general manager of the Baltimore Orioles in the International League, and in 1932 was hired by the New York Yankees to head the farm system and helped to keep the franchise on top by supplying it with a steady stream of talent. By 1948, Weiss was promoted to general manager. One of his first acts was to hire Casey Stengel as manager in October of that year. The Weiss-Stengel team won ten American League pennants and seven World Series in 12 years from 1949 through 1960. Included were five consecutive world championships beginning in their first year together. But Weiss and Stengel were unceremoniously fired by Yankees owner Dan Topping after losing the 1960 World Series. Weiss would serve as president and general manager of the Mets until 1966.

MARCH 15   The New York State Assembly approves a financing plan for New York City's new National League baseball team in Flushing Meadows. It had been hoped that the facility would be ready before or during the 1962 season, but delays in securing legislative approval from the city and state pushed those plans back to at least 1963. The franchise secured the Polo Grounds as a temporary home until the stadium in Flushing Meadows could be finished.

The Polo Grounds was located in the northeast part of Manhattan. On the southeast side of the ballpark, behind center field, was Eighth Avenue and the

Harlem River. Behind the third base side, was West 159th Street. Beyond the home plate northwest side, was Bridge Park, Harlem River Drive, Coogan's Bluff and the Croton Aqueduct. West 155th Street was on the first base side along with the Manhattan Field parking lot. A quarter-mile south and across the Harlem River stood Yankee Stadium. The New York Giants baseball team played on the site from 1883 through 1957, and shared the ballpark with the Yankees from 1912 through 1922. The Polo Grounds that existed in 1962 was built in 1911 and was the fifth ballpark that used the name. The location had previously been a polo field used by the Westchester Polo Association. It was also used by the New York Giants football team from 1925 through 1955 and the New York Titans of the American Football League from 1960 through 1963. In addition, there were five heavyweight boxing title bouts held at the Polo Grounds, won by Joe Louis (twice), Rocky Marciano and Floyd Patterson (twice). On the long and narrow lot, the Polo Grounds had one of the most unique field dimensions in baseball history. The left-field line in 1962 was only 279 feet long and the right-field foul pole was just 257 feet from home plate. The center-field wall was a distant 480 feet. With the exception of a two small bleacher sections behind center field, separated by the clubhouses, the stands were double-decked, similar to the shape of a horseshoe, all the way around the field. Capacity was 55,000.

MAY 8   New York's expansion baseball franchise announces that the team's nickname will be the Mets.

The Mets was short for Metropolitans, a name used by a New York baseball team in the American Association from 1884 through 1887. Other names considered were the Metros, Metro-Giants, Skyliners, Skyscrapers, Burros (for the five boroughs of New York), Rebels, Jets (the name wouldn't be attached to the football team until 1963), Continentals, Bees, Empires, Islanders (the hockey team didn't take the ice until 1972) and Avengers.

SEPTEMBER 29   The Mets announce that 71-year-old Casey Stengel would be the manager of the club.

A native of Kansas City, Charles (Casey) Stengel was a player or manager for all four of New York's major league teams in the modern era. He was a moderately successful outfielder with the Dodgers, Pirates, Phillies, Giants and Braves from 1912 until 1925. Stengel was a manager with the Dodgers in Brooklyn from 1934 through 1936 and the Braves in Boston from 1938 through 1943, but only one of those clubs finished above .500. His 1938 Braves finished at 77–75 and landed in fifth place in an eight-team league. Stengel became known more for his humor in the face of adversity than as a managerial tactician and drifted back to the minors as a manager. When George Weiss became general manager of the Yankees, he fired Bucky Harris as field manager after Harris had led the franchise to a world championship in 1947 and a 94–60 record in 1948. To the shock of nearly everyone, Weiss hired Stengel to replace Harris. The Yankees won the World Series in each of Stengel's first five years as manager. They reached the Fall Classic again four straight seasons beginning in 1955 and once more in 1960. The Yankees captured two more world championships in 1956 and 1958. After a seven-game loss to the Pirates in 1960, the organization fired Stengel along with general manager, George Weiss. The Yanks considered Stengel to be too old and had Ralph Houk waiting in the wings to take over as manager. Stengel would manage the Mets until July 1965, but had a record of only 175–404. Despite all of his success with the Yankees, Stengel's final record as manager was only 63 games above .500 (1,905–1,842).

OCTOBER 10   The Mets select 22 players in the expansion draft. The new Houston club, nicknamed the Colts, chose 23. The other eight teams in the National League each made 15 players available. Seven were required to be from the 25-man roster of August 31, 1961. The first player picked was Giants infielder Eddie Bressoud by Houston. The Mets followed with Giants catcher Hobie Landrith.

OCTOBER 11   The Mets purchase Johnny Antonelli from the Braves.

Antonelli was a hero in New York because of his 21–7 record for the 1954 world champion New York Giants and had won 16 games for the Giants as recently as 1959. He decided to retire rather than cast his lot with the Mets, however.

OCTOBER 16   The Mets purchase Billy Loes from the Giants.

OCTOBER 28   Ground is broken for the new ballpark in Flushing Meadows, which will later be known as Shea Stadium. Mayor Robert Wagner scooped out the first shovelful of dirt. Others on hand included Commissioner of Baseball, Ford Frick; National League president, Warren Giles; Mets president, George Weiss; New York Titans president, Harry Wismer; and former Dodgers and Giants players Gil Hodges, Billy Loes, Monte Irvin, Sid Gordon and Jim Hearn. It was expected that the stadium would be open in 1963, but two bitterly cold winters and 17 union strikes pushed the opening back to 1964.

NOVEMBER 16   The Mets logo is unveiled. Designed by sports cartoonist Ray Gatto, it has gone virtually unchanged through the club's history. The skyline in the background includes a church spire, symbolic of Brooklyn, which is known as the borough of churches. The second building from the left is the Williamsburg Savings Bank, the tallest building in Brooklyn. Next is the Woolworth Building. After a general skyline view of midtown Manhattan is the Empire State Building. At the far right is the United Nations Building.

NOVEMBER 23   Casey Stengel and Gil Hodges are among those on the Mets float in the Macy's Thanksgiving Day parade.

NOVEMBER 28   The Mets purchase Frank Thomas from the Braves.

Thomas was an All-Star with the Pirates in 1954, 1955 and 1958. He gave the Mets a solid season in 1962 with 34 homers and a .266 batting average as a left fielder. Thomas remained with the club until a trade to the Phillies in 1964.

DECEMBER 8   The Mets purchase Richie Ashburn from the Cubs.

A future Hall of Famer, Ashburn hit over .300 eight times for the Phillies between 1948 and 1958 and won the NL batting title in 1955 and 1958. He was a part-time outfielder with the Cubs in 1961, but had enough left to hit .306 in 135 games for the Mets in 1962. He decided to retire rather than return in 1963.

DECEMBER 15   The Mets send Lee Walls and cash to the Dodgers for Charlie Neal.

> *Neal was the Mets starting second baseman in 1962 and batted .260 with 11*
> *home runs. He was one of seven players from the 1957 Dodgers, the club's last*
> *year in Brooklyn, to later play for the Mets. The others were Gil Hodges, Duke*
> *Snider, Don Zimmer, Joe Pignatano, Roger Craig and Clem Labine.*

1962

Season in a Sentence

The Mets become a national punch line by losing a modern record 120 games.

Finish • Won • Lost • Pct • GB

Finish	Won	Lost	Pct	GB
Tenth	40	120	.250	60.5

Manager

Casey Stengel

Stats

Stats	Mets	AL	Rank
Batting Avg:	.240	.261	10
On-Base Pct:	.318	.327	8
Slugging Pct:	.361	.393	9
Home Runs:	139	6	
Stolen Bases:	59	7	
ERA:	5.04	3.94	10
Errors:	210	10	
Runs Scored:	617	9	
Runs Allowed:	948	10	

Starting Lineup

Choo-Choo Coleman, c
Marv Throneberry, 1b
Charlie Neal, 2b-ss
Felix Mantilla, 3b
Elio Chacon, ss
Frank Thomas, lf
Jim Hickman, cf
Richie Ashburn, rf-cf
Rod Kanehl, 2b
Joe Christopher, rf

Pitchers

Roger Craig, sp
Al Jackson, sp
Jay Hook, sp
Bob Miller, sp-rp
Craig Anderson, rp
Bob Moorhead, rp
Ray Daviault, rp
Ken McKenzie, rp

Attendance

922,530 (sixth in NL)

Club Leaders

Batting Avg:	Richie Ashburn	.306
On-Base Pct:	Richie Ashburn	.424
Slugging Pct:	Frank Thomas	.496
Home Runs:	Frank Thomas	34
RBI:	Frank Thomas	94
Runs:	Frank Thomas	69
Stolen Bases:	Richie Ashburn	12
	Elio Chacon	12
Wins:	Roger Craig	10
Strikeouts:	Roger Craig	118
	Al Jackson	118
ERA:	Al Jackson	4.40
Saves:	Craig Anderson	4

FEBRUARY 16   The Mets sign Clem Labine, most recently with the Pirates, as a free agent.

> *Labine played for the Dodgers from 1950 through 1960. George Weiss believed*
> *that the Mets needed recognizable names to attract fans and sprinkled the Mets*
> *roster with many former Yankees, Brooklyn Dodgers, New York Giants and*
> *National League All-Stars. In most instances the nostalgia trip didn't help the*
> *club win games, and Labine was a case in point. He lasted only three games with*
> *the Mets.*

FEBRUARY 19   In St. Petersburg, Florida, the Mets hold their first spring training drill.

St. Petersburg had been the spring training home of the Yankees from 1925 through 1961 and the St. Louis Cardinals since 1938. The Yanks moved to Ft. Lauderdale in 1962. St. Petersburg served as the Mets spring training headquarters until 1987, and during each of those 26 seasons, the Mets shared the city with the Cards.

MARCH 10   Three weeks after John Glenn becomes the first American to orbit the earth, the Mets play their first exhibition game, and lose 8–0 to the Cardinals in St. Petersburg.

MARCH 11   The Mets win for the first time, beating the Cardinals 4–3 in an exhibition game in St. Petersburg. Elio Chacon drove in Richie Ashburn with a wal-off single in the bottom of the ninth.

The Mets original uniforms contained elements from the Yankees, Dodgers and Giants. On the home jerseys, "Mets" was written in script in a style similar to the Dodgers uniforms in Dodgers blue. The blue was trimmed in Giants orange. The caps were blue with an intertwining "N" and "Y" that were borrowed from the former Giants hats when the club resided in the city. "Yankee" pinstripes were an added flourish. On the road shirts, "New York" was written in arched capitals letters, which again was heavily influenced by the 1950s uniforms of the Giants.

MARCH 22   The Mets and Yankees meet for the first time, and the Mets prevail 4–3 in St. Petersburg. The winning run scored in the ninth inning on a triple by Joe Christopher and a walk-off single from Richie Ashburn.

The Mets finished spring training with a 12–15 record. In a poll of 209 writers conducted by the Sporting News, *the Mets were a consensus pick to finish eighth among ten teams, ahead of the Phillies, who were 47–107 in 1961, and fellow expansion team Houston.*

APRIL 10   The Mets' first scheduled regular season game, against the Cardinals in St. Louis, is postponed because of rain.

APRIL 11   The Mets' first regular season game results in an 11–4 loss to the Cardinals in St. Louis. The starting lineup consisted of Richie Ashburn (cf), Felix Mantilla (ss), Charlie Neal (2b), Frank Thomas (lf), Gus Bell (rf), Gil Hodges (1b), Don Zimmer (3b), Hobie Landrith (c) and Roger Craig (p). Craig gave up two runs in the first inning. After the Mets scored twice in the top of the third to tie the score 2–2, the Cardinals responded with three in their half. Neal collected three hits, including a homer. Hodges also homered.

Mets achieving franchise firsts included Craig (losing pitcher), Bell (hit with a second-inning single), Ashburn (run scored), Neal (RBI and error), Hodges (home run) and Mantilla (double).

APRIL 12   The Mets are treated to a ticker tape parade on Broadway and a reception at City Hall.

APRIL 13   On Friday the 13th, the Mets play their first home game and lose 4–3 to the Pirates before 12,447 at the Polo Grounds. The game started at 2:15 p.m. It was cold and rainy and accompanied by a few snow flurries. Sherman Jones was the starting and losing pitcher. Frank Thomas homered in the losing cause.

APRIL 15   Facing Bob Friend, Felix Mantilla hits the first leadoff homer in club history, but the Mets lose 7–2 to the Pirates at the Polo Grounds.

> *Mets games were carried on radio over WABC and on television over WOR-TV. The announcers were Lindsay Nelson, Ralph Kiner and Bob Murphy. Nelson did Mets games until 1979, and Murphy until 2003. A Hall of Fame player who led the NL in home runs seven consecutive seasons from 1946 through 1952 as a Pirate, Kiner was still making guest shots in the broadcast booth at the age of 87 in 2010. Nelson was well-known nationally, mainly for his television work in college football and the NBA over NBC and CBS. Nelson was the play-by-play man for 26 Cotton Bowls on New Year's Day. Murphy previously announced games for the Red Sox (1954–59) and Orioles (1960–61). The broadcast booths at both Shea Stadium and Citi Field were named in his honor. Bob's brother Jack was a San Diego sportswriter who was influential in bringing the Chargers to San Diego from Los Angeles in 1961 and the creation of the Padres as an expansion team in 1969. The stadium where the two teams played was named Jack Murphy Stadium in recognition of his work. The facility was renamed Qualcomm Stadium in 1997.*

APRIL 17   The Mets play in extra innings for the first time and lose 5–2 in 11 innings to the Houston Colts at the Polo Grounds.

> *The Houston franchise was officially nicknamed the Colt .45s, and informally known as the Colts, from 1962 through 1964. The name was changed to Astros in 1965.*

APRIL 18   Ed Bouchee hits the first pinch-hit homer in Mets history, but the club loses 15–5 to the Cardinals at the Polo Grounds.

APRIL 22   The Mets record falls to 0–9 with a 4–3 loss to the Pirates in Pittsburgh.

APRIL 23   The Mets finally win their first game with a 9–1 decision over the Pirates in Pittsburgh. Jay Hook pitched the complete game victory.

APRIL 26   The Mets purchase Harry Chiti from the Indians. After playing in 15 games with the Mets, Chiti was sold back to the Indians on June 15. On the same day, the Mets traded Jim Marshall to the Pirates for Vinegar Bend Mizell.

APRIL 28   The Mets use five homers to defeat the Phillies 8–6 at the Polo Grounds. Charlie Neal led the way with two home runs. The others were struck by Jim Hickman, Gil Hodges and Charlie Neal. Three of the homers, by Thomas, Neal and Hodges, were struck consecutively in the sixth inning. It was also the Mets' first home win after seven defeats.

APRIL 29   Al Jackson pitches the first shutout in Mets history by beating the Phillies 8–0 in the first game of a double-header at the Polo Grounds. It was also the first twin bill in club history. The Mets scored seven runs in the fourth inning. Frank Thomas tied a major league record when he was hit twice by pitches in the inning from Art Mahaffey and Frank Sullivan. The Phillies won the second tilt 10–2.

MAY 6   The Mets win their first extra-inning game by beating the Phillies 7–5 in 12 innings in Philadelphia. Roger Craig recorded the first save in team history.

MAY 7	The Mets trade Don Zimmer to the Reds for Cliff Cook and Bob G. Miller.

MAY 9   The Mets send cash and a player to be named later to the Orioles for Marv Throneberry. Hobie Landrith was sent to Baltimore on June 7 to complete the transaction.

> *A first baseman, Marvin Eugene Throneberry's initials were "MET," so he was literally born to be a Met. Throneberry was 29 and in his sixth season in the majors when acquired by the Mets. He soon became the poster child for the ineptitude of the club with his atrocious play on defense and on the base paths. The fans fell in love with him and named Throneberry "Marvelous Marv." With his self-effacing humor, Throneberry took it all in stride and became a media favorite as well with one-liners.*

MAY 12   Hobie Landrith hits the first walk-off homer in Mets history which gives the club a 3–2 victory over the Braves in the first game of a double-header at the Polo Grounds. He accomplished the feat with a man on base, Warren Spahn on the mound and the Mets trailing 2–1 in the bottom of the ninth. Gil Hodges ended the second contest with a solo walk-off homer in the ninth, which lifted the Mets to an 8–7 triumph. It was the first time in major league history that a team won a double-header with two walk-off homers. The second was by the White Sox on July 25, 1967. It was also the first double-header sweep in Mets franchise history.

> *Craig Anderson was the winning pitcher in both games. The wins gave him a 3–1 record in the 1962 season and 7–4 in his career. Anderson proceeded to lose his last 16 decisions in 1962, to fall to 3–17, and his last 19 in the majors. He was 0–2 in 1963 and 0–1 in 1964 to finish his travels in the big leagues with a 7–23 record. During the 0–19 debacle, Anderson pitched in 43 games, 16 of them starts, and had a 6.11 ERA in 131 innings.*

MAY 15   The Mets take a thrilling 13-inning, 6–5 decision from the Cubs at the Polo Grounds. The Mets tied the score 4–4 with a two-out RBI-single from Gus Bell in the ninth. Chicago scored in the top of the tenth, but the Mets matched it in the bottom half. The Mets won in the 13th on a two-out, bases-loaded walk from Cal Koonce to Hobie Landrith.

MAY 16   The Mets win in extra innings for the second game in a row, this time on a walk-off single from Felix Mantilla in the 11th, which beats the Cubs 6–5 at the Polo Grounds. At 38 and running on bad knees, Gil Hodges tied the score 5–5 in the eighth with the first inside-the-park homer in Mets history. It was the only inside-the-park homer of his career.

MAY 20   The Mets sweep the Braves 7–6 and 9–6 in a double-header at County Stadium. In the opener, the Mets trailed 5–1 before scoring two runs in the eighth and four in the ninth to take a 7–5 lead, then survived a Milwaukee rally in the ninth for the win. All four of the ninth-inning runs scored with two out. Frank Thomas tied the score 5–5 with a two-run single. The other two tallies crossed the plate on an error.

> *The pair of wins gave the Mets a 12–19 record and 12 wins in their last 22 games, giving fans some hope the club would be respectable. Those illusions were wiped out with a 17-game losing streak which began on May 21.*

MAY 27   A seventh-inning brawl is the highlight of a 7–1 loss to the Giants in the first game of a double-header at Candlestick Park. Tensions were high because of a series of brushback pitches when Willie Mays spiked shortstop Elio Chacon while sliding into second base following a pick-off throw from Roger Craig. Chacon punched Mays, who responded by slamming Elio into the ground. Orlando Cepeda, still seething over a close pitch from Craig, rushed the mound and began raining punches on the Mets hurler. Chacon was the only player ejected. San Francisco also won the second game 6–5.

MAY 30   The Dodgers play a regular season game in New York for the first time since 1957 and beat the Mets 13–6 and 6–5 before a Memorial Day sellout crowd of 55,704 at the Polo Grounds. About half the crowd cheered for the Dodgers. In the sixth inning of the second game, the Mets pulled off the first triple play in club history. With the base runners on first and second moving with the pitch, Willie Davis lined to shortstop Elio Chacon, who threw to second baseman Charlie Neal for the force out at second. Neal in turn fired the ball to first baseman Gil Hodges to complete the triple play. Davis later hit a home run in the ninth to break the 5–5 tie.

JUNE 1   The Giants play a regular season game in New York for the first time since 1957 and beat the Mets 9–6 before 43,724 at the Polo Grounds.

JUNE 6   The Mets' losing streak extends to 17 with a 2–1 loss at the hands of the Phillies in Philadelphia.

JUNE 8   The Mets break their 17-game losing streak by beating the Cubs 4–3 in the first game of a double-header at Wrigley Field. Charlie Neal hit a sacrifice fly in the ninth to break a 3–3 tie. Chicago won the second tilt 3–2, which was called after eight innings due to darkness.

JUNE 15   The Mets purchase Gene Woodling from the Senators.

            Woodling was a member of the Yankees from 1949 through 1954, where he played on five winning World Series teams. Appearing in 81 games for the Mets over the remainder of the 1962 season, he became the first individual to play for both the Yankees and Mets.

JUNE 17   Marv Throneberry seals his legend as "Marvelous Marv" with his bumbling play during an 8–7 loss to the Cubs at the Polo Grounds. Playing first base in the top of the first, Throneberry got in the way of a runner during a rundown and was called for interference. It should have been the third out of the inning, and the Cubs went on to score four runs. In the bottom of the first, he hit an apparent triple, but was called out for failing to touch second base. When Casey Stengel went out to argue the play, first base coach Cookie Lavagetto said to forget it because Throneberry didn't touch first base either. Charlie Neal followed with a homer. Lou Brock of the Cubs became only the second player to homer into the center field bleachers at the Polo Grounds with a blast off Al Jackson. The Cubs also won the second contest 4–3.

            The bleachers were constructed in 1923 and were more than 450 feet from home plate. Prior to Brock, the only other batter to reach the seats during a regular season game was Joe Adcock of the Braves in 1953.

JUNE 18   Just one day after Lou Brock accomplishes the feat, Hank Aaron homers into the center field bleachers at the Polo Grounds with a grand slam off Jay Hook in the third inning of a 7–1 loss to the Braves. It was also the Mets 12th consecutive loss at home.

No one else homered into the bleachers before the ballpark closed at the end of the 1963 season.

JUNE 22   Al Jackson pitches a one-hitter to defeat the Colts 2–0 in the first game of a double-header at the Polo Grounds. The only Houston hit was a single by Joe Amalfitano with one out in the first inning. Jackson retired 22 batters in a row from the first through the eighth. Richie Ashburn scored both Mets runs, one of them on a homer off Dick Farrell leading off the first inning. The Mets collected only three hits in all. In the second game, the Mets made six errors and lost 16–3.

JUNE 23   The Mets clobber Houston 13–2 at the Polo Grounds. Richie Ashburn walloped two homers and scored four runs. One of the two homers was inside the park.

Ashburn hit only 29 homers in 9,736 career at-bats. He was homerless in 1,040 at-bats in 1960 and 1961 combined, but hit a career high seven with the Mets in 1962. Six of the seven were struck at the Polo Grounds.

JUNE 27   Richie Ashburn collects the 2,500th hit of his career with a single off Bob Friend in the fourth inning of a 6–5 loss to the Pirates in ten innings in Pittsburgh.

JUNE 29   The Mets collect only four hits, but beat the Dodgers 10–4 in Los Angeles. In the first inning, the Mets scored six times on seven walks and a single. Four Dodgers pitchers combined to walk 16 batters.

JUNE 30   Sandy Koufax pitches the first of his four career no-hitters by beating the Mets 2–0 in Los Angeles. He began the game by fanning Richie Ashburn, Rod Kanehl and Frank Thomas on nine pitches. Felix Mantilla made the last out by grounding into a forceout. Koufax struck out 13 in all.

JULY 6   Rod Kanehl hits a grand slam off Bobby Shantz in the eighth inning of a 10–3 win over the Cardinals at the Polo Grounds. It was the first grand slam in Mets history. Kanehl entered the game as a defensive replacement for Frank Thomas in left field in the top of the eighth.

JULY 7   Marv Throneberry hits a two-run, walk-off homer with one out in the ninth inning to beat the Cardinals 5–4 in the first game of a double-header at the Polo Grounds. St. Louis won the second tilt 3–2.

JULY 8   Stan Musial hits three homers for the Cardinals during a 15–1 rout of the Mets at the Polo Grounds. Counting a homer in his last at-bat the previous day, Musial hit four straight homers off Mets pitching.

Richie Ashburn was the first player in Mets history to be selected for the All-Star team. There were two All-Star Games played each season from 1959 through 1962. The first one in 1962 was played on July 10 at D.C. Stadium in Washington, and Ashburn didn't play. He pinch-hit in the seventh inning of the second game on July 30 at Wrigley Field and singled, but the National League lost 9–4.

JULY 24   On the first pitch of his first game with the Mets, Bob G. Miller gives up a walk-off homer to Del Crandall in the 12th inning, which results in a 5–4 loss to the Braves in Milwaukee.

JULY 26   The Mets extend their losing streak to 11 games with a 6–1 defeat at the hands of the Braves in Milwaukee.

JULY 27   The Mets end their 11-game losing streak by beating the Cardinals 1–0 in the first game of a double-header in St. Louis. Al Jackson pitched the shutout. The Cards win the second tilt 6–5.

AUGUST 1   Frank Thomas drives in six runs, four of them on a grand slam off Jack Hamilton in the fourth inning, but the Mets lose 11–9 to the Phillies at the Polo Grounds. Thomas also drew a bases-loaded walk in the first inning and hit a solo homer in the sixth.

AUGUST 2   Frank Thomas and Marv Throneberry each hit two homers, but the Mets lose 9–4 to the Phillies at the Polo Grounds.

AUGUST 3   The Mets hit five homers, but lose 8–6 to the Reds at the Polo Grounds. Frank Thomas hit two, giving him six homers in a span of three games. The other homers were struck by Charlie Neal, Marv Throneberry and Choo-Choo Coleman.

AUGUST 4   The Mets sweep the Reds 9–1 and 3–2 during the double-header at the Polo Grounds. The second contest was won on a walk-off homer by Frank Thomas in the 14th inning.

Cincinnati manager Fred Hutchinson, whose club was in pennant contention with the Dodgers and Giants, wasn't amused by the pair of losses. He sat in the dugout and fumed for 30 minutes and phoned the clubhouse to inform the players he wanted them dressed and gone before he arrived.

AUGUST 14   Al Jackson pitches all 15 innings of a 3–1 loss to the Phillies at the Polo Grounds.

AUGUST 15   The Mets hit two pinch-hit homers, but lose 8–7 to the Phillies in 13 innings in the first game of a double-header at the Polo Grounds. In the sixth inning, Choo-Choo Coleman pinch-hit for pitcher Craig Anderson and walloped a two-run homer. Coleman remained in the game as a catcher. In the eighth, Jim Hickman batted for Coleman and hit a three-run blast. Philadelphia also won the opener 9–3.

AUGUST 21   The Mets extend their losing streak to 13 games with an 8–6 loss to the Pirates in the first game of a double-header at the Polo Grounds, then break it with a 5–4 victory in the nightcap with a thrilling four-run rally in the ninth. Felix Mantilla singled in the first run. Marv Throneberry stepped to the plate against Roy Face with the Mets trailing 4–2 and two out, and walloped a three-run, walk-off homer for the victory.

The Mets played seven games in four days from August 18 through August 21.

AUGUST 28   Charlie Neal drives in both runs of a 2–0 win over the Phillies in the first game of a double-header in Philadelphia with singles in the first and seventh innings. Al Jackson pitched the shutout. The Phillies won the second tilt 10–1.

AUGUST 29   The Mets record their 100th loss of the season with a ten-inning, 3–2 defeat to the Phillies in Philadelphia.

Despite the mounting losses, the Mets drew 922,530 fans in 1962, to rank sixth among ten teams in the National League and 11th among the 20 in the majors. The crowds were also loud and enthusiastic.

SEPTEMBER 2   The Mets tie a major league record by using four catchers during a 4–3 win over the Cardinals in St. Louis. The four were starter Choo-Choo Coleman and reserves Chris Cannizzaro, Sammy Taylor and Joe Pignatano.

Cannizzaro and Taylor tied for the club lead in starts at the catching position with 42. Coleman had 37. Right field was also a revolving door. Joe Christopher led the Mets in starts in right in 1962 with 40.

SEPTEMBER 14   Choo-Choo Coleman hits a walk-off homer in the ninth inning to beat the Reds 10–9 at the Polo Grounds.

SEPTEMBER 22   Only 17, Ed Kranepool makes his major league debut during a 9–2 loss to the Cubs at the Polo Grounds and grounds out in the eighth inning after replacing Gil Hodges at first base. It was also Al Jackson's 20th loss of the season.

Kranepool was considered to be one of the best high school players in the country and signed with the Mets out of James Madison High School in the Bronx for $85,000. He never developed into the kind of player the club envisioned, but he appeared in at least one game in every Mets season from 1962 through 1979. Through 2010, he holds club records for most games played (1,853), most at-bats (5,436), most hits (1,418), most total bases (2,047), most doubles (225) and is fourth in RBI (614).

SEPTEMBER 26   Roger Craig records his 24th loss of the season by dropping a 6–3 decision to the Braves in Milwaukee.

SEPTEMBER 28   A crowd of just 595 watches the Mets lose 3–2 to the Cubs at Wrigley Field.

SEPTEMBER 29   After starting the season 0–12, Bob L. Miller finally wins his first game by defeating the Cubs 2–1 in Chicago.

SEPTEMBER 30   The Mets close the 1962 season by losing their 120th game with a 5–1 defeat to the Cubs in Chicago. In what would prove to be his last major league plate appearance, Joe Pignatano hit into a triple play.

The all-time record for losses in a season is 134 by the 1899 Cleveland Spiders. Overall, Cleveland was 20–134. Other clubs since 1900 with at least 115 defeats in a season are the 1916 Philadelphia Athletics (36–117), the 1935 Boston Braves (38–115) and the 2003 Detroit Tigers (43–119). The 1916 Athletics hold the all-time modern record for the worst winning percentage at .235. The 1935 Braves (.248) are the second worst. The 1962 Mets possess the third-worst winning percentage in modern times and the worst since 1935 at .250.

OCTOBER 11   The Mets purchase Ron Hunt from the Braves.

Hunt won the starting second base job at the age of 22 in 1963, batted .272 and was the runner-up to Pete Rose in the Rookie-of-the-Year voting. In 1964, Hunt was the first Met to start in an All-Star Game and hit .303.

NOVEMBER 26   A month after the end of the Cuban Missile Crisis, the Orioles draft Paul Blair from the Mets organization.

Blair was 18 and hit .228 in 122 games for the Mets farm club in Santa Barbara in 1962. The failure to protect him proved to be a huge mistake, as Blair played 1,947 major league games over 17 seasons, and appeared in four World Series with the Orioles.

NOVEMBER 30   The Mets trade Bob L. Miller to the Dodgers for Larry Burright and Tim Harkness.

DECEMBER 11   The Mets trade Felix Mantilla to the Red Sox for Pumpsie Green, Tracy Stallard and Al Moran.

1963

Season in a Sentence

With no where to go but up, the Mets win 11 more games than the previous season, but still lose 111 times.

Finish • Won • Lost • Pct • GB

Tenth   51   111   .315   48.0

Manager

Casey Stengel

Stats

Stats	Mets	AL	Rank
Batting Avg:	.219	.245	10
On-Base Pct:	.315	.364	9
Slugging Pct:	.315	.264	9
Home Runs:	96	9	
Stolen Bases:	41		9
ERA:	4.12	3.29	10
Errors:	210	10	
Runs Scored:	501	9	
Runs Allowed:	774	10	

Starting Lineup

Choo-Choo Coleman, c
Tim Harkness, 1b
Ron Hunt, 2b
Charlie Neal, 3b
Al Moran, ss
Frank Thomas, lf
Jim Hickman, cf-3b
Duke Snider, rf-lf
Ed Kranepool, rf

Pitchers

Al Jackson, sp
Roger Craig, sp
Carl Willey, sp
Tracy Stallard, sp-rp
Larry Bearnarth, rp
Galen Cisco, rp-sp
Jay Hook, sp-rp

Attendance

1,080,108 (fourth in NL)

Club Leaders

Batting Avg:	Ron Hunt	.272
On-Base Pct:	Ron Hunt	.334
Slugging Pct:	Ron Hunt	.396
Home Runs:	Jim Hickman	17
RBI:	Frank Thomas	60
Runs:	Ron Hunt	64
Stolen Bases:	Rod Kanehl	6
Wins:	Al Jackson	13
Strikeouts:	Al Jackson	142
ERA:	Roger Craig	3.78
Saves:	Larry Bearnarth	4

FEBRUARY 4   Mayor Robert Wagner signs a bill that officially changes the name of the Mets new stadium being constructed in Queens from Flushing Meadows Stadium to William A. Shea Municipal Stadium. The change was made to honor William Shea, who was instrumental in New York's efforts to obtain a National League team following the departure of the Dodgers and Giants in 1957.

MARCH 23   The Mets purchase Carl Willey from the Braves.

APRIL 1   The Mets purchase Duke Snider from the Dodgers.

              Snider played in seven All-Star Games and six World Series for the Dodgers, but was about finished as a productive player by the time he was acquired by the Mets. Snider hit .243 with 14 homers in 1963.

APRIL 9   The Mets begin the season by collecting only two hits off Ernie Broglio in a 7–0 loss to the Cardinals before 25,049 at the Polo Grounds.

              After an 0–9 start in 1962, the Mets begin the 1963 season 0–8. The club scored just nine runs in those eight defeats. The Mets rebounded with 13 wins in their next 20 games and were 13–15 on May 10, but went 38–96 over the rest of the season.

APRIL 19   The Mets win their first game of the season by scoring two runs in the ninth inning to defeat the Braves 5–4 at the Polo Grounds. Ron Hunt drove in both with a one-out, walk-off double.

APRIL 21   Trailing the Braves 5–4 in the eighth inning, Jim Hickman hits a grand slam off Claude Raymond in the eighth inning to lift the Mets to an 8–5 win in the first game of a double-header at the Polo Grounds. The Mets also won the second contest 9–2.

              The Mets won all four games of the series against the Braves. It was the first series sweep of three or more games in club history.

MAY 12   The Mets outlast the Reds 13–12 in the second game of a double-header at the Polo Grounds. The Mets broke a 6–6 tie with five runs in the fifth inning but allowed Cincinnati to score six times in the sixth to fall behind 12–11. The game was won with two tallies in the eighth, the second on a single by Choo-Choo Coleman. The Reds won the opener 3–0.

MAY 23   The Mets trade Gil Hodges to the Senators for Jimmy Piersall. Hodges was immediately named as manager of the Senators, replacing Mickey Vernon.

              As a rookie with the Red Sox in 1952, Piersall spent some time in a mental hospital because of a nervous breakdown and battled back to play as a regular in Boston, Cleveland and Washington for nine seasons beginning in 1953. His story was chronicled in a book called Fear Strikes Out, *and a subsequent movie of the same name was released in 1957. By 1963, Piersall was 33 and a part-time player. He batted only .194 with the Mets in 40 games before being released in July.*

MAY 30   Jay Hook pitches a two-hitter to defeat the Cubs 2–1 at the Polo Grounds. The only Chicago hits were a triple by Ken Hubbs in the first inning and a single from Don Landrum in the eighth.

JUNE 2

The Mets win both ends of a double-header against the Pirates at the Polo Grounds in extra innings. In the opener, the Mets won 21 in ten innings with the winning run crossing the plate on an error. In the nightcap, the Mets won 4–3 in ten innings on a walk-off homer by Jim Hickman.

JUNE 5

Trailing 9–1, the Mets force extra innings by scoring seven runs in the sixth inning and one in the eighth, but allow the Braves to score twice in the tenth resulting in an 11–9 loss at the Polo Grounds.

JUNE 7

With one out in the ninth inning and the Mets trailing 2–0, Duke Snider hits a three-run, walk-off homer for a 3–2 victory over the Cardinals at the Polo Grounds.

JUNE 14

Duke Snider collects his 400th career homer with a blow off Bob Purkey in the first inning of a 10–3 win over the Reds in Cincinnati. Ron Hunt garnered four hits and scored four runs.

JUNE 20

In the first Mayor's Trophy Game involving the Mets and the Yankees, the Mets win 6–2 before 52,430 in an exhibition game at Yankee Stadium. It was the second game of the day for the Yankees. During the afternoon, they defeated the Senators 5–4.

During the course of the game, boisterous Mets fans lofted cherry bombs and firecrackers, paraded homemade banners and tried to tear down the Yankees' 1962 world championship pennant. After the game, the Yankees found themselves prisoners in their own clubhouse as thousands of Mets fans stood outside the gate and chanted "Yankees Go Home." The game became an annual event to benefit New York's sandlot programs and was played every year from 1963 through 1979 and again in 1982 and 1983. The Mets and Yankees began playing regular season games against each other in 1997.

JUNE 23

Carl Willey pitches a two-hitter to defeat the Phillies 5–0 in the first game of a double-header at the Polo Grounds. The only Philadelphia hits were both triples by Johnny Callison in the fourth inning and Tony Taylor in the sixth. Jimmy Piersall provided the comic relief when he celebrated his 100th career homer by running the bases backwards (though in the proper order). The Mets completed the sweep by beating the Phillies 4–1 in the second game.

JUNE 26

Tim Harkness hits a walk-off grand slam off Jim Brewer with two out in the 14th inning to defeat the Cubs 8–6 at the Polo Grounds. Chicago scored twice in the top of the 14th on a two-out, inside-the-park homer by Billy Williams. The Mets loaded the bases on a single by Ron Hunt and walks to Jimmy Piersall and Sammy Taylor before the homer by Harkness. After the game, hundreds of fans stormed the center-field clubhouse and broke into a rousing ovation as Harkness stepped out for a curtain call.

The euphoria over the dramatic victory didn't last long. The Mets lost their next 15 games. From June 28 through August 6, the Mets were 5–32.

JULY 1

The Mets trade Charlie Neal and Sammy Taylor to the Reds for Jesse Gonder.

JULY 15   The Mets end a 15-game losing streak by beating Houston 14–5 in the first game of a double-header at the Polo Grounds. Carl Willey hit the first home run by a pitcher in club history with a grand slam against Ken Johnson in the second inning. Houston intentionally walked Larry Burright to load the bases before Willey came to the plate. The Colts took the second game 8–0.

Willey had an .099 batting average and two homers in 263 major league at-bats.

JULY 16   The Mets beat the Cardinals 4–3 at the Polo Grounds with a walk-off single from Norm Sherry in the ninth inning.

JULY 17   The Mets win with a walk-off hit for the second game in a row with an 11th-inning homer by Jim Hicks off Don Larsen, which beats the Giants 9–7 at the Polo Grounds.

JULY 28   The Mets tie a modern major league record by losing their 22nd game in a row on the road with an 8–2 defeat at the hands of the Colts in Houston.

The 22-game road losing streak began on June 16. The only other club to lose 22 in a row on the road since 1900 is the 1943 Philadelphia Athletics. The 1890 Pittsburgh Pirates hold the all-time record with 41.

JULY 30   On Casey Stengel's 73rd birthday, the Mets end their 22-game losing streak on the road by beating the Dodgers 5–1 in Los Angeles.

The Mets had a record of 7–47 against the Dodgers from 1962 through 1964.

AUGUST 4   Roger Craig loses his 18th decision in a row by falling 2–1 to the Braves in Milwaukee.

The loss dropped Craig to 2–20 on the season. The 18 straight defeats tied a National League record for a single season, set by Cliff Curtis of the Boston Braves in 1910. The all-time record is 19 by John Nabors of the Philadelphia Athletics in 1916. During the 18-game losing streak, Craig pitched 132 innings and had an ERA of 4.16 and changed his uniform number from 38 to 13 in attempt to change his luck.

AUGUST 7   Jim Hickman becomes the first Met in history to hit for the cycle during a 7–3 win over the Cardinals at the Polo Grounds. Batting out of the leadoff position, Hickman achieved the cycle in order with a single in the first inning, a double in the second and a triple in the fourth off Ernie Broglio and a homer against Barney Schultz in the sixth.

AUGUST 9   Jim Hickman hits a walk-off grand slam off Lindy McDaniel with two out in the ninth inning to defeat the Cubs 7–3 at the Polo Grounds. The blast also ended Roger Craig's 18-game losing streak.

AUGUST 20 In his first major league start, Grover Powell pitches a four-hit shutout to defeat the Phillies 4–0 in the first game of a double-header in Philadelphia. The Mets lost the second game 2–1 in 12 innings.

Powell had made five previous relief appearances and allowed two runs in six innings. His August 20 victory proved to be the only one of his career. Powell's stay in the majors lasted only 20 games, all of them in 1963, and four starting assignments. His final career numbers included a 1–1 record and a 2.72 ERA.

AUGUST 27 The Mets suffer an excruciating 2–1 loss to the Pirates in Pittsburgh. The Mets led 1–0 with one out in the ninth, Dick Schofield on first base and Manny Mota batting. Mota hit a bouncer up the middle, which center fielder Duke Carmel booted. Right fielder Joe Christopher fielded the ball and threw wildly to the plate in attempt to throw out Schofield. Catcher Jesse Gonder failed to purse the throw as Mota rounded third. Pitcher Galen Cisco rushed to the screen to retrieve the ball and threw to Gonder, who was out of position and missed the tag on Mota.

SEPTEMBER 1 Three days after the March on Washington and Martin Luther King's "I Have a Dream" speech, Tim Harkness ends a marathon against the Braves with a two-run, walk-off homer in the 16th inning for a 6–4 win. Larry Bearnarth pitched seven shutout innings of relief.

SEPTEMBER 2 Leading off the first inning, Pete Rose hits the first pitch from Jay Hook for a home run, and it holds up for a 1–0 Reds win in the second game of a double-header at the Polo Grounds. The Mets won the opener 5–3.

The second straight season of 100 or more losses failed to dim the enthusiasm of the fans. The Mets drew 1,080,108 at home in 1963 to rank fourth in the National League and eighth in the majors.

SEPTEMBER 10 In the eighth inning of a 4–2 win over the Giants at Shea Stadium, Carl Willey retires brothers Jesus, Matty and Felipe Alou in order. Jesus and Matty were in the game as pinch-hitters.

SEPTEMBER 15 The Mets stage their first Banner Day at the Polo Grounds as fans paraded on the field holding their homemade signs in between games of a double-header against Houston. The Mets lost both games 5–4 and 4–0.

Fans began bringing banners to games early in the 1962 season. At first, Mets management tried to discourage the practice by confiscating the banners, but soon embraced the idea.

SEPTEMBER 18 The last baseball game is played at the Polo Grounds, and the Mets lose 5–1 to the Phillies before a crowd of only 1,752.

SEPTEMBER 22 Willie McCovey hits three homers for the Giants during a 13–4 win over the Mets in San Francisco.

SEPTEMBER 27 The Colts field a starting lineup consisting of nine rookies and lose 10–3 to the Mets in Houston. Included was future Hall of Famer Joe Morgan, future Mets Rusty Staub and Jerry Grote, a 17-year-old pitcher Jay Dahl, who made his first, and only, major league appearance.

OCTOBER 10 In a special draft designed to help bolster the rosters of the Mets and Colts, the Mets select Jack Fisher from the roster of the Giants.

NOVEMBER 4 The Mets trade Roger Craig to the Cardinals for George Altman and Bill Wakefield.

DECEMBER 14   Three weeks after the assassination of President John Kennedy, the Jets play the last football game at the Polo Grounds and lose 19–10 to the Buffalo Bills before a crowd of only 5,826.

After the Polo Grounds was torn down, a public housing project went up on the site.

1964

Season in a Sentence

The Mets play their first season in brand new Shea Stadium, but it's the same old team on the field.

Finish • Won • Lost • Pct • GB

Tenth	53	109	.327	40.0

Manager

Casey Stengel

Stats

Stats	Mets	AL	Rank
Batting Avg:	.246	.254	6
On-Base Pct:	.296	.311	9
Slugging Pct:	.348	.374	8
Home Runs:	103	8	
Stolen Bases:	36	10	
ERA:	3.54	4.25	10
Errors:	167	7	
Runs Scored:	569	9	
Runs Allowed:	776	10	

Starting Lineup

Jesse Gonder, c
Ed Kranepool, 1b
Ron Hunt, 2b
Charley Smith, 3b
Roy McMillan, ss
George Altman, lf
Jim Hickman, cf
Joe Christopher, rf
Rod Kanehl, 2b-cf-3b
Larry Elliott, cf
Bobby Klaus, 3b-2b
Hawk Taylor, c

Pitchers

Al Jackson, sp
Jack Fisher, sp
Tracy Stallard, sp
Galen Cisco, sp
Bill Wakefield, rp
Larry Bearnarth, rp
Willard Hunter, rp

Attendance

1,732,597 (second in NL)

Club Leaders

Batting Avg:	Ron Hunt	.303
On-Base Pct:	Joe Christopher	.360
Slugging Pct:	Joe Christopher	.466
Home Runs:	Charley Smith	20
RBI:	Joe Christopher	76
Runs:	Joe Christopher	78
Stolen Bases:	Joe Christopher	6
	Ron Hunt	6
Wins:	Al Jackson	11
Strikeouts:	Tracy Stallard	118
ERA:	Tracy Stallard	3.79
Saves:	Willard Hunter	5

MARCH 6   A month after the Beatles make their historic appearance on *The Ed Sullivan Show*, the Mets play the Mexico City Red Devils in Mexico City and lose 6–4. The Mets played two more games in Mexico City, on March 7 and 8, and won both.

APRIL 3   In the seventh inning of the Mets 9–1 win over the Tigers in an exhibition game, pitcher Carl Willey has his jaw broken after being hit by a line drive off the bat of Gates Brown. Willey won only one more major league game.

APRIL 14   The Mets open the season with a 5–3 loss to the Phillies in Philadelphia. Al Jackson was the starting and losing pitcher. Joe Christopher homered in the losing cause.

On the same day, the Mets sold Duke Snider to the Giants.

APRIL 16   Shea Stadium is dedicated. In a symbolic gesture as part of the ceremonies, William Shea dumped bottles of water from the Harlem River and the Gowanus Canal over the infield. The Harlem River was adjacent to the Polo Grounds. The Gowanus Canal in Brooklyn was located next to Washington Park, which was the home of the Dodgers from 1898 through 1912.

APRIL 17   The Mets play their first game at Shea Stadium and lose 4–3 to the Pirates before 50,312. The Mets led 3–1 before Pittsburgh scored single runs in the fifth, seven and ninth innings. The first batter at the new ballpark was Dick Schofield, who faced Jack Fisher and popped out to second baseman Larry Burright. Willie Stargell hit the first homer with a blast off Fisher in the second.

Opening ceremonies included the introduction of former stars from the Giants and Dodgers, such as Bill Terry, Zack Wheat and Max Carey. A massive traffic snarl developed because of 3,000 commuter cars parked on the stadium lot earlier in the day. Disgruntled motorists parked their cars on the shoulders of the congested roadways leading to Shea and walked. When they returned to their cars, they found $15 tickets attached to the windshields. Shea Stadium was part of a trend in which municipalities built multi-purpose stadiums with a circular or semi-circular design to accommodate both baseball and football. The first was D. C. Stadium in Washington, which opened in 1961. Shea, home to both the Mets and the Jets, was the second. Others that followed included those constructed in Houston (1965), Oakland (1966), St. Louis (1966), Atlanta (1966), San Diego (1967), Cincinnati (1970), Pittsburgh (1970) and Philadelphia (1971). Shea was built along the Grand Concourse Parkway on the former site of Flushing Meadows Park next to the World's Fair site of 1939 and 1940. The World's Fair of 1964 and 1965 took place in the same location. Seating capacity for baseball in 1964 was 55,300. Outfield dimensions were 341 feet down each foul line and 410 feet to center field. It was the first stadium to be constructed without light towers, as the lights were placed along the roof line. It was also the first with motorized seating sections that could be moved for baseball and football. The stadium, to the very end, was dominated by the huge 175-foot-by-86-foot scoreboard in right-center, which in 1964 was by far the largest in North America. It was also the first equipped to show color images of players and the first to show moving pictures. The Mets drew 1,732,597 fans into Shea in the first season, the second-highest figure in the major leagues, despite fielding a club with a 53–109 record. The Yankees, who won their 14th AL title in 16 years during an exciting pennant race which went to the final weekday, attracted 1,305,638.

APRIL 19   After an 0–4 start, the Mets win their first game of the season with a 6–0 decision over the Pirates at Shea Stadium. Al Jackson pitched the shutout.

As a result of a union dispute, Shea Stadium lacked the usual telephone and telegraph connections with the outside world during the first few months of the season. Newspaper copy was handed to a runner, who raced to the World's Fair press center for transmission.

APRIL 23   In the fourth game at Shea, Ron Hunt hits the first home run by a Met, but it's the lone run of a 5–1 loss to the Cubs.

On the same day, the Mets sent Chico Fernandez, Bobby Catton and cash to the White Sox for Charley Smith.

MAY 2   Al Jackson pitches a two-hitter to defeat the Reds 3–0 at Crosley Field. The only Cincinnati hits were singles by Deron Johnson in the fifth inning and Jim Maloney in the sixth.

MAY 4   Ron Hunt is tagged out after barreling into Braves catcher Ed Bailey at the end of a 2–1 loss in Milwaukee. A rousing brawl ensued with Hunt wrestling Bailey to the ground. Umpire Bill Williams and 73-year-old Casey Stengel were both knocked flat on their backs while trying to act as peacemakers.

MAY 6   The Mets play a night game at Shea Stadium for the first time and lose 12–4 to the Reds.

          Among those at the game was Larry MacPhail, who was general manager of the Reds when that club staged the first night game in major league history in 1935. Franklin Delano Roosevelt, Jr. pressed the button that turned on the Shea Stadium lights. His father was president when he pressed a button in Washington that turned on the lights at Crosley Field in Cincinnati in 1935.

MAY 8   The Mets trade Jay Hook and Adrian Garrett to the Braves for Roy McMillan.

MAY 26   The Mets collect 23 hits and shock the Cubs 19–1 at Wrigley Field. The outburst came after the Mets had scored only 16 runs in their previous ten games. It was a great day for players named Smith. Batting out of the leadoff spot, first baseman Dick Smith garnered five hits, including a triple and a double, in six at-bats. It was the first five-hit game in Mets history. Third baseman Charley Smith (no relation) drove in five runs.

          Dick Smith is one of the most obscure players in baseball history with a five-hit game. After the five-hit game, he collected only three more hits in the majors in 36 at-bats. Smith had only 31 hits and a .218 batting average during a three-year, 76-game career.

MAY 31   The Mets and Giants play 32 innings in a double-header at Shea Stadium. San Francisco won the opener 5–3 in the conventional nine innings. The second tilt lasted 23 innings, and the Giants won again 8–6. It is the longest double-header in major league history by innings and time (nine hours and 52 minutes). The Giants led the second game 6–1 before the Mets scored two runs in the sixth inning and three in the seventh. The score was tied 6–6 on a two-out, three-run homer by Joe Christopher. There was no scoring for 15 consecutive innings, from the eighth through the 22nd. Relievers Tom Sturdivant (two innings), Frank Lary (two innings in his Mets debut), Larry Bearnarth (seven innings) and Galen Cisco (eight innings) combined to shutout the Giants for 19 straight innings. Gaylord Perry held the Mets without a run for ten innings, from the 13th through the 22nd. The Mets pulled off a triple play in the 14th. With the runners on first and second moving with the pitch, Orlando Cepeda lined to shortstop Roy McMillan, who stepped on second and threw to Ed Kranepool at first. Cisco was in his ninth inning of work when he retired the first two batters of the 23rd. A triple by Jim Davenport, an intentional walk, a double from Del Crandall and Jesus Alou's single scored two runs. Bob Hendley retired the

Mets in order in the 23rd. The Mets used 21 players and the Giants 19. Willie Mays even played shortstop for three innings. Catchers Chris Cannizzaro of the Mets and Tom Haller of the Giants played all 23 innings. The weariest player may have been Ed Kranepool, however, who played a double-header in Buffalo the day before and was told he was being recalled to the Mets. Kranepool drove all night and played all 32 innings of the twin bill.

Earlier on the same day, the Mets purchased Frank Lary from the Tigers.

JUNE 5   The Mets score seven runs in the third inning and beat the Dodgers 8–0 at Shea Stadium. Galen Cisco pitched the shutout.

Cisco played linebacker and fullback on Ohio State's national championship team in 1957. He was also the captain of the squad.

JUNE 9   After the Cubs score in the top of the 12th, the Mets respond with two in their half to win 6–5 at Shea Stadium. Amado Samuel drove in a run with a single, moved to second on a walk, and crossed the plate on Jesse Gonder's single. Larry Bearnarth was the winning pitcher. He entered the game as a reliever in the third inning and pitched nine consecutive scoreless innings before giving up the run in the 12th.

One of the fixtures at Shea Stadium from 1964 through 1981 was Karl Ehrhardt, also known as the "Sign Man." From a third base box, Ehrhardt held up 26-inch-by-20-inch signs with sayings to match the occasion. Ehrhardt would bring up to 60 signs to each game.

JUNE 21   On Father's Day, Jim Bunning of the Phillies pitches a perfect game to beat the Mets 6–0 in the first game of a double-header at Shea Stadium. In the ninth inning, Bunning retired Charley Smith on a pop-up to shortstop, then struck out pinch-hitters George Altman and John Stephenson. It was the first perfect game in the National League since 1880. Tracy Stallard, who gave up Roger Maris's 61st homer in 1961 while pitching for the Red Sox, was the losing pitcher. In the second game, the Mets were held to three hits by 18-year-old Rick Wise and lost 8–2.

It soon became apparent that nearby LaGuardia Airport would be a constant problem at Shea Stadium. Low-flying jets were a distraction to the players and an annoyance to the fans, and would continue to a problem at CitiField.

JUNE 26   The Mets score all eight of their runs of an 8–4 win over the Braves in Milwaukee in the second inning. Joe Christopher hit a grand slam off Bob Sadowski.

JUNE 29   Jesse Gonder hits a two-run homer with two out in the ninth to beat the Giants 4–3 in San Francisco.

JULY 7   Five days after Lyndon Johnson signs the Civil Rights Bill, which prohibits discrimination in voting, jobs and public accommodations, Shea Stadium plays host to one of the most exciting All-Star Games in history. The NL had a 3–1 lead at the end of the fifth inning with the help of home runs from Ken Boyer and Billy Williams, but the AL scored twice in the sixth and once in the seventh for a 4–3 advantage. Willie Mays led off the NL ninth and drew a walk off Dick Radatz. Mays proceeded to steal second, move to third on a single by Orlando Cepeda and cross the plate on an error to tie the score. With one out, Johnny Edwards was given an intentional walk. Radatz struck out Hank Aaron. It was the fifth strikeout for Radatz, who entered the contest in the seventh. Johnny Callison followed with a three-run, walk-off homer for the dramatic victory. Ron Hunt started at second base for the NL and singled in three at-bats. He was the first player in Mets history to start an All-Star Game.

The 1964 Midsummer Classic was the only one ever played at Shea Stadium. Future Hall of Famers on the rosters of the two clubs included Hank Aaron, Luis Aparicio, Jim Bunning, Orlando Cepeda, Roberto Clemente, Don Drysdale, Whitey Ford, Al Kaline, Harmon Killebrew, Sandy Koufax, Mickey Mantle, Juan Marichal, Willie Mays, Brooks Robinson, Willlie Stargell and Billy Williams.

JULY 9   Frank Thomas hits a two-out, two-run, pinch-hit, walk-off homer to down the Cardinals 4–3 at Shea Stadium. It was Thomas's first at-bat in five weeks because of a glandular infection.

JULY 12   The Mets sweep the Reds 1–0 and 5–1 at Shea Stadium. The lone run in the opener scored on back-to-back doubles by George Altman and Joe Christopher in the ninth inning. Galen Cisco pitched the shutout.

JULY 18   The Cardinals score 11 runs in the eighth inning off Bill Wakefield and Carl Willey and beat the Mets 15–7 in St. Louis.

JULY 25   The Mets trounce the Braves 10–0 at Shea Stadium. Tracy Stallard pitched the shutout.

JULY 26   The Mets lose 11–7 and 15–10 during a double-header against the Braves at Shea Stadium. In the second game, the Mets collected 20 hits and scored seven runs in the seventh inning to take a 10–7 lead but still wound up losing.

JULY 31   Frank Lary pitches a two-hitter to beat the Colts 3–0 in the first game of a double-header at Shea Stadium. The only Houston hits were singles by Bob Lillis with two out in the sixth inning and Nellie Fox with two out in the ninth. The Mets also won the second game 6–2.

AUGUST 7   The Mets trade Frank Thomas to the Phillies for Gary Kroll, Wayne Graham and cash.

AUGUST 8   The Mets trade Frank Lary to the Braves for Dennis Ribant.

AUGUST 18   Joe Christopher collects four extra base hits during a 7–3 win over the Pirates at Shea Stadium. Christopher had a triple in the first inning, a double in the third and another triple in the fifth off Joe Gibbon, and homered against Roy Face in the sixth.

AUGUST 23   Willard Hunter is the winning pitcher in both ends of a double-header as the Mets beat the Cubs 2–1 in ten innings and 5–4 in nine. Both were won with walk-off singles by Ed Kranepool in the opener and Charley Smith in the nightcap.

AUGUST 24   Before a standing-room-only crowd of 60,167 at Shea Stadium, the Yankees beat the Mets 6–4 in the Mayor's Trophy Game.

AUGUST 28   The Mets outslug the Cubs 12–10 in Chicago. A four-run rally in the eighth provided the winning margin.

SEPTEMBER 12   The Jets play at Shea Stadium for the first time and rout the Denver Broncos 30–6 before a crowd of 52,663, which at the time was an American Football League record.

SEPTEMBER 27   On the day the Warren Commission is released, citing Lee Harvey Oswald as the lone gunman in the assassination of President John Kennedy, Tracy Stallard records his 20th loss of 1964 by dropping a 4–1 decision to the Reds in the first game of a double-header at Shea Stadium. Cincinnati also won the second tilt 3–1.

SEPTEMBER 30   Jim Hickman has five hits in six at-bats, but the Mets lose 6–5 in 12 innings to the Braves in Milwaukee.

The Mets went into the final three-game series against the Cardinals in St. Louis with an opportunity to help decide the National League pennant-winner. Heading the series, the Cardinals were in first place one-half game ahead of the Reds. The Phillies were 2$\frac{1}{2}$ out and still had a mathematical chance to win. The Phils had led by 6$\frac{1}{2}$ games on September 21. The Mets traveled to St. Louis with a record of 51–108 and had lost eight in a row.

OCTOBER 2   Al Jackson pitches the Mets to a 1–0 win over the Cardinals in St. Louis. The lone run scored on a single by Ed Kranepool in the third inning.

OCTOBER 3   The Mets hit five homers and demolish the Cardinals 15–5 in St. Louis. The home runs were struck by Bobby Klaus, Joe Christopher, Charley Smith, Ed Kranepool and George Altman. Heading into the final day of the season, the Cardinals were tied for first place with the Reds and were one game up on the Phillies.

OCTOBER 4   The Cardinals clinch the NL pennant by beating the Mets 11–5 in St. Louis.

NOVEMBER 17   Two weeks after Lyndon Johnson defeats Barry Goldwater in the presidential election, the Mets hire Yogi Berra as a coach.

Rated by many as the greatest catcher of all-time, Berra played in 14 World Series with the Yankees from 1947 through 1963. He was named manager of the club in 1964 and won the AL pennant in his first season before losing to the Cardinals in seven games in the World Series. Despite the success, Berra was fired by the Yankees and replaced by Johnny Keane, who resigned as manager of the Cardinals after leading his club to the world championship. Berra would remain with the Mets for more than a decade as a coach (1965–71), player (1965) and manager (1972–75).

NOVEMBER 23   The Mets purchase Warren Spahn from the Braves.

Spahn came to the Mets with 356 career wins. He was 23–7 in 1963 at the age of 42, but slumped to 6–13 in 1964. In addition to playing for the Mets, Spahn served as pitching coach. He had a 4–12 record with the club before drawing his release in July 1965.

1965

Season in a Sentence

Casey Stengel retires and Mets fans anxious for progress are disappointed as the club loses 112 games.

Finish • Won • Lost • Pct • GB

Tenth 50 112 .309 47.0

Managers

Casey Stengel (31–64) and Wes Westrum (19–48)

Stats

Stats	Mets	AL	Rank
Batting Avg:	.221	.249	10
On-Base Pct:	.277	.311	10
Slugging Pct:	.327	.374	10
Home Runs:	107	9	
Stolen Bases:	28	10	
ERA:	4.06	3.54	10
Errors:	171	9	
Runs Scored:	495	10	
Runs Allowed:	752	10	

Starting Lineup

Chris Cannizzaro, c
Ed Kranepool, 1b
Chuck Hiller, 2b
Charley Smith, 3b
Roy McMillan, ss
Joe Christopher, lf-rf
Jim Hickman, cf
Johnny Lewis, rf
Ron Swoboda, lf
Bobby Klaus, 2b

Pitchers

Jack Fisher, sp
Al Jackson, sp
Warren Spahn, sp
Galen Cisco, rp-sp
Tug McGraw, rp
Tom Parsons, rp-sp
Gary Kroll, rp-sp

Attendance

1,768,389 (third in NL)

Club Leaders

Batting Avg:	Ed Kranepool	.253
On-Base Pct:	Johnny Lewis	.331
Slugging Pct:	Johnny Lewis	.384
Home Runs:	Ron Swoboda	19
RBIs:	Charley Smith	62
Runs:	Johnny Lewis	62
Stolen Bases:	Johnny Lewis	4
Wins:	Jack Fisher	8
	Al Jackson	8
Strikeouts:	Al Jackson	120
ERA:	Jack Fisher	3.94
Saves:	Dennis Ribant	3

JANUARY 15   The Mets trade George Altman to the Cubs for Billy Cowan.

MARCH 22   Gary Kroll (six innings) and Gordon Richardson (three innings) combine on a no-hitter to defeat the Pirates 6–0 in a spring training exhibition game in St. Petersburg.

MARCH 28   The Mets purchase Frank Lary from the Braves.

APRIL 12   The Mets open the season with a 6–1 loss to the Dodgers before 37,999 at Shea Stadium. Al Jackson was the starting and losing pitcher.

The Mets added uniform numbers to the fronts of the home and road uniforms in 1965.

APRIL 14   After the Astros score four runs in the top of the 11th with two out, the Mets counter with three in their half before falling 7–6 at Shea Stadium. In the Houston half of the 11th, Larry Bearnarth walked three straight batters and Al Spangler stole home. During the Mets' futile rally in the bottom half, Ron Swoboda homered in his second big-league at-bat.

APRIL 15   Bobby Klaus hits a walk-off homer in the tenth inning to defeat the Astros 5–4 at Shea Stadium. The Mets pulled off a triple play in the second inning. With Walt Bond on third base and Bob Aspromonte on first, Jimmy Wynn hit a fly ball to right fielder Johnny Lewis, whose one-bounce throw to catcher Chris Cannizzaro nailed Bond. Aspromonte tried to advance to second on the play and was thrown out by Cannizzaro to shortstop Roy McMillan.

The winning pitcher was 18-year-old Jim Bethke. He pitched only one big-league season and was 2–0 in 25 relief appearances. Bethke was still only 18 when he pitched his last big-league game.

APRIL 20   Warren Spahn pitches eight shutout innings before allowing two runs in the ninth to escape with a 3–2 win over the Dodgers in Los Angeles. During the ninth, Jim Lefebvre was Spahn's 2,500th career strikeout victim.

APRIL 23   Trailing 8–2, the Mets score two runs in the eighth inning, four in the ninth and one in the 11th to stun the Giants 9–8 at Candlestick Park. Both eighth-inning runs scored after two were out. Jim Hickman doubled in a run and scored on a single by Charley Smith. Ron Swoboda and Jesse Gonder began the ninth with back-to-back homers off Gaylord Perry. Swoboda's homer came in a pinch-hit role. Gonder entered the game as a pinch-hitter in the second inning and remained in the lineup as a catcher. Joe Christpoher singled in a run, and the score was tied 8–8 on a San Francisco error. Smith drove in the go-ahead run in the 11th with a sacrifice fly. The game ended at 3:10 a.m. Eastern Time.

APRIL 24   The Mets win with late-inning heroics for the second day in a row by scoring three runs in the ninth to beat the Giants 7–6 in San Francisco. With two out and runners on second and third, Johnny Lewis, representing the winning run, was walked intentionally. Danny Napoleon batted for Roy McMillan and hit a three-run triple to give the Mets the victory.

The game-winning hit came in Napoleon's third career plate appearance. He never hit another triple in a career that spanned two seasons, 80 games and 130 at-bats.

APRIL 27   The Mets play indoors for the first time in club history and lose 3–2 to the Astros in the Astrodome. The unfamiliarity of playing under a roof contributed to the defeat. With two out in the ninth, two Houston runners on base and the Mets leading 2–1, Eddie Kasko lifted a fly ball to left field that appeared to be the final out of the game. But Joe Christopher lost the ball in the roof panels, and it fell for a game-winning, two-run double.

APRIL 28   Lindsay Nelson broadcasts the game against the Astros from the gondola that hangs from the roof of the Astrodome, 208 feet above second base. The Mets lost 12–9.

APRIL 30   Ron Swoboda is robbed of an apparent home run during a 6–1 loss to the Reds in Cincinnati. The concrete outfield wall at Crosley Field had an eight-foot wooden extension added in 1964 to shield the batter's eyes from highway traffic. Balls hitting the extension were home runs. Swoboda's drive appeared to hit the wooden section of the fence, but second base umpire, Frank Secory, ruled it a double.

After the game, Yogi Berra said, "Anyone who can't tell the difference when a ball bounces off concrete and when it bounces off wood is deaf." Like many Berra quotes, this one took on a life of it's own. It has appeared in many baseball books with the world "blind" substituted for "deaf."

MAY 1   Yogi Berra plays in his first game since 1963 and grounds out as a pinch-hitter in the eighth inning of a 9–2 loss to the Reds in Cincinnati.

Berra was activated as a player on April 27. He appeared in four games, two of them starts as a catcher, before retiring as a player for good. Berra collected two hits in nine at-bats.

MAY 5   Phillies pitcher Jim Bunning hits a home run in the sixth inning off Warren Spahn for the only run of a 1–0 win over the Mets at Shea Stadium.

MAY 8   With a three-run homer in the first inning and a solo shot in the sixth, Ron Swoboda drives in all four runs of a 4–2 win over the Braves at Shea Stadium.

MAY 10   During an exhibition game against the U. S. Military Academy at West Point, Casey Stengel slips on a concrete walk while wearing his baseball spikes and fractures his right wrist.

MAY 23   The Mets blow a 7–0 lead by allowing two runs in the eighth inning, five in the ninth and one in the 12th to lose 8–7 to the Cardinals in St. Louis. Larry Bearnarth gave up all five runs in the ninth, the last three on a two-out, bases-loaded triple by Dal Maxvill.

JUNE 8   With the second overall pick in the very first amateur draft, the Mets select pitcher Les Rohr from West High School in Billings, Montana.

The Athletics picked first and drafted Rick Monday. Born in Lowestoft, England, Rohr pitched in only six games in the majors over three seasons, beginning in 1967. Other players drafted and signed by the Mets who later reached the majors were Joe Moock (second round), Ken Boswell (fourth round), Jim McAndrew (11th round), Nolan Ryan (12th round), Steve Renko (24th round), Don Shaw (35th round), Joe Campbell (44th round) and Joe Raziano (47th round). Ryan, of course, was by far the best of the bunch, but nearly all of his legendary success in baseball was achieved after being traded by the Mets. Ryan, Boswell and McAndrew played on the 1969 world championship team.

JUNE 13   The Mets extend their losing streak to ten games by dropping both ends of a double-header to the Dodgers at Shea Stadium by scores of 5–2 and 4–3.

JUNE 14   The Mets break their ten-game losing streak by breaking up Jim Maloney's no-hit bid in the 11th inning and winning 1–0 in Cincinnati. Through the first ten innings, Maloney not only had a no-hitter in progress but had walked only one and struck out 17. Johnny Lewis broke up the no-hitter and the shutout by homering to lead off the 11th. Before the inning was over, Maloney gave up a single to Roy McMillan and recorded his 18th strikeout. Frank Lary (eight innings) and Larry Bearnarth (three innings) combined on a seven-hit shutout.

After the victory, the Mets lost their next five games. The improbable victory was the club's only one in a span of 16 games.

JUNE 20   The Mets lone hit off Sandy Koufax is a fifth-inning home run by Jim Hickman in a 2–1 loss to the Dodgers in the first game of a double-header in Los Angeles. The Mets won the second contest 3–2.

JUNE 21   The Mets collect only two hits but beat the Dodgers 1–0 in Los Angeles. Claude Osteen had a no-hitter in progress until Joe Christopher singled in the seventh. The lone run scored on a homer by Billy Cowan leading off the ninth. Al Jackson hurled a three-hit shutout for the Mets.

From June 4 through June 27, the Mets scored only 34 runs in 24 games and had a record of 4–20. The wins were by scores of 2–1, 1–0, 3–2 and 1–0.

JULY 8   The Mets trade Frank Lary to the White Sox for Jimmie Schaffer.

JULY 19   The Mets release Warren Spahn. He signed with the Giants three days later.

JULY 21   Al Jackson pitches a two-hitter to defeat the Pirates 1–0 at Forbes Field. Jackson had a no-hitter in progress until Willie Stargell singled with one out in the eighth. Ozzie Virgil added another single in the ninth.

JULY 25   Stepping out of a friend's automobile after a late-night party, Casey Stengel falls and fractures his hip. Ironically, he was to have been honored between games of a double-header later that day at Shea Stadium for his 75th birthday. The birthday was actually on July 30, but the Mets were scheduled for a game in Philadelphia on that date. On July 27, Stengel underwent surgery and a metal ball was inserted in the hip to reduce the fracture. Coach Wes Westrum was named interim manager (see August 30, 1965).

JULY 29   The Mets clobber the Cubs 14–0 in the first game of a double-header at Wrigley Field. Johnny Lewis collected two homers, a double and a single and drove in four runs. Galen Cisco pitched the shutout. Lewis added three more hits in the second game, but the Mets lost 2–1 in 12 innings.

AUGUST 11 On the day in which riots begin in the Watts section of Los Angeles, resulting in the deaths of 34 people, the Mets lose 1–0 to the Dodgers at Dodger Stadium.

AUGUST 13 The Mets extend their losing streak to 11 by dropping a 3–2 decision to the Astros in Houston.

AUGUST 14 The Mets break their 11-game losing streak by beating the Astros 1–0 in ten innings in Houston. Galen Cisco (six innings) and Darrell Sutherland (four innings) combined on the shutout. Sutherland held the opposition without a hit to earn his first major league victory.

The Mets finished last in the NL in earned run average for the fourth straight year but managed five extra-inning shutouts. The others were on June 14, September 12, September 28 and October 2.

AUGUST 15   The Beatles play the first of their two historic concerts at Shea Stadium.

AUGUST 24   The Mets score three runs in the ninth inning to beat the Dodgers 4–3 at Shea Stadium. The Mets loaded the bases on a error and two singles before pinch-hitter John Stephenson walloped a three-run, walk-off double.

AUGUST 30   At a press conference, Casey Stengel announces that on medical advice he has decided to retire. He was named a vice-president in charge of the West Coast area. The interim tag was taken off Wes Westrum's title after the end of the season.

Even without the health issues, it's doubtful that Stengel would have returned in 1966. Fans and many front office executives were impatient with the club's lack of progress, and Stengel was frequently criticized for being out of touch. The only other individual in major league history to manage a club past his 75th birthday was Connie Mack. Westrum was an underrated catcher with the New York Giants from 1947 through 1957. He had a career batting average of just .217 but compiled a respectable on-base percentage of .356 because of his ability to draw walks, and at his peak twice hit more than 20 or more homers in a season. Westrum made the All-Star team in 1952 and 1953. He became a coach with the Giants after the club moved to San Francisco, from 1958 through 1963. Westrum came to the Mets during the 1963–64 offseason in an unusual trade of coaches. Mets coach Cookie Lavagetto wanted to be closer to his home in Oakland, and Westrum went back to New York in exchange. Westrum would guide the Mets through the end of the 1967 season. The Mets subsequently retired Stengel's number 37 in pregame ceremonies at Shea Stadium on September 2, the first so designated by the club.

Later, numbers were retired in honor of Gil Hodges (14) and Tom Seaver (41). Although not officially retired, the Mets haven't issued number 24 to anyone since Willie Mays last wore it as a player (1972–73) and coach (1974–79) with the exception of Kelvin Torve in 1990 and Rickey Henderson as a player in 1999 and 2000 and as a coach in 2007. Also, number 31 hasn't been issued to any Met since Mike Piazza last donned in 2005. Number 8 hasn't been issued since Gary Carter was elected to the Hall of Fame in 2003. In addition, number 42 is retired throughout baseball in honor of Jackie Robinson.

SEPTEMBER 3   Jim Hickman becomes the first Met to hit three homers in a game during a 6–3 win over the Cardinals in St. Louis. All three came off Ray Sadecki in consecutive plate appearances in the second, fourth and sixth innings. Hickman also singled against Nelson Briles in the eighth.

SEPTEMBER 10   Jim Hickman's homer in the fourth inning is the only Mets hit in a 3–1 loss to the Braves at Shea Stadium. The homer was struck off starter Wade Blasingame, who pitched five innings. Billy O'Dell (one inning) and Phil Niekro (three innings) completed the one-hitter. Jack Fisher suffered his 20th loss of the season.

Fisher was 8–24 in 1965.

SEPTEMBER 11   The Mets are not only held to one hit for the second game in a row but commit five errors in a 9–0 loss to the Braves at Shea Stadium. Tony Cloninger pitched the one-hitter.

SEPTEMBER 12   Dick Selma strikes out 13 batters and pitches a ten-inning, four-hit complete game shutout to beat the Braves 1–0 at Shea Stadium. The winning run scored on a walk-off single by Charley Smith.

Selma hurled his gem in his second major league game. He made his debut on September 3.

SEPTEMBER 28   The Mets outlast the Pirates to win 1–0 in 12 innings at Shea Stadium. Ron Hunt drove in the winning run with a single off Roy Face. Dennis Ribant (11 innings) and Darrell Sutherland (one inning) combined on the shutout.

The 11 innings of shutout ball came in Ribant's only start of the 1965 season. He made 18 relief appearances.

OCTOBER 2   The Mets play 27 innings in a double-header against the Phillies at Shea Stadium and fail to score. The opener was a 6–0 loss. The second tilt went 18 innings and ended in a 0–0 tie. It was called because of a National League rule that stipulated no inning could start after 1:00 a.m. Rob Gardner, who was 20 years old and pitching in his fifth big-league game, went 15 innings and allowed only five hits. Darrell Sutherland (two innings) and Dennis Ribant (one inning) completed the 18-inning shutout. Chris Short (15 innings), Gary Wagner (two innings) and Jack Baldschun (one inning) pitched for Philadelphia. Short struck out 18 batters, and 21 Mets in all went down on strikes.

The only longer 0–0 tie in major league history lasted 19 innings between the Reds and Dodgers in Brooklyn on September 11, 1946.

OCTOBER 3   On the last day of the season, Al Jackson records his 20th loss of the season with a 3–1 defeat at the hands of the Phillies in the first game of a double-header at Shea Stadium. The Mets also lost the second game 3–1 in 13 innings.

The Mets closed the season with back-to-back double-headers and scored only two runs in 49 innings. The club searched in vain for a winning combination all year. Counting pitchers, the Mets used 164 different starting lineups in the 164 games played, which included two ties. There were 16 different starting pitchers, seven catchers, three first basemen, three second basemen, seven third basemen, three shortstops, seven left fielders, six center fielders and eight right fielders. There were ten different starting leadoff batters. The center fielders combined for a batting average of .194. The Mets stole only 28 bases with Johnny Lewis and Joe Christopher tied for the team lead with four. Closing out a game was also a problem. The Mets had ten different pitchers record at least one save. Dennis Ribant was the club leader with three.

OCTOBER 19   The Mets trade Tom Parsons to the Astros for Jerry Grote.

The Mets pulled off a tremendous deal to acquire Grote, who played for the Mets from 1966 through 1977. At the end of the 2010 season, he ranked third all-time in franchise history in games played with 1,235.

OCTOBER 20   The Mets trade Al Jackson and Charley Smith to the Cardinals for Ken Boyer.

Boyer was named to seven NL All-Star teams and won the MVP Award in 1964, then went into a sudden decline in 1965. The Mets hoped that at 34, Boyer might have a few good seasons left, but in two years with the club he batted .258 with 17 homers in 192 games.

NOVEMBER 30   The Mets trade Joe Christopher to the Red Sox for Eddie Bressoud.

1966

Season in a Sentence

Progress of sorts is made as the Mets avoid last place and 100 losses for the first time.

Finish • Won • Lost • Pct • GB

Ninth   66   95   .410   28.5

Manager

Wes Westrum

Stats

Stats	Mets	AL	Rank
Batting Avg:	.239	256	10
On-Base Pct:	.301	.313	9
Slugging Pct:	.342	.384	10
Home Runs:	98	10	
Stolen Bases:	55	9	
ERA:	4.17	3.61	9
Errors:	159	7	
Runs Scored:	587	9	
Runs Allowed:	761	9	

Starting Lineup

Jerry Grote, c
Ed Kranepool, 1b
Ron Hunt, 2b
Ken Boyer, 3b
Ed Bressoud, ss
Ron Swoboda, lf
Cleon Jones, cf
Al Luplow, rf
Chuck Hiller, 2b
Roy McMillan, ss

Pitchers

Jack Fisher, sp
Dennis Ribant, sp
Bob Shaw, sp
Bob Friend, sp
Jack Hamilton, rp
Ron Gardner, rp-sp
Dick Selma, rp

Attendance

1,932,693 (second in NL)

Club Leaders

Batting Avg:	Ron Hunt	.277
On-Base Pct:	Ron Hunt	.356
Slugging Pct:	Ken Boyer	.415
Home Runs:	Ed Kranepool	16
RBI:	Ken Boyer	61
Runs:	Cleon Jones	74
Stolen Bases:	Cleon Jones	16
Wins:	Three tied with	11
Strikeouts:	Jack Fisher	127
ERA:	Dennis Ribant	3.20
Saves:	Jack Hamilton	13

FEBRUARY 22   The Mets trade Wayne Graham, Bobby Klaus and Jimmie Schaffer to the Phillies for Dick Stuart.

Stuart was one of the most colorful players of the era. In 1963 and 1964 combined, he hit 75 homers and drove in 232 runs for the Red Sox, but his atrocious fielding and "me first" attitude led to a trade to Philadelphia. Stuart led his league in errors for seven consecutive seasons beginning in 1958, which earned him the nickname "Dr. Strangeglove." He was in the starting lineup on Opening Day for the Mets in 1966, but after batting just .218 in 31 games, Stuart was released in June.

MARCH 5   The Major League Players Association hires Marvin Miller as the new executive director of the organization. Miller formally took office on March 1. Under Miller's leadership, the association would take actions that led to a revolution in player-owner relations, including free agency beginning in 1976.

APRIL 3   The Mets acquire Tom Seaver.

Seaver agreed to a contract with the Braves, but commissioner William Eckert ruled it invalid because it was signed before Seaver's season at the University of Southern California was completed. Seaver decided to go back to college, but the NCAA also ruled him ineligible. His father threatened to sue Major League Baseball, and Eckert allowed the other 19 teams to match the Braves' offer. The three teams who did so were the Mets, Indians and Phillies. Slips of paper with the names of the three teams were placed in a hat, and Eckert drew the Mets. Seaver made his major league debut in 1967. There is little argument that he is the greatest player in franchise history. In two stints with the club (1967–77 and 1983), Seaver was 198–124. He won the Cy Young Award in 1969, 1973 and 1975, and led the NL five times in strikeouts, three times in ERA and twice in wins. On the all-time franchise lists Seaver is first in wins, first in ERA (2.57), first in innings (3,045$^{1}/_{3}$), first in strikeouts (2,541), first in games started (395), first in complete games (171), first in shutouts (44), second in games pitched (401) and third in winning percentage (.615).

APRIL 11   The scheduled season opener against the Reds in Cincinnati is postponed due to rain. The showers continued, and eventually both contests of two-game opening series were postponed.

APRIL 14   The Mets get underway and lose 3–2 to the Braves before 52,812 at Shea Stadium. Jack Fisher took a 2–1 lead into the ninth inning before allowing two runs in the defeat.

APRIL 16   With a 2–1 record, the Mets move over the .500 mark for the first time in franchise history with a 5–4 win over the Braves at Shea Stadium. Ken Boyer tied the score 4–4 with a two-out, two-run double in the eighth. Ron Swoboda drew a walk from Billy O'Dell with the bases loaded in the ninth to score the winning run.

The Mets lost their next five games to fall to 2–6 and never got back to the .500 level in 1966.

APRIL 22   The Mets play in Atlanta for the first time and lose 8–4 to the Braves.

APRIL 26   The Mets outslug the Cubs 14–11 at Wrigley Field. The Mets were helped by five Chicago errors and made three of their own.

MAY 4   Jack Hamilton pitches a one-hitter to defeat the Cardinals 8–0 in St. Louis. The only hit off Hamilton was a bunt single by opposing pitcher Ray Sadecki in the third inning. Hamilton retired the last 19 batters to face him. It was also the last time that the Mets played in the first of three ballparks in St. Louis named Busch Stadium. It had served as the home of the Cards since 1920.

MAY 6   Cleon Jones hits a walk-off homer in the ninth inning to beat the Cubs 2–1 at Shea Stadium.

MAY 24   The Mets play on artificial turf for the first time and lose 5–3 to the Astros in Houston.

The Astrodome opened in 1965 with a conventional grass field, but players lost fly balls in the glare of the glass panels in the roof. The glass had to be painted, which killed the grass. The artificial surface, manufactured by Monsanto and named Astroturf, was the solution.

MAY 29   The Mets score three runs in the ninth inning to defeat the Dodgers 7–6 in Los Angeles. Pinch-hitter Hawk Taylor tied the score with a two-run double and scored on a two-out single by Roy McMillan.

JUNE 7   In one of the worst number one overall picks ever made, the Mets select catcher Steve Chilcott from Antelope Valley High School in Lancaster, California.

The two top prospects were considered to be Chilcott and Arizona State University outfielder Reggie Jackson. The Mets chose Chilcott. The Athletics, drafting second, picked Jackson. Chilcott played but never made the major leagues. Through 2010, the only other number one draft pick to retire without playing in the majors was Brien Taylor, who was chosen by the Yankees in 1991. Future major leaguers drafted and signed by the Mets in 1966 were Mike Jorgensen (fourth round), Ernie McAnally (20th round), Duffy Dyer (first round of the secondary phase) and Danny Frisella (third round of the secondary phase). The secondary phase consisted of players previously drafted but who did not sign with their original clubs. The Mets also drafted Ron Cey in the 19th round, but Cey decided to attend Washington State University instead of turning professional. Cey was drafted by the Dodgers in 1968.

JUNE 10   In his major league debut, Dick Rustek pitches a four-hit shutout to beat the Reds 4–0 at Shea Stadium. On the same day, the Mets purchased Bob Shaw from the Giants.

Rustek never won another major league game. His final major league numbers included eight games, three starts, a 1–2 won-lost record and a 3.00 ERA.

JUNE 15   The Mets purchase Bob Friend from the Yankees. It was the first transaction between the two New York clubs.

JUNE 16   The Braves pummel the Mets 17–1 in Atlanta.

JUNE 20   The Mets play at the second of three ballparks named Busch Stadium for the first time and lose 4–2 to the Cardinals. The second Busch Stadium served as the home of the Cards until 2005.

JUNE 22   Jack Fisher (nine innings) and Jack Hamilton (one inning) combine to beat the Cardinals 2–0 in ten innings in St. Louis. Cleon Jones drove in both runs on a two-out single off former Met Al Jackson.

JUNE 28   Both the Mets and the Phillies collect only two hits during a 1–0 loss at Shea Stadium. Bob Friend (eight innings) and Jack Hamilton (one inning) pitched for the Mets. The lone run scored on a homer by Bill White in the seventh inning. Jim Bunning hurled for the Phils.

JULY 1   Woodie Fryman of the Pirates faces the minimum 27 batters in beating the Mets 12–0 at Shea Stadium. Ron Hunt led off with a single and was out trying to steal second base. Fryman proceeded to retire the final 26 hitters to complete a one-hitter.

JULY 3   Ed Bressoud hits a grand slam off Bob Veale in the seventh inning, but the Mets lose 8–7 to the Pirates in the first game of a double-header at Shea Stadium. The Mets won the second tilt 9–8.

                  The Mets hit only two grand slams in 1966, and both were off Veale (see August 17, 1966).

JULY 10   Ron Hunt's sacrifice helps the National League win the All-Star Game 2–1 on a 105-degree day in St. Louis. Tim McCarver singled and went to second on Hunt's bunt. McCarver crossed the plate on a single from Maury Wills.

JULY 20   The Mets use three solo homers to beat the Giants 3–2 in ten innings in San Francisco. The three were by Al Luplow in the seventh and Roy McMillan in the eighth, both off Juan Marichal, and by Ron Swoboda against Bill Henry in the tenth.

JULY 21   The Mets rout the Giants 14–3 in San Francisco.

                  With an 18–14 record in July, the Mets completed the first winning month in club history.

JULY 25   Casey Stengel is formally inducted into the baseball Hall of Fame.

AUGUST 4   Trailing 6–1, the Mets score three runs in the eighth and four in the ninth to beat the Giants 8–6 at Shea Stadium. Jerry Stephenson drove in the first two runs in the eighth on a pinch-hit homer off Juan Marichal. Ken Boyer led off the ninth with another homer off Marichal, who was relieved by Lindy McDaniel. After singles by Ed Bressoud and Stephenson, McDaniel was replaced by Bill Henry. Ron Swoboda came into the game as a pinch-hitter and walloped a three-run, walk-off homer for the victory. It was Swoboda's second game-winning home run off Henry in two weeks (see July 20, 1966).

AUGUST 6   The Mets purchase Ralph Terry from the Athletics.

AUGUST 17   Down 7–1, the Mets score five runs in the fourth inning and two in the sixth to defeat the Pirates 8–7 at Shea Stadium. Batting for Ed Kranepool in the fourth inning, Hawk Taylor hit a pinch-hit grand slam off Bob Veale. The Mets took the lead on a two-run single from Ron Hunt in the sixth.

AUGUST 21   Tug McGraw pitches a two-hitter to defeat the Phillies 5–1 in the second game of a double-header at Connie Mack Stadium. The only Philadelphia hits were singles by Jim Bunning in the third inning and Harvey Kuenn in the fifth. The Mets also won the opener 6–5.

                  McGraw had a record of 4–19 with the Mets from 1965 through 1967, then spent the entire 1968 season in the minors. Returning in 1969 as a reliever, McGraw was instrumental in helping the club reach the World Series that season and in 1973, blending his toughness as a closer on the field with a whimsical sense of humor off the diamond.

AUGUST 23   The Beatles play at Shea Stadium for the second time.

SEPTEMBER 11   Nolan Ryan makes his major league debut by pitching the sixth and seventh innings of an 8–3 loss to the Braves at Shea Stadium. Ryan allowed a run and a hit, walked one and struck out three. The first of his 5,714 strikeout victims was Pat Jarvis.

> *Ryan was 20 when he made his major league debut. He was called up after going 17–4 in Greenville and Williamsport during the 1966 season in the Mets minor league system and had 327 strikeouts in 202 innings. Ryan pitched in two games for the Mets in 1966, then spent all of 1967 in the minors and performing military service in the Reserves before returning in 1968.*

SEPTEMBER 16   During a three-run rally in the ninth against the Dodgers in Los Angeles, Bud Harrelson breaks a 3–3 tie with a triple, then steals home. It was Harrelson's second triple of the game. The Mets allowed a run in the bottom half before closing out a 5–4 victory.

SEPTEMBER 17   Willie McCovey three homers for the Giants, including a three-run walkoff shot in the tenth off Larry Miller, to spark a 6–4 win over the Mets in San Francisco.

SEPTEMBER 18   Nolan Ryan makes his first major league start and allows four runs in only one inning of a 9–2 loss to the Astros in Houston.

SEPTEMBER 19   The Mets collect only three hits but beat the Astros 1–0 in ten innings in Houston. Bob Shaw pitched a four-hit complete game shutout. The Mets entered the tenth with only one hit off Chris Zachary, then scored on a single by Cleon Jones, a double from Ed Kranepool and a wild pitch.

SEPTEMBER 28   The Mets lose 4–1 and win 1–0 in a double-header against the Cubs at Shea Stadium. In the opener, the Mets completed a triple play in the sixth inning. With the runners on first and second moving with the pitch, Joe Amalfitano lined to third baseman Ed Bressoud. The triple play was completed on throws to second baseman Chuck Hiller and first baseman Jim Hickman. In the second game, Bob Shaw pitched a complete game shutout. The lone run scored in the seventh on a single by Cleon Jones.

SEPTEMBER 30   The Mets win 1–0 for the second game in a row, defeating the Astros at Shea Stadium. Houston's Larry Dierker came into the ninth with a no-hitter. Ed Bressoud led off the inning with a double and scored on a walk-off single from Ron Hunt. Jack Fisher pitched the shutout.

NOVEMBER 14   George Weiss resigns as president of the Mets and is replaced by 49-year-old Bing Devine.

> *Devine had been general manager of the Cardinals from 1957 through 1964. He was fired in August 1964 by St. Louis owner, August Busch, who was dissatisfied after the team had seemingly fallen out of contention after finishing second in 1963. But the Cardinals rallied to win the NL pennant and the World Series with players largely acquired in trades by Devine, including Lou Brock, Bill White and Julian Javier. Devine was hired by the Mets as Weiss's assistant and held the position for two years before being promoted to general manager.*

NOVEMBER 29   The Mets trade Ron Hunt and Jim Hickman to the Dodgers for Tommy Davis and Derrell Griffith.

After making the All-Star team as a starter in 1964, Hunt struggled with injuries in 1965 and 1966. He continued as a regular second baseman with the Dodgers, Giants and Expos until 1974. Hickman was the last of the players on the Opening Day roster in 1962 who was still with the club in 1966. He was a run-of-the-mill outfielder and first baseman for his first eight years in the majors before a breakout year with the Cubs in 1970 in which he hit .315 with 33 homers and 115 RBI. Hickman proved to be a one-year wonder, however. Davis won the NL batting title with the Dodgers in 1962 and 1963, but a broken ankle suffered in 1965 hampered his effectiveness. He played for ten big-league clubs from 1966 through 1976. In his lone season with the Mets, Davis hit .302 with 16 home runs.

DECEMBER 6   The Mets trade Gary Kolb and Dennis Ribant to the Pirates for Don Cardwell and Don Bosch.

Bosch was expected to be the solution for the Mets' center field problem, but batted an abysmal .157 in 204 at-bats over two seasons.

1967

Season in a Sentence

The Mets fall back into last place with 101 defeats and Gil Hodges is hired as manager following the resignation of Wes Westrum.

Finish • Won • Lost • Pct • GB

Tenth   61   101   .377   40.5

Managers

Wes Westrum (57–94) and Salty Parker (4–7)

Stats

Stats	Mets	AL	Rank
Batting Avg:	.238	.249	9
On-Base Pct:	.288	.310	10
Slugging Pct:	.325	.363	10
Home Runs:	83	9	
Stolen Bases:	58	7	
ERA:	3.73	3.38	9
Errors:	157	8	
Runs Scored:	498	9	
Runs Allowed:	672	9	

Starting Lineup

Jerry Grote, c
Ed Kranepool, 1b
Jerry Buchek, 2b
Ed Charles, 3b
Bud Harrelson, ss
Tommy Davis, lf
Cleon Jones, cf
Ron Swoboda, rf
Bob Johnson, 2b-1b

Pitchers

Tom Seaver, sp
Jack Fisher, sp
Don Cardwell, sp-rp
Bob Shaw, sp-rp
Ron Taylor, rp
Dick Selma, rp

Attendance

1,565,492 (third in NL)

Club Leaders

Batting Avg:	Tommy Davis	.302
On-Base Pct:	Tommy Davis	.342
Slugging Pct:	Tommy Davis	.440
Home Runs:	Tommy Davis	16
RBI:	Tommy Davis	73
Runs:	Tommy Davis	72
Stolen Bases:	Bud Harrelson	12
	Cleon Jones	12
Wins:	Tom Seaver	16
Strikeouts:	Tom Seaver	170
ERA:	Tom Seaver	2.76
Saves:	Ron Taylor	8

JANUARY 28   Thirteen days after the Green Bay Packers defeat the Kansas City Chiefs 35–10 in the first Super Bowl, the Mets select Ken Singleton in the first round and Tommy Moore in the tenth in the January amateur draft.

FEBRUARY 10   The Mets purchase Ron Taylor from the Astros.

MARCH 24   The Mets trade Derrell Griffith to the Astros for Sandy Alomar, Sr.

APRIL 1   The Mets send Ed Bressoud, Danny Napoleon and cash to the Cardinals for Jerry Buchek, Art Mahaffey and Tony Martinez.

APRIL 11   The Mets open the season with a 6–3 Opening Day loss to the Pirates before 31,510 at Shea Stadium. Pittsburgh broke a 3–3 tie in the ninth with three runs off starter Don Cardwell and reliever Don Shaw. Jerry Grote homered during the losing cause.

              On Opening Day, the outfield walls at Shea Stadium were painted an olive-hued white with dark green distance numbers. Following numerous complaints, the walls were painted dark green in May.

APRIL 13   Tom Seaver makes his major league debut and earns a no decision after allowing two runs in 5¹⁄₃ innings of a 3–2 win over the Pirates at Shea Stadium.

APRIL 20   Tom Seaver records his first major league victory by pitching 7¹⁄₃ innings of a 6–1 win over the Cubs at Shea Stadium.

              Seaver ended the season with the Rookie-of-the-Year Award, a 16–13 record, a 2.76 ERA and 18 complete games at the age of 22.

APRIL 30   The Mets collect only two hits but beat the Reds 2–0 in the first game of a double-header at Crosley Field. Don Cardwell pitched a three-hit shutout. Cincinnati won the second game 6–1.

MAY 1   The Mets purchase Jack Kralick from the Indians.

              On the same day, Samuel Timothy McGraw , the son of Mets pitcher Tug McGraw, was born in Start, Louisiana. Today, Tim McGraw is one of country music's greatest stars, but he didn't have a relationship with his birth father until he was 18. Tug and Tim's mother, Betty D'Agostino, lived in the same apartment building in Jacksonville, Florida, while Tug was pitching in the minors. When Betty became pregnant while still in high school, she was sent to Louisiana to live with relatives. For many years, Tim believed that his stepfather, Horace Smith, was his real father, until he found his birth certificate at the age of 11. Tug denied being Tim's father until Tim was 18, however. Tim attended the University of Louisiana at Monroe on a baseball scholarship before dropping out of school to pursue a music career. Tug died in 2004, and at the end of his life, had a close relationship with Tim.

MAY 2   After the Giants score in the top of the 12th, the Mets counter with two in their half to win 3–2 at Shea Stadium. Ed Kranepool drove in the tying run with a triple. Pinch-hitter John Sullivan won the contest with a walk-off single.

For the 1967 season, clear Plexiglas was placed in the outfield walls at Shea Stadium in front of the bullpens in right and left field to enabled fans to see who was warming up.

MAY 5
Jerry Buchek hits a walk-off homer in the ninth to beat the Astros 3–2 at Shea Stadium.

MAY 9
After three contests are postponed by rain on May 6 and 7, including a Sunday double-header, followed by an off day on Monday the eighth, the Mets win with a walk-off homer for the second game in a row. This time the hero was Tommy Davis, whose solo homer beat the Reds 3–2 in 11 innings at Shea Stadium.

MAY 10
The Mets purchase Bob Johnson and John Miller from the Orioles. On the same day, the Mets sent Larry Elliott and $50,000 to the Athletics for Ed Charles.

MAY 20
Pitcher Jack Hamilton hits a grand slam off Al Jackson in the second inning, but the Mets blow a 9–4 lead and lose 11–9 to the Cardinals at Shea Stadium.

MAY 26
Both teams collect only three hits each as the Mets edge the Braves 1–0 at Shea Stadium. Don Cardwell pitched a complete game shutout for New York. Jerry Buchek provided the lone run of the game with a homer in the second inning off Ken Johnson.

MAY 28
Tommy Davis collects four hits, including two homers and a double, and drives in five runs during a 6–3 win over the Braves at Shea Stadium.

JUNE 3
Bob Shaw pitches an 11-inning complete game and allows only three hits to beat the Giants 2–1 at Candlestick Park. The contest was scoreless through the first ten innings in a duel between Shaw and Bob Bolin. With two out in the top of the 11th, Bolin gave up a single to Cleon Jones and doubles to Johnny Lewis and Tommy Davis to give the Mets a 2–0 lead. The San Francisco run scored on a home run by Tom Haller with two out in the bottom half.

JUNE 6
The Mets win a pair of ten-inning games by scores of 1–0 and 3–2 in a double-header against the Pirates at Forbes Field. The winning run in the opener scored on a sacrifice fly by Ken Boyer. Tom Seaver (six innings), Ron Taylor (2²/₃ innings) and Don Shaw (1¹/₃ innings) combined on the shutout. In the nightcap, Ron Swoboda broke a 2–2 tie in the tenth with a home run. Both game-winning hits were struck off Roy Face.

On the same day, the Mets selected pitcher Jon Matlack from Henderson High School in West Chester, Pennsylvania with the fourth overall pick in the amateur draft. Matlack won 75 games over a five-year period for the Mets from 1972 through 1976. He was the NL Rookie-of-the-Year in 1972 and ranks second in Mets history in shutouts (26) and third in ERA (3.03). Others drafted and signed by the Mets during the regular phase in 1967 included Charlie Hudson (tenth round), Jesse Hudson (11th round), Dave Schneck (38th round) and Tom Robson (50th round). During the secondary phase, the Mets drafted Rich Folkers (first round), Rod Gaspar (second round), Gary Gentry (third round) and Rick Hacker (eighth round).

JUNE 11
Adolpho Phillips hits four homers, three of them in the second game, in leading the Cubs to a 5–3 and 18–10 double-header sweep of the Mets at Wrigley Field. The two teams combined for a National League record-tying 11 homers in the second contest.

In addition to the three by Phillips, Randy Hundley hit two and Ernie Banks and Ron Santo one each for Chicago. The Met home runs were struck by Bob Johnson, Ron Swoboda, Jerry Buchek and Jerry Grote.

JUNE 18   Tommie Reynolds hits a walk-off homer in the tenth inning to defeat the Cubs 4–3 at Shea Stadium. Reynolds entered the game in the eighth as a replacement for Ron Swoboda in right field.

JUNE 21   Jack Fisher pitches a two-hitter to defeat the Phillies 2–0 at Connie Mack Stadium. Gary Sutherland collected both Philadelphia hits with a double in the sixth inning and a single in the eighth.

JUNE 27   A scene from the movie *The Odd Couple* is filmed before a 5–2 win over the Pirates at Shea Stadium. In the scene, Oscar Madison, played by Walter Matthau, is called away from the press box by a phone call from Felix Unger, portrayed by Jack Lemmon. While on the phone, Madison misses the Mets pull off a game-ending triple play with Bill Mazeroski as the batter.

JULY 2   With one out in the ninth, Bud Harrelson singles, steals second, moves to third on an error and scores on a wild pitch to beat the Cardinals 5–4 at Shea Stadium.

JULY 4   The Mets beat Juan Marichal and the Giants 8–7 at Shea Stadium. Marichal came into the game with a 19–0 career record against the Mets.

JULY 9   Trailing the Braves 4–3 with two out and no one on base in the ninth, the Mets rally to win 5–4 at Shea Stadium. Jerry Buchek was sent in to bat for Bud Harrelson, who already had four hits in the game, including a double. Manager Wes Westrum's intuition proved to be correct as Buchek hit a pinch-hit home run to tie the score. Two walks and a single loaded the bases, and Claude Raymond walked Ron Swoboda to force across the winning run.

JULY 11   At Anaheim Stadium, Tom Seaver becomes the first Mets pitcher to appear in an All-Star Game. The NL took a 2–1 lead in the top of the 15th on a home run by Tony Perez. Seaver pitched the bottom of the 15th and allowed a one-out walk to Carl Yastrzemski before closing out the victory.

JULY 16   The Mets trade Jack Lamabe to the Cardinals for a player to be named later. Al Jackson was sent to the Mets on October 13, 1967 to complete the deal.

JULY 18   The Mets sweep the Astros 8–4 and 7–2 in a double-header at Shea Stadium. In the nightcap, the Mets had a 4–0 lead just four batters into the contest when Tommy Davis hit a grand slam off Dave Giusti. Tom Seaver struck out 12 batters.

JULY 22   The Mets trade Ken Boyer and Sandy Alomar, Sr. to the White Sox for J. C. Martin and Bill Southworth.

JULY 24   The day after riots begin in Detroit, which result in the deaths of 43 people, the Mets sell Bob Shaw to the Cubs.

AUGUST 2   The Mets purchase Cal Koonce from the Cubs.

AUGUST 8   The Mets score two runs in the ninth inning and one in the 11th to defeat the Braves
                  3–2 at Shea Stadium. In the ninth, Ed Kranepool doubled in a run and crossed the
                  plate on a two-out single from Ed Charles. Bob Johnson provided the game-winner
                  with walk-off homer.

AUGUST 11   Danny Frisella's first major league win is a 3–2 decision over the Pirates at Shea
                  Stadium and comes under unusual circumstances. Frisella went 6²/₃ innings, then
                  left for the airport to catch a plane for California where he had a meeting with his
                  Air National Guard unit the following morning.

AUGUST 14   The Mets beat Larry Jackson and the Phillies 8–3 in Philadelphia. Jackson came into
                  the contest with an 18–0 career record against the Mets.

AUGUST 17   Bud Harrelson's first major league homer is inside the park during a 14-inning, 6–5
                  loss to the Pirates at Forbes Field. The ball landed just inside the right foul line, and
                  Al Luplow, believing the ball was foul, failed to chase it down. When he learned the
                  umpires ruled the drive a fair ball, Luplow flew into a rage and Harrelson had plenty
                  of time to circle the bases. The Mets won the opener 6–5.

SEPTEMBER 21   With the club holding a record of 57–94, Wes Westrum resigns as manager. Coach
                  Salty Parker took over the reins on an interim basis for the remainder of the season.

                  *Westrum had a record of 142–239 as manager of the Mets, and team
                  management had already decided he wouldn't return in 1968. Westrum later
                  managed the Giants in 1974 and 1975.*

SEPTEMBER 22   Jerry Buchek drives in the last six runs of a ten-inning 8–5 win over the Astros in the
                  second game of a double-header at Shea Stadium. Buchek tied the score 5–5 with a
                  three-run homer with two out in the eighth. He came to bat again with two on in the
                  tenth and hit a three-run, walk-off homer. Houston won the opener 8–0.

SEPTEMBER 23   Jerry Buchek connects for a walk-off hit for the second game in a row, this time with
                  a single to defeat the Astros 1–0 at Shea Stadium. Tom Seaver pitched a three-hit
                  shutout.

OCTOBER 11   Gil Hodges becomes manager of the Mets.

                  *Perhaps the most beloved individual to ever play for the Brooklyn Dodgers,
                  Hodges was a popular choice. He was an original Met in 1962 and played
                  for the club at the start of the 1963 campaign before going to Washington as
                  manager of the Senators. Under Hodges, the Senators never had a winning
                  season, but he was praised for getting as much as possible out of a limited talent
                  base. In order to pry him away from Washington, the Mets paid the Senators
                  $100,000 and sent pitcher Bill Denehy in the exchange. Taking over a club that
                  was 61–101 in 1967, Hodges was a spectacular success guiding the Mets to
                  73–89 in 1968 and the world championship in 1969.*

NOVEMBER 8   The Mets trade Bob Johnson to the Reds for Art Shamsky.

DECEMBER 5   After only one year and 17 days on the job, Bing Devine resigns as president and
                  general manager of the Mets to return to St. Louis as general manager. In a front

office shuffling, Johnny Murphy became the vice-president and general manager with Joan Payson becoming president. Murphy was 59. He pitched for the Yankees from 1932 through 1946 and was named to three All-Star teams. He had been part of the Mets front office since 1961. Murphy helped put together the club that won the 1969 World Series but failed to live long enough to watch his club defend the title. Murphy died of a heart attack on January 14, 1970.

DECEMBER 15   The Mets trade Tommy Davis, Jack Fisher, Buddy Booker and Bill Wynne to the White Sox for Tommie Agee and Al Weis.

A childhood friend and high school teammate of Cleon Jones in Mobile, Alabama, Agee was the American League Rookie-of-the-Year, made the All-Star team and won a Gold Glove in 1966 but slumped in 1967. The slide continued into 1968, but Agee regained his form in 1969 and helped the Mets win the World Series. He continued as the Mets starting center fielder until a trade to the Cardinals after the 1973 season.

1968

Season in a Sentence

In Gil Hodges's first season as manager, the Mets ride an improved young pitching staff to their best season to date with 73 wins.

Finish • Won • Lost • Pct • GB

Ninth   73   89   .451   24.0

Manager

Gil Hodges

Stats

Stats	Mets	AL	Rank
Batting Avg:	.228	.243	10
On-Base Pct:	.281	.300	10
Slugging Pct:	.315	.341	10
Home Runs:	81	5	
Stolen Bases:	72	4	
ERA:	2.72	2.99	4
Errors:	133	4	
Runs Scored:	473	9	
Runs Allowed:	499	2	

Starting Lineup

Jerry Grote, c
Ed Kranepool, 1b
Ken Boswell, 2b
Ed Charles, 3b
Bud Harrelson, ss
Cleon Jones, lf
Tommie Agee, cf
Ron Swoboda, rf
Art Shamsky, lf
Al Weis, ss
J. C. Martin, c
Phil Linz, 2b

Pitchers

Jerry Koosman, sp
Tom Seaver, sp
Don Cardwell, sp
Dick Selma, sp-rp
Nolan Ryan, sp
Jim McAndrew, sp
Ron Taylor, rp
Cal Koonce, rp
Al Jackson, rp-sp

Attendance

1,781,657 (second In NL)

Club Leaders

Batting Avg:	Cleon Jones	.297
On-Base Pct:	Cleon Jones	.341
Slugging Pct:	Cleon Jones	.452
Home Runs:	Ed Charles	15
RBI:	Ron Swoboda	59
Runs:	Cleon Jones	63
Stolen Bases:	Cleon Jones	23
Wins:	Jerry Koosman	19
Strikeouts:	Tom Seaver	205
ERA:	Jerry Koosman	208
Saves:	Ron Taylor	13

MARCH 9   On the first pitch of the first exhibition game, Tommie Agee is hit behind the left ear by a pitch from Bob Gibson. The Mets lost 4–1 to the Cardinals in St. Petersburg.

Agee was in the Opening Day lineup, but was tentative at the plate and struggled all year. He began the regular season with only ten hits in his first 92 at-bats (a .109 batting average) and finished the season at .217 with five homers in 368 at-bats.

APRIL 9   The Mets scheduled season opener against the Giants in San Francisco is postponed because of the funeral of Martin Luther King, Jr., who was assassinated on April 4.

APRIL 10   The Mets blow a 4–1 lead and lose the season opener 5–4 to the Giants in San Francisco. The Mets still carried a 4–2 advantage into the bottom of the ninth with Tom Seaver pitching. After Willie Mays singled, moved to second on a passed ball and scored on a single from Jim Ray Hart, Seaver was replaced by Danny Frisella. Nate Oliver followed with a single and Jesus Alou hit a two-run, walk-off double, for the Giants victory. It was the Mets' seventh straight Opening Day loss in the club's seventh year of existence.

Seaver finished the season a 16–12 record and a 2.20 ERA in 278 innings.

APRIL 11   Jerry Koosman records his first major league victory by shutting out the Dodgers 4–0 in Los Angeles.

Koosman made nine appearances, three of them starts, in 1967. By rule, he was still considered a rookie in 1968 and put together a season with a 19–12 record, a 2.08 ERA, 17 complete games and seven shutouts. He finished second in the Rookie-of-the-Year balloting in a close vote with Johnny Bench. Koosman had 9 1/2 votes and Bench 10 1/2. One writer split his vote between the two. Koosman pitched for the Mets until 1978. From 1968 through 1976, he had a record of 129–100 with the club and was 140–137 overall. Through 2010, Koosman ranks fourth all-time in Mets history in ERA (3.09), third in wins, third in games pitched (376), second in games started (346), second in complete games (108), second in shutouts (26), second in innings (2,544 2/3) and third in strikeouts (1,799).

APRIL 14   Nolan Ryan records his first major league win by pitching 6 2/3 innings of a 4–0 win over the Astros in Houston.

APRIL 15   The Mets play 24 innings at the Astrodome and lose 1–0 to the Astros. It is the longest 1–0 game in major league history. Playing time was six hours and six minutes. Each team had 11 hits. Tom Seaver started for the Mets and allowed only two hits in ten innings. The New York relievers were Ron Taylor (one inning), Cal Koonce (one-third of an inning), Bill Short (one inning), Dick Selma (two-thirds of an inning), Al Jackson (three innings), Danny Frisella (five innings) and Les Rohr (2 1/3 innings). The pitchers for Houston were Don Wilson (nine innings), John Buzhardt (two innings), Danny Coombs (two innings), Jim Ray (seven innings) and Wade Blasingame (four innings). Ron Swoboda was 0-for-10 and struck out five times. Tommie Agee was also hitless in ten at-bats and fanned four times. Houston pitchers struck out 20 Mets in all. Jerry Grote of the Astros and Hal King of the Astros caught the entire game. Norm Miller led off the Houston 24th with a single and went to second on Rohr's balk. After an intentional walk to Jimmy Wynn, a ground out moved the runners to second and third. Johnny Bateman, pinch-hitting for King, drew an intentional walk to load the bases. Bob Aspromonte hit a grounder to shortstop Al Weis for what appeared to be an inning-ending double play, but the ball rolled through Weis's legs, and Miller scored the winning run.

APRIL 17   In the home opener, the Mets beat the Giants 3–0 before 52,079 at Shea Stadium. Jerry Koosman pitched his second straight shutout.

Over five games and 59 innings from April 11 through April 17, the Mets allowed only two runs but won only three of the five games by dropping two 1–0 decisions.

APRIL 19   Nolan Ryan strikes out 11 batters in $7^2/_3$ innings, but the Mets lose 3–2 to the Dodgers in Los Angeles. In the third inning, Ryan fanned Claude Osteen, Wes Parker and Zoilo Versalles on nine pitches.

APRIL 20   The Mets collect only two hits, but beat the Dodgers 3–2 at Shea Stadium. Both hits and all three runs came in the sixth inning on a single by Bud Harrelson, a walk to Art Shamsky and a three-run homer from Ron Swoboda.

APRIL 30   Ron Swoboda's third-inning homer off Chris Short is the lone run of a 1–0 win over the Phillies at Shea Stadium. Don Cardwell pitched the shutout.

MAY 10   Jerry Koosman pitches a two-hitter to defeat the Cubs 5–1 at Wrigley Field. The only Chicago hits were a double by Ron Santo in the second inning and a single from Ernie Banks in the third.

MAY 12   The Mets lose 4–3 and win 10–0 during a double-header against the Cubs in Chicago. Dick Selma pitched the game two shutout.

MAY 14   Nolan Ryan strikes out 14 batters during a 3–2 win over the Reds at Shea Stadium.

MAY 20   Two homers by Ed Charles off Bob Veale are enough to beat the Pirates 2–1 at Shea Stadium. The first was struck in the fourth inning. The second was a walk-off shot leading off the ninth.

MAY 21   The Mets outlast the Pirates 4–3 in 17 innings at Shea Stadium. There was no scoring by either team from the sixth through the 16th. The winning run scored on a single by Ken Boswell. Tom Seaver (11 innings), Cal Koonce (five innings) and Ron Taylor (one inning) pitched for the Mets.

MAY 25   A Weis hits his first homer since May 7, 1965 in the seventh inning of a 9–1 win over the Braves in Atlanta. Weis didn't hit another home run until July 15, 1969.

MAY 27   The National League votes to expand from 10 teams to 12 with the addition of franchises in San Diego and Montreal. The San Diego Padres and Montreal Expos began play in 1969.

JUNE 7   The Mets select shortstop Tim Foli from Notre Dame High School in Sherman Oaks, California, with the first overall pick in the amateur draft.

Foli played in 102 games for the Mets in 1970 and 1971 before being traded to the Expos. He played in the majors until 1985, including a return engagement with the Mets in 1978 and 1979. Foli earned the nickname "Crazy Horse" for his ferocious competitiveness and tantrums. He compiled a batting average of .251 in the majors with an on-base percentage of just .283 and a slugging percentage of .309 in 1,696 games. Other future major leaguers drafted and signed by the Mets in 1968 were Charlie Williams (seventh round), Hank Webb (tenth round), Don Rose (11th round) and John Milner (14th round). The Mets also drafted Burt Hooton (fifth round) and Mickey Rivers (eighth round of the secondary draft), but failed to sign either of them to a contract.

JUNE 8   The Mets game against the Giants in San Francisco is postponed out of respect to Robert Kennedy, who was shot on June 5 while campaigning in Los Angeles for the Democratic Party nomination. He died a day later.

JUNE 10   Tom Seaver pitches a ten-inning, four-hit shutout to beat the Dodgers 1–0 in Los Angeles. Al Weis drove in the lone run with a single.

JUNE 12   The Mets score two runs in the ninth inning to beat the Dodgers 2–1 in Los Angeles. J. C. Martin doubled in a run with one out and scored on a single by Jerry Grote.

Grote hit .282 in 1968 and was elected as the starting catcher in the All-Star Game. Cleon Jones led the Mets with a .297 average.

JUNE 18   Nolan Ryan strikes out 12 batters but loses 3–2 to the Astros in the first game of a double-header at Shea Stadium. The Mets also lost the second game 6–5.

JUNE 20   Tom Seaver strikes out 12 in 8²/₃ innings of a 5–3 win over the Astros at Shea Stadium.

JUNE 30   Tom Seaver pitches the Mets to a 1–0 win over the Astros in Houston.

JULY 6   Heading into the game with a .188 batting average in 85 at-bats, Phil Linz collects five hits, including a double, in six at-bats during an 11–6 win over the Phillies. With Linz's five hits and four by Cleon Jones, the Mets got nine hits out of the 1–2 spots in the batting order.

JULY 9   Tom Seaver and Jerry Koosman both pitch during the National League's 1–0 win in the All-Star Game at the Astrodome in Houston. Seaver pitched the seventh and eighth innings, allowed two hits and struck out five including Carl Yastrzemski and Mickey Mantle. Koosman entered the game with two out in the ninth and fanned Yastrzemski.

JULY 10   The National League votes to divide into two divisions in 1969 because of the addition of expansion teams in Montreal and San Diego. The Mets were placed in the Eastern Division with Chicago, Montreal, Philadelphia, Pittsburgh and St. Louis.

Chicago and St. Louis were placed in the Eastern Division and Cincinnati and Atlanta in the West in defiance of geographic logic because of the shortsightedness of Mets chairman of the board M. Donald Grant. At the time, the three biggest road draws in baseball were the Dodgers, Giants and Cardinals. Grant insisted that at least one of them be placed in the same division as the Mets. Being the easternmost of the three, St. Louis thus moved into the Eastern Division, but the Cardinals would agree only if long-standing rival Chicago was included. Shortly after division play began, the Cardinals fell from their perch as one of the NL's best teams, while the Reds became one of the top attractions in baseball.

JULY 21   Jerry Koosman strikes out 12 batters and beats the Cardinals 1–0 in the second game of a double-header in St. Louis. The lone run scored on a single by J. C. Martin in the sixth inning. The Cards won the opener 2–0. Making his major league debut, Jim McAndrew went six innings and allowed a run.

> *The Mets were shutout in each of McAndrew's first four major league starts as the club lost 2–0 to the Dodgers on August 4, 1–0 against the Giants on August 10 and 1–0 versus the Astros on August 17. Over his first nine starts, the Mets scored just six runs on McAndrew's behalf. He was 2–7 despite an ERA of 2.17. Both of his wins were by 1–0 scores. A native of Lost Nation, Iowa, McAndrew had a degree in psychology from the University of Iowa. He pitched for the club until 1973 and had a 36–49 record as a Met.*

JULY 23   The Mets defeat the Braves 2–1 with solo homers from Ed Kranepool in the second inning and Ron Swoboda in the sixth.

JULY 26   Ron Swoboda drives in both runs of a 2–0 win over the Reds at Shea Stadium without collecting a hit. Swoboda drove in runners from third base with groundouts in the second and fourth innings. Jerry Koosman pitched the shutout.

AUGUST 6   With two out in the ninth, two runners on base and the score 1–1, third baseman Kevin Collins hits his first major league homer to beat the Astros 4–1 in Houston.

AUGUST 7   A fourth-inning brawl is the highlight of a 4–3 loss to the Astros in the Astrodome. On a close play at third, Houston's Doug Rader slid into third and elbowed Kevin Collins in the face. As Collins was being carried off the field on a stretcher, the two teams began swinging at each other. Rader was the chief target and was unceremoniously decked by Don Cardwell. Tommie Agee rushed in from center field and sent two Houston players to the turf with punches, and Cleon Jones felled John Bateman.

AUGUST 9   The Mets score three runs in the ninth inning off Juan Marichal to beat the Giants 5–4 in San Francisco. The final two tallies crossed the plate on a two-out error by third baseman Jim Davenport.

AUGUST 13   Bud Harrelson scores both runs of a 2–0 win over the Dodgers at Shea Stadium. Don Cardwell (eight innings), Bill Short (one-third of an inning) and Cal Koonce (two-thirds of an inning) combined on the shutout.

> *Harrelson was born on June 6, 1944, the same day as the D-Day invasion of France.*

AUGUST 16   The Astros arrive in New York City and Doug Rader is provided with around-the-clock police protection following threatening phone calls and letters as a result of his altercation with Kevin Collins nine days earlier.

AUGUST 19   The Mets lose 1–0 to the Giants in a 17-inning marathon at Shea Stadium. Jerry Koosman (12 innings) and Ron Taylor (five innings) pitched for the Mets. Bob Bolin (11 innings), Frank Linzy (five innings) and Mike McCormick (one inning) combined on the San Francisco shutout. Former-Met Ron Hunt drove in the lone run with two out in the 17th.

Taylor played in the majors from 1962 through 1972 and was a member of world championship teams with the Cardinals in 1964 and the Mets in 1969. After his playing career ended, Taylor went back to school to become a doctor. He was the team physician for the Toronto Blue Jays when that club won world championships in 1992 and 1993.

AUGUST 26   On the first day of the Democratic National Convention in Chicago, which features bloody clashes between antiwar demonstrators and police, Jim McAndrew earns his first major league victory by beating Steve Carlton and the Cardinals 1–0 in St. Louis. The lone run scored on a sacrifice fly by Cleon Jones in the eighth inning.

AUGUST 29   Cal Koonce (6$^{1}/_{3}$ innings) and Ron Taylor (2$^{2}/_{3}$ innings) combine on a two-hitter to beat the Reds 2–0 at Shea Stadium. The only Cincinnati hits were singles by Fred Whitfield in the second inning and Vada Pinson in the seventh.

AUGUST 30   Art Shamsky hits a grand slam off Nelson Briles in the fifth inning of an 8–2 win over the Cardinals at Shea Stadium.

Shamsky played for the Mets from 1968 through 1971. The pet bulldog of actor Brad Garrett's character Robert Barone in the TV series Everybody Loves Raymond, *which aired from 1996 through 2005, was named Shamsky in honor of the ballplayer.*

SEPTEMBER 10   Billy Williams hits three homers for the Cubs during an 8–1 win over the Mets in Chicago.

SEPTEMBER 11   Jim McAndrew (8$^{1}/_{3}$ innings), Bill Short (one-third of an inning) and Cal Koonce (one-third of an inning) combine on a two-hitter to defeat the Cubs 1–0 at Wrigley Field. The only Chicago hits were singles by Glenn Beckert in the fourth inning and Don Kessinger with one out in the ninth. The lone run of the game scored in the fourth inning on doubles by J. C. Martin and Jerry Grote.

SEPTEMBER 13   Art Shamsky hits a homer and a triple and scores both runs of a 2–0 win over the Pirates at Shea Stadium. Jerry Koosman pitched the shutout.

SEPTEMBER 17   Jim McAndrew pitches a two-hitter to defeat the Cubs 3–2 at Shea Stadium. The only Chicago hits were a two-run double by Willie Smith in the fourth inning and a single from Al Spangler in the eighth.

SEPTEMBER 24   During a 7–4 loss to the Braves in Atlanta, Gil Hodges is rushed to the hospital with a mild heart attack. He remained in the hospital for a month and spent another month recuperating in Florida.

SEPTEMBER 29   On the last day of the season, Richie Allen hits three homers for the Phillies during a 10–3 win over the Mets at Shea Stadium.

OCTOBER 14   In the expansion draft, the Mets lose Dick Selma, Jerry Morales and Larry Stahl to the Padres and Don Shaw and Ernie McAnally to the Expos.

OCTOBER 28   A week before Richard Nixon defeats Hubert Humphrey in the Presidential election, 19-year-old Mets farmhand Mike McCready dies of injuries suffered in a car crash three days earlier. McCready had just been added to the 40-man roster.

1969

Season in a Sentence

The Mets exceed the wildest imaginations of their most optimistic fans by overcoming a 9½-game deficit to the Cubs to win the NL East pennant, sweeping the Braves in the Championship Series, then stunning the heavily favored Orioles in the World Series.

Finish • Won • Lost • Pct • GB

First   100   62   .617   +8.0

National League Championship Series

The Mets defeated the Atlanta Braves three games to none.

World Series

The Mets defeated the Baltimore Orioles four games to one.

Manager

Gil Hodges

Stats	Mets • AL • Rank		
Batting Avg:	.242	.250	7
On-Base Pct:	.311	.319	10
Slugging Pct:	.351	.369	11
Home Runs:	109	8	
Stolen Bases:	66	8	
ERA	2.99	3.59	2
Errors:	122	2	
Runs Scored:	632	9	
Runs Allowed:	541	2	

Starting Lineup

Jerry Grote, c
Ed Kranepool, 1b
Ken Boswell, 2b
Wayne Garrett, 3b
Bud Harrelson, ss
Cleon Jones, lf
Tommie Agee, cf
Ron Swoboda, rf
Art Shamsky, rf
Al Weis, ss-2b
Rod Gaspar, rf
Donn Clendenon, 1b

Pitchers

Tom Seaver, sp
Jerry Koosman, sp
Gary Gentry, sp
Don Cardwell, sp
Jim McAndrew, sp
Ron Taylor, rp
Tug McGraw, rp
Nolan Ryan, rp-sp
Cal Koonce, rp

Attendance

2,175,373 (first in NL)

Club Leaders

Batting Avg:	Cleon Jones	.340
On-Base Pct:	Cleon Jones	.422
Slugging Pct:	Cleon Jones	.482
Home Runs:	Tommie Agee	26
RBI:	Tommie Agee	76
Runs:	Tommie Agee	97
Stolen Bases:	Cleon Jones	16
Wins:	Tom Seaver	25
Strikeouts:	Tom Seaver	208
ERA:	Tom Seaver	2.21
Saves:	Ron Taylor	13

APRIL 8   Three months after the Jets upset the Colts in Super Bowl III, the Mets open the season with an 11–10 loss to the Expos before 44,541 at Shea Stadium. It was the first game in the history of the Expos franchise and the eighth consecutive Opening Day loss for the Mets. Tom Seaver was the starting pitcher and allowed four runs, two of them earned, in five innings. The Mets took a 6–4 lead in the fourth on a three-run double from Tommie Agee, but allowed seven unanswered runs and trailed 11–6 heading into the ninth. The Mets scored four runs in the ninth after two were out, the last three on a pinch-hit homer by Duffy Dyer, but the rally fell a run short. Jerry Grote scored three runs in the losing cause.

The homer was the first of Dyer's career. It came in his second big-league game after making his debut on September 21, 1968.

APRIL 10   Tommie Agee hits two homers, one of them a shot about halfway up in the fifth deck at Shea Stadium, during a 4–2 win over the Expos.

A marker was painted on the concrete where the ball landed. The marker remained there until the last Mets game played at the facility in 2008. It was removed during the demolition of Shea Stadium and was sold to a private collector.

APRIL 27   Cleon Jones breaks up a scoreless deadlock with a three-run, walk-off homer with one out in the ninth inning that beats the Cubs 3–0 at Shea Stadium. Jim McAndrew (five innings) and Tug McGraw (four innings) combined on the shutout.

Jones batted .340 with 12 home runs in 1969.

APRIL 29   The Mets play a regular season game outside of the United States for the first time and beat the Expos 2–0 at Jarry Park in Montreal. Both runs scored on solo homers by Ed Kranepool off Mudcat Grant in the second and sixth innings. Jerry Koosman ($4^{1}/_{3}$ innings) and Nolan Ryan ($4^{2}/_{3}$ innings) combined on the shutout.

Koosman left the game with a shoulder injury and didn't pitch again until May 24. He still ended the season with a 17–9 record and a 2.28 ERA in 241 innings and completed 16 of his 32 starts.

MAY 14   Trailing 3–1, the Mets explode for eight runs in the eighth inning to defeat the Braves 9–3 at Shea Stadium. The only Met hit during the first seven innings off Phil Niekro was a triple by Ken Boswell leading off the seventh. The eight runs in the eighth were created with only four hits. Cleon Jones hit a grand slam off George Stone.

MAY 27   The Mets play the Padres for the first time and lose 3–2 at Shea Stadium.

Following the defeat, it appeared as though the Mets were headed for their eighth straight losing season. The club had a record of 18–23 and was in fourth place nine games behind the Cubs. The next day, the Mets began an 11-game winning streak.

MAY 28   The Mets edge the Padres 1–0 in 11 innings at Shea Stadium. Jerry Koosman pitched ten innings, allowed only four hits and struck out 15. Tug McGraw hurled the 11th. Bud Harrelson drove in the winning run with a walk-off single.

JUNE 1   Joe Gibbon of the Giants walks four batters in the ninth, one intentional, handing the Mets a 5–4 win at Shea Stadium. With two out and a runner on third, Gibbon issued an intentional pass to Cleon Jones, then walked Amos Otis and Ron Swoboda to force across the winning run.

JUNE 4   The Mets outlast the Dodgers to win 1–0 in 15 innings at Shea Stadium. The Mets won despite collecting only three hits in the first 14 innings off Bill Singer (nine innings), Jim Brewer (two innings) and Al McBean (three innings). After three relief appearances with the Mets, Jack DiLauro made his first big-league start and allowed only two hits in nine innings. Tug McGraw (four innings) and Ron Taylor (two innings) were the New York relievers. Pete Mikkelsen pitched the 15th for Los Angeles. Bud Harrelson walked to open the inning. He was forced at second on a grounder By Tommie Agee, who scored on Wayne Garrett's single and an error by center fielder Willie Davis.

> *DiLauro began his career by pitching 17²/₃ consecutive shutout innings over three relief appearances and two starts. The 1969 season was his only one with the Mets and the first of two in the majors. He made 23 appearances, four of them starting assignments, in a New York uniform and had a 1–4 record and a 2.40 ERA.*

JUNE 5   With the fourth overall pick in the amateur draft, the Mets select pitcher Randy Sterling from Key West High School in Key West, Florida.

> *Sterling proved to be a complete bust. His major league career lasted only three games in 1974. Other future major leaguers drafted and signed by the Mets in 1969 were Joe Nolan (second round), Lute Barnes (21st round), Buzz Capra (27th round), George Theodore (31st round) and Larry Fritz (third round of the secondary phase).*

JUNE 6   The Mets play in San Diego for the first time and beat the Padres 5–3. It was the Mets' eighth win in a row.

JUNE 8   Tom Seaver strikes out 14 batters in seven innings during a 3–2 triumph over the Padres in San Diego. It was the Mets' tenth victory in succession.

> *Seaver won his first career Cy Young Award in 1969 with a record of 25–7, an ERA of 2.21 and 208 strikeouts in 273¹/₃ innings. He also finished second in the MVP voting to Willie McCovey. Both Seaver and McCovey received 11 first place votes, out of 24 cast, but McCovey had five more second place votes and won with 265 points to Seaver's 243.*

JUNE 10   The Mets extend their winning steak to 11 games by beating the Giants 9–4 in San Francisco.

> *With the exception of the Padres, a first-year expansion team, the Mets fielded the youngest roster in the National League in 1969. The eight players with the most plate appearances were Jerry Grote (age 26), Ed Kranepool (24), Ken Boswell (23), Bud Harrelson (25), Wayne Garrett (21), Cleon Jones (26), Tommie Agee (26) and Ron Swoboda (25). Key pitchers included Tom Seaver (24), Jerry Koosman (24), Gary Gentry (22), Jim McAndrew (25), Tug McGraw (24) and Nolan Ryan (22).*

JUNE 13   The Mets sell Al Jackson to the Reds.

JUNE 15   The Mets trade Steve Renko, Kevin Collins, Dave Colon and Bill Carden to the Expos for Donn Clendenon.

> *The Mets traded four prospects to acquire Clendenon, who helped spark the drive to the pennant by solidifying the first base position in a platoon with Ed Kranepool.*

JUNE 17   Gary Gentry pitches a two-hitter to defeat the Phillies 1–0 in the first game of a double-header at Connie Mack Stadium. The only Philadelphia hits were singles by Larry Hisle in the sixth inning and Johnny Callison in the seventh. The lone run scored on a single by J. C. Martin in the seventh. The Phils won the second tilt 7–3.

JUNE 19   A two-out, two-run single by Ken Boswell beats the Phillies 6–5 in Philadelphia.

JUNE 22   The Mets sweep the Cardinals 5–1 and 1–0 in a double-header at Shea Stadium. In the opener, Ron Swoboda struck out five times in five plate appearances against three different St. Louis pitchers. Jerry Koosman pitched the game-two shutout. The lone run scored in the seventh inning on a triple by Bud Harrelson and a double from Tommie Agee.

JUNE 24   Jim McAndrew (eight innings) and Ron Taylor (one inning) combine on a two-hitter to defeat the Phillies 5–0 in the second game of a double-header at Shea Stadium. The only Philadelphia hits were back-to-back singles by Terry Harmon and Vic Roznovsky in the sixth inning. The Mets also won the opener 2–1.

JULY 2   The Mets score two runs in the 14th inning to beat the Cardinals 6–4 in St. Louis. Tommie Agee scored the go-ahead run on a single from Ken Boswell. An insurance run was added on a bases-loaded walk by Ron Willis to Wayne Garrett.

JULY 6   The Mets fall behind 6–1 in the second inning, then rally to defeat the Pirates 8–7 in Pittsburgh. Donn Clendenon put the Mets into the lead with a three-run homer in the sixth.

JULY 8   The Mets score three runs off Ferguson Jenkins in the ninth inning to defeat the Cubs 4–3 at Shea Stadium. Three doubles by Ken Boswell, Donn Clendenon and Cleon Jones produced the first two runs and tied the score 3–3. Clendenon's two-bagger came in a pinch-hit role. Two of the doubles were gifts on misplayed fly balls by center fielder Don Young. Ed Kranepool drove in the winning run with a two-out, walk-off single.

JULY 9   Tom Seaver loses a chance at a perfect game in the ninth inning but beats the Cubs 4–0 at Shea Stadium. Seaver retired the first 25 batters to face him, 11 of them on strikeouts. With one out in the ninth, center fielder Jimmy Qualls stepped to the plate and lined a clean single to left. Qualls was playing in only his 18th major league game and was in the lineup in place of Don Young, whose defensive lapses had caused the Cubs a victory the night before. Qualls proved to be the only Chicago base runner as Seaver retired Willie Smith and Don Kessinger to close out the win, which put the Mets only 3½ games behind the-first place Cubs.

Qualls finished his career with only 31 hits and a .223 batting average.

JULY 13   The Mets sweep a double-header against the Expos at Shea Stadium by scores of 4–3 and 9–7. In the second game, Tommie Agee hit two homers, drove in four runs and scored four.

Agee hit .271 with 26 homers in 1969.

JULY 15   Al Weis hits his first home run since May 25, 1968 during a 5–4 win over the Cubs in Chicago. The three-run shot in the fourth inning broke a 1–1 tie.

JULY 16 — Al Weis homers for the second game in a row during a 9–5 triumph over the Cubs in Chicago.

> *The homers in back-to-back games were the only ones hit by Weis in 247 at-bats in 1969. He had only seven regular season homers in 1,768 at-bats over a ten-year career with the White Sox and Mets. All seven were accomplished on the road. Weis did hit a home run at home during the World Series, however (see October 16, 1969).*

JULY 18 — A brawl highlights a 5–2 win over the Expos at Jarry. In the fifth inning, Cleon Jones was tagged out at the plate by Montreal catcher Ron Brand. As he got to his feet, Jones became tangled with Brand and threw two punches. While trying to retaliate, Brand hit umpire Charlie Williams in the face. After both dugouts emptied, skirmishes broke out all over the field, but only Jones was ejected.

JULY 22 — Two days after Neil Armstrong becomes the first man to walk on the moon, Cleon Jones collects two singles and scores two runs in four at-bats during the National League's 9–3 win in the All-Star Game at RFK Stadium in Washington. Jerry Koosman hurled 1 2/3 shutout innings.

JULY 30 — The Mets lose 16–3 and 11–5 in a double-header against the Astros at Shea Stadium. In the opener, Houston scored 11 runs during a ninth-inning rally that included two grand slams. The bases-loaded homers were belted by Denis Menke off Cal Koonce and Jimmy Wynn off Ron Taylor. Relief pitcher Fred Gladding kept the rally alive with a single off Taylor. It was Gladding's only hit in 63 career at-bats. In the second contest, the Astros scored ten runs in the third inning against Gary Gentry and Nolan Ryan.

AUGUST 2 — The Mets edge the Braves 1–0 at Shea Stadium. Jim McAndrew (seven innings) and Tug McGraw (two innings) combined on the shutout. Cleon Jones, in the role of a pinch-hitter, drove in the lone run with a single in the seventh inning.

AUGUST 3 — Jerry Grote hits a walk-off homer in the 11th inning to down the Braves 6–5 at Shea Stadium. The Mets erased a 5–0 Atlanta lead with five runs in the sixth inning.

AUGUST 5 — The Mets score eight runs in the third inning and clobber the Reds 10–1 in Cincinnati.

> *At the end of play on August 13, the Mets had a record of 62–51 and were in third place in the NL East, 9 1/2 games behind the Cubs. The Cardinals were in second, 8 1/2 back of Chicago. St. Louis seemed to be the biggest threat to the Cubs' perch atop the division. The Cards won the NL pennant in 1967 and 1968 and had 28 victories their last 36 games prior to August 13. The Mets had seven losing seasons in the seven years of their existence and had established themselves as a universal symbol of failure. The Mets had also lost 14 of their previous 24 games. Over the remainder of the season, however, the Mets had a record of 38–11 while the Cubs were 18–27. Over those final 49 games, the Mets allowed only 116 runs.*

AUGUST 16 — On the second day of the Woodstock Music Festival, the Mets sweep the Padres 2–0 and 2–1 during a double-header at Shea Stadium. Tom Seaver (eight innings) and Ron Taylor (one inning) combined on the shutout in the opener.

AUGUST 17   The Mets sweep the Padres in a double-header at Shea Stadium for the second day in a row, this time by a pair of 3–2 scores.

AUGUST 19   Tommie Agee hits a walk-off homer off Juan Marichal with one out in the 14th inning to defeat the Giants 1–0 at Shea Stadium. Marichal pitched a complete game and allowed only four hits. Gary Gentry (ten innings) and Tug McGraw (four innings) combined on a five-hit shutout for the Mets. The victory was achieved with the help of an unusual bit of strategy by Gil Hodges. With Willie McCovey batting with two out in the 13th, the Mets manager employed a four-man outfield by moving third baseman Bobby Pfeil to guard the left-field line. Left fielder Cleon Jones moved to left-center, and made a leaping catch against the left-field wall. It would have been impossible for Jones to reach the ball with a three-man outfield.

AUGUST 20   Jim McAndrew hurls a two-hitter to defeat the Giants 6–0 at Shea Stadium. The only San Francisco hits were both collected by Don Mason on a double in the first inning and a triple in the third.

             The Mets allowed only five runs in seven games from August 14 through August 20.

AUGUST 27   Jerry Koosman pitches a two-hitter to defeat the Padres 4–1 in San Diego. The only hits off Koosman were a home run by Ollie Brown and a single from Al Ferrara, both with two out in the first inning.

AUGUST 30   Donn Clendenon's tenth-inning homer off Gaylord Perry beats the Giants 3–2 in San Francisco.

SEPTEMBER 5 Tom Seaver records his 20th win of the season with a 5–1 decision over the Phillies at Shea Stadium.

SEPTEMBER 7 The Mets defeat the Phillies 9–3 at Shea Stadium. The first pitch by Philadelphia pitcher Billy Champion in the bottom of the first sent Tommie Agee into the dirt. Agee hit the next pitch for a home run. The victory put the Mets 2½ games behind the Cubs with a two-game series against the division-leaders at Shea Stadium coming up next on the schedule.

SEPTEMBER 8 Jerry Koosman strikes out 13 batters and the Mets beat the Cubs 3–2 at Shea Stadium to pull within 1½ games of first place. Chicago starting pitcher Bill Hands set the tone with his first pitch of the first inning, which sent Tommie Agee sprawling in the dirt. Agee responded with a two-run homer in the third inning to give the Mets a 2–0 lead. With the score 2–2 in the sixth, Agee doubled and scored on a single by Wayne Garrett. The play led to a heated argument as the Cubs claimed that catcher Randy Hundley tagged Agee before he touched the plate.

SEPTEMBER 9 The Mets are only one-half game out of first place after beating the Cubs 7–1 at Shea Stadium. During the game, someone released a black cat in front of the Cubs dugout, a fitting metaphor for the lack of luck the Cubs had in September 1969.

SEPTEMBER 10 The Mets take over first place by sweeping the Expos 3–2 and 7–1 at Shea Stadium. Coupled with the Cubs' 6–2 loss to the Phillies in Philadelphia, the Mets had a lead of one game.

SEPTEMBER 11   Gary Gentry shuts out the Expos 4–0 at Shea Stadium.

SEPTEMBER 12   The Mets record their second and third shutouts in a span of three days by beating the Pirates twice by 1–0 scores in Pittsburgh. Pitchers drove in both New York runs. In the opener, Jerry Koosman not only pitched a three-hit shutout, but drove in the lone run with a single off Bob Moose in the fifth inning. In the second tilt, starter Don Cardwell went eight innings and Tug McGraw pitched the ninth. Cardwell's single in the second against Doc Ellis provided the only run.

SEPTEMBER 13   The Mets extend their winning streak to ten games by beating the Pirates 5–2 in Pittsburgh. Ron Swoboda broke a 1–1 tie with a grand slam off Chuck Hartenstein in the eighth inning. Pittsburgh issued an intentional walk to Donn Clendenon to get to Swoboda.

SEPTEMBER 15   The Mets win an extraordinary 4–3 decision over the Cardinals in St. Louis. Steve Carlton struck out 19 Mets batters, and Met fielders made four errors. At the time, the modern record for strikeouts by a pitcher in a nine-inning game was 18 by Bob Feller, Sandy Koufax (twice) and Don Wilson. Carlton fanned the last four batters he faced, but wound up a loser because Ron Swoboda walloped a pair of two-run homers in the fourth and eighth innings. The win gave the Mets a 4½-game lead in the pennant race.

SEPTEMBER 18   Ed Kranepool drives in both runs of a 2–0 win over the Expos in Montreal with a single in the first inning and a homer in the sixth. Tom Seaver pitched the shutout.

SEPTEMBER 20   Bob Moose of the Pirates pitches a no-hitter to beat the Mets 4–0 at Shea Stadium. He walked three and struck out six. The last out was a ground out by Art Shamsky from second baseman Dave Cash to first baseman Al Oliver.

SEPTEMBER 24   The Mets clinch the Eastern Division pennant with a 6–0 win over the Cardinals at Shea Stadium. Donn Clendenon homered twice. Gary Gentry pitched the shutout.

                After the game, Mets fans stormed the field and tore up the sod, a scene that would be repeated twice more in the coming weeks, following wins in the NLCS and the World Series.

SEPTEMBER 26   Jerry Koosman records the second straight shutout by a Mets pitcher by beating the Phillies 5–0 in Philadelphia.

SEPTEMBER 27   Tom Seaver records his 25th victory by defeating the Phillies 1–0 in Philadelphia. It was the Mets' third consecutive shutout. Bobby Pfeil drove in the lone run of the game with a single in the eighth inning.

SEPTEMBER 28   The Mets run their shutout streak to four straight games with a 2–0 victory over the Phillies in Philadelphia. Gary Gentry (five innings), Nolan Ryan (three innings) and Ron Taylor (one inning) combined on the whitewashing.

                Over five games from September 23 through September 28, the Mets combined for 42 consecutive scoreless innings.

OCTOBER 1   The Mets collect their 100th win of the season by beating the Cubs 6–5 in 12 innings in Chicago. The winning run scored on a double by Bud Harrelson and a single from Art Shamsky.

The Mets met the Braves in the first National League Championship Series in history. Managed by Luman Harris, the Braves were 93–69 in 1969.

OCTOBER 4   The Mets open the Championship Series by beating the Braves 9–5 in Atlanta. The starting pitchers were a pair of future Hall of Famers coming off one of the best seasons of their long careers with Tom Seaver (25–7) matched against Phil Niekro (23–13). Neither pitched particularly well. The Mets took a 4–3 lead in the fourth inning on a two-run triple by Bud Harrelson, but solo homers from Tony Gonzalez in the fifth and Hank Aaron in the seventh gave Atlanta a 5–4 advantage. The Mets erupted for five runs in the eighth off Niekro. Wayne Garrett doubled and scored on a single by Cleon Jones. A single by Art Shamsky, a stolen base from Jones and an error produced another run. With the bases loaded, J. C. Martin batted for Seaver and hit a three-run single to cap the victory.

The series was telecast nationally by NBC. Announcers were Jim Simpson and Sandy Koufax in games one and two and Curt Gowdy and Tony Kubek in game three.

OCTOBER 5   The Mets score in each of the first five innings and wallop the Braves 11–6. Tommie Agee, Ken Boswell and Cleon Jones homered. Agee scored three runs and Jones also doubled and singled. Art Shamsky collected three hits for the second game in a row. The 11 runs matched a season high.

OCTOBER 6   The Mets complete the sweep of the Braves with a 7–4 win before 54,195 at Shea Stadium. With the Mets trailing 2–0 in the third inning, Gary Gentry was relieved by Nolan Ryan, who pitched seven innings for the win. New York took a 6–4 lead with three runs in the fifth. Ryan started the rally with a single and scored on a homer by Wayne Garrett. It was Garrett's first homer since May 6.

The Mets had recorded nine shutouts in the last 21 regular season games, but surrendered 15 runs in the NLCS against the Braves. Fortunately, the hitters made up for it with 27 runs of their own. The only other time all year the Mets scored as many as 27 runs in three straight games was in the first week of July. The opponent in the World Series was the Baltimore Orioles. Managed by Earl Weaver, the Orioles were 108–54 in 1969 and swept the Twins in the ALCS. The Orioles were heavy favorites.

OCTOBER 11   The Mets open the World Series by losing 4–1 to the Orioles at Memorial Stadium in Baltimore. Don Buford led off the first inning with a home run off Tom Seaver just over the glove of a leaping Ron Swoboda in right field. Mike Cuellar, a 23-game winner in 1969, pitched a complete game for the Orioles.

The series was telecast nationally over NBC. Announcers were Curt Gowdy and Bill O'Donnell in games one and two and Gowdy and Lindsay Nelson in games three, four and five. The World Series has been telecast since 1947 and has been in color since 1955, but few of the early transmissions were saved on tape, and most of those are in black-and-white. The 1969 World Series is believed to be the first in which every game was saved for posterity with games three, four and five saved in color. They are thought to be the oldest surviving color telecasts of a World Series.

OCTOBER 12   The Mets even the series by beating the Orioles 2–1 in Baltimore behind the two-hit pitching of Jerry Koosman (8$^2/_3$ innings) and Ron Taylor (one-third of an inning). Donn Clendenon provided the first run of the game with a homer in the fourth off Dave McNally. Koosman carried a no-hitter into the seventh before Paul Blair singled, stole second and scored on a single from Brooks Robinson. The winning run scored on three straight singles with two out from Ed Charles, Jerry Grote and Al Weis.

Weis was the surprise package of the 1969 World Series, with five hits, including a homer, in 11 at-bats for an average of .455. Weis hit .215 during the regular season.

OCTOBER 14   The Mets take a two-games-to-one lead with a 5–0 win over the Orioles before 56,355 at Shea Stadium. Gary Gentry (6$^2/_3$ innings) and Nolan Ryan (2$^1/_3$ innings) combined on the shutout. Both needed help from center fielder Tommie Agee, who saved five runs with a pair of tremendous catches. With two out in the fourth and two runners on base, Agee made a backhanded catch off a drive from Elrod Hendricks at the base of the wall in left center. The bases were loaded, two were out in the seventh and Paul Blair was at bat when Agee made a belly-sliding catch in right center. Gentry helped his own cause with a two-run double in the second off Jim Palmer. Agee and Ed Kranepool homered. Agee's shot led off the first inning.

The appearance by Ryan, then 22 years old, would prove to be the only one in a World Series during his 27-year major league career.

OCTOBER 15   The Mets move to within one victory of a world championship with a ten-inning, 2–1 triumph over the Orioles before 57,367 at Shea Stadium. Donn Clendenon homered in the second inning off Mike Cuellar which gave the Mets a 1–0 lead. It held up until the ninth. Tom Seaver gave up singles to Frank Robinson and Boog Powell, which set the stage for Brooks Robinson's slicing liner to right on which Ron Swoboda made a daring, sliding catch. Frank Robinson scored after the play. In the tenth, Jerry Grote reached second when left fielder Don Buford misplayed his drive into a double. Al Weis was intentionally walked and J. C. Martin went to the plate to bat for Seaver. Martin's bunt was fielded by pitcher Pete Richert, whose throw struck Martin and bounced into the outfield, allowing Grote to score. Replays later showed that Martin was running illegally inside the base line.

The game was played Moratorium Day, which featured large demonstrations across the country to protest the war in Vietnam. New York Mayor John Lindsay, a critic of the war, ordered all flags in New York City to be flown at half-staff to honor those who had died in the War. But Baseball Commissioner Bowie Kuhn ordered that the flag at Shea Stadium be flown at full-staff.

OCTOBER 16   The Mets complete their miracle season with a 5–3 win over the Orioles before 57,397 at Shea Stadium to claim the world championship. Baltimore pitcher Dave McNally started the scoring with a two-run homer in the third inning, and Frank Robinson followed with a solo shot. The Orioles would not score again, however.

The Mets narrowed the gap to 3–2 with two runs in the sixth. Cleon Jones was hit in the foot by a pitch from McNally. At first, plate umpire Lou DiMuro ruled the ball missed Jones. Gil Hodges retrieved the ball, however, and showed DiMuro that it had a spot of shoe polish on it. At that point, Jones was sent to first. Donn Clendenon followed with a home run, his third of the series. Light-hitting Al Weis homered in the seventh to tie the score 3–3. In the eighth, Ron Swoboda doubled in a run and scored when first baseman Boog Powell fumbled a grounder by Jerry Grote and his toss to first was dropped by pitcher Eddie Watt. The final out was recorded when Koosman induced future Mets manager Dave Johnson to fly out to right fielder Ron Swoboda. The Mets made a quick dash to the clubhouse as frenzied fans stormed the field after the final out and staged a celebration of their won. The sod was decimated.

The 1969 World Series was the second major upset of a Baltimore team during the year. The previous January, the Jets upended the Baltimore Colts 16–7 in Super Bowl III. New Yorkers celebrated again the following May when the Knicks won their first NBA title over the Los Angeles Lakers after outlasting the Baltimore Bullets in seven games in the Eastern Conference semifinals.

OCTOBER 19   The Mets appear on The Ed Sullivan Show and sing "You Gotta Have Heart." Pitcher Jack DiLauro did an impression of Sullivan. Other guests included the rock band Smith, singer Lana Cantrell, the Don Ellis Band, comedians Bill Dana and Joan Rivers, Topo Gigio, and Tanya the Elephant.

OCTOBER 20   The Mets are honored with a ticker-tape parade on Broadway.

DECEMBER 3   The Mets trade Amos Otis and Bob Johnson to the Royals for Joe Foy.

The Mets hoped that Foy would solve the club's third base problem and dealt two prospects to acquire him. The trade proved to be a disaster. Foy lasted only one year with the Mets and hit just .236 with six home runs. The Mets had wanted Otis to move from the outfield to third base, but he refused. He was also unimpressive as a Met, hitting just .178 in 168 at-bats over two seasons. But Otis was only 23 when traded and had plenty of time to prove his potential. One of the most underrated players of the 1970s, he made five All-Star teams and won three Gold Gloves while in Kansas City and was a regular in center field from 1970 until 1982.

DECEMBER 10   The Mets trade Jim Gosger and Bob Heise to the Giants for Ray Sadecki and Dave Marshall.

THE STATE OF THE METS

The Mets won the world championship in 1969 with one of the youngest teams in baseball, and the future looked bright. With the notable exception of Tom Seaver, most of the young players on the 1969 world champions peaked early in their careers, however, and Nolan Ryan was traded to the Angels in 1971. The Mets were on a treadmill early in the 1970s with 83 wins in each of the first three seasons and 82 in 1973. The 1973 team won the NL East with an 82–79 record and reached the World Series. From there it was mostly downhill. The Mets finished last in the NL East in 1977, 1978 and 1979. Overall, the club was 763–850 during the decade, a winning percentage of .473, which ranked ninth in the NL and exceeded only the Braves, Expos and Padres. National League champions were the Reds (1970, 1972, 1975 and 1976), Pirates (1971 and 1979), Mets (1973) and Dodgers (1974, 1977 and 1978). NL East pennant-winners were the Pirates (1970, 1971, 1972, 1974, 1975 and 1979), Mets (1973) and Phillies (1976, 1977 and 1978).

THE BEST TEAM

In terms of winning percentage, the 1972 Mets were the best with an 83–73 record. But the 1973 club had the best overall success, rising from last place in late-August to win the NL East. The club then upset the Reds in the NLCS and took the Athletics to seven games in the World Series.

THE WORST TEAM

The 1979 Mets stumbled to a mark of 63–99.

THE BEST MOMENT

The Mets completed their upset of the Reds in the 1973 NLCS with a win in game five by a 7–2 score at Shea Stadium.

THE WORST MOMENT

On April 2, 1972, just days before the start of the regular season, Gil Hodges died of a heart attack.

THE ALL-DECADE TEAM • YEARS W/METS

John Stearns, c	1975–84
John Milner, 1b	1971–77
Felix Millan, 2b	1973–77
Wayne Garrett, 3b	1969–76
Bud Harrelson, ss	1965–77
Cleon Jones, lf	1963; 1965–75
Lee Mazzilli, cf	1976–81; 1986–89
Rusty Staub, rf	1972–75; 1981–85
Tom Seaver, p	1967–77; 1983
Jerry Koosman, p	1967–78
Jon Matlack, p	1971–77
Tug McGraw, p	1965–67; 1969–74

Note the number of players whose last year with the club was 1977, which marked a time of transition in Mets history. Mazzilli is the only member of the All-Decade Team who was with the team in 1978 and 1979. Seaver is in the Hall of Fame. Seaver, Koosman, Harrelson and Jones were also on the 1960s All-Decade Team. Other outstanding Mets players included first baseman Ed Kranepool (1962–79), center fielder Tommie Agee (1968–72), second baseman Ken Boswell (1967–74), catcher Jerry Grote (1966–77) and pitcher Craig Swan (1973–84).

THE DECADE LEADERS

Batting Avg:	Cleon Jones	.279
On-Base Pct:	Lee Mazzilli	.362
Slugging Pct:	Rusty Staub	.428
Home Runs:	Rusty Staub	62
RBI:	Ed Kranepool	322
Runs:	Bud Harrelson	328
Stolen Bases:	Lee Mazzilli	81
Wins:	Tom Seaver	132
Strikeouts:	Tom Seaver	1,803
ERA:	Tom Seaver	2.54
Saves:	Tug McGraw	73

THE HOME FIELD

Shea Stadium opened in 1964 as the home for the Mets and Jets. The Yankees moved in for two seasons in 1974 and 1975 while Yankee Stadium was being rebuilt. And the Giants also played at Shea in 1975 while Giants Stadium in the New Jersey Meadowlands was under construction. The Mets led the National League in attendance in 1969, 1970, 1971 and 1972, but the fan base began to become disillusioned mid-decade. In 1977, the Mets ranked tenth among 12 teams, the first time that the franchise was in the bottom half of the circuit in attendance since 1962 when it was sixth among the ten clubs. By 1979, the Mets were next-to-last in attendance with a figure of 778,905, a huge drop from the peak of 2,697,479 in 1970.

THE GAME YOU WISHED YOU HAD SEEN

On April 22, 1970, Tom Seaver struck out 19 Padres during a 2–1 win, including a major league record ten in succession.

THE WAY THE GAME WAS PLAYED

During the 1970s, speed and defense ruled, in part because of new stadiums with more distant fences and artificial turf. Opening in the NL during the decade were Riverfront Stadium in Cincinnati, Three Rivers Stadium in Pittsburgh, Veterans Stadium in Philadelphia and Olympic Stadium in Montreal. The average number of stolen bases per team rose from 87 in 1970 to 124 in 1979, while home runs declined from 140 to 119. The increased importance of relief pitching was underscored in 1970 when for the first time in major league history there were more saves recorded than complete games.

THE MANAGEMENT

Joan Payson was the principal owner from the club's inception in 1961 until her death in October 1975. Her daughter, Lorinda de Roulet, took over as president of the club until 1980. Chairman of the Board M. Donald Grant made many of the key decisions, particularly following the death of Mrs. Payson. General managers were Bob Scheffing (1970–74) and Jim McDonald (197–80). Field managers were Gil Hodges (1968–71), Yogi Berra (1972–75), Roy McMillan (1975), Joe Frazier (1976–77) and Joe Torre (1977–81).

THE BEST PLAYER MOVE

The best move was the drafting of Lee Mazzilli in the first round of the amateur draft in 1973. The best trade sent Gary Gentry and Danny Frisella to the Braves for Felix Millan and George Stone in December 1972.

THE WORST PLAYER MOVE

One of the worst trades in baseball history was perpetrated on December 10, 1971 when the Mets sent Nolan Ryan, Leroy Stanton, Don Rose and Francisco Estrada to the Angels for Jim Fregosi.

1970

Season in a Sentence

In a frustrating season, the defending world champions win only 83 games and finish in third place, six games behind the pennant-winning Pirates.

Finish • Won • Lost • Pct • GB

Third   83   79   .512   6.0

Manager

Gil Hodges

Stats

Stats	Mets	AL	Rank
Batting Avg:	.249	.258	9
On-Base Pct:	.333	.329	4
Slugging Pct:	.370	.392	10
Home Runs:	120	9	
Stolen Bases:	118	2	
ERA:	3.45	4.05	1
Errors:	124	2	
Runs Scored:	695	9	
Runs Allowed:	630	1	

Starting Lineup

Jerry Grote, c
Donn Clendenon, 1b
Ken Boswell, 2b
Wayne Garrett, 3b-2b
Bud Harrelson, ss
Cleon Jones, lf
Tommie Agee, cf
Art Shamsky, rf-1b
Joy Foy, 3b
Ron Swoboda, rf
Ken Singleton, lf-rf

Pitchers

Tom Seaver, sp
Jerry Koosman, sp
Jim McAndrew, sp
Gary Gentry, sp
Ray Sadecki, sp-rp
Nolan Ryan, sp-rp
Ron Taylor, rp
Tug McGraw, rp

Attendance

2,697,479 (first in NL)

Club Leaders

Batting Avg:	Tommie Agee	.286
On-Base Pct:	Cleon Jones	.352
Slugging Pct:	Tommie Agee	.469
Home Runs:	Tommie Agee	24
RBI:	Donn Clendenon	97
Runs:	Tommie Agee	107
Stolen Bases:	Tommie Agee	31
Wins:	Tom Seaver	18
Strikeouts:	Tom Seaver	283
ERA:	Tom Seaver	2.82
Saves:	Ron Taylor	13

JANUARY 16   General manager Johnny Murphy dies at the age of 61 from his second heart attack in 16 days.

Bob Scheffing was named to replace Murphy. Scheffing had been a part of the Tigers organization as a manager, scout and radio broadcaster since 1961. Previously, he played in the majors as a catcher with the Cubs, Reds and Cardinals from 1941 through 1951 and managed the Cubs from 1957 through 1959. Scheffing remained as general manager through the end of the 1974 season. The club won the NL pennant in 1973 during his tenure, but he's best remembered for trading Nolan Ryan to the Angels in December 1971. Scheffing also presided over a series of amateur drafts that netted little in the way of talent, setting the stage for the abysmal clubs of the late-1970s and early 1980s.

MARCH 31   During a visit to the White House, Baseball Commissioner Bowie Kuhn presents a 1969 Mets world championship ring to president Richard Nixon.

APRIL 7   The Mets open with their first Opening Day win in club history by defeating the Pirates 5–3 in 11 innings in Pittsburgh. The two runs in the 11th scored on a pinch-hit single by Donn Clendenon. Tom Seaver was the starting pitcher and went eight innings. Tommie Agee collected three hits.

After an 0–8 record on Opening Day during the 1960s, the Mets were 18–2 in openers in the 1970s and 1980s. The only losses during that period were in 1974 and 1984.

APRIL 9   The Mets play at Forbes Field for the last time and lose 2–1 to the Pirates.

APRIL 14   In the home opener, the Mets lose 6–4 in ten innings to the Pirates before 41,679 at Shea Stadium.

             Before the game, the Mets received their World Series rings, and the world championship pennant was run up the flagpole.

APRIL 17   With a shot off Grant Jackson, Bud Harrelson hits the first outside-the-park home run of his career during a 6–0 win over the Phillies at Shea Stadium. It came in his 1,500th career at-bat. Harrelson's only previous home run was inside-the-park on August 17, 1967. He didn't hit another home run of any description until May 1, 1972.

APRIL 18   Nolan Ryan strikes out 15 batters during a one-hitter, which beats the Phillies 7–0 at Shea Stadium. The only Philadelphia hit was a single by Denny Doyle leading off the first inning. Ryan walked six.

APRIL 22   In a spectacular performance, Tom Seaver strikes out 19 batters, including ten in a row, and pitches a two-hitter to defeat the Padres 2–1 at Shea Stadium. At the time, the modern record for consecutive strikeouts was eight, and the mark for most strikeouts in a nine-inning game was 19 by Steve Carlton against the Mets on September 15, 1969. San Diego tied the score 1–1 on a home run by Al Ferrara in the second inning. The Mets broke the deadlock with a run in the third. The second hit off Seaver was a single by Dave Campbell in the fourth. Seaver ended the sixth with a strikeout of Ferrara, his tenth of the game. It was the start of Seaver's ten strikeouts in succession. He fanned Nate Colbert, Campbell and Jerry Morales in the seventh, Bob Barton, Ramon Webster and Ivan Murrell in the eighth, and Van Kelly, Cito Gaston and Ferrara in the ninth.

             The ten consecutive strikeouts is still the major league record. Seaver shared the record of 19 strikeouts in a nine-inning game until Roger Clemens fanned 20 in 1986.

APRIL 24   The Mets lose 1–0 to the Dodgers in 15 innings in Los Angeles. Jerry Koosman (nine innings) and Ron Taylor (five innings) pitched shutout ball until Ray Lamb surrendered a run in the 15th on a single by Tom Haller.

APRIL 25   In his first start since pitching a one-hitter on April 18, Nolan Ryan hurls a two-hitter but loses 1–0 to the Dodgers in Los Angeles. It was the Mets second straight 1–0 defeat. The only hits off Ryan were singles by Ted Sizemore in the first inning and Maury Wills in the third.

APRIL 28   Dave Marshall hits a grand slam off Gaylord Perry in the first inning to spark a 5–2 win over the Giants at Shea Stadium.

MAY 9   Five days after four students are killed by National Guardsmen on the campus of Kent State University, the Mets break a 4–4 tie with eight runs in the fifth inning and defeat the Giants 14–5 at Shea Stadium. The fifth inning rally was achieved with a double and eight singles. There were five singles in succession, and Duffy Dyer accounted for two of the three outs by striking out twice. Tommie Agee extended his batting streak to 20 games during the contest.

MAY 11   Tom Seaver strikes out 12 batters, but the Mets lose 3–0 to the Expos at Shea Stadium.

The loss was Seaver's first after a 6–0 start. Counting his last ten regular season decisions in 1969, Seaver won 16 in a row. The 16–0 record came in 18 starts and included an ERA of 1.63 in 154$^1/_3$ innings and 13 complete games. Seaver finished the 1970 season with an 18–12 record and league-leading figures in earned run average (2.82) and strikeouts (283). He also pitched 290$^2/_3$ innings and completed 19 of his 36 starts.

MAY 13   Gary Gentry pitches a one-hitter to defeat the Cubs 4–0 in Chicago. Gentry had a no-hitter in progress until Ernie Banks singled with two out in the eighth inning. After a long run, left fielder Dave Marshall got glove on Banks's looping fly, but couldn't hold it.

MAY 15   Tom Seaver records the second Mets one-hitter in as many games in a 4–0 victory over the Phillies at Connie Mack Stadium. The only Philadelphia hit was a single by Mike Compton in the third inning.

MAY 16   Jerry Koosman makes it three shutouts in a row for Mets pitchers by beating the Phillies 6–0 in Philadelphia.

MAY 18   The Mets allow five runs in the ninth inning and lose 8–4 to the Expos at Jarry Park. The Mets broke a 1–1 tie with three consecutive homers in the eighth inning by Dave Marshall, Joe Foy and Jerry Grote off Bill Stoneman. Montreal scored two times in the bottom of the eighth to pull within a run. In the ninth, Rusty Staub doubled in a run off Tug McGraw to tie the game once more. After an intentional walk, Cal Koonce replaced McGraw, and allowed a walkoff grand slam to Bob Bailey.

MAY 23   The Mets set a franchise record with four triples, but lose 14–8 to the Cubs in Chicago. The three-baggers were collected by Ron Swoboda, Al Weis, Ken Boswell and Tommie Agee.

MAY 24   Nolan Ryan pitches a two-hitter to defeat the Cubs 3–1 in the second game of a double-header at Wrigley Field. The only Chicago hits were singles by Don Kessinger in the first inning and Billy Williams in the third. The Cubs won the opener 3–1.

MAY 31   The Mets sweep the Astros 14–4 and 4–3 in a double-header at Shea Stadium. In the opener, Ron Swoboda hit two homers and drove in five runs. The second game went 14 innings. Duffy Dyer drove in the winning run with a pinch-hit single.

JUNE 4   In the first round of the amateur draft, the Mets select shortstop George Ambrow from Poly High School in Long Beach, California.

Ambrow failed to reach the majors, setting the stage for the worst draft year in club history. In the regular phase in June, the only future big leaguer drafted by the club was 20th-round selection Bruce Bosclair. The club drafted Roy Staiger in the secondary phase in January and Brent Strom in the June secondary draft, and neither proved to be impact players.

JUNE 7   The Mets play at Crosley Field in Cincinnati for the last time and lose 10–2 to the Reds.

JUNE 8   A two-run homer by Art Shamsky off Jack Billingham in the sixth inning accounts for the only two runs of a 2–0 win over the Astros in Houston. Jim McAndrew pitched the shutout.

          On the same day, the Mets sold Cal Koonce to the Red Sox.

JUNE 12   Tommie Agee collects two homers and two singles and scores four runs during an 8–1 triumph over the Braves at Shea Stadium.

JUNE 19   The Mets score seven runs in the first inning off Jim Bunning and trounce the Phillies 13–3 at Shea Stadium. All seven runs in the opening inning scored after two were out on six straight hits, which included four singles, a double and a triple.

JUNE 23   The Mets outlast the Cubs 12–10 in ten innings at Wrigley Field. The Mets scored seven runs in the fourth to take an 8–4 lead, then fell behind 10–8. Two runs in the ninth inning and two in the tenth won the game. Both ninth-inning tallies scored on a two-out single by Ken Boswell. Duffy Dyer walloped a two-run homer in the tenth for the victory.

JUNE 24   The Mets sweep the Cubs 9–5 and 6–1 in a double-header at Wrigley Field. Nolan Ryan (seven innings) and Tug McGraw (two innings) combined on a two-hitter in the second game. The only Chicago hits were singles by Don Kessinger leading off the first inning and Ernie Banks in the eighth.

JUNE 29   The Mets score two runs in the ninth inning to defeat the Pirates 3–2 at Shea Stadium. Dave Marshall drove in the tying run with a single and later scored in a sacrifice fly by Donn Clendenon.

          The Mets closed the month of June with a 40–33 record and a two-game lead in the NL East.

JULY 6   Tommie Agee hits for the cycle during a 10–3 win over the Cardinals at Shea Stadium. Agee singled in the third inning and homered in the fourth off Jerry Reuss, doubled in the fifth against Chuck Hartenstein, and tripled in the seventh facing Frank Linzy.

JULY 9   Ron Swoboda hits a grand slam off Rich Nye in the third inning of a 7–1 victory over the Expos at Shea Stadium.

JULY 12   The Mets sell Don Cardwell to the Braves.

JULY 14   Gil Hodges manages the National League to a 12-inning, 5–4 win in the All-Star Game at Riverfront Stadium in Cincinnati. Tom Seaver started for the NL and pitched three shutout innings. Bud Harrelson added two hits in three at-bats. The game ended on one of the most famous plays in All-Star history as Pete Rose bowled over AL catcher Ray Fosse with the winning run.

JULY 18 | The Mets score three runs in the ninth inning to down the Dodgers 4–3 in Los Angeles. Cleon Jones drove in the go-ahead run with a sacrifice fly.

JULY 19 | Joe Foy collects five hits in five at-bats and drives in five runs during a ten-inning, 7–6 win over the Giants in the second game of a double-header at Candlestick Park. Foy had two homers, a double and two singles. Foy's second homer was struck in the tenth and broke the 6–6 deadlock. San Francisco won the opener 5–3.

JULY 21 | The Mets are held without a hit by Clay Kirby for the first eight innings, but win 3–0 in San Diego. The Mets scratched out a run in the first inning on walks to Tommie Agee and Ken Singleton, a double steal and a grounder by Art Shamsky. Trailing 1–0, San Diego manager Preston Gomez pinch-hit for Kirby in the eighth. Jack Baldschun pitched the ninth for the Padres and gave up a lead-off single to Bud Harrelson to break up the no-hitter. Before the inning was over, Baldschun gave up two more hits and a pair of runs. Jim McAndrew hurled a three-hitter for the Mets.

JULY 24 | Tommie Agee climaxes a game against the Dodgers with a two-out steal of home in the tenth inning, which lifts the Mets to a 2–1 victory.

Agee hit .286 with 24 homers and 107 runs scored in 1970.

JULY 28 | Donn Clendenon hits a pair of three-run homers and a sacrifice fly to account for seven runs batted in during a 12–2 thrashing of the Giants at Shea Stadium.

AUGUST 1 | Tom Seaver strikes out 13 batters during a 4–2 win over the Padres at Shea Stadium.

AUGUST 4 | Nolan Ryan strikes out 13 batters and pitches a three-hitter to defeat the Cubs 4–0 at Shea Stadium.

AUGUST 7 | The Mets play at Three Rivers Stadium in Pittsburgh for the first time and lose 6–1 to the Pirates.

AUGUST 8 | Tommie Agee collects five hits in five at-bats as the Mets outslug the Pirates 12–9 in Pittsburgh. Agee had a triple, two doubles and two singles and scored four runs.

AUGUST 11 | The Mets play at Riverfront Stadium in Cincinnati for the first time and lose 8–1 to the Reds.

AUGUST 15 | The Mets suffer a shocking 3–2 defeat at the hands of the Braves in Atlanta. With one out in the ninth and Tony Gonzalez on third base and Rico Carty on second, Tom Seaver struck out Bob Tillman swinging for the second out. But the ball sailed past catcher Jerry Grote for a wild pitch, and by the time Grote retrieved the ball, both Gonzalez and Carty scored.

AUGUST 23 | The Mets score three runs in the ninth inning to defeat the Reds 5–4 in the first game of a double-header at Shea Stadium. The game ended on a two-out. bases-loaded walk by Wayne Granger to Joe Foy. Cincinnati won the second contest 7–5.

SEPTEMBER 9 | Nolan Ryan strikes out 13 batters in eight innings, but the Mets lose 3–2 to the Phillies in the first game of a double-header in Philadelphia. Ray Sadecki fanned 12 in the second tilt and defeated the Phils 3–1.

SEPTEMBER 10   Cleon Jones hits a walkoff triple in the 14th inning to beat the Phillies 3–2 at Shea Stadium.

SEPTEMBER 15   Cleon Jones extends his hitting streak to 23 games during a ten-inning, 5–4 loss to the Expos in Montreal.

During the streak, Jones collected 40 hits and compiled a batting average of .408.

SEPTEMBER 18   The Mets purchase Dean Chance from the Indians.

SEPTEMBER 20   Jerry Koosman pitches a two-hitter to beat the Pirates 4–1 in the first game of a double-header at Shea Stadium. The only Pittsburgh hits were a home run by Jose Pagan in the sixth inning and a single from Willie Stargell in the eighth.

The Mets were in a virtual tie for first place with the Pirates on September 14, then lost contests to the Expos on September 15 and 16 in Montreal to fall two games out. A four-game series against Pittsburgh in New York from September 18 through 20 resulted in three defeats.

SEPTEMBER 22   Tommie Agee hits a two-run single in the ninth inning to defeat the Phillies 7–6 in Philadelphia.

SEPTEMBER 23   The Mets play at Connie Mack Stadium for the last time, and defeat the Phillies 5–4.

The Mets headed for a three-game series against the Pirates in Pittsburgh beginning on September 24 trailing by two games. The Mets lost all three and in the process were eliminated from the pennant race.

SEPTEMBER 28   The Mets score two runs in the ninth and three in the tenth to defeat the Cubs 6–3 at Shea Stadium. With two out and no one on base in the ninth, Cleon Jones singled and Donn Clendenon homered to tie the score 3–3. In the tenth, Wayne Garrett walloped a three-run walkoff home run off Hoyt Wilhelm with two out. Center fielder Leroy Stanton made his major league debut and tripled leading off the first inning, but had to leave the game when he was hit in the head by the relay throw.

NOVEMBER 30   The Senators draft Joe Foy from the Mets organization.

DECEMBER 1   The Mets trade Ron Herbel to the Braves for Bob Aspromonte.

1971

Season in a Sentence

The Mets are 45–29 at the end of June, but a 13–31 stretch in July and August knocks the club out of contention.

Finish • Won • Lost • Pct • GB

Third (tie) 83   79   .512   14.0

Manager

Gil Hodges

Stats

Stats	Mets	AL	Rank
Batting Avg:	.249	.252	6
On-Base Pct:	.319	.316	6
Slugging Pct:	.351	.366	8
Home Runs:	98	7	
Stolen Bases:	89	4	
ERA:	3.00	3.47	1
Errors:	114	3	
Runs Scored:	588	8	
Runs Allowed:	550	1	

Starting Lineup

Jerry Grote, c
Ed Kranepool, 1b
Ken Boswell, 2b
Bob Aspromonte, 3b
Bud Harrelson, ss
Cleon Jones, lf
Tommie Agee, cf
Ken Singleton, rf
Tim Foli, 2b-3b
Donn Clendenon, 1b
Dave Marshall, rf-lf
Wayne Garrett, 3b
Don Hahn, cf

Pitchers

Tom Seaver, sp
Gary Gentry, sp
Nolan Ryan, sp
Ray Sadecki, sp-rp
Jerry Koosman, sp
Danny Frisella, rp
Tug McGraw, rp
Charlie Williams, rp
Jim McAndrew, rp-sp
Ron Taylor, rp

Attendance

2,266,680 (first in NL)

Club Leaders

Batting Avg:	Cleon Jones	.319
On-Base Pct:	Cleon Jones	.382
Slugging Pct:	Cleon Jones	.473
Home Runs:	Three tied with	14
RBI:	Cleon Jones	69
Runs:	Cleon Jones	63
Stolen Bases:	Tommie Agee	28
	Bud Harrelson	28
Wins:	Tom Seaver	20
Strikeouts:	Tom Seaver	289
ERA:	Tom Seaver	1.76
Saves:	Danny Frisella	12

MARCH 30   The Mets trade Dean Chance and Bill Denehy to the Tigers for Jerry Robertson.

MARCH 31   The Mets trade Ron Swoboda and Rich Hacker to the Expos for Don Hahn.

APRIL 6   The Mets open the season with a rain-shortened, five-inning 4–2 win over the Expos before 26,079 at Shea Stadium. Tom Seaver, making his fourth Opening Day start in a row, earned his first Opening Day victory.

APRIL 10   The Mets edge the Reds 3–2 in 11 innings at Shea Stadium. The winning run scored on a bases-loaded wild pitch by Wayne Granger with Jerry Grote at the plate.

APRIL 11   The Mets beat the Reds in 11 innings at Shea Stadium for the second game in a row, this time with a 1–0 decision. The winning run scored on a walk-off homer by Jerry Grote off Wayne Granger, who was the losing pitcher for the second day in succession. Tom Seaver (nine innings) and Tug McGraw (two innings) combined on the shutout.

Seaver was 20–12 in 1971 with league-leading figures in ERA (a career-low 1.76) and strikeouts (a career-high 289 in 286¹/₃ innings). He compiled 21 complete games (another career-best) in 35 starts.

APRIL 16   Tom Seaver strikes out 14 batters and pitches a three-hitter to beat the Pirates 1–0 at Shea Stadium. The lone run scored in the fourth inning on a home run by Donn Clendenon off Doc Ellis.

APRIL 18   Gary Gentry pitches a one-hitter to defeat the Pirates 5–2 at Three Rivers Stadium. The two Pittsburgh runs scored in the sixth inning on a walk, a triple by Roberto Clemente and a sacrifice fly.

APRIL 24   Tommie Agee hits a grand slam off Milt Pappas in the seventh inning, but the Mets lose 7–5 to the Cubs in Chicago.

APRIL 26   The Mets hammer the Cardinals 12–2 in St. Louis.

MAY 2   After the Astros score three runs in the ninth inning to tie the score, the Mets pull out a 6–5 win in Houston with a run in the tenth. The winning tally scored on a double by Ken Boswell and a triple from Bob Aspromonte.

MAY 3   Tommie Agee's walkoff single in the 11th inning beats the Cubs 3–2 at Shea Stadium. The Mets were saved in the bottom of the ninth by an umpire's call. With the bases loaded, one out and the score 2–2, third base umpire Stan Landes called a balk on Tug McGraw to give the Cubs an apparent victory. But home plate umpire Mel Steiner said he called time before McGraw's balk, which nullified the call by Landes. It was the Mets' second straight extra inning win.

MAY 11   Dave Marshall hits a grand slam off George Culver in the sixth inning of an 8–1 win over the Astros at Shea Stadium.

On May 15, the Mets had a 21–10 record and a 2¹/₂-game lead in the NL East, but dropped out of first place with a five-game losing streak, which began on May 16.

MAY 17   In Atlanta, Donn Clendenon homers in the top of the tenth to give the Mets a 3–2 lead, but Ralph Garr of the Braves counters with a pair of home runs in the tenth off Tom Seaver and in the 12th against Ron Taylor to hand the Mets a 4–3 defeat.

MAY 19   The Mets play at Veterans Stadium in Philadelphia for the first time and lose 4–1 to the Phillies.

MAY 22   The Mets rally in the late innings to beat the Braves 8–7 at Shea Stadium. Atlanta scored three times in the ninth to take a 6–4 lead, but the Mets countered in the bottom half to tie the score. Bud Harrelson drove in the game-tying run with a two-out single. The Braves scored in the tenth, but again the Mets deadlocked the contest in the bottom half on three straight singles, the last of them by Ken Boswell. Donn Clendenon gave the Mets the 8–7 victory with a walkoff single in the 11th.

MAY 26   The Mets lose a frustrating 3–2 decision to the Phillies in 11 innings at Shea Stadium. Gary Gentry had a one-hitter in progress before giving two runs and three hits in the ninth to tie the score 2–2. Larry Bowa drove in the winning run with a single off Tug McGraw in the 11th.

During the game, one of the warm-up throws from third baseman Tim Foli hit first baseman Ed Kranepool, who refused to throw the ball to Foli anymore, and the two had to be separated by teammates in the dugout.

MAY 29   The Mets sweep the Padres 5–1 and 2–1 during a double-header in San Diego. Nolan Ryan struck out 16 batters in the second game.

At the end of May, Ryan had a 6–1 record and an earned run average of 1.08. At the age of 24, Ryan finally seemed to have become a consistent pitcher. From July 5 through the end of the season, however, Ryan was 2–10, compiled an ERA of 6.94, and walked 62 batters in 59²/₃ innings. He finished the year with a 10–14 record and a 3.97 ERA. The performance caused the Mets to give up on Ryan and package him in a trade (see December 10, 1971).

JUNE 8   In the first round of the amateur draft, the Mets select second baseman Rich Puig from Hillsborough High School in Tampa, Florida.

For the second straight year, the Mets made a series of horrible picks in the draft. Puig played in only 11 major league games, all with the Mets in 1974, and was hitless in ten at-bats. The only other future major leaguers drafted and signed by the Mets in 1971 were Rich Baldwin (ninth round) and Mark DeJohn (23rd round), neither of whom ever had to worry about being besieged by autograph seekers.

JUNE 18   Gary Gentry pitches a two-hitter to defeat the Phillies 2–0 at Shea Stadium. The only Philadelphia hits were singles by Tim McCarver in the fourth inning and Oscar Gamble in the seventh. The only two runs of the game crossed the plate on a home run by Ken Singleton off Ken Reynolds in the second inning. It was one of only three New York hits in the game.

JUNE 19   The Mets outlast the Phillies 6–5 in 15 innings at Shea Stadium. The Phils scored in the top of the 14th on a steal of home by Larry Bowa. The Mets countered in the bottom half on a one-out home run by Ken Singleton. The winning run scored on a two-out, walk-off homer in the 15th from Donn Clendenon.

JUNE 20   The Mets score three runs in the ninth inning without a batter being retired to beat the Phillies 7–6 in the first game of a double-header at Shea Stadium. The three tallies were accounted for by five singles strung together by Tim Foli, Dave Marshall, Bud Harrelson, Don Hahn and Duffy Dyer off Darrell Brandon. Philadelphia won the second game 9–7 in 11 innings.

JUNE 25   Cleon Jones ties a National League record for most walks in a double-header with six as the Mets sweep the Expos 4–1 and 4–2 in Montreal.

JUNE 29   Tom Seaver strikes out 13 batters during a 3–0 win over the Phillies in Philadelphia. The three Mets runs scored on solo homers by Jerry Grote in the fourth inning and back-to-back shots from Cleon Jones and Ed Kranepool. All three were struck off Barry Lersch.

The Mets ended the month of June with a record of 45–29 and were two games behind the first-place Pirates. But the Mets soon spiraled into a terrible slump and were 13–31 from July 1 through August 15.

JULY 17   Prior to a 2–1 loss to the Astros in Houston, Gary Gentry and Jim McAndrew collide in the outfield. Gentry needed 16 stitches to close cuts in the face, and McAndrew required 20.

JULY 29   Nolan Ryan walks nine batters in five innings of a 3–1 loss to the Cardinals at Shea Stadium. The contest was shortened to eight innings by rain.

AUGUST 5   The Mets leave 18 men on base and lose 2–1 to the Braves in 17 innings in Atlanta. Sonny Jackson drove in the winning run with a single off Ron Taylor.

AUGUST 7   The Mets reach the 20-run plateau for the first time in club history and smother the Braves 20–6 in Atlanta. The Mets scored three runs in the first inning, seven in the second, three in the fifth, three in the sixth, two in the seventh and two in the ninth. There were 21 New York hits in all on two homers, a double and 18 singles. Ken Boswell was the offensive star with four hits in five at-bats and five runs batted in. Boswell hit a grand slam off Mike McQueen in the second.

AUGUST 8   The day after scoring 20 runs, the Mets lose 5–0 to Phil Niekro and the Braves in Atlanta.

AUGUST 10   Tug McGraw strikes out nine batters in a four-inning relief appearance that closes out a 6–4 win over the Padres in San Diego.

AUGUST 11   The Mets waste a brilliant pitching performance by Tom Seaver and lose 1–0 to the Padres in San Diego. Seaver pitched ten innings, allowed only three hits and struck out 14. Danny Frisella took the loss.

Over eight starts from August 6 through September 11, Seaver was 7–0 and had an 0.62 ERA in 73 innings. Included was a streak of 27 consecutive scoreless innings.

AUGUST 21   Cleon Jones hits a walk-off homer in the ninth inning to defeat the Padres 2–1 at Shea Stadium.

AUGUST 28   For the second Saturday in a row, Cleon Jones belts a walk-off homer in the ninth inning, this time to down the Dodgers 2–1 in the second game of a double-header at Shea Stadium. The Mets also won the opener 9–2.

Jones batted .319 with 14 homers in 1971.

AUGUST 31   Nolan Ryan strikes out 12 batters in six innings, but the Mets lose 2–1 to the Cardinals in St. Louis.

SEPTEMBER 6   Tom Seaver pitches a two-hitter and strikes out 12 batters to defeat the Expos 7–0 at Jarry Park. The only Montreal hits were a single by Ron Hunt in the first inning and a double from Gary Sutherland in the fifth.

SEPTEMBER 17   The Mets defeat the Pirates 3–0 in Pittsburgh with three solo homers. They were each struck off Nelson Briles by Ted Martinez leading off the first inning, Ken Singleton in the second and Ed Kranepool in the fourth. The homer by Martinez was the first of his career and the only one he hit in 1971.

SEPTEMBER 25   The Mets outlast the Pirates 2–1 in 15 innings at Shea Stadium. Bob Aspromonte drove in the winning run with a single with two out in the 15th. Jon Matlack (eight innings), Tug McGraw (five innings) and Danny Frisella (two innings) pitched for the Mets.

SEPTEMBER 26   Tom Seaver pitches a one-hitter to defeat the Pirates 3–1 at Shea Stadium. The only Pittsburgh hit was a single by Vic Davalillo leading off the seventh.

SEPTEMBER 30   On the last day of the season, Tom Seaver records his 20th win with a 6–1 decision over the Cardinals at Shea Stadium.

OCTOBER 18   The Mets trade Art Shamsky, Jim Bibby, Rich Folkers and Charlie Hudson to the Cardinals for Harry Parker, Chuck Taylor, Jim Beauchamp and Chip Coulter.

Bibby was nearly 27 and had kicked around the Mets minor league system since 1965 without receiving a call-up to the parent club. After the trade, he went on to win 111 games with the Cardinals, Rangers, Indians and Pirates. None of the players acquired in the deal had any kind of long-term success with the Mets.

OCTOBER 20   The Mets sell Ron Taylor to the Expos.

OCTOBER 28   The Mets release Donn Clendenon.

DECEMBER 10   The Mets trade Nolan Ryan, Leroy Stanton, Don Rose and Frank Estrada to the Angels for Jim Fregosi.

The trade would prove to be one of the worst ever made by a major league club. Fregosi was 29 and had been named to six American League All-Star teams as a shortstop with the Angels between 1964 and 1970. During the 1970 season, he collected 22 homers, drove in 82 runs and batted .278. In 1971, however, Fregosi developed a tumor on his foot that required surgery, and he batted only .233 with five home runs. The Mets hoped that Fregosi was young enough to recover his previous form and would fill a hole at third base. That plan failed to materialize as Fregosi was never again a regular. He broke his thumb in spring training and was overweight for most of the 1972 season. Overall, Fregosi played in only 146 games as a Met before being sold to the Rangers in July 1973 and hit .233 with five homers, coincidentally the same numbers he posted in his last season with the Angels. Ryan seemed to have tapped his enormous potential early in the 1971 season (see May 29, 1971), but by the end of the year the Mets had all but given up hope that he would develop into a consistent winner. His numbers over five seasons as a Met included a 29–38 record and a 3.58 ERA. He was 24 at the time of the infamous trade. It didn't take long for the Mets to realize they had made a monumental miscalculation. In 1972, Ryan was 19–16 with a 2.28 ERA, nine shutouts, and 329 strikeouts in 284 innings. After leaving New York, Ryan played for another 22 seasons with the Angels, Astros and Rangers. By the time his career was over, Ryan had a major league records for most strikeouts (5,714) and no-hitters (seven) in a career along with a 324–292 record and eight All-Star selections. He was a first ballot Hall of Famer in 1999. It seems astonishing today that the Mets not only traded Ryan for Fregosi but sent three others along with him in the transaction.

1972

Season in a Sentence

Following the death of Gil Hodges during spring training, the Mets roar to a 25–7 start under new manager Yogi Berra and bring Willie Mays back to New York, but fade to a distant third by the end of the year.

Finish • Won • Lost • Pct • GB

Third   83   73   .532   13.5

Manager

Yogi Berra

Stats

Stats	Mets	AL	Rank
Batting Avg:	.225	.248	12
On-Base Pct:	.307	.315	9
Slugging Pct:	.332	.365	10
Home Runs:	105	7	
Stolen Bases:	41	12	
ERA:	3.26	3.45	5
Errors:	116	2	
Runs Scored:	528	9	
Runs Allowed:	578	5	

Starting Lineup

Duffy Dyer, c
Ed Kranepool, 1b
Ken Boswell, 2b
Jim Fregosi, 3b
Bud Harrelson, ss
John Milner, lf
Tommie Agee, cf
Rusty Staub, rf
Cleon Jones, lf
Wayne Garrett, 3b
Ted Martinez, 2b-ss
Willie Mays, cf
Jerry Grote, c

Pitchers

Tom Seaver, sp
Jon Matlack, sp
Jerry Koosman, sp
Jim McAndrew, sp
Gary Gentry, sp
Tug McGraw, rp

Attendance

2,134,185 (first in NL)

Club Leaders

Batting Avg:	Tommie Agee	.227
On-Base Pct:	Tommie Agee	.317
Slugging Pct:	Tommie Agee	.374
Home Runs:	John Milner	17
RBI:	Cleon Jones	52
Runs:	John Milner	52
	Tommie Agee	52
Stolen Bases:	Bud Harrelson	12
Wins:	Tom Seaver	21
Strikeouts:	Tom Seaver	249
ERA:	Jon Matlack	2.32
Saves:	Tug McGraw	27

APRIL 1   Just five days prior to the scheduled opening of the season, the players go on strike. The major point of contention was over an increase in the players' pension fund. The players and owners did not come to an agreement until April 15, which canceled the Mets first six games of the season. Play began on April 15.

APRIL 2   After playing a round of golf with his coaches in West Palm Beach, Florida, on Easter Sunday, Gil Hodges suffers a heart attack in the parking lot of the Ramada Inn and dies suddenly two days before his 48th birthday.

APRIL 6   On the day that Gil Hodges is buried at Holy Cross Cemetery in Brooklyn, the Mets announce that Yogi Berra will be his successor as manager. The Mets also reported the trade of Ken Singleton, Tim Foli and Mike Jorgensen to the Expos for Rusty Staub.

The Mets were roundly criticized for callously making the announcements on the same day of Hodges' burial. Known more for his witticisms, many true, some exaggerated, than for his baseball acumen, Berra had been a coach with the Mets since 1965. After a Hall of Fame playing career with the Yankees from 1946 through 1963, Yogi was named manager of the Yanks for the 1964 season. Despite leading the team to the American League pennant, Berra was unceremoniously fired, leading to his appointment with the Mets. He served as manager of the club until 1975 and won the National League pennant in 1973. Staub solidified a right-field position that had been a problem for the Mets almost continuously since the franchise's inception in 1962. He was the starter in right field until a trade to the Tigers following the 1975 season. As well as Staub played in New York, the Mets would have been better served by keeping Singleton. He was a starter in right for the Expos and Orioles until 1984, and played in three All-Star Games and two World Series while in Baltimore.

APRIL 15   The Mets win the strike-delayed opener 4–0 over the Pirates before only 15,893 at Shea Stadium. Tom Seaver (six innings) and Tug McGraw (three innings) combined on the shutout. McGraw retired all nine batters he faced. Ed Kranepool drove in three runs with a two-run homer and a sacrifice fly.

APRIL 21   Bud Harrelson has a hand in both runs of a 2–0 win over the Cubs at Shea Stadium. In the fifth inning, Harrelson singled in a run against Burt Hooton, advanced to second on an error and scored on a single from Ken Boswell. It was Hooton's first start since pitching a no-hitter against the Phillies on April 16. Tom Seaver pitched the shutout.

                  Seaver began the season by pitching 21 consecutive scoreless innings. He finished the year with a 21–12 record, a 2.92 ERA and 249 strikeouts in 262 innings.

APRIL 28   Tommie Agee hits a grand slam off Jim Brewer in the eighth inning of a 6–1 win over the Dodgers at Shea Stadium. Agee was the first batter Brewer faced after relieving Bill Singer.

MAY 1   Tom Seaver strikes out 12 batters in $6^2/_3$ innings but also gives up four runs, as the Mets beat the Giants 7–4 in San Francisco.

MAY 2   Gary Gentry pitches a two-hitter to defeat the Giants 4–2 at Candlestick Park. The only two San Francisco hits were triples by Bobby Bonds leading off the fourth and ninth innings. Bonds scored following both three-baggers on a ground out in the fourth and a sacrifice fly in the ninth.

MAY 7   The Mets rally from a 6–0 deficit with five runs in the eighth inning, one in the ninth and two in the tenth for a thrilling 8–6 victory over the Padres at Shea Stadium. The five runs in the eighth were driven in by five different players. Tommie Agee had a hand in all three late-inning rallies. He hit a double in the eighth and drove in the tying run with a single in the ninth. Agee capped the comeback with a two-run, walk-off homer in the tenth.

MAY 10   After a scheduled day off and a postponement due to rain, the Mets win in extra innings for the second game in a row, this time with a 4–3 decision over the Dodgers in 14 innings at Shea Stadium. In the 14th, Bud Harrelson singled, stole second, went to third on a wild pitch and crossed the plate on a single from Ted Martinez. Tug McGraw pitched five shutout innings.

MAY 11   The Mets trade Charlie Williams to the Giants for Willie Mays.

Mays was 41 years old at the time of the trade and a part-time player with the Giants, holding a batting of average of .184 in 49 at-bats. The Giants, with one of the lowest home attendance figures in the majors, could no longer afford his salary, which was $165,000 annually. Despite his declining skills, Mets fans were delirious over the fact that Mays would be back in New York, where he played with the Giants from 1951 through 1957. At first, he seemed to be rejuvenated by his return to the Big Apple. He had eight hits, two of them game-winning homers, in his first 19 at-bats as a Met. After 49 games with the club, Mays had a batting average of .286 with five homers and an on-base percentage of .432. But nagging injuries took a toll, and Willie hit only .218 from August 5 through the end of the 1972 season and .211 in 66 games in 1973. He retired at the end of the 1973 campaign.

MAY 13   Buzz Capra (eight innings) and Tug McGraw (one inning) combine to shut out the Giants for a 1–0 win at Shea Stadium. McGraw struck out all three batters he faced in the ninth inning, setting down Bobby Bonds, Dave Kingman and Ken Henderson. It was Capra's third career start. He not only pitched eight shutout innings but drove in the lone run of the game with a two-out single in the second off Juan Marichal.

McGraw began the year by allowing only one run in 26 innings over 11 relief appearances. His final numbers included an 8–6 record, 27 saves and a 1.70 ERA in 54 games and 106 innings.

MAY 14   In his first game with the Mets, Willie Mays breaks a 4–4 tie against his former Giants teammates with a fifth-inning homer off Don Carrithers, which lifts his new club to a 5–4 win at Shea Stadium. Mays played first base and hit in the lead-off spot in the batting order. Facing Sam McDowell, Mays walked and struck out in the two plate appearances prior to the home run.

MAY 17   The Mets score six runs in the third inning for a 9–0 lead and rout the Expos 12–2 at Shea Stadium.

MAY 21   The Mets extend their winning streak to 11 games with a 4–3 decision over the Phillies in Philadelphia. A two-run homer by Willie Mays off Steve Carlton in the eighth inning erased a 3–2 deficit. Tom Seaver was the winning pitcher.

The Mets closed the day with a 25–7 record and a six-game lead in the NL East.

MAY 25   The Mets outlast the Cubs 3–2 in 14 innings in Chicago. Willie Mays drove in the deciding run with a two-out single. Tug McGraw pitched five scoreless innings of relief.

MAY 29   The Mets score four runs in the ninth inning to defeat the Cardinals 7–6 in St. Louis. Ken Boswell tied the score 6–6 with a one-out, three-run homer. The winning run scored on Tommie Agee's single, a walk, a hit batsman and a passed ball.

JUNE 3   Rusty Staub is hit in the hand by a pitch from George Stone during a 5–2 win over the Braves at Shea Stadium.

Staub remained in the game and played in every contest until June 18. The hand grew progressively worse, however, and by June 18 he could no longer grip a bat, and it was determined that the hand was broken. Staub played in only one game between June 18 and September 18. Injuries plagued the club throughout the last two-thirds of the season. On June 2, the club was 31–12 and possessed a 5½-game lead in the NL East. From June 3 through September 7, the Mets compiled a record of 35–53 and slipped far out of contention for the pennant. In mid-July, the entire starting outfield of Staub, Tommie Agee and Cleon Jones was out of action at the same time. No Mets player accumulated as many as 500 plate appearances during the season.

JUNE 6   In the first round of the amateur draft, the Mets select Philip Bengston from Richwoods High School in Peoria, Illinois.

Bengston never reached the majors. The only significant player drafted and signed by the Mets in 1972 was third-rounder Craig Swan. Other future major leaguers included Brock Pemberton (sixth round), Craig Cacek (ninth round), Ron Hodges (second round of the January draft) and Randy Tate (fifth round of the January draft).

JULY 1   Two weeks after the break-in of the Democratic Party headquarters at the Watergate complex in Washington, Dave Marshall drives in both runs of a 2–0 win over the Expos in Montreal with a single in the third inning and a homer in the fifth, both off Mike Torrez. Jerry Koosman pitched the shutout.

JULY 4   Tom Seaver is two outs from a no-hitter in the first game of a double-header against the Padres at Shea Stadium. Leron Lee broke up Seaver's no-hit bid with a single with one out in the ninth. Seaver had to settle for a one-hit, 2–0 victory. He struck out 11. Both New York runs scored in the third inning when Clay Kirby walked four straight batters, the last two to Jim Fregosi and Ed Kranepool with the bases loaded. San Diego won the second tilt 4–2.

JULY 6   The Mets collect only two hits in 14 innings and lose 1–0 to the Padres at Shea Stadium. A walk by Tug McGraw to Jerry Morales with the bases loaded forced across the lone run. Jerry Koosman started for the Mets, pitched ten innings, and struck out 12. Steve Arlin (ten innings) and Gary Ross (four innings) pitched for San Diego. The only New York hits were singles by Dave Marshall in the fourth inning and Jim Fregosi in the 12th.

JULY 14   Stepping to the plate for the third plate appearance of his first major league game, right fielder Dave Schneck erases a 2–1, sixth-inning deficit with a two-run homer, which gives the Mets a 3–2 win over the Padres in San Diego.

JULY 21   In his first game in San Francisco since becoming a Met, Willie Mays hits his 650th career homer during a 3–1 win. The milestone was struck in the fifth inning off Jim Barr.

JULY 25   In the All-Star Game in Atlanta, Tug McGraw pitches shutout ball the ninth and tenth innings to help the National League to a 4–3 win. McGraw allowed one hit and fanned four. Reggie Jackson and Carlton Fisk were among McGraw's strikeout victims. Joe Morgan drove in the winning run with a single.

JULY 27   The Mets edge the Pirates 1–0 in ten innings in the first game of a double-header in Pittsburgh. The lone run scored on a double from Cleon Jones, Ed Kranepool's single and a sacrifice fly by Wayne Garrett off Nelson Briles. Jon Matlack pitched a complete game and allowed only four hits.

               Matlack was the NL Rookie of the Year in 1972. At the age of 22, he had a 15–10 record and a 2.32 earned run average.

AUGUST 1   The Mets defeat the Phillies 3–2 in an 18-inning marathon in the first game of a double-header at Shea Stadium. Cleon Jones drove in all three New York runs with a sacrifice fly in the sixth inning, a homer in the eighth, and a single in the 18th. Jon Matlack ($8^2/_3$ innings), Tug McGraw ($6^1/_3$ innings) and Ray Sadecki (three innings) pitched for the Mets. The annual Banner Day parade was scheduled for between games of the twin bill, and those with banners had to wait about three hours longer than they had anticipated because of the 18-inning contest. Philadelphia won the second game 4–1.

               The usage patterns of relievers in 1972 were much different than today. McGraw made ten appearances of three or more innings that season and pitched in four contests of at least five innings.

AUGUST 6   The Mets lambaste the Cubs 12–2 in Chicago.

AUGUST 7   Ted Sizemore hits a walkoff, inside-the-park homer in the 13th inning to beat the Mets 3–2 in St. Louis. Cleon Jones missed an attempt at a shoestring catch in left field and allowed Sizemore's drive to roll to the wall. It was the only hit allowed by Tug McGaw, who fanned six in four innings of work.

               During the afternoon, Yogi Berra was in Cooperstown for his induction into the Hall of Fame. He flew to St. Louis in time to witness the defeat.

AUGUST 12   The Mets beat the Cubs 2–1 in Chicago with solo homers by Willie Mays in the sixth inning and Tommie Agee in the tenth. Both were struck off Burt Hooton.

AUGUST 21   A two-run, walk-off homer with two out in the ninth inning by Jim Beauchamp beats the Astros 4–2 at Shea Stadium. It was his second homer of the game, and the outburst occurred on his 33rd birthday. The homers were the first two of five that Beauchamp collected in 1972.

AUGUST 22   Jim Beauchamp drives in all four Mets runs, two of them with his third homer in two days, during a 4–2 win over the Astros at Shea Stadium. His two-run single with two out in the eighth inning broke the 2–2 tie.

AUGUST 27   The Mets take a 10–0 lead after six innings and defeat the Braves 13–6 in Atlanta.

The win broke a three-game losing streak, which tied for the longest of the season. The Mets had 12 three-game losing streaks in 1972 and broke each of them with a victory.

AUGUST 29   The Mets hit three solo homers off Jack Billingham and defeat the Reds 3–0 in Cincinnati. The home runs were belted by Ed Kranepool and Ken Boswell in the fourth inning and Tommie Agee in the eighth. Jim McAndrew (8²/₃ innings) and Tug McGraw (one-third of an inning) combined on the shutout.

SEPTEMBER 2   Down 8–0 after seven innings, the Mets explode for seven runs in the eighth inning and four in the ninth to shock the Astros 11–8 in Houston. The key hits in the eighth were a three-run homer by Ken Boswell and a two-run single from Wayne Garrett. Cleon Jones broke an 8–8 tie in the ninth by driving in two teammates with a single.

SEPTEMBER 8   John Milner collects five hits, including a homer and a double, in five at-bats, during an 8–2 triumph over the Cardinals in the first game of a double-header at Shea Stadium. S. Louis won the second contest 9–4 in 13 innings.

SEPTEMBER 16   Five Mets pitchers combine to walk 15 batters during an 18–5 drubbing at the hands of the Cubs in Chicago. The five offending pitchers were Tom Seaver, Brent Strom, Hank Webb, Bob Rauch and Danny Frisella. Rauch, a rookie in his lone season in the majors, walked five in 1²/₃ innings.

SEPTEMBER 18   A walkoff single by Duffy Dyer in the ninth inning off Nelson Briles beats the Pirates 1–0 at Shea Stadium. Jon Matlack pitched the shutout.

SEPTEMBER 20   Tom Seaver strikes out 15 batters during a 4–1 victory over the Pirates at Shea Stadium.

SEPTEMBER 29   Tom Seaver records his 20th win of the season with a 1–0 decision over the Pirates at Three Rivers Stadium. Seaver pitched a two-hitter and fanned 13. The only Pittsburgh hits were singles by Al Oliver in the fourth inning and Richie Hebner in the seventh. Tommie Agee drove in the lone run of the game with a single off Nelson Briles in the ninth inning.

Briles lost three games to the Mets by 1–0 scores in 1972. The other two were on July 27 and September 18.

SEPTEMBER 30   Jon Matlack surrenders Roberto Clemente's 3,000th career hit during a 5–0 loss to the Pirates in Pittsburgh. The milestone was a double in the fourth inning.

Clemente never collected another regular season hit. He died in a plane crash on December 31 off the coast of Puerto Rico. Clemente was delivering supplies to earthquake victims in Nicaragua.

OCTOBER 2   In the first game of a double-header in Montreal, Bill Stoneman of the Expos pitches a no-hitter to defeat the Mets 7–0. He walked seven and struck out nine. The last out was recorded when Don Hahn grounded into a force-out at second base. The Mets won the second tilt 2–1.

No Mets player collected 100 hits in 1972. Tommie Agee led the club with 96.

NOVEMBER 2   Five days before Richard Nixon defeats George McGovern in the Presidential election, the Mets trade Gary Gentry and Danny Frisella to the Braves for Felix Millan and George Stone.

Most of the trades completed by the Mets during the 1970s had a detrimental effect on the club, but this one turned out well. Gentry and Frisella did little in Atlanta while Millan was the Mets starting second baseman for four years. Frisella was a member of the Milwaukee Brewers when he was killed in a dune buggy accident in Phoenix, Arizona, on January 1, 1977.

NOVEMBER 27   The Mets trade Tommie Agee to the Astros for Rich Chiles and Buddy Harris.

Agee played his way out of New York by batting .227 and by complaining loudly about losing playing time in center field to Willie Mays. The 1973 campaign was his last in the majors, and Agee hit just .222 with the Astros and Cardinals.

1973

Season in a Sentence

The Mets rise from a last-place predicament on August 30 to win the NL East, upset the Reds in the Championship Series and take the defending world champion A's to seven games in the World Series.

Finish • Won • Lost • Pct • GB

First   82   79   .509   +1.5

National League Championship Series

The Mets defeated the Cincinnati Reds three games to two.

World Series

The Mets lost to the Oakland Athletics four games to three.

Manager

Yogi Berra

Stats

Stats	Mets	AL	Rank
Batting Avg:	.246	.254	11
On-Base Pct:	.315	.322	8
Slugging Pct:	.338	.376	12
Home Runs:	85	11	
Stolen Bases:	27	11	
ERA:	3.26	3.66	2
Errors:	126	4	
Runs Scored:	608	11	
Runs Allowed:	588	2	

Starting Lineup

Jerry Grote, c
John Milner, 1b
Felix Millan, 2b
Wayne Garrett, 3b
Bud Harrelson, ss
Cleon Jones, lf
Don Hahn, cf
Rusty Staub, rf
Ed Kranepool, 1b-lf
Ted Martinez, ss-cf
Willie Mays, cf

Pitchers

Tom Seaver, sp
Jerry Koosman, sp
Jon Matlack, sp
George Stone, sp
Tug McGraw, rp
Ray Sadecki, rp-sp
Harry Parker, rp

Attendance

1,912,390 (third in NL)

Club Leaders

Batting Avg:	Felix Millan	.290
On-Base Pct:	Rusty Staub	.361
Slugging Pct:	John Milner	.432
Home Runs:	John Milner	23
RBI:	Rusty Staub	76
Runs:	Felix Millan	82
Stolen Bases:	Wayne Garrett	6
Wins:	Tom Seaver	19
Strikeouts:	Tom Seaver	251
ERA:	Tom Seaver	2.08
Saves:	Tug McGraw	25

APRIL 6   The Mets open the season with a 3–0 win over the Phillies before 27,326 at Shea Stadium. Tom Seaver (7^2/$_3$ innings) and Tug McGraw (1^1/$_3$ innings) combined on the shutout. Cleon Jones drove in all three runs with a two-run homer in the fourth inning and a solo shot in the seventh, both off Steve Carlton. Eleven ceremonial first balls were thrown by eleven former prisoners of war (Vietnam).

           The Mets began the season by winning their first four games.

APRIL 22   The Mets score seven runs in the third inning on the way to a 13–3 trouncing of the Expos in the second game of a double-header at Shea Stadium. Montreal won the opener 2–1 in ten innings.

           With the changing times, facial hair was permissible in baseball for the first time since the turn-of-the-century. The Oakland A's started the trend in the sport in 1972, when at the urging of owner Charlie Finley, nearly every player on the team grew a mustache. Among the 1973 Mets with mustaches were Felix Millan, Ken Boswell, Cleon Jones and Ed Kranepool.

APRIL 27   The game between the Braves and Mets in Atlanta takes only one hour and 37 minutes making it the shortest game of nine innings or more by time in Mets history. Pat Dobson outdueled Tom Seaver for the 2–0 Atlanta win.

APRIL 29   Jerry Koosman pitches the Mets to a 1–0 victory over the Braves in Atlanta. The lone run scored in the second inning on a sacrifice fly by Jerry Grote.

MAY 2   Tom Seaver strikes out 13 batters in six inning, but also allows four runs, and the Mets lose 6–1 to the Reds at Shea Stadium.

MAY 3   Four batters into the first inning, the Mets have a 4–0 lead thanks to a grand slam by Rusty Staub off Jim McGlothlin, but wind up losing 6–5 to the Reds at Shea Stadium.

MAY 8   In the seventh inning of a 10–6 loss to the Braves at Shea Stadium, Jon Matlack is carried off the field after being hit in the head by a line drive off the bat of Marty Perez. Matlack suffered a hairline fracture of the skull, but returned to action 11 days later.

MAY 12   Tom Seaver pitches a two-hitter and beats the Pirates 6–0 at Three Rivers Stadium. The only Pittsburgh hits were a single by opposing pitcher Bob Moose in the third inning and a triple from Willie Stargell in the seventh.

           Seaver had a 19–10 record and pitched 290 innings in 1973. He posted league-leading figures in ERA (2.08), strikeouts (251) and complete games (18) which earned him his second Cy Young Award.

MAY 14   The Mets purchase Jerry May from the Royals.

           A catcher, May was acquired because Jerry Grote broke his arm. May made his Mets debut on May 24, and left the contest in the seventh inning with a sprained right wrist. He returned five days later, but on June 3 went on the disabled list with a pulled hamstring muscle and never played another major league game. May appeared in four games with the club, and was injured in two of them.

MAY 24

The Mets win 7–3 over the Dodgers in a 19-inning encounter in Los Angeles. The Dodgers took a 3–1 lead in the third inning, but the Mets tied the contest with runs in the seventh and eighth and didn't allow a run over the final 16 innings. The Mets pitchers were Tom Seaver (six innings), Phil Hennigan (one inning), Tug McGraw (five innings), George Stone (six innings) and Jim McAndrew (one inning). The 3–3 tie was broken in the 19th on a single by Cleon Jones and a double from Rusty Staub. It was Staub's fifth hit in nine at-bats. Before the inning concluded, the Mets added three more runs. Willie Davis collected six hits in nine at-bats for the Dodgers. The game ended at 4:44 a.m. New York time.

The Mets lost 12 of their next 15 games to fall to 23–29, nine games out of first.

MAY 29

Tom Seaver strikes out 16 batters and beats the Giants 5–2 in San Francisco. The Mets trailed 2–1 heading into the ninth inning, but pulled out a victory with four runs.

JUNE 5

In the first round of the amateur draft, the Mets select outfielder Lee Mazzilli from Lincoln High School in Brooklyn, New York.

The Brooklyn native was the son of welterweight boxer Libero Mazzilli. In addition to playing baseball in his youth, Lee was an eight-time speed skating champion in his age group. He played for the Mets from 1976 through 1981 and again from 1985 through 1987. During his first tour, Mazzilli was the star of a string of last-place teams and became one of the most popular players in franchise history, particularly with female fans because of his striking good looks. On his return to New York, he was a part-time player during a period in which the Mets were the premier team in baseball. Other future major leaguers drafted and signed by the Mets in 1973 were Jackson Todd (second round) and Mardie Cornejo (21st round).

JUNE 8

The Mets complete a double play in which six fielders handle the ball in the seventh inning of a 4–2 win over the Dodgers at Shea Stadium. With Davey Lopes the base runner on first and Tom Paciorek on third, Lopes became involved in a rundown after an attempted pickoff by Jon Matlack. Lopes kept evading the tags of the New York defense while trying to allow Paciorek a chance to go home. Rusty Staub joined the pursuit from right field and put the tag on Lopez near second base. Paciorek headed for home and was out on a thrown from Staub to catcher Duffy Dyer. Others involved in the double play were first baseman John Milner, second baseman Felix Millan and shortstop Jim Fregosi.

JUNE 16

The Mets defeat the Padres 5–2 on POW Night at Shea Stadium. A total of 152 former Vietnam prisoners of war were introduced to the crowd prior to the game.

JUNE 27

The Mets score seven runs in the first inning and hang on to beat the Phillies 7–6 in the first game of a double-header at Shea Stadium. The seven-run rally was achieved with nine hits, eight of them singles. Buzz Capra pitched four innings of no-hit relief just hours after attending the burial of his father in Illinois. Philadelphia won the second game 7–1.

JULY 6

Ron Schueler of the Braves takes a no-hitter into the ninth inning before beating the Mets 2–0 with a two-hitter. Ron Hodges broke up the no-hit bid by leading off the ninth with a single.

JULY 7 — Left fielder George Theodore suffers a dislocated right hip after colliding with Don Hahn trying to haul in Ralph Garr's long drive. Garr scored on an inside-the-park homer, and the Mets lost 9–8 to the Braves at Shea Stadium.

> *On July 8, the Mets were 34–46 and 12 games out of first. Before the July 9 game, Board Chairman M. Donald Grant addressed the team. Grant talked of confidence, faith and the club "believing in itself." After Grant left, Tug McGraw leapt to his feet and shouted: "You gotta believe! You gotta believe!" It became a Mets battle cry as the club pulled out of last place to win the pennant.*

JULY 9 — The Mets eke out a 12-inning 2–1 win over the Astros at Shea Stadium. The Mets trailed 1–0 with two out in the ninth when pinch-hitter Jim Beauchamp singled a run. Felix Millan singled in the winning run.

JULY 10 — Jon Matlack pitches a one-hitter to defeat the Astros 1–0 at Shea Stadium. The only Houston hit was a double by Tommy Helms in the sixth inning. Duffy Dyer drove in the lone run with a single in the second inning.

JULY 11 — The Mets sell Jim Fregosi to the Rangers.

JULY 17 — In one of the greatest comebacks in club history, the Mets score seven runs in the ninth inning to defeat the Braves 8–7 in Atlanta. With one out in the ninth, Rusty Staub hit a two-run homer to make the score 7–3. After a single from Cleon Jones, John Milner homered and it was 7–5. Ron Hodges then grounded out and the Mets were down to their last out with no one on base. After Don Hahn singled to keep the rally alive, pinch-hitters Ed Kranepool walked and Jim Beauchamp singled to produce a run. Beauchamp scored all the way from first base on a two-run single by Willie Mays to give the Mets an 8–7 lead and the improbable victory.

JULY 18 — Rusty Staub hits two homers and drives in five runs during a 12–2 trouncing of the Braves in Atlanta.

> *Shortly after arriving in New York, Staub opened a restaurant called "Rusty's" on the upper East Side at 73rd Street and Third Avenue. It was best-known for its' annual rib-eating contest. The established closed during the 1980s.*

JULY 28 — John Milner hits a grand slam off Mike Torrez in the first inning of an 11–3 win over the Cardinals at Shea Stadium.

AUGUST 8 — Jon Matlack pitches a two-hitter to defeat the Dodgers 1–0 in Los Angeles. The only hits off Matlack were singles by Willie Davis in the first inning and Manny Mota in the fourth. Jerry Grote drove in the lone run with a single in the second inning.

AUGUST 15 — Tom Seaver pitches a two-hitter to defeat the Padres 7–0 in San Diego. The only hits off Seaver were singles by Derrel Thomas in the fifth inning and Jerry Morales in the sixth.

AUGUST 17 — Willie Mays hits the last of his 660 career homers during a ten-inning, 2–1 loss to the Reds at Shea Stadium. It was struck off Don Gullett.

AUGUST 18 — The Mets hammer the Reds 12–1 at Shea Stadium.

AUGUST 20 — Tom Seaver pitches 12 innings and allows only two runs while striking out 12 batters, but the Mets end up losing 8–3 in 16 innings to the Reds at Shea Stadium. Tug McGraw gave up five runs in the 16th.

> *At the end of the game, McGraw had a 5.45 ERA in 77²/₃ innings. Over the remainder of the 1973 season, he pitched in 19 games and 41 innings and compiled an earned run average of 0.88.*

AUGUST 22 — After trailing 3–2 in the ninth with two out and a runner on second base, the Mets beat the Dodgers 4–3 at Shea Stadium on three consecutive singles from Felix Millan, Rusty Staub and John Milner.

AUGUST 24 — Jerry Koosman pitches a ten-inning shutout to beat the Giants 1–0 at Shea Stadium. Felix Millan drove in the lone run with a walkoff single off Juan Marichal.

> *The Mets lost their next two games to fall to 58–70 and were in last place. Fortunately, there were no outstanding teams in the NL East in 1973, and the Mets were only 6¹/₂ games out of first. At that point, the Cardinals led the division with a record of 65–64. The Mets were 24–9 over the rest of the regular season.*

AUGUST 27 — Rusty Staub hits a grand slam off Steve Arlin in the fifth inning of a 6–5 win over the Padres at Shea Stadium. Tug McGraw closed out the victory by striking out four of the five batters to face him in the eighth and ninth innings.

AUGUST 31 — The Mets move out of last place with a ten-inning, 6–4 decision over the Cardinals in St. Louis.

SEPTEMBER 3 — Jerry Koosman shuts out the Phillies 5–0 in the first game of a double-header at Shea Stadium. Philadelphia won the second game 6–3.

> *Koosman pitched 31²/₃ consecutive scoreless innings from August 19 through September 7.*

SEPTEMBER 4 — Tom Seaver strikes out 13 batters during a 7–1 triumph over the Phillies at Shea Stadium.

SEPTEMBER 7 — The Mets sweep the Expos 1–0 and 4–2 at Jarry Park. In the opener, Wayne Garrett provided the lone run by leading off the first inning with a home run off Steve Renko. Jon Matlack (8²/₃ innings) and Tug McGraw (one-third of an inning) combined on the shutout. The second game went 15 innings. Don Hahn broke a 1–1 tie in the 15th with a sacrifice fly. The Mets added two insurance runs before Montreal scored in the bottom half. The first game was also delayed for 11 minutes in the third inning because the sun setting over the rim of the ballpark made it impossible for the first basemen to see the ball thrown from the other infielders.

SEPTEMBER 13 — Tom Seaver pitches 11 innings and strikes out 12 during a 12-inning 4–2 victory over the Phillies in Philadelphia. Wayne Garrett broke the 2–2 deadlock with an RBI-single.

SEPTEMBER 18 — Trailing 4–1, the Mets erupt for five runs in the ninth inning and beat the Pirates 6–5 in Pittsburgh. Felix Millan drove in two runs with a triple and scored on a single from pinch-hitter Ron Hodges. Don Hahn broke the 4–4 two with a two-run single.

Bob Apodaca made his major league debut as a reliever in the ninth and walked the first two Pittsburgh batters to face him. Buzz Capra relieved Apodaca and walked two more, one intentionally, before pitching out of the jam.

After the win, the Mets were 74–77, in fourth place, and 2¹/2 games out of first. It was part of an unusual five-game series against the Pirates, in which the first two contests were played in Pittsburgh and the last three in New York.

SEPTEMBER 19   John Milner hits two homers and drive in five runs during a 7–3 triumph over the Pirates at Shea Stadium.

SEPTEMBER 20   The Mets outlast the Pirates with a thrilling 13-inning, 4–3 win over the Pirates at Shea Stadium. With two out in the ninth inning, Duffy Dyer hit a double which tied the score 3–3. The Pirates missed taking a 5–3 lead in the 13th by an inch. With two out and Richie Zisk on first base, Dave Augustine lined a Ray Sadecki pitch deep to left field. The ball hit the pointed edge of the wall, bounced straight up in the air, and into the glove of Cleon Jones. Jones fired to third baseman Wayne Garrett, whose relay throw to Ron Hodges at the plate nipped Zisk and preserved the tie. A single by Ron Hodges brought home the winning run. Augustine completed his career with 29 major league at-bats, and never hit a home run.

On the same day, Willie Mays announced his retirement as a player, effective at the end of the season.

SEPTEMBER 21   The Mets take first place with a 10–2 win over the Pirates at Shea Stadium. The Mets had a record of 77–77.

SEPTEMBER 22   A two-run homer by Wayne Garrett in the second inning provides both runs of a 2–0 win over the Cardinals at Shea Stadium. Jon Matlack pitched the shutout.

SEPTEMBER 23   The Mets purchase Bob L. Miller from the Tigers. Miller was an original Met and had a 1–12 record with the club in 1962.

SEPTEMBER 25   The Mets hold retirement ceremonies for Willie Mays before a 2–1 win over the Expos at Shea Stadium. Mays told the crowd of 53,603 "it's time to say goodbye to America."

At the close of play on September 27, the Mets were 80–78 and held a one game lead over the Pirates. Remaining on the schedule was four games against the Cubs in Chicago.

SEPTEMBER 28   The game against the Cubs in Chicago is postponed by rain, forcing the two clubs to play double-headers on Saturday the 29th and Sunday the 30th to close the season. The Pirates lost 3–2 to the Expos to fall 1¹/2 games back. The Cards were still mathematically alive in third place just two games back.

SEPTEMBER 29   The double-header against the Cubs in Chicago is postponed by more rain, which extends the regular season by one day to Monday, October 1 if the NL East race isn't settled on Sunday the 30th. The Cardinals defeated the Phillies 7–1 in St. Louis to leapfrog into second place 1¹/2 games back of the Mets and ahead of the Pirates, who lost 6–4 to the Expos.

SEPTEMBER 30   The Mets lose 1–0 and win 9–2 in a double-header against the Cubs in Chicago. The Cardinals beat the Phillies 3–1 in St. Louis. At the conclusion of play, the Mets were 81–79 and the Cardinals 81–81. The Mets needed one win in a double-header against the Cubs on October 1 to clinch the NL East. If the Mets lost both, an one-game playoff between the Mets and Cards was scheduled to determine the pennant-winner.

OCTOBER 1   The Mets defeat the Cubs 6–4 at Wrigley Field to clinch the NL East pennant. Tom Seaver pitched six innings for the win. Tug McGraw hurled three innings of shutout relief. Rusty Staub contributed four hits and Cleon Jones homered. The second game of the scheduled double-header was canceled because it no longer had a bearing on the pennant race.

The Mets met the Cincinnati Reds in the National League Championship Series. managed by Sparky Anderson, the Reds were 99–63 in 1973 and were the National League champions in both 1970 and 1972.

OCTOBER 6   The Mets open the Championship Series with a 2–1 loss to the Reds at Riverfront Stadium in Cincinnati. The Mets struck first when Tom Seaver doubled in a run in the second inning. Seaver struck out 13 batters without issuing a walk, but gave up home runs to Pete Rose in the eighth inning and Johnny Bench in the ninth for the loss.

The series was telecast nationally by NBC. Curt Gowdy and Tony Kubek were the announcers in games one and two and Jim Simpson and Maury Wills in games three, four and five.

OCTOBER 7   Jon Matlack evens the series by beating the Reds 5–0 with a two-hitter at Riverfront Stadium. Andy Kosco collected both Cincinnati hits with singles in the second and seventh innings. The Mets broke open a close game with four runs in the ninth. Rusty Staub contributed a home run.

OCTOBER 8   In a game which will forever be remembered for the fight between Bud Harrelson and Pete Rose, the Mets move within one win of the NL pennant with a 9–2 victory before 53,967 at Shea Stadium. The Mets scored five times in the second for a 6–0 lead and cruised to the win. Rusty Staub homered twice and drove in four runs. Jerry Koosman pitched a complete game.

In the fifth inning, Rose slid hard into Harrelson in an attempt to break up a double play and the two exchanged punches. Players from both teams rushed onto the field, and play was held up for several minutes. Reds pitcher Pedro Borbon battled Mets pitcher Buzz Capra, and after the fight was over, Borbon accidentally donned Capra's cap. Recognizing his mistake, Borbon took a bite out of the headgear. Neither Rose nor Harrelson was ejected. When Rose returned to left field, fans began throwing bottles and other assorted debris at him, prompting Sparky Anderson to pull him off the field. After umpires threatened a forfeit if the activity continued, Yogi Berra, Willie Mays, Tom Seaver, Cleon Jones and Rusty Staub went out to left field and pleaded with the fans to desist. The appeal was successful and the game continued.

OCTOBER 9   The Reds even the series at two games apiece with a 2–1 win over the Mets before 50,786 at Shea Stadium. Pete Rose gained a measure of revenge with a 12th-inning homer off Harry Parker for the game-winner.

OCTOBER 10   On the day that Spiro Agnew resigns as vice-president due to financial improprieties, the Mets take the National League pennant by beating the Reds 7–2 before 50,323 at Shea Stadium. The Mets broke a 2–2 tie with four runs in the fifth inning. Cleon Jones collected three hits, including a double. Tom Seaver pitched a complete game. In the seventh inning, Mets fans began to crowd into the field-level boxes in order to rush the field at game's end to celebrate. The crowd became so uncontrollable the game had to be halted in the ninth inning so the wives of the Reds players and Cincinnati club officials could be escorted to safety under the stands. The game ended with Dan Driessen grounding out with Pete Rose the base runner on first. At least 5,000 mobbed the field after the game, virtually destroying the grass and the outfield wall.

The Mets played the Oakland Athletics in the World Series. Managed by Dick Williams, the A's were 94–68 in 1973. Oakland won the 1972 World Series in seven games over the Cincinnati Reds.

OCTOBER 13   The Mets open the World Series with a 2–1 loss to the Athletics in Oakland. Both A's runs scored in the third inning. The first crossed the plate on a double by pitcher Ken Holtzmann and an error by second baseman Felix Millan on a grounder by Bert Campaneris. Jon Matlack took the defeat.

The series was telecast nationally over NBC. The announcers were Curt Gowdy, Tony Kubek and Monty Moore during games one, two, six and seven, and Gowdy, Kubek and Lindsay Nelson in games three, four and five.

OCTOBER 14   The Mets even the series by defeating the Athletics 10–7 in 12 innings in Oakland. The Mets took a 6–3 lead with four runs in the sixth inning, but the A's scored a run in the seventh and two in the ninth after two were out to tie. Willie Mays, who had entered the game as a pinch-runner for Rusty Staub in the ninth, drove in the tie-breaking run with a single in the 12th. It proved to be the last hit and RBI of his career. The Mets added three insurance runs before Oakland plated a run in the bottom half. Cleon Jones homered, singled twice, and scored three runs. Wayne Garrett also homered. Bud Harrelson collected three hits, including a double which ignited the 12th-inning rally.

Willie Mays and Oakland second baseman Mike Andrews were the focus of attention for their miscues on the field. Fielders on both teams battled a blinding sun through the first two games of the Series, which were played on a Saturday and Sunday afternoon. Every ball hit into the air was an adventure and fielders approached them like men searching for a light switch in a dark room. In the bottom of the ninth, Mays lost sight of a fly ball by Deron Johnson and fell down on the warning track. Johnson reached second base for a double and led the two-run Oakland rally which tied the score. Mays played in only one more game, as a pinch-hitter in the third game of the Series. Andrews made two key errors on successive plays in the 12th which helped the Mets score four times. Charlie Finley placed Andrews on the disabled list, citing an injury which proved to be non-existent. Commissioner Bowie Kuhn reinstated Andrews and disciplined Finley with a substantial fine. Andrews played as a pinch-hitter in game four and received a standing ovation from the Shea Stadium crowd.

OCTOBER 16   The A's take a two games to one lead with an 11-inning, 3–2 win over the Mets before 54,817 at Shea Stadium. The Mets scored twice in the first inning, with the first coming on Wayne Garrett's leadoff homer off Catfish Hunter. Oakland tied the score with runs in the sixth and eighth. Tom Seaver pitched eight innings and struck out 12 before exiting for a pinch-hitter. The winning run in the 11th scored on a walk from Harry Parker to Ted Kubiak, a passed ball by Jerry Grote, and a single from Bert Campaneris.

Between games two and three, A's manager Dick Williams told reporters he would not be returning to manage the club in 1974.

OCTOBER 17   The Mets even the series with a 6–1 victory over the Athletics before 54,817 at Shea Stadium. Rusty Staub hit a homer and three singles and drove in five of the six New York runs. Jerry Grote collected three hits. Jon Matlack went eight innings and allowed only three hits.

OCTOBER 18   The Mets move within one win of a world championship with a 2–0 victory over the Athletics before 54,817 at Shea Stadium. The Mets scored their runs in the second and sixth inning. Jerry Koosman ($6^2/_3$ innings) and Tug McGraw ($2^1/_3$ innings) combined on the shutout.

OCTOBER 20   The Athletics force a seventh game by beating the Mets 3–1 in Oakland. Reggie Jackson gave the A's a 2–0 lead with RBIs in the first and third innings off Tom Seaver.

OCTOBER 21   The Athletics take the world championship by beating the Mets 5–2 in Oakland. The A's took a 4–0 lead with four runs in the third inning on a pair of two-run homers by Bert Campaneris and Reggie Jackson off Jon Matlack.

Al Dark replaced Dick Williams as manager of the Athletics in 1974 and led the franchise to its' third consecutive world championship.

DECEMBER 20   The Mets trade Jim McAndrew to the Padres for Steve Simpson.

1974

Season in a Sentence

The youthful mythmakers of the 1969 world championship season begin to show their age and the Mets fade to fifth place with 91 defeats.

Finish • Won • Lost • Pct • GB

Fifth   71   91   .438   17.0

Manager

Yogi Berra

Stats

Stats	Mets	AL	Rank
Batting Avg:	.235	.255	11
On-Base Pct:	.311	.326	11
Slugging Pct:	.329	.367	12
Home Runs:	96	8	
Stolen Bases:	43	12	
ERA:	3.42	3.62	4
Errors:	158	8	
Runs Scored:	572	11	
Runs Allowed:	646	6	

Starting Lineup

Jerry Grote, c
John Milner, 1b
Felix Millan, 2b
Wayne Garrett, 3b
Bud Harrelson, ss
Cleon Jones, lf
Don Hahn, cf
Rusty Staub, rf
Ted Martinez, ss
Dave Schneck, cf
Ken Boswell, 2b-3b
Ed Kranepool, lf-1b

Pitchers

Jerry Koosman, sp
Jon Matlack, sp
Tom Seaver, sp
Harry Parker, rp-sp
Bob Apodaca, rp
Tug McGraw, rp
Bob L. Miller, rp
Ray Sadecki, rp

Attendance

1,722,209 (fifth in NL)

Club Leaders

Batting Avg:	Cleon Jones	.282
On-Base Pct:	Rusty Staub	.347
Slugging Pct:	Cleon Jones	.421
Home Runs:	John Milner	20
RBI:	Rusty Staub	78
Runs:	John Milner	70
Stolen Bases:	John Milner	10
Wins:	Jerry Koosman	15
Strikeouts:	Tom Seaver	201
ERA:	Jon Matlack	2.41
Saves:	Harry Parker	4

JANUARY 5   Due to heavy financial losses, Rhinegold Beer announces it will close its Brooklyn-based plant. As a result, the brewery was forced to end its' 13-year sponsorship of Mets games on radio and television.

MARCH 9   In the midst of the streaking craze, two young men take a nude romp across the field during the ninth inning of a 4–1 win over the Cardinals in St. Petersburg. One of the streakers took the cap of centerfielder Dave Schneck.

MARCH 27   The Mets sell Buzz Capra to the Braves.

Capra had a 5–10 record over three seasons with the Mets. In 1974, he was brilliant in Atlanta with a 16–8 mark and a league-leading ERA of 2.28. But Capra proved to be a one-year wonder and posted a 10–19 won-lost ledger from 1975 through the end of his career in 1977.

APRIL 6   Mike Schmidt hits a two-run, walk-off homer off Tug McGraw with one out in the ninth to lift the Phillies to a 5–4 win over the Mets in the season opener in Philadelphia. Tom Seaver was the starter and went seven innings. Bud Harrelson collected three hits, one of them a double, in the losing cause.

On the same day, the Yankees played their first home game at Shea Stadium and defeated the Indians 6–1. The Yankees used Shea as their home field in 1974 and 1975 while Yankee Stadium was being rebuilt.

APRIL 9   The day after Hank Aaron hits his 715th homer to break Babe Ruth's career record, the Mets' scheduled home opener against the Cardinals is postponed by rain.

APRIL 10   The 1973 National League pennant is raised before the home opener in which the Mets defeat the Cardinals 3–2 before 17,154 at Shea Stadium. Jerry Grote homered.

After a 2–1 start, the Mets lost seven in a row and were 3–11 on April 28.

MAY 1   The Mets waste a brilliant pitching performance from Tom Seaver and lose 2–1 in 14 innings to the Dodgers in Los Angeles. Seaver pitched 12 innings, allowed a run and only three hits, and struck out 16. The only hits off Seaver were a homer by Steve Garvey in the fifth, and singles from Bill Russell in the eighth and Bill Buckner in the 12th. Garvey drove in the winning run with a walk-off single off Harry Parker.

Seaver suffered through a tough year, posting an 11–11 record and a 3.20 ERA.

MAY 5   John Milner hits a two-run, walk-off homer in the tenth inning to defeat the Padres 6–4 at Shea Stadium.

MAY 8   Jon Matlack strikes out 12 batters without issuing a walk during a 4–2 victory over the Giants at Shea Stadium.

MAY 17   Tom Seaver strikes out 13 batters without issuing a walk during a 5–0 triumph over the Expos at Shea Stadium.

MAY 26   The Mets score four times with two out in the ninth inning to defeat the Pirates 5–3 in Pittsburgh. Felix Millan tied the score with a two-run single. Following a pair of walks, John Milner drove in two more with another single.

JUNE 5   In the first round of the amateur draft, the Mets select pitcher Cliff Speck from Beaverton High School in Beaverton, Oregon.

Speck didn't pitch in the majors until 1986, when he appeared in 13 games with the Braves. The Mets received little of quality in the draft in 1974. The only other future major leaguers drafted and signed were Dwight Bernard (second round), John Pacella (fourth round), Bob Myrick (20th round) and Ned Yost (first round of the secondary draft).

JUNE 8   The Mets edge the Astros 6–5 in 14 innings in Houston. The winning run scored when John Milner doubled, moved to third on a single by Ray Sadecki, and crossed the plate on Wayne Garrett's ground out.

JUNE 14   The Mets purchase Jack Aker from the Braves.

JUNE 21   Three solo homers beats the Phillies 3–1 in Philadelphia. John Milner homered twice off Steve Carlton in consecutive at-bats in the fourth and sixth innings. Rusty Staub added another home run against Mac Scarce in the eighth.

JUNE 29   Jon Matlack pitches a one-hitter to beat the Cardinals 4–0 at Shea Stadium. The only St. Louis hit was a single by opposing pitcher John Curtis in the third inning.

Matlack led the league in shutouts with seven and had a 2.41 ERA, but received little batting support from his teammates and finished with a record of 13–15.

JULY 8   Harry Parker walks nine batters and allows four hits in eight innings of a 2–1 win over the Padres at Shea Stadium.

JULY 20   George Theodore, Cleon Jones and Rusty Staub hit consecutive homers off Lowell Palmer in the fifth inning of a 10–2 victory over the Padres in San Diego.

JULY 23   Yogi Berra manages the National League to a 7–2 victory in the All-Star Game at Three Rivers Stadium in Pittsburgh.

AUGUST 12 Four days after Richard Nixon resigns as President, John Milner hits a long home run off Andy Messersmith which lands two-thirds of the way up the right field scoreboard at Shea Stadium. The Mets beat the Dodgers 3–1.

AUGUST 25 Ray Sadecki not only pitches a complete game shutout to defeat the Braves 1–0 in Atlanta, but drives in the game's lone run with a single off Phil Niekro in the fifth inning.

AUGUST 26 The Mets score three runs in the ninth inning to down the Astros 5–4 at Shea Stadium. Ted Martinez doubled in the first run, moved to third on an error, and crossed the plate on a bunt single from Felix Millan. Rusty Staub drove in the winning run with a two-out single.

AUGUST 27 Left fielder Benny Ayala homers in his first major league plate appearance to spark the Mets to a 4–2 win over the Astros at Shea Stadium. The pitcher was Tom Griffin.

Ayala hit three homers in 102 at-bats for the Mets over three seasons. He ended his big-league career in 1985 with 38 home runs.

SEPTEMBER 1 Tug McGraw pitches the only shutout of his 19-year major league career with a 3–0 decision over the Braves at Shea Stadium.

McGraw pitched in 824 games during his career and made 39 starts.

SEPTEMBER 3 The Mets sweep the Cubs 2–0 and 11–4 in Chicago. In the opener, John Milner drove in both runs with a single in the first inning and a single in the sixth. Jon Matlack pitched the shutout.

SEPTEMBER 11 The Mets lose 4–3 to the Cardinals in 25 innings at Shea Stadium. The only longer game in major league history went 26 innings and took place on May 1, 1920 between the Brooklyn Dodgers and Boston Braves. That one ended in a 1–1 tie before being called on account of darkness. The Mets-Cardinals encounter lasted seven hours and four minutes and ended at 3:13 a.m. Among those in attendance was Commissioner Bowie Kuhn and his wife. With two out in the ninth, a St. Louis runner on first base, and the Mets leading 3–1, Jerry Koosman gave up a two-run homer to Ken Reitz. There was no scoring over the next 15 innings by either team.

After Koosman went nine innings, the Mets relievers from the tenth through the 24th were Harry Parker (three innings), Bob L. Miller (one inning), Bob Apodaca (three innings) and Jerry Cram (eight innings). Hank Webb started the 25th for the Mets. It was his first major league appearance in 1974 after spending most of the season at Class AAA Tidewater. Bake McBride singled to begin the inning and scored all the way from first base when Webb's pick-off attempt sailed past first baseman John Milner to give the Cards a 4–3 lead. In the bottom of the 25th, Brock Pemberton singled with two out for his first major league hit, but was stranded when John Milner struck out to end the game. The Mets failed to score over the last 20 innings. Claude Osteen pitched 9²/₃ innings of relief for the Cardinals. There were 50 players used by the two teams, 26 of them by the Cardinals.

Ed Sudol was the home plate umpire. He was also the home plate umpire during the Mets' 23-inning marathon against the Giants on May 30, 1964 and the 24-inning affair versus the Astros on April 15, 1968. Ed Kranepool played in all three of those games. The contest is still tied for the second-longest in major league history. Another 25-inning game took place on May 8 and 9, 1984 between the White Sox and Brewers on Chicago. In that game, the two clubs played 17 innings before the umpires suspended the game because of a 1:00 a.m. curfew. Play continued the following evening with eight more innings. Chicago won 5–4. Tom Seaver pitched in the 25th inning for the White Sox, his first relief appearance since 1976, then went nine innings in the regularly scheduled game the same day and won 5–4.

OCTOBER 1   Tom Seaver strikes out 14 batters, but the Mets lose 2–1 to the Phillies at Shea Stadium.

On the same day, 45-year-old Joe McDonald succeeded Bob Scheffing as general manager. Scheffing had earlier announced his retirement. McDonald began working for the Mets in 1962 as a statistician. He was the farm director when promoted to general manager. McDonald would remain in the position until 1980, a period in which the Mets had a notable lack of success.

OCTOBER 13   The Mets trade Ray Sadecki and Tommie Moore to the Cardinals for Joe Torre.

Torre followed Ken Boyer, Joe Foy and Jim Fregosi as another aging veteran acquired to fix the club's long-standing problem at third base. A native of Brooklyn, Torre broke into the majors as a catcher in 1961. He was converted into a third baseman by the Cardinals in 1970, a position he hadn't played since high school, and won the NL MVP award in 1971 by batting .363. In 1973, Torre was named to the All-Star team for the ninth time. By 1975, however, he was 34 and had slowed down considerably. Unable to withstand the rigors of playing third base, Torre was moved back across the diamond to first a year later. In three seasons as a player with the Mets, he hit .267 with 12 homers in 722 at-bats. In May 1977, he was named manager of the club, a job he held until 1981.

OCTOBER 23   The Mets embark on a three-week goodwill tour of Japan. The Mets won nine and lost seven on the trip.

OCTOBER 29   The Mets trade Ken Boswell to the Astros for Bob Gallagher.

DECEMBER 3   The Mets trade Tug McGraw, Don Hahn and Dave Schneck to the Phillies for
Del Unser, John Stearns and Mac Scarce.

*McGraw suffered through subpar seasons in both 1973 and 1974, but
rebounded and pitched in the Phillies bullpen until 1984. He was a key member
of Philadelphia's World Series teams of 1980 and 1983. Stearns was the second
overall pick of the Phillies in the 1973 draft and was an all-Big Eight selection
as a defensive back at the University of Colorado. He was also drafted by the
Buffalo Bills. Stearns was the Mets starting catcher from 1977 through 1982 and
was named to four All-Star teams while with the club before injuries prematurely
ended his career.*

1975

Season in a Sentence

The Mets rebound from the
nightmare of 1974 with a winning
season, but it's not enough to
save Yogi Berra's job.

Finish • Won • Lost • Pct • GB

Third (tie) 82   80   .506 10.5

Managers

Yogi Berra (56–53) and
Roy McMillan (26–27)

Stats

Stats	Mets	AL	Rank
Batting Avg:	.256	.257	7
On-Base Pct:	.319	.327	9
Slugging Pct:	.361	.369	8
Home Runs:	81	11	
Stolen Bases:	32	12	
ERA:	3.39	3.62	4
Errors:	151	5	
Runs Scored:	646	9	
Runs Allowed:	625	4	

Starting Lineup

Jerry Grote, c
Ed Kranepool, 1b
Felix Millan, 2b
Joe Torre, 3b
Mike Phillips, ss
Dave Kingman, lf
Del Unser, cf
Rusty Staub, rf
Wayne Garrett, 3b
John Milner, lf-1b

Pitchers

Tom Seaver, sp
Jon Matlack, sp
Jerry Koosman, sp
Randy Tate, sp
Hank Webb, sp-rp
Bob Apodaca, rp
Rick Baldwin, rp

Attendance

1,730,566 (fourth in NL)

Club Leaders

Batting Avg:	Del Unser	.294
On-Base Pct:	Rusty Staub	.371
Slugging Pct:	Dave Kingman	.494
Home Runs:	Dave Kingman	36
RBI:	Rusty Staub	105
Runs:	Rusty Staub	93
Stolen Bases:	Dave Kingman	7
Wins:	Tom Seaver	22
Strikeouts:	Tom Seaver	243
ERA:	Tom Seaver	2.38
Saves:	Bob Apodaca	13

FEBRUARY 28   The Mets purchase Dave Kingman from the Giants for $150,000.

*At the time Kingman was acquired, the only two Mets players with 25 or more
homers in a season were Frank Thomas with 34 in 1962 and Tommie Agee with
26 in 1969. Kingman clubbed 36 in 1975 and 37 in 1976, although it came with*

batting averages of .231 and .238 and some abysmal defense. He was popular with Mets fans but was unhappy in New York and requested a trade. That was granted with a deal to the Padres in June 1977.

APRIL 8   In his Mets debut, Joe Torre hits a walk-off single off Steve Carlton in the ninth inning to beat the Phillies 2–1 before an Opening Day crowd of 18,257. In the second plate appearance of his first game with the Mets, Dave Kingman homered in the fourth inning. Tom Seaver pitched a complete game.

Seaver rebounded from his 11–11 season in 1974 by winning the Cy Young Award in 1975 with a record of 22–9, a 2.38 ERA and a league-leading 243 strikeouts in 280^1/$_3$ innings.

APRIL 12   The Mets sign Jesus Alou, most recently with the Athletics, as a free agent.

APRIL 17   The Mets break a five-game losing streak by scoring six runs in the first inning and beat the Cardinals 14–7 in St. Louis.

"Mets" was written in script across the front of the team's road uniforms for the first time in 1975. The previous scheme from 1962 through 1974 had "New York" written in fancy block letters.

APRIL 20   The Mets sweep the Cubs 8–6 and 4–3 in a double-header at Shea Stadium. In the opener, Jack Heidemann hit his first home run since September 3, 1970 when he was playing for the Indians.

APRIL 23   Rusty Staub hits a grand slam off Bob Gibson in the fifth inning of a 7–1 victory over the Cardinals at Shea Stadium.

Staub batted .282 with 19 homers and 105 RBIs in 1975. Staub was the first player in club history to drive in at least 100 runs in a season.

APRIL 25   The Mets score five runs on only three hits and beat the Expos 5–3 in Montreal.

APRIL 27   Trailing 6–1, the Mets bust loose for six runs in the seventh inning and defeat the Expos 7–6 in Montreal. Five of the seventh-inning runs crossed the plate after two were out. Dave Kingman broke the 6–6 tie with a single.

MAY 20   Joe Torre collects a homer, two doubles and a single in five at-bats during a 6–2 victory over the Reds in Cincinnati.

MAY 26   Wayne Garrett hits a three-run, pinch-hit, walk-off homer in the ninth inning to defeat the Dodgers 6–3 at Shea Stadium.

JUNE 2   Dave Kingman has a hand in both runs of a 2–0 win over the Astros at Shea Stadium. In the second inning, Kingman tripled in a run and scored on a sacrifice fly by Jerry Grote. It was Kingman's only triple of the season. Jon Matlack pitched the shutout.

JUNE 3   Dave Kingman rips a 480-foot home run into the Shea Stadium parking lot off Ken Forsch in the fourth inning of a 4–3 win over the Astros.

*On the same day, the Mets selected catcher Butch Benton from Godby High
School in Tallahassee, Florida, in the first round of the amateur draft. Benton
made his major league debut with the Mets in 1978 and played for three clubs
before his last game in 1985. He played in a total of only 51 games, however,
and batted just .162. The rest of the June draft was a wasted exercise, as the
Mets didn't sign a single player who would play in the majors.*

JUNE 4   Jerry Koosman pitches the Mets to a 1–0 win over the Astros at Shea Stadium.
          Ed Kranepool drove in the lone run with a single in the first inning.

JUNE 8   The Mets outlast the Braves 7–6 in 14 innings at Shea Stadium. The winning run
          scored when Felix Millan singled, advanced to third on an error and crossed the plate
          on a wild pitch.

JUNE 12   Felix Millan drives in both runs of a 2–0 win over the Dodgers in Los Angeles with
          RBI-doubles off Don Sutton in the sixth and eighth innings. Jon Matlack pitched
          the shutout.

JUNE 24   After being shutout in their three previous games and held without a run over
          35 innings in four contests, the Mets beat the Cardinals 5–1 at Shea Stadium.

JULY 4   The Mets score three runs in the ninth inning off Tug McGraw to beat the Phillies
          4–3 in Philadelphia. Dave Kingman led off the ninth with a home run. After Cleon
          Jones singled, McGraw retired two batters before former battery mate Jerry Grote
          walloped a two-run homer for the win.

JULY 9   Rusty Staub homers in the tenth inning to down the Braves 2–1 in Atlanta.

JULY 11   The Braves beat the Mets 9–8 during a strange afternoon in Atlanta. In pre-game
          ceremonies, 34 couples were married at home plate and a wrestling match was
          staged. During the game, Tom Seaver and Jerry Koosman both appeared as relievers.
          It was Seaver's only relief appearance between 1971 and 1985.

JULY 15   Jon Matlack is named co-MVP of the All-Star Game with Bill Madlock of the Cubs
          for his role in the National League's 6–3 win at County Stadium in Milwaukee.
          Matlack pitched shutout ball in the seventh and eight and struck out four, including
          Rod Carew and Fred Lynn.

JULY 20   After falling behind 7–1 in the fifth inning, the Mets rally to beat the Astros 10–9 at
          Shea Stadium. Dave Kingman was the star of the comeback with six runs batted in.
          He drove in the first four New York runs on a ground out in the second inning and
          a three-run homer in the fifth. With the Mets trailing 9–8 and two-out in the eighth,
          Kingman blasted a two-run home run to provide the winning margin.

JULY 21   Joe Torre ties a major league record by grounding into four double plays during a
          6–2 loss to the Astros at Shea Stadium. The four double plays came in the first, third,
          sixth and eighth innings with Ken Forsch pitching, and each followed a single by
          Felix Millan.

JULY 24   Tom Seaver records his 2,000th career shutout by fanning Dan Driessen in the
          second inning of a 2–1 loss to the Reds at Shea Stadium.

JULY 26   Bill Madlock collects six hits in six at-bats for the Cubs, but the Mets emerge with a ten-inning, 9–8 victory in Chicago.

JULY 27   The Mets release Cleon Jones.

A starter in left field from 1966 through 1974, Jones had been an enigma for years because he seldom seemed to put forth his best effort. He started the 1975 season recovering from a knee injury and was sent to St. Petersburg to work out on his own. In the wee hours of the morning, Jones was arrested for indecent exposure when found sleeping in the nude with a young woman. Even though the case was dismissed for insufficient evidence, Board Chairman M. Donald Grant fined Jones $2,000 for "breaking training rules" and "betraying the image of the club" and forced Jones to make a public apology at a press conference on May 13. Grant was severely criticized by fans and the media alike by further embarrassing Jones. On July 18, Cleon pinch-hit during a game against the Braves and Shea Stadium and was told to finish the contest in left field and refused. The Mets suspended him four days later after Yogi Berra made it clear he would not play Jones again under any circumstances. When Berra refused to reconsider, Jones was released. Jones signed with the White Sox and played 12 games in Chicago in 1976 before ending his career.

JULY 28   The Mets acquire Skip Lockwood from the Athletics.

Lockwood turned into a surprising find, as he served as an effective closer for the Mets closer through 1979. He was originally signed as a third baseman with the Athletics in 1964 and was converted into a pitcher four years later. At the time Lockwood was acquired by the Mets, he had a career record of 30–60.

AUGUST 4   Randy Tate suffers a tough 4–3 loss to the Expos at Shea Stadium. Tate had a no-hitter in progress until Jim Lyttle singled with one out in the eighth. Tate still had a shutout with two out in the inning and 13 strikeouts over the course of the game, but Gary Carter singled in a run and Mike Jorgensen belted a three-run homer.

The 1975 season was Tate's only one as a major leaguer. He went to bat 41 times without a base hit. No one in baseball history has more career at-bats with a batting average of .000.

AUGUST 6   The Mets score seven runs in the sixth inning and defeat the Expos 9–6 in a contest at Shea Stadium called in the eighth inning by rain. The seven runs scored on only three hits which were back-to-back-to-back doubles by Del Unser, Felix Millan and Ed Kranepool. Montreal walked five, hit a batter, and made two errors.

The game was the first following the dismissal of Yogi Berra. With the club holding a record of 56–53, the Mets fired Yogi Berra as manager. First base coach Roy McMillan was appointed as interim manager to finish the season. Chairman of the board M. Donald Grant said that the Mets were "trying to salvage something from the season." McMillan was 46 and had played for the Mets from 1964 through 1966. He managed for three years in the Mets farm system, coached for the three seasons with the Milwaukee Brewers, then returned to the Mets as a coach under Berra in 1973. The Mets continued to flounder under McMillan, however, and the club hired Joe Frazier as manager (see October 3, 1975). McMillan served as a coach under Frazier in 1976, before being fired by the club. Berra returned to the Yankees, first as a coach (1976–83), then as a manager (1984–85).

AUGUST 10   Reliever Ken Sanders is forced to leave a 2–1 loss to the Dodgers at Shea Stadium when a throw from John Stearns strikes Sanders above the left eye. Sanders had just entered the game in the eighth inning when struck during his warm-ups pitches and leaves without facing a batter.

AUGUST 24   Ed Halicki pitches a no-hitter to beat the Mets 6–0 in the second game of a double-header in San Francisco. Halicki walked two and struck out ten. The final out was recorded on a ground out by Wayne Garrett to first baseman Willie Montanez unassisted. In the opener, Dave Kingman belted a grand slam off Jim Barr in the fifth inning of a 9–5 victory.

AUGUST 29   Six runs in the first inning off Don Sutton are enough to beat the Dodgers 6–1 in Los Angeles.

              At the conclusion of the game, the Mets were 71–62 and were four games behind the first-place Pirates, but ten losses in the next 12 games shattered any illusions that the Mets would win the NL East.

SEPTEMBER 1   Tom Seaver earns his 20th win of the season with a 3–0 decision over the Pirates at Shea Stadium.

SEPTEMBER 15 Rookie outfielder Mike Vail runs his hitting streak to 23 games during a 3–2 win over the Expos at Shea Stadium.

              Vail's hitting streak began on August 22 in his third major league game and second start. He collected 36 hits during the during the streak and batted .364. Vail broke his foot playing basketball during the following offseason, however, (see February 15, 1976) and was never a regular over a full season. He played for the Mets until 1977 before going to the Indians on waivers. Cleveland was the second of Vail's seven teams during a career which ended in 1984.

SEPTEMBER 16 The Mets need 18 innings to beat the Expos 4–3 at Shea Stadium. The Mets trailed 3–2 with two out in the ninth and no one on base when Mike Phillips hit a single, John Milner walked, and Del Unser singled to tie the score 3–3. There was no more scoring until the 18th. The game ended when Unser drew a bases loaded walk from Don Demola. Jon Matlack pitched the first nine innings. Over the last nine, relievers Bob Apodaca (two innings), Ken Sanders (three innings) and Rick Baldwin (four innings) allowed only two hits. Mike Vail's 23-game hitting streak came to an end when he was hitless in seven at-bats against five Montreal pitchers.

              Phillips was the Mets regular shortstop in 1975 because Bud Harrelson was limited to 35 games with injuries. Mets shortstops made 46 errors during the season.

SEPTEMBER 18 Dave Kingman's two-run, walk-off homer with two out in the ninth inning beats the Cubs 7–5 at Shea Stadium.

SEPTEMBER 20   A two-run, walk-off homer by Ron Hodges in the 12th inning defeats the Phillies 9–7 at Shea Stadium. Hodges entered the game in the sixth inning after starting catcher Jerry Grote was lifted for a pinch-runner. Rusty Staub collected five hits, including a double and a homer, in six at-bats.

No relation to Gil Hodges, Ron played 12 seasons for the Mets from 1973 through 1984, but accumulated 200 or more plate appearances in only two of them. His career high was 305 in 1983.

SEPTEMBER 24   Tom Seaver holds the Cubs hitless for $8^2/_3$ innings and the Mets lose 1–0 to the Cubs in 11 innings at Wrigley Field. Seaver stuck out Don Kessinger and Rick Monday to open the ninth before Joe Wallis broke up the no-hitter bid with a two-out single. Wallis was a rookie with 15 major league hits. Seaver closed out the ninth without allowing another hit, but the game went to extra innings because the Mets couldn't score off Rick Reuschel. Seaver surrendered two hits in the tenth and was lifted for a pinch-hitter in the 11th. Skip Lockwood loaded the bases in the bottom of the 11th before walking Bill Madlock to force in the winning run.

The game was the third in which Seaver pitched eight no-hit innings, only to surrender a hit in the ninth. The first was on July 9, 1969 when Jimmy Qualls, another obscure Chicago outfielder, singled with one out. The other no-hit spoiler was Leron Lee of the Padres on July 4, 1972. Seaver pitched a no-hitter with the Reds in 1978.

SEPTEMBER 26   The Mets play a pair of 12-inning games in Philadelphia, and emerge with a 4–3 loss and a 3–2 victory against the Phillies. In the second game, Jerry Koosman pitched 11 innings and allowed a run and four hits. Because of numerous rain delays, the second tilt ended at 3:14 a.m.

SEPTEMBER 29   Casey Stengel dies from cancer at the age of 85 in Glendale, California.

OCTOBER 3   The Mets name 53-year-old Joe Frazier as manager replacing Roy McMillan.

Frazier made his major league debut as a player as an outfielder with the Indians in 1947, then went back to the minors for seven years, before returning to play for the Cardinals, Reds and Orioles from 1954 through 1956. He appeared in 217 big-league games, most of them as a pinch-hitter. Frazier began managing in the minors in 1966, joined the Mets organization in 1969, and worked his way up from Class A to Class AAA Tidewater, where he won the International League pennant in 1975. In his first season with the Mets, Frazier guided the club to an 86–76 record, but was fired after a 15–30 start in 1977.

OCTOBER 4   Mets owner and team president Joan Payson dies from complications from a stroke suffered the previous June. She had been principal owner since the club's inception. Well-liked by nearly everyone, Payson was a passionate baseball fan and was seen often from a box seat at Shea Stadium cheering wildly for her team, even during the incessant losing seasons during the early years of the franchise. Presidency of the club passed to her daughter, Lorinda de Roulet. Lorinda had little interest in the team, however, and board chairman M. Donald Grant was given an increased role in the operation of the Mets until the club was sold in 1980.

OCTOBER 12   The New York Giants play at Shea Stadium for the first time and lose 13–7 to the Dallas Cowboys.

The Giants played at Yankee Stadium from 1956 through 1972 but had to find another home field when the facility underwent a massive remodeling which wasn't completed until 1976. The Giants didn't return to Yankee Stadium, however, and instead moved into Giants Stadium in East Rutherford, New Jersey for the 1976 season. Meanwhile, the Giants played at the Yale Bowl in New Haven, Connecticut in 1973 and 1974 and Shea Stadium in 1975. Shea was the home of the Mets, Yankees, Jets and Giants in 1975. The Jets remained at Shea until 1984 when they joined the Giants in East Rutherford.

DECEMBER 12   The Mets trade Rusty Staub and Bill Laxton to the Tigers for Mickey Lolich and Billy Baldwin.

Staub was 31 and could still hit, but was a liability on defense. He played mostly as a designated hitter in Detroit. Rusty returned to New York to play for the Mets again from 1981 through 1985, mainly as a pinch-hitter. Lolich was 35 and had 207 career wins at the time of the trade, but was about finished. He was 8–13 in his only season as a Met.

1976

Season in a Sentence

The Mets win 86 games, the most since 1969, but draw fewer fans than in any season since 1963, and finish in third place 15 games out of first.

Finish • Won • Lost • Pct • GB

| Third | 86 | 76 | .531 | 15.0 |

Manager

Joe Frazier

Stats

Stats	Mets	AL	Rank
Batting Avg:	.246	.255	9
On-Base Pct:	.319	.320	7
Slugging Pct:	.352	.361	6
Home Runs:	102	5	
Stolen Bases:	66	12	
ERA:	2.94	3.50	1
Errors:	131	4	
Runs Scored:	615	7	
Runs Allowed:	538	1	

Starting Lineup

Jerry Grote, c
Ed Kranepool, 1b
Felix Millan, 2b
Roy Staiger, 3b
Bud Harrelson, ss
John Milner, lf
Del Unser, cf
Dave Kingman, rf
Joe Torre, 1b
Bruce Bosclair, cf-lf
Wayne Garrett, 3b
Mike Phillips, ss

Pitchers

Jerry Koosman, sp
Jon Matlack, sp
Tom Seaver, sp
Mickey Lolich, sp
Craig Swan, sp
Skip Lockwood, rp
Bob Apodaca, rp

Attendance

1,468.754 (fifth in NL)

Club Leaders

Batting Avg:	Felix Millan	.282
On-Base Pct:	John Milner	.362
Slugging Pct:	Dave Kingman	.506
Home Runs:	Dave Kingman	37
RBI:	Dave Kingman	86
Runs:	Dave Kingman	70
Stolen Bases:	Bud Harrelson	9
	Bruce Bosclair	9
Wins:	Jerry Koosman	21
Strikeouts:	Tom Seaver	235
ERA:	Tom Seaver	2.59
Saves:	Skip Lockwood	19

JANUARY 7 In the January amateur draft, the Mets select future major leaguers Jody Davis in the third round and Kim Seaman in the fourth.

FEBRUARY 15 Mike Vail breaks his foot playing basketball at Old Dominion College. Counted upon to be a starting outfielder, Vail didn't play until June and batted just .217.

FEBRUARY 24 The Mets trade George Stone to the Rangers for Bill Hands.

MARCH 28 The Mets virtually consummate a trade which would send Tom Seaver to the Dodgers for Don Sutton. A reporter broke the story, however, and the public outrage caused the Mets to back out of the deal. Following acrimonious contract negotiations, Seaver signed a three-year contract worth $225,000 per year.

Seaver had a record of 14–11 in 1976, but led the league in strikeouts (235 in 271 innings) and was third in earned run average (2.59).

APRIL 9 The Mets open the season with a 3–2 win over the Expos before 17,013 at Shea Stadium. Tom Seaver went seven innings for the win.

APRIL 10   Jon Matlack shuts out the Expos 1–0 at Shea Stadium. The lone run scored in the fourth inning on a triple by Bud Harrelson and a double from Felix Millan.

APRIL 14   Dave Kingman hits the longest home run in Wrigley Field history during a 6–5 loss to the Cubs. The drive was struck off Tom Dettore and carried an estimated 550 feet over Waveland Avenue, and after bouncing a few times, struck the side of a house three doors down from the corner on the east side of Kenmore Avenue. The residents of the home poured out onto the front porch to see what was knocking at their wall. Kingman hit the same house when he was playing for the Cubs in 1979 with a drive off Ron Reed of the Phillies.

APRIL 15   After falling behind 7–2 in the third inning, the Mets rally to beat the Cubs 10–8 in Chicago. With the Mets still down 8–7 and one out in the ninth, Dave Kingman belted a three-run homer off Tom Dettore to win the game. It was Kingman's second homer of the game and the second day in a row he homered off Dettore.

APRIL 17   The Mets collect 21 hits and clobber the Pirates 17–1 in Pittsburgh.

APRIL 19   The Mets outlast the Cardinals 4–3 in 17 innings in St. Louis. Del Unser's home run in the 17th was the game-winner. Relievers Skip Lockwood (four innings), Ken Sanders (two innings) and Bob Apodaca (three innings) combined to shut out the Cards over the final nine innings.

APRIL 20   The Mets beat the Cardinals 8–0 in St. Louis in a game that featured a free-for-all over hit batsmen. After Del Unser homered in the first inning, Cardinals pitcher Lynn McGlothlen hit him in the third. In the bottom of the inning Jon Matlack threw over McGlothlen's head. When Matlack led off the fourth, McGlothlen drilled him with a pitch that set off a brawl. The league suspended McGlothlen for five days.

APRIL 27   Down 5–1, the Mets score a run in the seventh inning, another in the eighth, and three in the ninth to beat the Braves 6–5 at Shea Stadium. The three ninth-inning runs scored with two out. John Milner drove in the first run with a single. Bruce Bosclair followed with a two-run, walkoff double.

Milner collected 24 hits in his first 48 at-bats in 1976, for a batting average of .500, but faded to .271 by the end of the season.

APRIL 28   Dave Kingman's three-run homer off Andy Messersmith in the first inning provides all of the runs needed in a 3–0 win over the Braves at Shea Stadium. Craig Swan pitched the shutout and struck out 11.

MAY 7   Dave Kingman hits two homers and drives in five runs during a 6–2 win over the Padres at Shea Stadium.

The Mets had a record of 18–9 on May 8, but lost 22 of their next 30 games to slide out of pennant contention.

MAY 12   Dave Kingman collects two homers, a double and a single in five at-bats during a 6–3 triumph over the Braves in Atlanta.

MAY 21   Wayne Garrett drives in all four Mets runs during a 4–3 win over the Expos at Jarry Park. He tied the score 2–2 with a two-run homer in the seventh. After Montreal took a 3–2 lead in the eighth, Garrett belted a two-run double in the ninth for the win.

MAY 27   The Mets score four runs in the ninth inning to defeat the Phillies 5–2 in Philadelphia. The Mets were trailing 2–1 with two out in the ninth when Wayne Garrett belted a three-run triple. Garrett scored on Roy Staiger's double.

MAY 31   The Mets trounce the Pirates 13–2 at Shea Stadium.

JUNE 4   Dave Kingman hits homers in three consecutive plate appearances and drives in eight runs during an 11–0 thrashing of the Dodgers in Los Angeles. Kingman hit a two-run homer off Burt Hooton in the fourth inning to give the Mets a 2–0 lead. Kingman added a three-run shit against Hooton in the fifth. Facing Al Downing in the seventh, Kingman struck another three-run home run. He batted again in the ninth against Downing with a chance at a record-tying fourth homer, but struck out. Tom Seaver pitched a three-hit shutout.

JUNE 8   In the first round of the amateur draft, the Mets select outfielder Tom Thurberg from South Weymouth High School in Weymouth, Massachusetts.

          Thurberg never reached the majors. Future big leaguers drafted and signed by the Mets in the June 1976 draft were Mike Scott (second round), Neil Allen (11th round) and Dave von Ohlen (17th round).

JUNE 17   The Mets use brilliant pitching from Craig Swan and Skip Lockwood to beat the Dodgers 1–0 in 14 innings at Shea Stadium. Swan pitched ten innings and allowed only three hits. Lockwood hurled four hitless innings and struck out six. Dave Kingman ended the game with a walk-off homer off Charlie Hough.

JUNE 18   Tom Seaver pitches a two-hitter and defeats the Giants 3–2 at Shea Stadium. Darrell Evans broke up the no-hit bid with a homer leading off the fifth inning. Derrel Thomas tripled in the sixth and scored to give San Francisco a 2–1 lead. Ed Kranepool hit a two-run homer in the bottom half to provide the winning margin.

JUNE 25   Mike Phillips hits for the cycle during a 7–4 win over the Cubs in Chicago. Phillips began the game by striking out leading off the first inning against Ray Burris. It was Phillips's 21st consecutive hitless at-bat dating back to June 6 and dropped his batting average to .204. Phillips broke out of the slump in a big way with a double in the third, a triple in the fifth and a homer in the seventh, all off Burris. The homer was Phillips's first of the year. He completed the cycle with a single facing Mike Garman in the eighth.

          Phillips finished the year with a .256 average in 383 at-bats. He hit four home runs, three of them during the three-game June series at Wrigley Field.

JUNE 26   John Milner hits a grand slam off Bill Bonham in the third inning of a 10–2 victory over the Cubs in Chicago.

JUNE 27   The Mets explode for eight runs in the second inning and wallop the Cubs 13–3 in Chicago.

July 1	John Milner hits a grand slam off Mike Wallace during a 13–0 trouncing of the Cardinals at Shea Stadium. It was Milner's second grand slam in six days. The Mets scores the 13 runs on only nine hits.
July 2	Jerry Koosman strikes out 12 and pitches a three-hitter to beat the Cubs 2–1 at Shea Stadium.
July 4	On the day the nation celebrates the Bicentennial, the resourceful Mets score nine runs on only six hits and beat the Cubs 9–4 in the first game of a double-header at Wrigley Field. It was the club's tenth win in a row. With the victory, the Mets were 43–37 on the 1976 season. The winning streak ended with a 4–2 loss in the nightcap.
July 7	The Mets collect 20 hits and beat the Astros 12–4 in Houston.
July 12	An agreement is reached between players and owners which makes free agency a reality for the first time. A player could declare himself a free agent after his contract expired and he had six years of major league experience. Because of the tight-fisted policies of M. Donald Grant, it would be several years before the Mets were active participants in signing premier free agents, however.
July 18	Mickey Lolich pitches a two-hitter to defeat the Braves 2–0 at Shea Stadium. The only Atlanta hits were singles by Darrell Chaney in the third inning and Jimmy Wynn in the fourth.
July 19	Dave Kingman tears ligaments in his right thumb while diving for a ball in the outfield during a 4–2 loss to the Braves at Shea Stadium. *Kingman had 32 homers at the time of the injury and was on a pace to hit 56 for the season. He didn't return to the lineup until August 27, and finished the season with 37 home runs.*
July 21	The Mets trade Wayne Garrett and Del Unser to the Expos for Pepe Mangual and Jim Dwyer.
July 23	Two days after being traded, Del Unser beats his former teammates with an 11th-inning walk-off homer off Skip Lockwood to lift the Expos to a 3–2 win over the Mets in Montreal.
August 15	Jerry Koosman shuts down the Big Red Machine for a 1–0 win over Cincinnati at Shea Stadium. The lone run scored on a single by Bruce Boisclair in the fifth inning.
August 21	Jon Matlack defeats the Padres 1–0 in San Diego. Jerry Grote drove in the lone run with a double in the seventh inning.
September 1	Jerry Koosman beats the Giants 1–0 at Shea Stadium. The lone run scored on back-to-back doubles by Felix Millan and John Milner in the eighth inning.
September 3	Tom Seaver records the Mets fourth 1–0 win in less than three weeks by defeating the Phillies at Shea Stadium. The lone run scored on a single by Roy Staiger off Steve Carlton in the fourth inning.

SEPTEMBER 7   The Mets lambaste the Cubs 11–0 in Chicago. Lee Mazzilli made his major league debut replacing John Milner in left field and grounded out in his lone plate appearance.

SEPTEMBER 8   The Mets score six runs in the ninth inning and defeat the Cubs 11–5 in Chicago. In his second major league plate appearance, Lee Mazzilli hit a three-run, pinch-hit homer.

SEPTEMBER 11   Jerry Koosman hurls a two-hitter to beat the Cardinals 4–1 at Busch Stadium. The only St. Louis hits were singles by Jerry Mumphrey in the sixth inning and Ted Simmons in the seventh.

SEPTEMBER 13   In Pittsburgh, the Mets score all five of their runs of a 5–0 win over the Pirates in the seventh inning. Tom Seaver pitched a complete game and struck out 12.

SEPTEMBER 16   Jerry Koosman records his 20th win of the season with a 4–1 decision over the Cardinals at Shea Stadium. He also struck out 13 batters.

> *After posting a 19–12 record as a rookie in 1968 and a 17–9 mark in 1969, Koosman was 72–69 from 1970 through 1975. He rebounded to a 21–10 record and a 2.49 earned run average in 1976. But Koosman struggled mightily on a couple of terrible Mets teams the next two seasons. He was 8–20 in 1977 and 3–15 in 1978, despite posting ERAs near the league average.*

SEPTEMBER 19   Dave Kingman hits two homers and drives in five runs during a 7–6 triumph over the Pirates at Shea Stadium. Skip Lockwood struck out seven in a three-inning relief appearance.

SEPTEMBER 20   With the Mets trailing 4–3 and two out and no one on base against the Pirates at Shea Stadium, John Milner singles and Lee Mazzilli belts a two-run, walk-off homer for a 5–4 victory.

SEPTEMBER 24   Billy Baldwin hits a pinch-hit, walk-off homer in the ninth inning to defeat the Cubs 4–3 at Shea Stadium. It was Baldwin's only homer in 22 at-bats as a member of the Mets and the last of five he hit as a major leaguer.

SEPTEMBER 27   John Milner hits a grand slam off Larry Landreth in the sixth inning of a 10–3 win over the Expos at Shea Stadium. The contest was called in the eighth inning by rain. It was Milner's third grand slam of the season.

DECEMBER 8   A month after Jimmy Carter defeats Gerald Ford in the Presidential election, the Mets trade Jim Dwyer to the Cubs and receive Shawn Mallory from the Royals as part of a three-team trade.

1977

Season in a Sentence

During a 98-loss season, the Mets hire Joe Torre as manager and trade Tom Seaver and Dave Kingman, then further overhaul the roster during the offseason.

Finish • Won • Lost • Pct • GB

Sixth   64   98   .395   37.0

Managers

Joe Frazier (15–30) and Joe Torre (49–68)

Stats

Stats	Mets	AL	Rank
Batting Avg:	.244	.262	12
On-Base Pct:	.313	.328	12
Slugging Pct:	.346	.396	12
Home Runs:	88	12	
Stolen Bases:	98	8	
ERA:	3.77	3.91	6
Errors:	134	5	
Runs Scored:	587	12	
Runs Allowed:	663	3	

Starting Lineup

John Stearns, c
John Milner, 1b
Felix Millan, 2b
Len Randle, 3b
Bud Harrelson, ss
Steve Henderson, lf
Lee Mazzilli, cf
Bruce Bosclair, rf
Ed Kranepool, 1b
Mike Vail, rf
Doug Flynn, ss
Dave Kingman, lf-rf

Pitchers

Jerry Koosman, sp
Nino Espinosa, sp
Jon Matlack, sp
Craig Swan, sp
Pat Zachry, sp
Tom Seaver, sp
Skip Lockwood, rp
Bob Myrick, rp
Bob Apodaca, rp

Attendance

1,066,825 (tenth in AL)

Club Leaders

Batting Avg:	Len Randle	.304
On-Base Pct:	Len Randle	.383
Slugging Pct:	Len Randle	.404
Home Runs:	Three tied with	12
RBIs:	Steve Henderson	65
Runs:	Len Randle	78
Stolen Bases:	Len Randle	33
Wins:	Nino Espinosa	10
Strikeouts:	Jerry Koosman	192
ERA:	Nino Espinosa	3.42
Saves:	Skip Lockwood	20

MARCH 31   The Mets sign Ray Sadecki, most recently with the Brewers, as a free agent. Sadecki previously pitched for the Mets from 1970 through 1974. His return engagement lasted only four games.

APRIL 7   The Mets open the season with a 5–3 win over the Cubs at Wrigley Field. John Stearns broke a 2–2 tie with a two-run single in the sixth inning. Tom Seaver went seven innings and was the winning pitcher. It was his tenth consecutive Opening Day start. Skip Lockwood retired all six batters he faced in relief of Seaver.

In his first full season in the majors, Stearns took over for Jerry Grote as the Mets starting catcher and batted .251 with 12 homers.

APRIL 17   Tom Seaver pitches a one-hitter to defeat the Cubs 6–0 at Shea Stadium. The only Chicago hit was a single by Steve Ontiveros in the sixth inning.

APRIL 26   The Mets trade Rick Auerbach to the Rangers for Len Randle.

Randle was involved in an ugly incident with the Rangers during spring training in 1977 while preparing for his seventh season with the club. After Texas *manager Frank Lucchesi called Randle a punk, Randle responded by punching Lucchesi. Randle was charged with assault, and Lucchesi was fired. Later, Lucchesi sued Randle for $200,000. Randle was one of the few bright spots for the Mets in 1977, batting .304 as a third baseman. But his 1978 numbers included a .233 average and just two home runs, and Randle was released.*

APRIL 29   Dave Kingman drives in six runs with three-run homers in the first and fifth innings to spark a 9–2 victory over the Padres in San Diego.

The Mets were 9–9 on May 1, then lost 22 of their next 30 games.

MAY 18   Jerry Koosman hits his first home run since 1968 and pitches a complete game to beat the Giants 8–1 at Shea Stadium.

MAY 31   With the club holding a record of 15–30, the Mets fire Joe Frazier as manager and hire Joe Torre.

Frazier guided the club to an 86–76 record in 1976, but the slow start in 1977 and lack of support in the front office doomed his term as manager. He never managed another major league team. Torre was 36 and in his 17th, and last, year as a player. He had been with the Mets since being acquired in a trade with the Cardinals in October 1974. The 6–2 victory over the Expos at Shea Stadium on May 31 was Torre's first in a managerial career that would last more than three decades. His stint with the Mets was less than successful, however. Before being fired in 1981, none of his teams had a winning record and he was 286–420 overall for a winning percentage of .405.

JUNE 1   John Stearns hits a grand slam off Jackie Brown in the fifth inning of a 6–4 win over the Expos in Montreal. It was also the first time that the Mets played at Olympic Stadium.

JUNE 4   Jerry Grote drives in both runs of a 2–0 win over the Phillies at Shea Stadium with singles in the fourth and sixth innings off Steve Carlton. Nino Espinosa ($7^1/_3$ innings) and Skip Lockwood ($1^2/_3$ innings) combined on the shutout.

JUNE 7   In the first round of the amateur draft, the Mets select shortstop Wally Backman from Aloha High School in Aloha, Oregon. University of South Carolina outfielder Mookie Wilson was added in the second round.

The Mets made an important step toward stabilizing the franchise on draft day in 1977, as both Backman and Wilson became regulars on the strong clubs of the mid-1980s, including the 1986 world champions. Other future major leaguers drafted and signed by the Mets that year were Alfredo Martinez (fifth round) and Brent Gaff (sixth round). The best amateur player signed by the Mets in 1977 was undrafted free agent Jeff Reardon out of the University of Massachusetts. Reardon made his major league debut in 1979 and went on to become one of the best relievers in the game.

JUNE 11   With the help of some shoddy defense by the Astros, the Mets score two runs in the ninth inning and two in the tenth to win 6–4 in the second game of a double-header at the Astrodome. Both runs in the ninth scored after two were out on a pair of errors by Houston first baseman Bob Watson and third baseman Enos Cabell. The go-ahead tally in the tenth crossed the plate on an error by catcher Ed Herrmann. The Astros won the opener 4–1. Dave Kingman struck out six times during the twin bill.

JUNE 15   The Mets make three deals in one day. Tom Seaver was traded to the Reds for Pat Zachry, Steve Henderson, Doug Flynn and Dan Norman. Dave Kingman was dealt to the Padres for Bobby Valentine and Paul Siebert. Mike Phillips went to the Cardinals for Joel Youngblood.

 ## The Midnight Massacre

The Mets made two bold trades on June 15, 1977 in what has become known in Mets lore as "The Midnight Massacre" for the late hour in which the deals were announced. Franchise icon Tom Seaver was dealt to the Cincinnati Reds for Pat Zachry, Steve Henderson, Doug Flynn and Dan Norman. On the same day, Dave Kingman, the only Met to hit 30 or more homers in a season between 1962 and 1985, was traded to the Padres for Bobby Valentine and Paul Siebert.

Seaver and Kingman both signed three-year contracts prior to the 1976 season. They could not anticipate that the players and owners would come to agreement during the summer of 1976 in which free agency would become a reality for the first time. Those whose contracts had expired and had at least six years of experience could declare themselves a free agent and sign with the highest bidder.

The first free agents signed during the 1976–77 offseason and dramatically increased salaries (from an average of $60,300 per player in 1976 to $87,314 in 1977). Seaver and Kingman were upset on two fronts. First, they saw others with far fewer career accomplishments sign contracts for far more money. Also Mets management, led by Chairman of the Board M. Donald Grant, did not seriously bid on the free agents in an attempt to improve a club that was 86–76 in 1976.

Seaver and Kingman wanted contracts in line with what the free agents were commanding, but Grant refused to re-negotiate their deals. The spat became public with Seaver and Grant sniping at each other in the media. Grant went so far as to call Seaver an "ingrate." Most of the New York media, and more importantly the fans, sided with the players. With the June 15 trade deadline looming, Seaver and Kingman both demanded to be sent elsewhere, and Grant made the decision to trade them both. It didn't help that Kingman was hitting .209 with nine homers in 211 at-bats during the first third of the 1977 season, which greatly diminished his trade value. (During the 1977 season, Kingman played for the Mets, Padres, Angels and Yankees. After the season ended, he signed a free agent deal with the Cubs.)

Because of bad trades and poor drafts, the talent on the Mets roster was in such a sad state during the late 1970s that keeping Seaver and Kingman wouldn't have turned the club into a winning team, much less a pennant contender. Nonetheless, the trades were a disaster, particularly from a public relations standpoint. Fans reacted angrily to the trade of Seaver, who was the Mets' first true star and had been the face of the team since his rookie season in 1967. The fact that one of his nicknames was "The Franchise" speaks volumes about his importance to the club. Grant received phone calls threatening his life and hired a bodyguard to protect him.

From the time of the trade through end of the 1981 season, Seaver had a record of 70–33 with the Reds. Recovering from an off-year in 1977, Kingman continued to be a productive hitter for another five years and led the NL in home runs in 1978 (with the Cubs) and in 1981 (in a return engagement with the Mets).

The Mets received little of substance in exchange for the two stars. Henderson was a regular in left until 1980 and hit .287 as a Met, but collected only 35 homers in 497 games.

Zachry was 41–46 in six seasons in New York with an ERA around the league average. Flynn was a starting second baseman through 1981, but hit .234 with on-base percentage of .264 and a slugging percentage of .292 as a member of the Mets. Valentine batted .222 with two homers in 243 at-bats with the club. Norman, an outfielder, and Siebert, a pitcher, were seldom-used reserves.

With Seaver and Kingman gone, local hero Lee Mazzilli became the only gate attraction on the roster. Attendance, which peaked at 2,697,479 in 1970, declined rapidly throughout the 1970s. The club drew 1,912,390 in 1973, 1,066,825 in 1977 and just 788,905 in 1979. Excluding strike-shortened seasons, the only other franchise in baseball history to lose more than 1.9 million fans in less than ten years is the Toronto Blue Jays from 1993 through 2002. In honor of the man who authorized the trades of Seaver and Kingman, Shea Stadium became known as "Grant's Tomb."

JUNE 18   Joe Torre formally retires as an active player.

JUNE 21   Steve Henderson hits a three-run, walk-off homer in the 11th inning to defeat the Braves 5–2 at Shea Stadium. It was Henderson's first major league home run.

The win gave Joe Torre was 14–7 record as manager. The Mets lost 15 of their next 17 games, however.

JULY 9   The Mets outlast the Expos for a 7–5 victory in 17 innings at Shea Stadium. Montreal scored in the top of the 11th for a 5–4 lead, but Steve Henderson responded in the bottom half with a home run, which tied the score. Len Randle won the game with a two-out, two-run, walk-off homer in the 17th. The win broke a nine-game losing streak.

JULY 13   The New York City electrical power blackout of 1977 strikes during a game between the Mets and Cubs at Shea Stadium.

The lights went out at 9:31 p.m. with Len Randle at bat for the Mets, Ray Burris pitching and the Cubs leading 2–1 in the bottom of the sixth. An auxiliary generator kept the public address system and some of the lights in the seating area operating, but it wasn't powerful enough to keep the field lights turned on. Joel Youngblood and Craig Swan drove their vehicles onto the field, and Mets players entertained the crowd with a shadowy infield drill illuminated by the headlights. Other players signed autographs along the box-seat railings. Organist Jane Jarvis played "White Christmas" in the sweltering heat. The game was suspended at 10:52 p.m. with the intention of completing it before the regularly scheduled contest the next evening. The two teams showered and changed into their street clothes in dark clubhouses. Cubs players went back to the Waldorf-Astoria Hotel. With the elevators out, players had to take the stairs to their rooms, some as high as the 17th floor, while holding candles. Power was restored at 10:03 a.m. the following day, but went out again at 11:53. The suspended game was finally finished two months later on the Cubs' next trip to New York (see September 16, 1977). The blackout lasted 25 hours and resulted in city-wide looting and arson. There were few problems at Shea, however, as the fans filed out of the darkened stadium without incident.

JULY 17	Steve Henderson hits a grand slam off Kent Tekulve in the seventh inning of a 9–3 win over the Pirates in the second game of a double-header at Shea Stadium. Pittsburgh won the opener 3–1. *The Mets and Pirates played five games in a little over 48 hours with a twi-night double-header on Friday the 15th, a single game on Saturday the 16th and an afternoon twin bill on Sunday the 17th.*
JULY 24	With the Mets leading 3–2 and two out in the ninth in Los Angeles, right fielder Bruce Bosclair drops a fly ball off the bat of Davey Lopes in foul territory for an error. Given new life, Lopes walloped a three-run homer for a 5–3 Dodgers win.
JULY 25	Craig Swan pitches a three-hit shutout to beat the Dodgers 1–0 in Los Angeles. The lone run scored on a double by Steve Henderson in the first inning.
AUGUST 3	The Mets score two runs in the ninth inning and one in the 14th to defeat the Dodgers 4–3 at Shea Stadium. The two runs in the ninth came after two were out. With runners on first and second, Mike Vail singled in a run, and after Joel Youngblood singled to load the bases, Doug Flynn drew a walk from Lance Rautzhan to tie the score. Lee Mazzilli drove in the winning run with a single in the 14th.
AUGUST 12	At Three Rivers Stadium, the Mets not only drop ends both games of a double-header to the Pirates 3–2 and 6–5 in 12 innings, but also lose Felix Millan to a season-ending injury suffered in a fight. In the opener, Pittsburgh catcher Ed Ott slid hard into Millan trying to break up a double play. Millan responded by punching Ott in the face with the ball still in his hand. Ott retaliated by lifting Millan off the ground and slamming him to the turf. Millan sustained a broken collarbone and a separated shoulder. He never appeared in another major league game in the U.S. Millan played with the Taiyo Whales in Japan from 1978 through 1980 and won a batting title with a .346 average in 1979 before retiring.
AUGUST 21	Tom Seaver pitches at Shea Stadium for the first time as a member of the opposition and hurls a complete game to lead the Reds to a 5–1 win over the Mets. The game drew 46,265, which was the largest crowd of the year at Shea.
AUGUST 31	The Mets trade Jerry Grote to the Dodgers for Dan Smith and Randy Rogers.
SEPTEMBER 14	Nino Espinosa not only pitches a three-hit shutout, but drives in the lone run of a 1–0 win over the Phillies in Philadelphia with a fifth-inning single off Steve Carlton.
SEPTEMBER 16	The game interrupted by the July 13 blackout is completed. It was picked up where it left off with the Cubs leading 2–1 in the bottom of the sixth inning. The Mets tied the score 2–2 in the seventh, but the Cubs won 5–2 with two runs in the eighth and one in the ninth. Ray Burris, who pitched $5^1/_3$ innings on July 13 and $3^2/_3$ innings on September 16, was credited with a complete game that took 66 days to complete. The Mets and Cubs were supposed to play another game after the completion of the suspended contest, but it was rained out.
SEPTEMBER 17	With one out in the ninth inning and the Mets trailing the Cubs 4–2 in the first game of a double-header at Shea Stadium, Ed Kranepool pinch-hits for Joel Youngblood and whacks a three-run walkoff double for a 5–4 win. Chicago won the second tilt 4–3.

SEPTEMBER 21   Jerry Koosman loses his 20th decision of the season with a 4–0 defeat at the hands of the Pirates at Shea Stadium.

SEPTEMBER 25   The United States Olympic Committee chooses Los Angeles over New York City as the site of the 1984 Olympics. Many accused Mets chairman of the board, M. Donald Grant, with undermining New York's efforts. As part of the Olympic plan, Shea Stadium was to be expanded to 90,000 seats. During the expansion, the Mets would have been required to play at Yankee Stadium for one season. Grant was opposed to the idea.

SEPTEMBER 26   In an unusual move, the last-place Mets purchase Doc Medich from the Mariners on waivers with less than a week left in the season. Medich pitched only one game with the Mets before declaring himself a free agent and signing with the Rangers.

OCTOBER 24   Mets pitcher Bob Myrick breaks his ankle slipping on a tennis ball while playing with his dog at his home in Glenwood Landing, Long Island.

NOVEMBER 30   The Mets sign Elliott Maddox, most recently with the Yankees, as a free agent.

DECEMBER 7   The Mets purchase Tim Foli from the Giants.

DECEMBER 8   As part of a four-team trade, the Mets send Jon Matlack to the Rangers and John Milner to the Pirates and receive Willie Montanez from the Braves and Tom Grieve and Ken Henderson from the Rangers.

> *After winning 75 games for the Mets from 1972 through 1976, Matlack slipped to 7–15 in 1977. He was 15–13 with a 2.27 ERA in Texas in 1978, but was ineffective over the remainder of his career, which ended in 1983. Both Milner and Montanez were disappointments with their new clubs. Montanez batted only .247 with 22 homers in 268 games over two seasons with the Mets. Henderson played only seven games with the Mets.*

1978

Season in a Sentence

The promotional slogan "Bring Your Kids to See Our Kids" fails to result in success at the box office as a rebuilding club loses 96 games.

Finish • Won • Lost • Pct • GB

Sixth   66   96   .407   24.0

Manager

Joe Torre

Stats

Stats	Mets	AL	Rank
Batting Avg:	.245	.254	11
On-Base Pct:	.314	.320	8
Slugging Pct:	.352	.372	11
Home Runs:	86	8	
Stolen Bases:	100	8	
ERA:	3.87	3.57	10
Errors:	132	2	
Runs Scored:	607	8	
Runs Allowed:	690	10	

Starting Lineup

John Stearns, c
Willie Montanez, 1b
Doug Flynn, 2b-ss
Len Randle, 3b
Tim Foli, ss
Steve Henderson, lf
Lee Mazzilli, cf
Elliott Maddox, rf
Joel Youngblood, rf
Bruce Bosclair, rf-2b

Pitchers

Nino Espinosa, rp
Craig Swan, sp
Pat Zachry, sp
Jerry Koosman, sp
Mike Bruhert, sp
Skip Lockwood, rp
Kevin Kobel, rp-sp
Dale Murray, rp

Attendance

1,007,328 (tenth in NL)

Club Leaders

Batting Avg:	Lee Mazzilli	.273
On-Base Pct:	John Stearns	.364
Slugging Pct:	Lee Mazzilli	.432
Home Runs:	Willie Montanez	17
RBI:	Willie Montanez	96
Runs:	Steve Henderson	83
Stolen Bases:	John Stearns	25
Wins:	Nino Espinosa	11
Strikeouts:	Jerry Koosman	160
ERA:	Craig Swan	2.43
Saves:	Skip Lockwood	15

MARCH 24   The Mets trade Bud Harrelson to the Phillies for Fred Andrews and cash.

Harrelson hit only .178 in 269 at-bats for the Mets in 1977 and, at age 33, no longer fit into the club's youth movement. He played three more major league seasons as a utility infielder. Harrelson returned to the Mets as a coach (1982 and 1985–90) and manager (1990–91).

APRIL 7   The Mets beat the Expos 3–1 before an Opening Day crowd of only 11,736. Jerry Koosman pitched a complete game.

The outfield fences were extended from foul line to foul line at Shea Stadium in 1978, cutting the distance in the corners from 341 feet to 338 feet. Previously, the corners had a brick wall with an orange line. If a ball struck above the line, it was a home run.

APRIL 8   The Mets score two runs in the eighth inning and two in the ninth to beat the Expos 6–5 at Shea Stadium. In the eighth, Lee Mazzilli hit a two-out, two-run homer to pull the Mets within a run. In the ninth, Ed Kranepool pinch-hit with two out and walloped a two-run, walk-off home run for the victory.

APRIL 9   Steve Henderson hits a grand slam off Stan Bahnsen in the sixth inning of a 6–5 win over the Expos in the first game of a double-header at Shea Stadium. Montreal won the second tilt 5–0.

The Mets altered their uniform design in 1978. The new shirts were pullovers, replacing the previous button-down fronts. Orange and blue striping trim was added to the sleeve ends and the collar.

APRIL 19   Pat Zachry pitches a two-hitter to beat the Cardinals 2–0 at Busch Memorial Stadium. The only St. Louis hits were back-to-back singles by Keith Hernandez and Jerry Morales in the second inning. The Mets also collected just two hits off Mark Littell and Pete Vuckovich. Bruce Bosclair drove in both New York runs with a sacrifice fly in the first inning and a single in the third.

APRIL 26   The Mets waste excellent pitching from Craig Swan (seven innings), Skip Lockwood (three innings) and Bob Myrick (one inning) to lose 1–0 to the Pirates in 11 innings at Shea Stadium. The three hurlers combined to allow only four hits. The lone run scored on a home run from Ed Ott off Myrick.

Swan's ERA of 2.43 in 207$^{1}/_{3}$ innings led the National League. His won-lost record was 9–6.

APRIL 29   Pete Rose collects three homers among his five hits during a 14–7 Reds win over the Mets at Shea Stadium. It was Rose's only multi-homer game between 1970 and the end of his career in 1985.

MAY 18   Len Randle scores five runs during a ten-inning, 8–7 triumph over the Braves at Shea Stadium. In six plate appearances, Randle drew three walks and hit a triple, a double and a single. In the tenth, Randle crossed the plate with a winning run on Steve Henderson's single.

MAY 21   After allowing five runs in the top of the first inning, the Mets rally to beat the Phillies 6–5 with a run in the second inning, two in the fourth, one in the sixth, one in the eighth and one in the tenth. Steve Henderson drove in the winning run with a double.

MAY 30   In his first major league start, Silvio Martinez of the Cardinals pitches a one-hitter to beat the Cardinals 8–2 at Shea Stadium. The lone New York hit was a home run by Steve Henderson in the seventh inning.

JUNE 5   The Mets score three runs in the ninth inning to defeat the Dodgers 9–8 at Shea Stadium. With two out, Tim Foli doubled in two runs to tie the score 8–8. The winning run crossed the plate on an error by shortstop Bill Russell.

JUNE 6   With the third overall pick in the amateur draft, the Mets select outfielder Hubie Brooks from Arizona State University.

Brooks was converted into a third baseman and made his major league debut in 1980. He played five seasons for the Mets at the start of a career that lasted until 1994. Brooks's final big-league numbers included a .269 batting average and 149 homers in 1,645 games and All-Star Game appearances as a member of the

Expos in 1986 and 1987. Other future major leaguers drafted and signed by the Mets in 1978 were Brian Giles (second round), Mike Fitzgerald (sixth round), Randy Johnson (11th round) and Rick Anderson (24th round). The Brian Giles chosen was not the future All-Star outfielder, but a second baseman who played in 287 major league contests. The Randy Johnson drafted by the Mets was likewise not the future 300-game winner, but a third-baseman who lasted three years in the majors.

JUNE 13   Len Randle hits a two-run single off Rollie Fingers in the ninth inning to defeat the Padres 3–2 in San Diego.

JUNE 30   A collision between John Stearns and Dave Parker caps a 6–5 win over the Pirates at Three Rivers. Parker tripled in two runs with one out to pull Pittsburgh within a run. Parker tried to score following a fly ball by Bill Robinson to right fielder Joel Youngblood and was tagged out by Stearns. The Mets catcher escaped from the impact unscathed while Parker suffered a broken cheekbone and didn't play again for two weeks.

Stearns batted .264 with 15 homers and 25 stolen bases in 1978. The 25 steals broke the NL record for a catcher set by Johnny Kling of the Cubs in 1902.

JULY 4   Pat Zachry pitches a two-hitter to beat the Phillies 4–0 in the first game of a double-header at Shea Stadium. Zachry had a no-hitter in progress until Garry Maddox singled with two out in the seventh. Ted Sizemore added another single in the ninth. All four Mets runs scored on a grand slam by Lee Mazzilli off Larry Christenson with two out in the eighth. In the second game, Craig Swan struck out 13 batters, but the Mets lost 3–2 on Jose Cardenal's two-run, two-out homer in the ninth.

With the win, Zachry had a 10–3 record on a team that was 34–46. He didn't win again in 1978, however. On July 24, frustrated after being taken out against the Reds at Shea Stadium, Zachry kicked the dugout steps and broke his foot. He ended the year at 10–6.

JULY 7   Trailing 6–0, the Mets score seven runs in the fifth inning, but wind up losing 9–7 to the Cubs at Shea Stadium. The seven-run rally featured back-to-back triples by Joel Youngblood and Len Randle and a three-run homer from Willie Montanez.

JULY 8   Kevin Kobel wins his first major league game since 1974, when he was a member of the Brewers, by pitching 6$\frac{1}{3}$ innings of a 7–0 decision over the Cubs at Shea Stadium.

JULY 26   Joel Youngblood hits a homer and a triple and drives in five runs during a 12–3 victory over the Reds at Shea Stadium. Pete Rose extended his National League-record hitting streak to 39 games.

Rose headed into the series with his hitting streak at 36 games. The modern NL record was 37, set by Tommy Holmes of the Boston Braves in 1945. Rose tied the mark on July 24 and broke it on July 25. Holmes attended the games in which Rose tied and broke the record. With Rose as the attraction, the three games against Cincinnati drew 93,989 on a Monday, Tuesday and Wednesday. It was the largest crowd for a series at Shea all year. Pete's streak eventually reached 44 games.

AUGUST 9   Joel Youngblood collects five hits, including two doubles and a triple, during a 10–3 victory over the Expos in Montreal.

AUGUST 21   Jerry Koosman strikes out 13 batters in ten innings, but the Mets lose 4–2 to the Giants in 11 innings at Shea Stadium.

SEPTEMBER 3   Lee Mazzilli collects two homers and two singles in five at-bats to lead the Mets to an 8–5 win over the Dodgers in Los Angeles. The homers came from opposite sides of the plate. The switch-hitting Mazzilli hit from the right side leading off the first inning against Tommy John, and from the right side off Charlie Hough in the seventh.

SEPTEMBER 9   Kevin Kobel pitches a two-hitter to defeat the Pirates 4–1 at Shea Stadium. The only Pittsburgh hits were a double by Bill Robinson in the second inning and a homer from Willie Stargell in the eighth.

SEPTEMBER 10   The Mets outslug the Pirates 11–9 at Shea Stadium. Elliott Maddox broke the 9–9 tie with a single in the eighth inning.

SEPTEMBER 14   After falling behind 6–0, the Mets rally with two runs in the third inning, two in the fourth and three in the sixth to beat the Expos 7–6 at Shea Stadium. The three tallies in the sixth came on a two-out, three-run, pinch-hit home run from Ed Kranepool.

SEPTEMBER 17   Elliott Maddox accounts for both runs of a 2–0 win over the Phillies in Philadelphia. In the first inning, Maddox singled in Lee Mazzilli, moved to second on a balk and crossed the plate on a single from John Stearns. Mike Bruhert pitched the shutout.

                The shutout was Bruhert's only career complete game and his last big-league win. The 1978 season was his only one in the majors, and Bruhert was 4–11 with a 4.78 earned run average.

NOVEMBER 9   Mets president Lorinda de Roulet announces that M. Donald Grant would be relieved of his duties as chairman of the board effective January 1, 1979. At that time, Mrs. de Roulet assumed Grant's duties. Grant had become one of the most unpopular individuals in New York for his trades of Tom Seaver, Dave Kingman, Rusty Staub, Nolan Ryan and Amos Otis. Grant also refused to enter into the free agent market, which began during the 1976–77 offseason. It didn't help that the decline of the Mets during the last half of the 1970s coincided with the rise of the free-spending Yankees, who in 1976 won their first AL pennant in 12 years and followed with World Series victories in 1977 and 1978.

DECEMBER 5   The Mets trade Tom Grieve and Kim Seaman to the Cardinals for Pete Falcone.

DECEMBER 8   The Mets trade Jerry Koosman to the Twins for Jesse Orosco and Greg Field.

                Koosman was 11–35 for the Mets the previous two seasons combined and desired to be traded to the Twins so he could be close to his Appleton, Minnesota, home. He revived his career in his home state with a 20–13 record in 1979 and 16–13 in 1980. In the long run, however, the Mets made a terrific deal, as Orosco was the club's closer through the glory days of the 1980s. On the all-time franchise lists, Orosco ranks second in ERA (2.73), third in saves (107) and fifth in games pitched (372).

1979

Season in a Sentence

Despite playing in the nation's largest city, the Mets rank 24th among 26 major league teams in attendance, as 99 defeats turn the fans away.

Finish • Won • Lost • Pct • GB

Sixth   63   99   .389   35.0

Manager

Joe Torre

Stats

Stats	Mets	AL	Rank
Batting Avg:	.250	.261	10
On-Base Pct:	.313	.325	11
Slugging Pct:	.350	.385	10
Home Runs:	74	11	
Stolen Bases:	135	4	
ERA:	3.84	3.73	8
Errors:	140	8	
Runs Scored:	593	11	
Runs Allowed:	706	7	

Starting Lineup

John Stearns, c
Willie Montanez, 1b
Doug Flynn, 2b
Richie Hebner, 3b
Frank Taveras, ss
Steve Henderson, lf
Lee Mazzilli, cf
Joel Youngblood, rf-lf
Elliott Maddox, rf-cf
Alex Trevino, c

Pitchers

Craig Swan, sp
Pete Falcone, sp
Kevin Kobel, sp
Dock Ellis, sp
Tom Hausman, sp-rp
Skip Lockwood, rp
Neil Allen, rp
Dale Murray, rp

Attendance

788,905 (11th in NL)

Club Leaders

Batting Avg:	Lee Mazzilli	.303
On-Base Pct:	Lee Mazzilli	.395
Slugging Pct:	Lee Mazzilli	.449
Home Runs:	Joel Youngblood	16
RBI:	Lee Mazzilli	79
	Richie Hebner	79
Runs:	Joel Youngblood	90
Stolen Bases:	Frank Taveras	42
Wins:	Craig Swan	14
Strikeouts:	Craig Swan	145
ERA:	Craig Swan	3.29
Saves:	Skip Lockwood	9

JANUARY 22   Lindsay Nelson, the voice of the Mets on radio and television since 1962, announces he will not be returning to the club for the upcoming season. He took a position as an announcer with the Giants. Nelson, Bob Murphy and Ralph Kiner had been the Mets' only announcers since the club's inception in 1962. Murphy and Kiner would continue to announce the club's games on radio and television into the 21st century, but replacing Nelson proved to be difficult and led to a period of instability. Broadcasters joining Murphy and Kiner from 1979 through 1984 included Steve Albert (1979–81), Bob Goldsholl (1980), Art Shamsky (1981), Lorn Brown (1982), Jiggs McDonald (1982) and Steve LaMar (1982–84).

MARCH 27   The Mets trade Nino Espinosa to the Phillies for Richie Hebner and Jose Moreno.

Garrett Morris, one of the cast members of Saturday Night Live, *filmed several segments during spring training camp featuring Mets players. Morris played his character Chico Escuela, a fictional Hispanic player with a limited command of the English language. Escuela's catchphrase was "baseball been berry berry good to me." During camp, Escuela's unsuccessful comeback was documented following a tell-all book he wrote called* Bad Stuff 'Bout the Mets. *For example, Escuela accused Ed Kranepool of borrowing his soap and failing to return it.*

APRIL 5   Eight days after the nuclear disaster at Three Mile Island, the Mets open the season with a 10–6 win over the Cubs in Chicago. Richie Hebner's Mets debut was spectacular, with a home run, two doubles and a single along with four runs batted in. Craig Swan went eight innings and was the winning pitcher.

Names were added to the backs of the Mets jerseys for the first time in 1979.

APRIL 10   In the home opener, the Mets lose 3–2 to the Expos in 14 innings before 10,406 at Shea Stadium.

The Mets had a new mascot in 1979—a mule named "Mettle" that was occasionally ridden around the warning track by Bebe De Roulet, the daughter of club owner, Lorinda de Roulet. Mettle was kept in a pen near the right-field bullpen. An object of derision, Mettle lasted only one year at Shea. A positive change at the ballpark was a new matrix scoreboard in left-center field to display statistics. In addition, the original wooden seats were removed and replaced by new ones made of plastic.

APRIL 11   A fight erupts between John Stearns and Garry Carter in the ninth inning of a 3–2 loss to the Expos at Shea Stadium. Carter was tagged out after attempting to score from first base on a throwing error by pitcher Pete Falcone, and during the subsequent collision at the plate, Stearns felt that Carter had unnecessarily elbowed him. The two began exchanging punches, and both benches emptied. Both Stearns and Carter were ejected.

APRIL 19   The Mets trade Tim Foli and Greg Field to the Pirates for Frank Taveras.

APRIL 24   With the regular umpires on strike, the replacement umps make a mess of things during a 10–3 win over the Giants at Shea Stadium. It took 28 minutes for Dave Pallone, Phil Lospitalier, Merrill Hadry and Jerry Loeber to decide whether or not Jack Clark caught Lee Mazzilli's sinking liner to right field. After reversing themselves twice, the umpires ruled that Clark caught the ball.

APRIL 25   Craig Swan pitches a two-hitter to defeat the Giants 2–0 at Shea Stadium. The only San Francisco hits were a double by Roger Metzger in the third inning and a single from Marc Hill in the eighth.

MAY 1   Frank Taveras strikes out five times in five plate appearances during a 10–5 loss to the Padres at Shea Stadium. Facing Gaylord Perry in the second inning, Doug Flynn hit his first home run since 1976. It ended a streak of 967 homerless at-bats.

Flynn hit only seven home runs in 3,853 career at-bats.

MAY 13   Skip Lockwood loses his 13th consecutive decision dating back to 1978 with a ten-inning, 5–4 defeat at the hands of the Padres in San Diego. Lockwood lost his last nine games in 1978 and the first four in 1979.

MAY 20   The Mets take a thrilling 11-inning, 8–7 decision from the Cardinals at Shea Stadium. St. Louis scored three runs in the top of the tenth inning to take a 7–4 lead, but Richie Hebner hit a three-run homer with one out in the bottom half to tie the score 7–7. Frank Tavares drove in the winning run with a single. Neil Allen received credit for his first major league victory.

MAY 25   The game between the Mets and Pirates at Shea Stadium is postponed by dense fog in the bottom of the 11th inning with the score 3–3. Umpires halted play when Pittsburgh left fielder Bill Robinson could not locate Joel Youngblood's routine fly ball, which fell for a triple. The game was postponed when conditions failed to improve after a wait of one hour and 18 minutes.

JUNE 5   With the second overall pick in the amateur draft, the Mets select pitcher Tim Leary from UCLA.

Leary was 4–4 in three seasons with the Mets before being traded to the Brewers. He finished his career with a record of 78–105. The only other future major leaguers drafted and signed by the Mets in 1979 were Jeff Bettendorf (second round), Ron Gardenhire (sixth round) and Dave Smith (27th round).

JUNE 12   The Mets collect ten runs in the sixth inning of a 12–6 win over the Reds at Shea Stadium. The Reds garnered five runs in the top of the fifth to take a 5–2 lead. The ten-run rally in the bottom half was accomplished with only five hits. Cincinnati helped out with three walks, one intentional, and two errors. Doug Flynn capped the run-explosion with a three-run, inside-the-park homer.

The ten-run rally marked the first time that the Mets reached double digits in a single inning. It didn't happen again until June 30, 2000.

JUNE 15   Craig Swan pitches a two-hitter to defeat the Braves 2–1 at Shea Stadium. The only Atlanta hits were a single by Roland Office in the fifth inning and a homer from Jeff Burroughs in the seventh.

On the same day, the Mets traded Mike Bruhert and Bob Myrick to the Rangers for Dock Ellis.

JUNE 16   Doug Flynn scores both runs of a 2–0 win over the Braves at Shea Stadium. Flynn homered in the sixth inning. Kevin Kobel hurled a three-hit shutout.

JUNE 18   The Mets score twice in the first inning against the Astros in Houston, but don't dent the plate again and lose 3–2 in 18 innings. The Mets left 19 men on base. In his seventh inning on the mound, Tom Hausman failed to retire a batter in the 18th. Craig Reynolds drove in the winning run with a single.

JUNE 27   The Mets score five runs in the ninth inning to beat the Pirates 12–9 at Three Rivers Stadium. Willie Montanez and Steve Henderson tied the score 9–9 with back-to-back homers to start the ninth. A double by Doug Flynn and a single from Elliott Maddox broke the deadlock. Richie Hebner drove in two insurance runs with a single.

JUNE 30   The Mets and Cubs combine for 11 runs in the 11th inning before the Mets escape with a 9–8 win at Wrigley Field. In the top of the 11th, Joe Youngblood and Lee Mazzilli each belted two-run homers and Steve Henderson added a two-run triple for a 9–3 lead. In the bottom half, Chicago scored five times, four of them on a grand slam by Mike Vail off Dale Murray.

JULY 6   The Mets hit a club-record four triples, but lose 6–5 in 12 innings to the Padres in San Diego. Frank Taveras hit two of the three-baggers, with Joel Youngblood and Steve Henderson adding the others.

JULY 12   The Mets erupt for eight runs in the first inning and rout the Dodgers 12–5 at Shea Stadium. The eight runs were accomplished with only four hits. Los Angeles walked three and made two errors. Lee Mazzilli made two of the three outs.

JULY 17   Lee Mazzilli is the MVP of the National League's 7–6 win in the All-Star Game at the Kingdome in Seattle. Mazzilli entered the game as a pinch-hitter for Gary Matthews in the eighth inning and tied the score 6–6 with an opposite field homer off Jim Kern, which barely cleared the left-field wall down the line. In the ninth, Mazzilli faced Ron Guidry with the bases loaded and walked to force home the winning run.

              Mazzilli's homer was the first by a Met in an All-Star Game. He finished the year with a .303 batting average and 15 homers.

JULY 27   Dave Kingman hits two homers for the Cubs during a 4–2 win over the Mets at Shea Stadium.

JULY 28   Dave Kingman hits three more homers for the Cubs, giving him five in consecutive games, but the Mets survive the barrage to win 6–4 at Shea Stadium.

AUGUST 2   The Mets purchase Jose Cardenal from the Phillies.

AUGUST 12   The Mets trade Willie Montanez to the Rangers for Ed Lynch and Mike Jorgensen.

AUGUST 14   The Mets pummel the Braves 18–5 in Atlanta. Lee Mazzilli tied a franchise record by scoring five runs. He reached base on a home run, a triple, two walks and a fielder's choice.

              The Mets had a record of 7–33 from August 17 through September 23 to sink the club's record to 56–98. From August 1 through the end of the year, the Mets were 4–32 at Shea. The club lost its 99th game of the season on September 25, but won the last six to avoid a 100-loss season.

AUGUST 18   Frank Taveras hits the only outside-the-park home run of his career during a 4–3 loss to the Mets in Cincinnati. It was struck off Mike LaCoss in the sixth inning.

              Taveras hit only two home runs in 4,043 career at-bats. The other one was inside-the-park as a member of the Pirates on August 5, 1977. That was also struck in Cincinnati.

AUGUST 20   The Mets purchase Ray Burris from the Yankees.

AUGUST 21   An apparent 5–0 win over the Astros at Shea Stadium ends in chaos. With Pete Falcone pitching and two out in the ninth, Jeff Leonard flew out to center field but Frank Taveras called time before the pitch. Leonard went back to the plate and singled. The Mets had only eight men on the field, however, because first baseman Ed Kranepool had left for the clubhouse believing the game had ended. Leonard was sent back to bat again, and flied out.

The Astros filed a protest, and NL president Chub Feeney ruled that Leonard should be awarded a single and that the game should resume before the regularly scheduled contest on August 22. Kevin Kobel recorded the final out, then started the scheduled game and lost 3–1. The ruling by Feeney cost Falcone a shutout.

SEPTEMBER 8   The Mets outlast the Pirates 3–2 in 15 innings at Shea Stadium. John Stearns drove in the winning run with a single.

SEPTEMBER 20   The Mets play a double-header for the third day in a row and lose 6–3 and 2–0 to the Expos at Shea Stadium. The Mets lost 2–0 and 2–1 in 11 innings against the Cubs on September 18 and 3–1 and 4–1 to the Expos on September 19.

The Mets a played double-header again on September 22 versus the Cardinals at Shea and on September 25 against the Cubs in Chicago. Playing 12 games in eight days, the Mets were 2–10.

SEPTEMBER 21   The Mets sell Dock Ellis to the Pirates.

SEPTEMBER 25   The Mets score a run in the ninth inning and one in the tenth to defeat the Cubs 4–3 in the second game of a double-header at Wrigley Field. With two out in the ninth, Richie Hebner drove in the winning run with a single off Bruce Sutter. Steve Henderson drove in the winning run with another single against Dick Tidrow in the tenth. Chicago won the opener 11–3.

OCTOBER 3   As part of his seven-day tour of North America, Pope John Paul II makes an appearance at Shea Stadium. It rained hard all morning, but the showers stopped at almost the precise moment the Pontiff entered the stadium.

OCTOBER 29   Willie Mays signs a ten-year contract to work for the Bally Corporation, which operates gambling casinos in Atlantic City. As a result of his association with Bally, Mays was banned from working in Organized Baseball following a ruling from Commissioner Bowie Kuhn. At the time, Mays was employed by the Mets as a goodwill ambassador and a part-time coach.

OCTOBER 31   The Mets trade Richie Hebner to the Tigers for Phil Mankowski and Jerry Morales.

NOVEMBER 27   Three weeks after Iranian militants seize the U. S. Embassy in Teheran, taking 52 hostages, Skip Lockwood signs with the Red Sox as a free agent.

DECEMBER 10   The Mets trade Jody Davis to the Cardinals for Ray Searage.

THE STATE OF THE METS

The Mets were 63–99 in 1979 and drew fewer fans in a non-strike season than at any time in history. By 1983, progress was imperceptible, as the Mets finished at 68–94. But the losing seasons resulted in early draft choices, and the Mets made some terrific selections. Things changed dramatically with 90 wins in 1984, the first of seven straight winning seasons. The summit came in 1986 when the Mets were 10–54 during the regular season and won the world championship. Overall, the Mets were 816–743 during the 1980s, a winning percentage of .523, which ranked third in the NL to the Cardinals (.529) and Dodgers (.527). National League champions were the Phillies (1980 and 1983), Dodgers (1981 and 1988), Cardinals (1982, 1985 and 1987), Padres (1984), Mets (1986) and Giants (1989). The NL East pennant winners were the Phillies (1980 and 1983), Expos (1981), Cardinals (1982, 1985 and 1987), Cubs (1984 and 1989) and Mets (1986 and 1988).

THE BEST TEAM

The 1986 club was the best in franchise history, with a record of 108–54 during the regular season, followed by thrilling wins over the Astros in the NLCS and the Red Sox in the World Series.

THE WORST TEAM

The 1982 Mets were 65–97. The club didn't have a winning percentage above .420 in any season from 1977 through 1983.

THE BEST MOMENT

The best moment was the final out of the 1986 World Series and Jesse Orosco leaping in the air in sheer joy.

THE WORST MOMENT

After posting the best record in the National League in 1988, the Mets lost the National League Championship Series to the Dodgers.

THE ALL-DECADE TEAM • YEARS W/METS

Gary Carter, c	1985–89
Keith Hernandez, 1b	1983–89
Wally Backman, 2b	1980–88
Howard Johnson, 3b	1985–93
Kevin Elster, ss	1988–92
Kevin McReynolds, lf	1987–91
Mookie Wilson, cf	1980–89
Darryl Strawberry, rf	1983–90
Dwight Gooden, p	1984–94
Sid Fernandez, p	1984–93
Ron Darling, p	1983–91
Jesse Orosco, p	1979, 1981–87

With the exception of McReynolds and Elster, each of the players on the All-Decade Team were key contributors to the 1986 world championship team. Other outstanding players on the Mets during the decade included left fielder George Foster (1982–86), center fielder Lenny Dykstra (1985–89) and third baseman Hubie Brooks (1980–84).

THE DECADE LEADERS

Batting Avg:	Keith Hernandez	.297
On-Base Pct:	Keith Hernandez	.387
Slugging Pct:	Darryl Strawberry	.520
Home Runs:	Darryl Strawberry	215
RBI:	Darryl Strawberry	625
Runs:	Darryl Strawberry	570
Stolen Bases:	Mookie Wilson	281
Wins:	Dwight Gooden	100
Strikeouts:	Dwight Gooden	1,168
ERA:	Jesse Orosco	2.60
Saves:	Jesse Orosco	107

THE HOME FIELD

Shea Stadium was in its 17th season in 1980. The success of the team made it the place to be once more, as attendance rose from 788,905 in 1979 to a peak of 3,055,455 in 1988. In 1983, the Mets finished last in the NL in attendance. By 1988, the club was first. There were several changes to the physical structure of the stadium. In 1980, the orange and blue steel panels were removed from the exterior of the stadium, and large blue wind shields were installed. The Big Apple Top Hat was built behind the center-field wall in 1981, and every Met home run was followed with a Big Apple rising out of the hat. A giant Diamond Vision video display debuted in left-center field in 1982 to display statistics and other information. In 1984, the Jets played their last season at Shea, making the Mets the only tenant. In mid-decade 50 suites were added on the press level. The entire outside of the stadium was painted blue, and six neon outlines of baseball players were placed on the exterior. A new scoreboard was built in 1988 into the shell of the old one in right field. Auxiliary scoreboards were installed along the facade of the loge section down the right- and left-field lines.

THE GAME YOU WISHED YOU HAD SEEN

The best day to be at Shea Stadium during the ballpark's 45-year history was on October 25, 1986, when the Mets scored three runs in the tenth inning to beat the Red Sox 6–5 in game six of the World Series.

THE WAY THE GAME WAS PLAYED

The 1980s had a little something for everyone. Trends that surfaced during the 1970s continued, with teams emphasizing speed over power. Earned run averages hovered around 3.60. The 1987 season combined the speed numbers of the dead ball era with the power numbers of the 1950s. NL teams averaged more than 150 homers and 150 steals, the only time that ever occurred. But the offensive bubble burst sharply afterward, and in 1988 and 1989, the NL experienced its lowest batting averages in 20 years.

THE MANAGEMENT

The Doubleday Corporation purchased the stagnating franchise in January 1980. Nelson Doubleday assumed the title of Chairman of the Board with Fred Wilpon serving as President and CEO. Doubleday and Wilpon bought the club from the Doubleday Corporation in 1986. Frank Cashen was the general manager from 1980 through 1990. Field managers were Joe Torre (1977–81), George Bamberger (1982–83), Frank Howard (1983) and Davey Johnson (1984–90).

THE BEST PLAYER MOVE

The best player move was the drafting of Darryl Strawberry in 1980. The best trade brought Keith Hernandez from the Cardinals for Neil Allen and Rick Ownbey in 1983.

THE WORST PLAYER MOVE

The worst trade sent five players, including Rick Aguilera and Kevin Tapani, to the Twins for Frank Viola in July 1989.

1980

Season in a Sentence

After a promising start, the Mets lose 33 of their last 44 games to post 95 or more defeats for the fourth year in a row.

Finish • Won • Lost • Pct • GB

Fifth   67   95   .414 24.0

Manager

Joe Torre

Stats

Stats	Mets	AL	Rank
Batting Avg:	.257	.259	7
On-Base Pct:	.319	.320	9
Slugging Pct:	.345	.374	10
Home Runs:	61	12	
Stolen Bases:	158	5	
ERA:	3.85	3.60	9
Errors:	154	9	
Runs Scored:	611	10	
Runs Allowed:	702	10	

Starting Lineup

Alex Trevino, c
Lee Mazzilli, 1b-cf
Doug Flynn, 2b
Elliott Maddox, 3b
Frank Taveras, ss
Steve Henderson, lf
Jerry Morales, cf
Joel Youngblood, rf
Mike Jorgensen, 1b
John Stearns, c
Claudell Washington, rf

Pitchers

Mark Bomback, sp-rp
Ray Burris, sp
Pete Falcone, sp
Pat Zachry, sp
Craig Swan, sp
Neil Allen, rp
Tom Hausman, rp
Jeff Reardon, rp
John Pacella, rp-sp

Attendance

1,192,073 (ninth in NL)

Club Leaders

Batting Avg:	Steve Henderson	.290
On-Base Pct:	Lee Mazzilli	.370
Slugging Pct:	Lee Mazzilli	.431
Home Runs:	Lee Mazzilli	16
RBI:	Lee Mazzilli	76
Runs:	Lee Mazzilli	82
Stolen Bases:	Lee Mazzilli	41
Wins:	Mark Bomback	10
Strikeouts:	Pete Falcone	109
ERA:	Pat Zachry	3.01
Saves:	Neil Allen	22

JANUARY 24   The huge New York publishing firm of Doubleday and Company buys the Mets for $21.1 million. At the time, it was the largest sum ever paid for a baseball team. Until the sale, the Mets had been owned by the Payson family since the inception of the franchise. Joan Payson operated the club until her death in October 1975, relying heavily on M. Donald Grant, who served as chairman of the board. After Joan's death, ownership passed to her husband Charles Payson and daughter Lorinda de Roulet. Neither had much interest in running the franchise, and Grant took on a more substantial role. Grant's frugal policies and a string of last-place teams during the last three years of the 1970s alienated the fan base, and attendance dropped alarmingly by nearly two million over the course of the 1970s. The corresponding financial losses caused the Payson family to unload the team. Nelson Doubleday, Jr., a 46-year-old Princeton graduate and head of the publishing firm, became the chairman of the board. His company owned 80 percent of the stock. Fred Wilpon, the 43-year-old chairman of a Long Island real estate firm, owned $6^{1}/_{2}$ percent of the Mets and was named president. It took a few years to revive the dormant franchise, but the Doubleday Corporation turned the perennial losers of the late 1970s and early 1980s into a perennial pennant contenders.

FEBRUARY 21   The day prior to the U.S. hockey team's "Miracle on Ice" win over the Soviet Union in the Olympics, the Mets fire Joe McDonald as general manager and hire 53-year-old Frank Cashen.

Cashen had been a part of the Baltimore Orioles as an executive vice-president and helped put together the World Series teams of 1966, 1969, 1970 and 1971. Cashen served as the Orioles" general manager from 1971 through 1975, following the resignation of Harry Dalton. Cashen was out of baseball from 1975 through 1979 when he was as an assistant to Commissioner Bowie Kuhn. Cashen served as the general manager of the Mets until 1990 and guided the franchise through its most successful period.

APRIL 10   The Mets open the season with a 5–2 win over the Cubs before 12,219 at Shea Stadium. Craig Swan pitched seven innings for the victory.

The Mets hired ad man Jerry Della Femina to try to bring fans back into the ballpark. Full-page ads were taken out in the New York papers with the slogan "The Magic Is Back." Della Femina made several unflattering comments about the Yankees during the campaign, which led to a $5,000 fine from Commissioner Bowie Kuhn for "conduct detrimental to baseball." The campaign was a moderate success as attendance at Shea increased from 788,905 in 1979 to 1,192,073 in 1980.

APRIL 15   The Mets commit six errors during a 7–3 loss to the Expos in Montreal. Third baseman Phil Mankowski made two errors in the first inning of his first game with the club.

The Mets began telecasting games over cable in 1980 on SportsChannel.

APRIL 19   The Mets blow a 9–1 lead and lose 12–9 to the Cubs at Wrigley Field. Chicago overcame the eight-run deficit with four runs in the sixth inning against Mark Bomback and seven in the eighth off Neil Allen. Dave Kingman hit a two-run homer in the sixth and a grand slam in the eighth.

APRIL 30   Mark Bomback pitches a two-hitter to beat the Phillies 2–0 at Shea Stadium. The only Philadelphia hits were singles by Mike Schmidt in the second inning and Garry Maddox in the seventh.

The gem came in Bomback's third major league start and second with the Mets. It was his only career shutout.

MAY 1   Pete Falcone strikes out the first six batters he faces, but winds up losing 2–1 to the Phillies at Shea Stadium. Falcone fanned Lonnie Smith, Pete Rose, Garry Maddox, Mike Schmidt, Greg Luzinski and Bob Boone. The Mets hurler had a total of eight strikeouts in seven innings.

MAY 2   Ray Burris (eight innings) and Jeff Reardon (one inning) combine on a two-hitter but the Mets lose 1–0 to the Padres at Shea Stadium. Jerry Mumphrey had both San Diego hits with singles in the second and seventh innings.

MAY 7   The Mets and Reds play in extra innings for the third game in a row at Shea Stadium. The Mets won 3–2 in ten innings on May 5, and Cincinnati was victorious 12–10 in 14 innings on May 6 and 3–2 in 12 innings on May 7.

MAY 28   Ten days after the volcanic eruption of Mt. St. Helens in the state of Washington, the Mets eliminate a 5–0 deficit with six runs in the eighth inning and won 6–5 over the Cardinals in St. Louis. All six runs crossed the plate after two were out and on just three hits. Cardinals pitchers walked five. John Stearns drove in the first two with a bases-loaded single. Elliott Maddox tied the contest 5–5 with a three-run double. Second baseman Jose Moreno drove in the game-winning run with another one-base hit. It was only the third major league game and first career hit for Moreno, who entered the game in the seventh inning during a double switch.

JUNE 3   With the first overall pick in the amateur draft, the Mets select outfielder Darryl Strawberry from Crenshaw High School in Los Angeles, California.

Strawberry made his major league debut in 1983 and made an immediate impact. After winning the Rookie-of-the-Year award, Strawberry was an All-Star in each of his last seven seasons with the Mets from 1984 through 1990. On the all-time franchise lists, Strawberry ranks first in home runs (252), first in RBI (733), first in runs (662), first in walks (580), second in total bases (2,028), second in slugging percentage (.520) and fourth in stolen bases (191). The Mets also drafted Billy Beane and John Gibbons in the first round as a result of free agent compensation for losing Andy Hassler and Skip Lockwood. Other future major leaguers drafted and signed by the Mets in 1980 were Jay Tibbs (second round), Ronn Reynolds (fifth round), Jeff Bittinger (seventh round), Lloyd McClendon (eighth round) and Rick Ownbey (13th round). The club also signed Kevin Mitchell as an undrafted free agent.

JUNE 4   Pat Zachry (seven innings) and Neil Allen (three innings) combine to allow only three hits, but the Mets lose 1–0 to the Cardinals at Shea Stadium. The lone run scored on a home run by Ken Reitz leading off the tenth.

JUNE 6   The Mets score eight runs in the second inning and defeat the Pirates 9–4 at Shea Stadium. The Mets collected seven hits in the game—six of them, all singles—during the eight-run second.

JUNE 7   The Mets trade Jesse Anderson to the White Sox for Claudell Washington.

JUNE 10   The Mets rally from a 4–0 deficit to defeat the Dodgers 5–4 in a game at Shea Stadium marked by a benches-clearing brawl. In the second inning, Ron Cey took exception at being drilled in the hip by a pitch from Pat Zachry and charged the mound. Cey tackled Zachry at the knees, causing players from both teams to storm the field. After order was restored, Cey was ejected.

JUNE 11   Mike Jorgensen hits a walk-off grand slam off Rick Sutcliffe with two out in the tenth inning to beat the Dodgers 6–2 at Shea Stadium. Jorgensen entered the game in the ninth as a replacement for John Stearns, who was making a rare appearance as a first baseman.

JUNE 12   After falling behind 5–0, the Mets score four runs in the fifth inning and two in the sixth to defeat the Dodgers 6–5 at Shea Stadium. Mike Jorgensen and John Stearns began the sixth with walks. Elliott Maddox laid down a bunt, and both Jorgensen and Stearns crossed the plate following pitcher Bobby Castillo's wild throw to first base.

During the game, two inebriated fans jumped onto the playing field. While police were unable to catch them, John Stearns jumped from behind the plate and ran into left field in pursuit. Utilizing his football skills from his days as an All-Big Eight defensive back at the University of Colorado, Stearns tackled one of the two fans.

JUNE 14   The Mets score five runs in the ninth inning to stun the Giants 7–6 at Shea Stadium. The Mets trailed 6–0 before scoring single runs in the sixth and eighth. With two out in the ninth, the Mets were still behind 6–2 with Greg Minton pitching for San Francisco and Doug Flynn the runner on second base. Flynn scored on Lee Mazzilli's single. After Frank Taveras walked, Claudell Washington singled home Mazzilli. Allen Ripley was called in to relieve Minton and faced Steve Henderson. Believe it or not, Ripley gave up a three-run homer to Henderson to lift the Mets to the victory.

The win gave the Mets a record of 27–28 after a 9–18 start. The club was still one game under .500 at 56–57 on August 13, then lost 35 of their next 42 games.

JUNE 22   Claudell Washington hits three homers during a 9–6 win over the Dodgers in Los Angeles. Facing Dave Goltz, Washington hit a two-run homer in the first inning, struck out in the third and hit another two-run blast in the fifth. With Charlie Hough on the mound, Washington hit a solo homer in the seventh. With a chance at a record-tying fourth home run in the ninth, Washington stroked a single off Bobby Castillo.

The outburst came in Washington's seventh game, and fifth start, as a member of the Mets. During his first six games with the club, he collected only one hit, a single, in 17 at-bats. Washington hit ten homers with the Mets before departing to the Braves as a free agent at the end of the season.

JUNE 28   The Mets win a pair of games in their last at-bat during a double-header against the Phillies in Philadelphia. In the opener, John Stearns drove in the winning run with a double in the 11th inning for a 2–1 victory. In the nightcap, Steve Henderson's single in the ninth broke a 4–4 tie and lifted the Mets to a 5–4 triumph.

JULY 2   John Pacella (7¹⁄₃ innings) and Neil Allen (1²⁄₃ innings) combine to win a two-hitter to defeat the Cubs 7–1 at Shea Stadium. Both Chicago hits went for extra bases in the fifth inning on a double by Barry Foote and a triple from Mike Tyson.

The victory was only the second for Pacella during a six-year career with five teams in which he posted a 4–10 record and a 5.73 ERA.

JULY 4   John Stearns is ejected from a 6–5 loss to the Expos in the second game of a double-header at Shea Stadium. In the first inning, Montreal pitcher Bill Gullickson brushed back Mike Jorgensen. As Jorgensen motioned his disapproval, Stearns ran out of the dugout and tackled Gullickson. The Mets won the opener 9–5. Lee Mazzilli homered in the eighth inning, giving him home runs in four consecutive games.

Mazzilli hit only two home runs in the first 71 games of the season through June 30, then pounded out 11 homers in 19 contests from July 1 through July 20. He finished the season with 16 homers in 152 games.

JULY 13   Lee Mazzilli collects six hits, including two homers and a double, in eight at-bats as
                 the Mets sweep the Cardinals 7–4 and 10–4 in a double-header at Shea Stadium.

JULY 19   The Mets collect 20 hits and rout the Reds 13–3 in Cincinnati. Playing in his
                 fifth game, and first start, with the Mets, shortstop Bill Almon garnered four hits,
                 including a triple, and scored four runs in six at-bats. They were his first four hits as
                 a Met. A former number-one overall pick in the amateur draft in 1974, Almon was
                 signed by the Mets on July 11 following his release by the Expos. Roy Lee Jackson
                 pitched a three-hitter and struck out 12.

                 *Almon hit .170 in 120 at-bats with the Mets and was released during the
                 following offseason. The win for Jackson was his only one in 1980 and came in
                 his third game and first start after being recalled from Class AAA Tidewater.
                 He finished the season 1–7.*

JULY 25   John Stearns drives in both runs of a 2–0 win over the Reds at Shea Stadium.
                 Pat Zachry pitched the shutout.

AUGUST 5   Doug Flynn ties a modern major league record with three triples during an 11–5
                 loss to the Expos in Montreal. Flynn tripled in the third and fifth inning off Bill
                 Gullickson and in the eighth off Elias Sosa.

AUGUST 26   The Mets lose 8–6 in 18 innings to the Padres at Shea Stadium. The Mets sent the
                 game into extra innings when Joel Youngblood drove in a run with a pinch-hit double
                 off Rollie Fingers with two out in the ninth to deadlock the contest 6–6. There was no
                 more scoring until the 18th when San Diego garnered two runs off Pete Falcone.

AUGUST 30   The Mets score seven runs in the sixth inning and beat the Giants 9–5 in San Francisco.

SEPTEMBER 12   The Mets extend their losing streak to 13 games by dropping a 10–5 decision to the
                 Cubs in 14 innings at Shea Stadium. It was also the 17th consecutive game in which
                 the Mets failed to hit a home run.

                 The Mets hit only 61 homers in 1980, a franchise low for a non-strike season.

SEPTEMBER 14   The Mets score four runs in the ninth inning off Bruce Sutter to beat the Cubs
                 10–7 at Shea Stadium. The game ended on a one-out, three-run homer by Steve
                 Henderson.

SEPTEMBER 29   With two out in the ninth inning, Joel Youngblood hits a two-run, walk-off homer to
                 defeat the Phillies 5–4 at Shea Stadium.

SEPTEMBER 30   A crowd of 1,754, the smallest in Shea Stadium history, watches the Mets beat the
                 Pirates 3–2.

NOVEMBER 15   A week after Ronald Reagan defeats Jimmy Carter in the presidential election,
                 Claudell Washington signs a contract as a free agent with the Braves.

DECEMBER 12   Four days following the murder of John Lennon in New York City, the Mets trade
                 Roy Lee Jackson to the Blue Jays for Bob Bailor.

DECEMBER 15   The Mets trade Jose Moreno and John Pacella to the Padres for Randy Jones.

DECEMBER 16   The Mets sign Rusty Staub, most recently with the Rangers, as a free agent.

> *Staub previously played for the Mets from 1972 through 1975. In his return, which lasted five seasons, he was used as a spare outfielder and pinch-hitter.*

1981

Season in a Sentence

Joe Torre is fired at the end of another losing season, which is interrupted for nearly two months by a player's strike.

Finish • Won • Lost • Pct • GB

| * | 41 | 62 | .398 | * |

* Because of the strike, the season was split into two halves. The Mets were 17–34, in fifth place and 15 games behind in the first half. In the second half, the Mets were 24–28, in fourth place and 5¹/₂ games behind.

Manager

Joe Torre

Stats

Stats	Mets	AL	Rank
Batting Avg:	.248	.255	9
On-Base Pct:	.308	.319	10
Slugging Pct:	.356	.364	8
Home Runs:	57	7	
Stolen Bases:	103	3	
ERA:	3.55	3.49	6
Errors:	130	12	
Runs Scored:	348	12	
Runs Allowed:	432	8	

Starting Lineup

John Stearns, c
Dave Kingman, 1b-lf
Doug Flynn, 2b
Hubie Brooks, 3b
Frank Taveras, ss
Lee Mazzilli, lf-cf
Mookie Wilson, cf
Ellis Valentine, rf
Rusty Staub, 1b
Alex Trevino, c
Joel Youngblood, rf

Pitchers

Pat Zachry, sp
Mike Scott, sp
Ed Lynch, sp
Greg Harris, sp
Randy Jones, sp
Neil Allen, rp
Pete Falcone, rp

Attendance

704,244 (seventh in NL)

Club Leaders

Batting Avg:	Mookie Wilson	.271
On-Base Pct:	Hubie Brooks	.345
Slugging Pct:	Dave Kingman	.456
Home Runs:	Dave Kingman	22
RBI:	Dave Kingman	59
Runs:	Mookie Wilson	49
Stolen Bases:	Mookie Wilson	24
Wins:	Pat Zachry	7
Strikeouts:	Pat Zachry	76
ERA:	Mike Scott	3.90
Saves:	Neil Allen	18

JANUARY 5   The Mets sign Dave Roberts, most recently with the Mariners, as a free agent.

JANUARY 13   In the winter amateur draft, the Mets select Randy Milligan in the first round of the regular phase and Herm Winningham in the first round of the secondary phase.

FEBRUARY 17   A month after 52 American hostages are released after 444 days of captivity in Iran, Jerry Morales signs a contract as a free agent with the Cubs.

FEBRUARY 18   Ray Burris signs a contract as a free agent with the Expos.

FEBRUARY 28   The Mets trade Steve Henderson to the Cubs for Dave Kingman.

Kingman had previously played for the Mets from 1975 through 1977. In his return engagement, Kingman accounted for 22 of the club's 57 homers in 1981, but batted only .221. During the 1982 season, Kingman led the NL in homers with 37, but his average slipped to just .204 and he led the circuit in strikeouts with 156. The Mets released him in 1983 after hitting ten homers and batting .198 in 100 games.

MARCH 31   The day after President Ronald Reagan is shot by John Hinckley, the Mets trade Juan Berenguer to the Royals for Marvell Wynne and John Skinner.

APRIL 9   The Mets open the season with a 2–0 win over the Cubs at Wrigley Field. Both runs scored off solo homers by Lee Mazzilli and Rusty Staub off Rick Reuschel in the fourth inning. It was Staub's first game as a Met since 1975. Pat Zachry (5 2/3 innings), Tom Hausman (one-third of an inning) and Neil Allen (three innings) combined on the shutout.

APRIL 15   In the home opener, the Mets down the Cardinals 5–3 before 15,205 at Shea Stadium.

APRIL 26   Craig Swan suffers a freak injury in the first inning of a 7–6 loss to the Expos in the second game of a double-header at Olympic Stadium. While Tim Raines was attempting to steal second, the throw from catcher Ron Hodges drilled Swan in the ribs, fracturing one of them. Swan didn't pitch again until June 2. Montreal also won the opener 8–4.

MAY 20   The Mets break a nine-game losing streak by beating the Giants 4–3 in ten innings in San Francisco. Heading into the contest, the Mets had a record of 8–24.

MAY 25   Dave Kingman hits a grand slam off Dick Ruthven in the second inning of a 13–3 trouncing of the Phillies at Shea Stadium.

MAY 29   The Mets trade Jeff Reardon and Dan Norman to the Expos for Ellis Valentine.

The Mets made a horrible decision in trading Reardon, who was only 25 at the time he was sent packing to Montreal. Reardon would go on to record 357 saves after leaving the Mets before his career ended in 1994. Valentine flopped in New York with a .261 average and 13 homers in 159 games over two seasons.

JUNE 8   In the first round of the amateur draft, the Mets select outfielder Terry Blocker from Tennessee State University.

Taken with the fourth overall pick, Blocker played only 18 games as a Met, all in 1985, and collected one hit in 16 at-bats. He finished his career in 1989 with a .205 average and two home runs in 118 games. Other future major leaguers drafted and signed by the Mets were John Christensen (second round),

Dave Cochrane (fourth round), Mark Carreon (eighth round), Lenny Dykstra (13th round) and Lou Thornton (19th round). The Mets let a huge draft-day plum get away, however. Roger Clemens from San Jacinto Junior College was picked in the 12th round. Clemens decided to attend the University of Texas instead of signing with the Mets. He was drafted in the first round by the Red Sox in 1983 with the 19th overall pick after the Mets passed him up to take third baseman Eddie Williams.

JUNE 11   With a midnight strike deadline looming, the Mets lose 5–2 to the Reds at Shea Stadium.

JUNE 12   The major league players begin a strike that lasts 50 days and wipes out nearly months of the 1981 baseball season. The strike reduced the Mets schedule to 105 games (including two ties).

JULY 31   Just two days after Prince Charles marries Lady Diana Spencer in London, the players and owners hammer out an agreement that ends the strike.

AUGUST 6   The owners vote to split the 1981 pennant race, with the winners of the two halves of the season competing in an extra round of playoffs for the division title. The standings when the strike was called comprised the first half.

AUGUST 10   In the first game following the strike, the Mets take a thrilling 13–inning, 7–5 decision over the Cubs at Wrigley Field. The score was 1–1 after ten innings. Dave Kingman belted a three-run homer in the top of the 11th, but Chicago countered with three tallies in their half. Both teams scored once in the 12th before the Mets put the game away in the 13th. Ellis Valentine broke the 5–5 tie by bringing Joel Youngblood across the plate with an RBI-single.

AUGUST 19   The Mets sign Mike Marshall, most recently with the Twins, as a free agent.

AUGUST 22   With the Mets trailing 4–1 and two out in the eighth inning, Dave Kingman hits a grand slam off Frank Pastore, which leads to a 7–4 win over the Reds in Cincinnati.

SEPTEMBER 16 Steve Carlton strikes out 15 batters, but the Mets survive to win 5–4 over the Phillies at Shea Stadium. John Stearns put the Mets into the lead with a two-run homer in the eighth. It was his first home run since August 18, 1979, a drought covering 197 games and 684 official at-bats.

SEPTEMBER 20 The Mets score two runs in the ninth inning to beat the Cardinals 7–6 at Shea Stadium. Over the first five innings, the Mets collected 20 hits, but left 13 men on base while scoring only five runs. In the ninth, Bruce Sutter retired the first two batters to face him before Frank Taveras singled and Mookie Wilson walloped a two-run, walk-off homer.

SEPTEMBER 24 Ellis Valentine hits two homers and a double and drives in five runs, but the Mets lose 10–9 to the Cubs in Chicago.

SEPTEMBER 29 Pete Falcone hits a home run and pitches a shutout to defeat the Phillies 7–0 in Philadelphia. The homer was struck off Mark Davis in the third inning and was the only one of Falcone's career in 416 at-bats.

OCTOBER 4   The Mets dismiss Joe Torre as manager.

Torre was hired in May 1977 and had a 286–420 record as manager of the Mets while trying to rebuild a losing club that had little in the way of talent, either on the parent club or in the farm system. Three weeks later, Torre was hired by the Braves as manager, and the club bolted out of the gate in 1982 with 13 straight wins. At the end of the year, the Braves had the NL West title. Torre managed the Braves until 1984 and the Cardinals from 1990 through 1995. When he was hired by the Yankees as manager for the 1996 season, Torre had not been a part of a World Series team in 17 years as a player and 14 as a manager. That situation was rectified quickly, as in his first season with the Yanks, Torre led the franchise to their first World Series since 1981 and beat the Braves in six games. He followed with three more World Championships in 1998, 1999 and 2000 and an AL pennant in 2001 before losing a seven-game series with the Diamondbacks. After leaving New York at the end of the 2007 season, Torre managed the Dodgers from 2008 through 2010.

OCTOBER 20   The Mets name 56-year-old George Bamberger as manager.

A native of Staten Island, Bamburger was a highly successful pitching coach with the Orioles from 1968 through 1977 before being hired as manager of the Brewers. Taking over a franchise that had never won more than 76 games in a season since it moved to Milwaukee in 1970, Bamburger was 93–69 in 1978. He followed that with a 95–66 record in 1979 before a heart attack sidelined him in 1980. Bamburger couldn't revive the Mets, however. The club was 65–97 in 1982 and fired him after a 16–30 start in 1983.

DECEMBER 11   The Mets send Frank Taveras and cash to the Expos for Steve Ratzer. On the same day, the Mets traded Doug Flynn and Dan Boitano to the Rangers for Jim Kern.

1982

Season in a Sentence

The season begins promisingly with the acquisition of George Foster and a 34–30 record on June 20, but a second-half collapse includes a 15-game losing streak.

Finish • Won • Lost • Pct • GB

Sixth   65   97   .401   27.0

Manager

George Bamburger

Stats

Stats	Mets	AL	Rank
Batting Avg:	.247	.258	11
On-Base Pct:	.305	.319	11
Slugging Pct:	.350	.373	10
Home Runs:	97	9	
Stolen Bases:	137	8	
ERA:	3.88	3.60	11
Errors:	175	12	
Runs Scored:	609	10	
Runs Allowed:	723	12	

Starting Lineup

John Stearns, c
Dave Kingman, 1b
Bob Bailor, 2b-ss
Hubie Brooks, 3b
Ron Gardenhire, ss
George Foster, lf
Mookie Wilson, cf
Ellis Valentine, rf
Wally Backman, 2b
Ron Hodges, c
Rusty Staub, rf-lf-1b

Pitchers

Craig Swan, sp-rp
Charlie Puleo, sp-rp
Pete Falcone, sp-rp
Mike Scott, sp-rp
Randy Jones, sp
Nail Allen, rp
Ed Lynch, rp
Pat Zachry, rp-sp
Jesse Orosco, rp

Attendance

1,323,036 (ninth in NL)

Club Leaders

Batting Avg:	Mookie Wilson	.279
On-Base Pct:	Mookie Wilson	.314
Slugging Pct:	Dave Kingman	.432
Home Runs:	Dave Kingman	37
RBI:	Dave Kingman	99
Runs:	Mookie Wilson	90
Stolen Bases:	Mookie Wilson	58
Wins:	Craig Swan	11
Strikeouts:	Pete Falcone	101
ERA:	Craig Swan	3.35
Saves:	Neil Allen	19

FEBRUARY 10   The Mets trade Jim Kern, Alex Trevino and Greg Harris to the Reds for George Foster.

The deal was made because the Reds failed to meet Foster's salary demands. There was a great deal of excitement over his arrival because it seemed that the Mets were finally willing to spend money to put a winning team on the field. With a $10 million contract over five years, Foster became the second-highest paid player in baseball, behind only Dave Winfield of the Yankees. Foster was 33 at the time of the trade, had made the All-Star team in five of the six previous seasons, and won Most Valuable Player honors in 1977 when he belted 52 homers, drove in 149 runs and batted .320. Foster was coming off a strike-shortened 1981 season in which he hit 22 homers and drove in 90 runs in 108 games and finished third in the MVP balloting. He seemed to be on a track to the Hall of Fame. In 1981, respected baseball historians Lawrence Ritter and Donald Honig included Foster in their book The 100 Greatest Players of All-Time. *It was expected that Foster and Dave Kingman would give the Mets one of the best one-two home run punches in baseball, but those hopes weren't realized as Foster flopped miserably in New York. In his first season as a Met, he batted .247 with 13 home runs in 151 games. Foster failed to improve significantly before a trade to the White Sox in 1986. Fortunately, the Mets were hurt only* *in the pocketbook as the three traded for Foster accomplished little of substance while in Cincinnati.*

APRIL 1   The Mets trade Lee Mazzilli to the Rangers for Ron Darling and Walt Terrell.

There were hoots over the deal from Mets fans despite Mazzilli's off-year in 1981 because he was one of the most popular players on the roster. He was dealt for two pitchers who had not yet pitched above the Class AA level, but the trade proved to be very beneficial. Mazzilli was only 27 at the time of the transaction, but was never again a regular afterward. He returned to the Mets as a part-time player from 1986 through 1989. Darling made his major league debut in 1983. He was 72–39 with the Mets from 1984 through 1988. Overall, Darling ranks fourth in wins in Mets history with 99. He is also fourth in innings (1,620) and fifth in games started (241). Terrell gave the club two effective seasons before going to the Tigers for Howard Johnson following the 1984 season.

APRIL 8   The Mets open the season with a 7–2 win over the Phillies in Philadelphia. Bob Bailor was the offensive star with three hits, including two doubles and three RBI in four at-bats. Randy Jones, who drew the start after posting a record of 1–8 in 1981, was the winning pitcher after hurling six innings.

Early in the 1982 campaign, Jones seemed to have his career back on track at the level he showed as a Cy Young winner with the Padres in 1976. He was 6–2 with a 2.74 ERA on May 23. From May 28 through the end of the season, however, Jones had a 1–8 record and a 7.91 earned run average in 38$\frac{2}{3}$ innings. The 1982 season proved to be his last in the majors.

APRIL 13   In the home opener, the Mets defeat the Phillies 5–2 before 40,845 at Shea Stadium. Dave Kingman homered.

APRIL 24   The Mets edge the Expos 1–0 in Montreal. The lone run scored in the seventh inning on back-to-back doubles by Gary Rajsich and John Stearns. Charlie Puleo (6$\frac{1}{3}$ innings), Pete Falcone (one inning) and Neil Allen (1$\frac{2}{3}$ innings) combined on the shutout.

Stearns batted .293 for the Mets in 1982, but an elbow injury suffered in August all but ended his career. After 1982 he appeared in only 12 major league games, only three of which were as a starter, before his playing days ended in 1984.

APRIL 28   The Mets outlast the Padres to win 5–4 in 15 innings in San Diego. The winning run scored on a triple by Mookie Wilson and a sacrifice fly from Bob Bailor. Relievers Craig Swan, Neil Allen and Pete Falcone combined to pitch 11 shutout innings while surrendering only three hits.

MAY 2   A two-run homer by George Foster in the first inning provides both runs of a 2–0 win over the Giants in the second game of a double-header in San Francisco. Randy Jones (eight innings) and Neil Allen (one inning) combined on the shutout. The Giants won the opener 4–3.

MAY 9   Pinch-hitting for Craig Swan with two out in the ninth inning, Rusty Staub hits a walk-off homer to defeat the Giants 6–5 at Shea Stadium.

MAY 10   Pinch-hitting for Randy Jones with two out in the ninth inning, Bob Bailor strokes a
            two-run, walk-off double to turn to 2–1 deficit into a 3–2 triumph over the Padres at
            Shea Stadium.

MAY 16   The Mets erupt for nine runs in the sixth inning and defeat the Dodgers 13–4 at
            Shea Stadium. The rally was achieved with six hits, all of them singles. The Dodgers
            contributed with three errors, three walks and a balk.

MAY 22   The Mets hang on to beat the Astros 6–5 in 12 innings in Houston. The Mets seemed
            to have the game in the bag with a 5–1 lead heading into the ninth, but Craig Swan
            loaded the bases and Neil Allen surrendered a grand slam to Terry Puhl.

MAY 28   Dave Kingman strikes out five times in five at-bats during an 8–3 loss to the Astros at
            Shea Stadium.

JUNE 7   With the fifth overall pick in the amateur draft, the Mets select pitcher Dwight
            Gooden from Hillsborough High School in Tampa, Florida.

            *The Mets had one of the best drafts in club history in 1982. Gooden made his
            major league debut in 1984 and had an immediate impact by becoming one of
            the most dominating pitchers in baseball at the tender age of 19. Other future
            major leaguers drafted and signed by the Mets in the regular phase included
            Floyd Youmans (second round), Roger McDowell (third round), Gerald Young
            (fifth round), Greg Olson (seventh round), Joe Redfield (ninth round), Mickey
            Weston (12th round), Barry Lyons (15th round), Steve Springer (20th round)
            and Wes Gardner (22nd round). In addition, Randy Myers was taken in the first
            round of the secondary phase. Rafael Palmeiro was chosen in the eighth round
            out of Jackson High School in Miami, but opted to attend Mississippi State
            University instead of signing with the Mets. He was drafted in the first round by
            the Cubs in 1985.*

JUNE 18   The Mets score five runs in the ninth inning to beat the Cardinals 5–3 in the first
            game of a double-header in St. Louis. Bruce Sutter loaded the bases before Ellis
            Valentine drove in two runs with a single. George Foster tied the score with another
            single. Jim Kaat relieved Sutter and gave up a two-out, two-run single to Wally
            Backman, which broke the deadlock. The Cards won the second tilt 4–3.

JUNE 19   George Foster collects five hits, including a homer and a double, in five at-bats during
            an 8–5 victory over the Cardinals in St. Louis.

            *The Mets had a 34–30 record on June 20 and were in third place, three games
            out of first. The club was 31–67 the rest of the way, however.*

JUNE 21   Craig Swan gets into a shoving match with six-foot-eight-inch third base coach Frank
            Howard. The incident occurred after Swan complained loudly about the club's travel
            arrangements on a trip from St. Louis to New York.

JULY 24   The Mets strike with two runs in the ninth inning to defeat the Padres 4–3 in San
            Diego. Rusty Staub tied the score with a pinch-double. Bob Bailor broke the 3–3
            deadlock with an RBI-single.

AUGUST 3   The Mets complete a triple play in the eighth inning of a 5–0 loss to the Cubs in
                Chicago. With runners on first and second and Larry Bowa at bat, shortstop Bob
                Bailor made a running catch with his back to the plate. Both runners believed the
                ball would drop for a hit and were far off their respective bases when Bailor snared
                the ball. Bailor threw to second baseman Wally Backman for the force at second.
                Backman in turn fired to first baseman Dave Kingman for the third out. Bailor started
                the game as a second baseman but moved to short in the fourth inning following an
                injury to Ron Gardenhire. It was the first triple play for the Mets since 1966.

AUGUST 4   Joel Youngblood plays for two teams in one day. He was the starting center fielder
                for the Mets against the Cubs in Chicago and singled in two runs off Ferguson
                Jenkins in the third inning. In the fourth, Youngblood was pulled from the game and
                informed he had been traded to the Expos for a player to be named later. The Mets
                went on to win 7–4. Youngblood flew to Philadelphia where the Expos were playing
                the Phillies that evening. He made it to Veterans Stadium in time to enter the contest
                as a right fielder in the sixth inning. Youngblood contributed a single against Steve
                Carlton, but Montreal lost 5–4.

                *The only other players to play for two teams in one day are Max Flack and
                Cliff Heathcote on May 30, 1922. In between games of a double-header in
                Chicago, Flack went from the Cubs to the Cardinals in exchange for Heathcote.
                Youngblood is the only individual to play for two teams in two different cities in
                a single day. He is also the only one to collect a hit for two different teams in a
                day, and he accomplished the feat off two future Hall of Famers.*

AUGUST 13   Wally Backman breaks his left clavicle after falling off a bicycle while riding with
                his wife, Margie, near their home in the Fresh Meadows neighborhood in Queens.
                Backman didn't play again for the rest of the season.

AUGUST 20   After Brian Giles homers in the top of the tenth, the Braves rally for two runs in the
                bottom half to beat the Mets 2–1 in Atlanta. The home run was the first by Giles in
                the major leagues. It was the Mets' third straight extra-inning loss. The club fell to
                the Reds 7–6 in 14 innings on August 18 and 3–1 in ten innings on August 19, both
                in Cincinnati.

AUGUST 31   The Mets extend their losing streak to 15 games by dropping a 2–0 decision to the
                Astros at Shea Stadium.

SEPTEMBER 1   The Mets break their 15-game losing streak by downing the Astros 5–1 at Shea
                Stadium.

SEPTEMBER 5   The Mets score seven runs in the second inning and beat the Reds 10–2 at Shea
                Stadium. The seven runs were accomplished on only three hits. Ellis Valentine
                capped the outburst with a three-run homer.

SEPTEMBER 8   Ron Hodges hits a grand slam off Grant Jackson in the ninth inning of a 9–1 win
                over the Pirates in Pittsburgh.

SEPTEMBER 21   Ron Gardenhire hits a walk-off homer in the tenth inning to defeat the Expos 2–1 at
                Shea Stadium.

SEPTEMBER 29   The Mets pull off a triple play in the third inning of a 4–1 loss to the Cubs at Shea Stadium. With runners on first and second, Keith Moreland lined to second baseman Brian Giles, who stepped on second for the force and threw to first baseman Rusty Staub for the third out. It was the club's second triple play of the season, and both came in losses against the Cubs (see August 3, 1982).

OCTOBER 1   The Mets beat the Phillies 1–0 at Veterans Stadium in a ten-inning affair that features only three hits. In one of the best pitching performances in franchise history, Terry Leach pitched a complete game for the Mets and allowed only a fifth-inning triple to Luis Aguayo. Philadelphia's John Denny allowed New York only one hit through the first nine innings, a single in the second by Dave Kingman. Denny was relieved by Porfi Altamirano in the tenth. Altamirano gave up a walk to Dave Kingman, a single to Gary Rajsich and a sacrifice fly by Hubie Brooks to break the 0–0 tie.

                Rick Ownbey was the scheduled starting pitcher but was scratched because of a blister on his finger. When Leach stepped to the mound, he had made only one previous major league start and 40 relief appearances. The only other start was on August 15, 1981. After spending all of 1983 and 1984 in the minors, Leach didn't pitch again in the big leagues until June 21, 1985. He would eventually settle in as a capable reliever and posted an 11–1 record for the Mets in 1987 and was 7–2 in 1988. Leach lasted in the majors until 1993. In 2000, he published an autobiography titled Things Happen for a Reason: The True Story of an Itinerant Life in Baseball *with Bob Clark.*

DECEMBER 10   The Mets trade Mike Scott to the Astros for Danny Heep.

                The Scott trade is one of the worst in franchise history. Scott was 27 at the time of the trade and had a 14–27 lifetime record and a 4.64 ERA. He struggled for two more seasons in Houston before suddenly blossoming into an All-Star. From 1985 through 1989, Scott was 86–49 for the Astros. Heep batted .263 with 21 homers in 399 games as an outfielder over four seasons in a Mets uniform.

DECEMBER 16   The Mets trade Charlie Puleo, Lloyd McClendon and Jason Felice to the Reds for Tom Seaver.

                Tom Terrific was back after a 5½-year absence (see June 15, 1977). The Reds soured on him after a 5–13 season in 1982. Seaver was 9–14 with the Mets in 1983 before moving to the White Sox (see January 20, 1984).

DECEMBER 20   Pete Falcone signs with the Braves as a free agent.

DECEMBER 28   The Mets trade Pat Zachry to the Dodgers for Jorge Orta.

1983

Season in a Sentence

The Mets hire Davey Johnson as manager after finishing another disappointing season with 94 defeats, the most in the National League.

Finish • Won • Lost • Pct • GB

Sixth   68   94   .420   22.0

Managers

George Bamburger (16–30) and Frank Howard (52–64)

Stats

Stats	Mets	AL	Rank
Batting Avg:	.241	.255	11
On-Base Pct:	.300	.322	12
Slugging Pct:	.344	.376	12
Home Runs:	112	7	
Stolen Bases:	141	8	
ERA:	3.68	3.63	8
Errors:	151	8	
Runs Scored:	575	12	
Runs Allowed:	680	8	

Starting Lineup

Ron Hodges, c
Keith Hernandez, 1b
Brian Giles, 2b
Hubie Brooks, 3b
Jose Oquendo, ss
George Foster, lf
Mookie Wilson, cf
Darryl Strawberry, rf
Bob Bailor, ss-2b
Danny Heep, rf
Dave Kingman, 1b

Pitchers

Tom Seaver, sp
Mike Torrez, sp
Ed Lynch, sp
Walt Terrell, sp
Craig Swan, sp
Jesse Orosco, rp
Doug Sisk, rp
Scott Holman, rp
Carlos Diaz, rp

Attendance

1,112,774 (12th in NL)

Club Leaders

Batting Avg:	Mookie Wilson	.271
On-Base Pct:	Darryl Strawberry	.336
Slugging Pct:	Darryl Strawberry	.512
Home Runs:	George Foster	28
RBI:	George Foster	90
Runs:	Mookie Wilson	91
Stolen Bases:	Mookie Wilson	54
Wins:	Mike Torrez	10
	Ed Lynch	10
Strikeouts:	Tom Seaver	135
ERA:	Tom Seaver	3.55
Saves:	Jesse Orosco	17

JANUARY 13   The Mets trade Mike Davis to the Red Sox for Mike Torrez.

JANUARY 21   Ellis Valentine signs with the Angels as a free agent.

FEBRUARY 4   The Mets trade Jorge Orta to the Blue Jays for Steve Senteney.

APRIL 5   The Mets open the season with a 2–0 win over the Phillies before 46,687 at Shea Stadium. Tom Seaver made his first appearance with the Mets since 1977 and pitched six shutout innings. Doug Sisk went the final three innings and picked up the victory. The Mets scored both runs in the seventh off Steve Carlton. Right fielder Mike Howard drove in the first tally with a single.

> *Seaver was making the 14th Opening Day start of his career, tying the major league record for pitchers set by Walter Johnson of the Senators. Johnson made his starts in 14 of 17 seasons between 1910 and 1926. Seaver drew the Opening Day assignment ten years in row with the Mets from 1968 through 1977 and started for the Reds in 1978, 1979 and 1981. He would break Johnson's record by starting on Opening Day for the White Sox in 1985 and 1986. At the other end of the spectrum, the Opening Day start for Mike Howard proved to be the last game*

of his major league career, as he was sent to the minors and never returned. The plate appearance in which he drove in the game-winning run was also his last in a big-league game. Overall, he played in 48 games in the majors, all with the Mets, and accumulated 88 plate appearances from 1981 through 1983.

APRIL 13   The Mets give up five runs in the ninth inning and lose 10–9 to the Phillies at Veterans Stadium. With two out in the ninth, Rick Ownbey walked Len Matuszek to load the bases. Jesse Orosco came on in relief and issued a walk to Bill Robinson to force in a run and make the score 9–6. Neil Allen followed Orosco and surrendered a grand slam to Bo Diaz to end the game.

Bud Harrelson, Steve Zabriskie and Tim McCarver joined the Mets television announcing team on SportsChannel and WOR-TV in 1983. Harrelson lasted only a year before becoming a coach with the team. Zabriskie remained until 1989 and McCarver until 1998.

APRIL 22   Scott Holman, Doug Sisk and Neil Allen combine to walk 12 batters without a strikeout during a 5–4 loss to the Braves in Atlanta.

MAY 7   The Mets use dramatic home runs to take a thrilling 12-inning, 7–4 decision from the Reds at Shea Stadium. With two out in the ninth inning, Dave Kingman belted a two-run homer to tie the score 3–3. After Cincinnati scored in the top of the tenth, Hubie Brooks hit a solo homer with two out in the bottom half to deadlock the contest at 4–4. After the first two batters off the 12th were retired, Darryl Strawberry (in his major league debut) and Mike Jorgensen walked before George Foster walloped a three-run, walk-off homer.

Only 21 in 1983, Strawberry struggled early and hit only .161 in his first 87 at-bats. But by the end of the year, he earned the Rookie-of-the-Year award with a .257 batting average, 26 homers and 74 RBI.

MAY 9   After the Reds score five runs in the top of the first inning, the Mets rally to win 10–5 at Shea Stadium.

JUNE 3   With the club holding a record of 16–30, George Bamberger resigns as manager.

In his statement to the media, Bamberger said "the nature of managing is to suffer, and I probably suffered enough." Third base coach Frank Howard was named as interim manager to replace Bamberger. After failing to lure Earl Weaver out of retirement, General Manager Frank Cashen gave Howard the post for the remainder of the season. As a player from 1958 through 1973, the six-foot-eight–inch Howard was a feared power hitter while playing for the Dodgers, Senators and Rangers. He hit 382 lifetime homers and twice led the AL in the category. Howard had been a coach with the Mets since 1982 after previously serving under Bamberger as a coach with the Brewers. Howard was replaced as manager by Davey Johnson at the end of the 1983 campaign. Howard coached under Johnson in 1984 before moving back to the Brewers. He later returned to the Mets as a coach from 1994 through 1996. Bamberger managed the Milwaukee club again in 1985 and 1986 and had a record of 142–171.

June 6   With the fourth overall pick in the amateur draft, the Mets select third baseman Eddie Williams from Hoover High School in San Diego, California.

Williams attended the same high school as Ted Williams, but all similarities ended there. Williams was traded by the Mets before reaching the majors, which he did with the Indians in 1986. He played for six more clubs through 1998 and appeared in 395 games with a batting average of .252 and 39 homers. Stan Jefferson and Calvin Schiraldi were also drafted in the first round as compensation picks for the loss of Pete Falcone to free agency. Other future major leaguers drafted and signed by the Mets in 1983 were Dave Magadan (second round), Rick Aguilera (third round), David West (fourth round), Marcus Lawton (sixth round), Jeff Innis (13th round) and Joe Klink (36th round). The Mets also drafted Matt Williams in the 27th round, but Williams chose to attend the University of Nevada at Las Vegas instead of turning pro. He was drafted in the first round by the Giants in 1987.

June 9   Bob Bailor hits a two-run double in the 11th inning to defeat the Cubs 6–4 in Chicago.

June 10   The Mets win in extra innings for the second day in a row when Dave Kingman belts a two-run, walk-off homer in the 17th inning to down the Expos 4–2 at Shea Stadium. Neil Allen (three innings) and Rick Ownbey (four innings) pitched shutout relief. Five days later, both would be packaged in a deal to the Cardinals for Keith Hernandez.

June 14   Rusty Staub hits a walk-off, pinch-hit single in the tenth inning to beat the Cubs 4–3 at Shea Stadium.

Staub tied a major league record with eight consecutive pinch-hits from June 11 through June 26. Overall, Staub had 24 hits and 25 RBI in a pinch-hit role in 1983.

June 15   The Mets trade Neil Allen and Rick Ownbey to the Cardinals for Keith Hernandez and sell Mike Jorgensen to the Braves.

The Mets pulled off a brilliant deal in acquiring Hernandez, who was the club's starting first baseman until 1988. He was an immediate fan favorite, as hit he hit .443 in his first 61 at-bats with the club. While in New York, Hernandez won six Gold Gloves, appeared in three All-Star Games and was in the top ten in the MVP balloting three times. He had been a two-time All-Star in St. Louis and was the Most Valuable Player in the National League in 1979. As durable as they come, Hernandez missed only ten games from 1977 through 1982. But Hernandez had a strained relationship with Cards manager Whitey Herzog over Keith's involvement with drugs, particularly cocaine. Also, Herzog loved players who scrapped and rolled in the dirt, and Hernandez was never that type of individual. While with the Mets, Hernandez kicked his drug habit and became a leader in the clubhouse. On the all-time Mets career lists, Hernandez ranks third in batting average (.297) and fourth in on-base percentage (.387). Allen and Ownbey were never more than mediocre pitchers at best, both before and after the trade. Allen was 58–70 during his major league career, and Ownbey had a dismal record of 3–11.

JUNE 28	Hubie Brooks collects five hits, including a double, in six at-bats during a 10–1 thrashing of the Cardinals in St. Louis. Darryl Strawberry contributed two homers and five RBI.
JULY 21	Mike Torrez walks ten batters in just 3⅓ innings of a 6–1 loss to the Reds in Cincinnati.
JULY 22	Keith Hernandez and Darryl Strawberry hit home runs in the ninth inning to defeat the Reds 3–2 in Cincinnati.
JULY 25	The Mets erupt with four runs with two out in the ninth inning to down the Braves 5–4 at Shea Stadium. With two away, runners on first and second and the Mets trailing 4–1, Hubie Brooks singled in a run off Steve Bedrosian. Keith Hernandez followed with another run-scoring single to pull the Mets within a run. George Foster ended the contest with a two-run, walk-off double.
JULY 26	Mookie Wilson hits a walk-off homer to beat the Braves 2–1 at Shea Stadium.
JULY 31	Jesse Orosco is the winning pitcher in both ends of a double-header as the Mets take a pair of 12-inning decisions from the Pirates at Shea Stadium. In the opener, New York trailed 6–1 before scoring a run in the seventh inning, four in the eighth and one in the 12th. Bob Bailor drove in the winning run with a single. Orosco pitched the final four innings. In the second tilt, the Mets collected only three hits, but won 1–0. Pittsburgh's Jose DeLeon carried a no-hitter into the ninth before Hubie Brooks singled with one out. In the 12th, Mookie Wilson singled and moved to second on a sacrifice. Keith Hernandez drew an intentional walk. George Foster grounded to shortstop Dale Berra, who flipped to second baseman Johnny Ray for the force of Hernandez. Wilson kept running and scored all the way from second on the play, just beating Berra's throw to the plate. Mike Torrez (11 innings) and Orosco (one inning) combined on the shutout.

Orosco was 13–7 with 17 saves, and a 1.47 ERA in 62 games and 110 innings in 1983. From July 22 through August 27, he threw 27⅔ consecutive scoreless innings.

AUGUST 6	Mets pitcher Walt Terrell drives in all four runs of a 4–1 win over the Cubs with a pair of two-run homers. Terrell homered off Ferguson Jenkins in the third and fourth innings.

Terrell is the only pitcher in Mets history to hit two homers in a game. He pitched most of his career in the American League and didn't bat because of the designated hitter. Terrell finished his stay in the majors with three home runs, all of them in 1983, over 192 at-bats. The pair of homers on August 5 were the first two of the trio. The other one was hit on August 23.

AUGUST 7	Hubie Brooks hits a two-run homer in the tenth inning to defeat the Cubs 6–4 in Chicago.
AUGUST 8	The Mets win in extra innings for the second day in a row with a 6–5, ten-inning decision over the Expos in Montreal.

| AUGUST 14 | George Foster hits a grand slam off Chuck Rainey in the third inning of a 5–2 win over the Cubs at Shea Stadium. |

AUGUST 14   George Foster hits a grand slam off Chuck Rainey in the third inning of a 5–2 win over the Cubs at Shea Stadium.

AUGUST 19   Down 6–3, the Mets score a run in the eighth inning, two in the ninth and one in the tenth to beat the Giants 7–6 in San Francisco. George Foster ripped a two-run homer in the ninth to tie the score. A double by Ron Hodges drove home the game winner.

AUGUST 20   The Mets score all seven of their runs in a 7–2 win over the Giants in San Francisco during a fifth-inning outburst. George Foster clubbed a grand slam off Mark Calvert. It was Foster's second grand slam in seven days.

SEPTEMBER 3   The Mets need 15 innings to beat the Padres 4–3 at Shea Stadium. The winning run crossed the plate on a sacrifice fly by Brian Giles.

SEPTEMBER 5   George Foster smacks a three-run, walk-off homer with one out in the ninth inning to defeat the Phillies 6–5 at Shea Stadium.

SEPTEMBER 13   Mets catcher Mike Fitzgerald hits a home run in his first major league plate appearance to spark a 5–1 win over the Phillies in Philadelphia. The blow was struck off Tony Ghelfi, who was making the last of his three big-league appearances.

Fitzgerald spent the first two years of his ten seasons in the majors with the Mets and hit three home runs in 380 at-bats. He had 48 homers in 2,316 at-bats during his career.

SEPTEMBER 17   Mookie Wilson collects two triples, a double and a single in five at-bats, but the Mets blow a 6–1 lead and lose 7–6 to the Cubs at Shea Stadium.

SEPTEMBER 19   The Mets rally with two runs in the ninth inning and one in the tenth to defeat the Pirates 5–4 at Shea Stadium. Ron Hodges drove in the tying run in the ninth with a two-out double. In the tenth, Mookie Wilson singled, stole second and crossed the plate on a walk-off single by Hubie Brooks.

OCTOBER 1   A first-inning homer by Danny Heep off Charlie Lea holds up for a 1–0 win over the Expos at Shea Stadium. Walt Terrell pitched the complete game shutout.

OCTOBER 2   On the last day of the season, the Mets score two runs in the ninth inning to beat the Expos 5–4 at Shea Stadium. Rusty Staub stepped to the plate as a pinch-hitter with two out in the ninth, two men on base and the Mets trailing 4–3. Staub stroked a two-run double to win the game.

OCTOBER 13   The Mets name 40-year-old Davey Johnson as manager.

Johnson succeeded Frank Howard, who finished the 1983 season as interim manager. Johnson was a player in the majors from 1965 through 1978 and was the starting second baseman for the Orioles in the World Series in 1966, 1969, 1970 and 1971. He managed three seasons in the minors from 1981 through 1983, the last of which was with the Mets Class AAA farm team at Tidewater. Johnson took over a Mets club that hadn't lost fewer than 90 games in a non-strike season since 1976. The Mets from 1977 through 1983 were the first franchise in over 25 years to post seven consecutive seasons with a winning percentage of .420 or worse. The last team to do so was the St. Louis Browns from 1947 through 1953. (It hasn't happened since 1983.) The fans were apathetic from listening to years of empty promises of improvement from club management, and the Mets finished last in the National League in attendance in 1983. Johnson had an immediate impact by guiding the club to a 90–72 record in 1984, 98 wins in 1985, and 108 regular season victories and a world championship in 1986. Before being fired in May 1990, he had a record of 595–417, a winning percentage of .588, as skipper of the Mets.

DECEMBER 8   The Mets trade Bob Bailor and Carlos Diaz to the Dodgers for Sid Fernandez and Ross Jones.

The Mets acquired Fernandez in another tremendous deal. He pitched ten seasons with the club and had a record of 98–78. On the all-time franchise lists, he ranks fifth in wins, fifth in innings pitched (1,584²/₃), fourth in strikeouts (1,449) and fourth in games started (250).

DECEMBER 10   The Jets play at Shea Stadium for the last time and lose 34–7 to the Pittsburgh Steelers. The Jets moved to Giants Stadium in 1984.

1984

Season in a Sentence

With an infusion of young pitching led by Dwight Gooden along with the managing of Davey Johnson, the long-dormant franchise exceeds all expectations with a 90-win season.

Finish • Won • Lost • Pct • GB

Second   90   72   .556   6.5

Manager

Davey Johnson

Stats

Stats	Mets	AL	Rank
Batting Avg:	.257	.255	6
On-Base Pct:	.320	.319	5
Slugging Pct:	.369	.369	6
Home Runs:	107	6	
Stolen Bases:	149	6	
ERA:	3.60	3.59	8
Errors:	129	4	
Runs Scored:	652	6	
Runs Allowed:	676	9	

Starting Lineup

Mike Fitzgerald, c
Keith Hernandez, 1b
Wally Backman, 2b
Hubie Brooks, 3b
Jose Oquendo, ss
George Foster, lf
Mookie Wilson, cf
Darryl Strawberry, rf
Danny Heep, lf-rf
Kelvin Chapman, 2b

Pitchers

Dwight Gooden, sp
Walt Terrell, sp
Ron Darling, sp
Bruce Berenyi, sp
Sid Fernandez, sp
Jesse Orosco, rp
Doug Sisk, rp
Ed Lynch, rp-sp
Brent Gaff, rp

Attendance

1,842,695 (sixth in NL)

Club Leaders

Batting Avg:	Keith Hernandez	.311
On-Base Pct:	Keith Hernandez	.409
Slugging Pct:	Darryl Strawberry	.467
Home Runs:	Darryl Strawberry	26
RBI:	Darryl Strawberry	97
Runs:	Mookie Wilson	88
Stolen Bases:	Mookie Wilson	46
Wins:	Dwight Gooden	17
Strikeouts:	Dwight Gooden	276
ERA:	Dwight Gooden	2.60
Saves:	Jesse Orosco	31

JANUARY 17   In the winter amateur draft, the Mets select future major leaguers Kevin Elster (second round), Scott Little (seventh round) and Brian Givens (tenth round).

JANUARY 20   The Mets lose Tom Seaver in the free agent compensation draft.

At the time, rules called for teams that lost a Class A free agent to select a player from a list submitted by the other 25 big-league clubs. Each team was allowed to protect 26 players. The Mets wanted to protect as many of their young pitching prospects as possible and failed to protect Seaver, believing that no one would draft a 40-year-old pitcher who had a 14–27 record the previous two seasons. The White Sox were allowed to select a player because of the loss of Dennis Lamp to the Blue Jays and stunned the Mets by jumping at the chance to choose Seaver. Commissioner Bowie Kuhn even stepped in and tried to persuade the Sox from selecting Seaver because of what Kuhn believed would have a negative impact on baseball in general and the Mets franchise in particular. Seaver was livid that the Mets failed to place him on their protected list, as he hoped to end his storied career in New York where it began. Mets fans were likewise outraged. Seaver considered retiring before the White Sox re-negotiated his contract.

He gave the Sox two solid seasons. In 1984 and 1985 combined, Seaver was 31–22 and his ERA was 3.56. Seaver also won his 300th career game in a White Sox uniform. The 1986 season, which was spent with both the White Sox and the Red Sox, would be Seaver's last in the majors.

JANUARY 27 The Mets sign Dick Tidrow, most recently with the White Sox, as a free agent.

APRIL 2 The Mets open the season with an 8–1 loss to the Reds in Cincinnati. Mike Torrez drew the assignment as the starting pitcher and gave up six runs in only 1⅓ innings.

The loss was the first by the Mets on Opening Day since 1974. The club wouldn't lose in the season opener again until 1990.

APRIL 6 George Foster collects a homer, two doubles and a single and drives in four runs during an 8–1 victory over the Astros in Houston.

A mathematics major in college, Davey Johnson was among the first managers to use computers to spot trends and exploit match-ups.

APRIL 7 Dwight Gooden makes his major league debut and earns a victory after pitching five innings of a 3–2 win over the Astros in Houston.

At 19, Gooden was the second-youngest player in the majors in 1984. The previous season, he had a 19–4 record with 300 strikeouts in 191 innings at Class A Lynchburg. By the end of the 1984 campaign, Gooden had pitched in the All-Star Game and won the Rookie-of-Year Award by drawing 23 of the 24 first-place votes on the strength of a 17–9 record, a 2.60 ERA and a league-leading 276 strikeouts in 218 innings. The strikeouts set a major league record for rookies, which still stands. The previous mark was 245 by Herb Score of the Cleveland Indians in 1955. The performance in which Gooden struck out 11.4 batters per nine innings earned him the nickname "Dr. K." The 11.4 strikeouts per nine innings also broke the previous record of 10.7 by Sam McDowell with the Indians in 1965. (Gooden's record stood until Nolan Ryan recorded 11.5 strikeouts per nine innings with the Astros in 1987.) It would be the only season of Gooden's career, however, in which he would strike out more than a batter an inning.

APRIL 17 In the home opener, the Mets lose 10–0 to the Expos before 46,636 at Shea Stadium.

Fran Healy became a part of the Mets TV announcing crew in 1984, a job he held until 2005.

APRIL 18 The Mets score two runs in the ninth inning to defeat the Expos 5–4 at Shea Stadium. With two out in the ninth, the Mets trailed 4–3 and had a runner on second base. After John Gibbons and pinch-hitter Ron Hodges walked to load the bases, Wally Backman brought two home with a walk-off double.

APRIL 28 Shortstop Ross Jones hits a walk-off double in the ninth inning to beat the Phillies 4–3 at Shea Stadium. Jones entered the game as part of a double switch in the eighth. The RBI proved to be his only one in 13 plate appearances with the Mets.

Shortstop was a weak spot for the Mets throughout much of the 1980s. In 1984, Jose Oquendo led the club in games started at the position with 55.

APRIL 29   Prior to a 6–2 win over the Phillies at Shea Stadium, Darryl Strawberry is presented the 1983 Rookie-of-the-Year Award. In honor of the occasion, each fan at Shea was given a free strawberry sundae, provided by Carvel. The Mets ordered 2,187 gallons of ice cream and 2,275 pounds of strawberries. The losing pitcher was Jerry Koosman, who was making his first appearance at Shea since 1978.

MAY 1   The Mets score seven runs in the fifth inning of an 8–1 triumph over the Cubs at Shea Stadium.

MAY 15   After trailing 5–0 in the fourth inning, the Mets rally to win 7–6 in 11 innings against the Giants in San Francisco. Keith Hernandez drove in the winning run with a sacrifice fly.

            Hernandez batted .311 with 15 homers in 1984.

MAY 25   Dwight Gooden strikes out 14 batters in eight innings of a 2–1 victory over the Dodgers at Shea Stadium.

JUNE 2   The 24-game hitting streak of Hubie Brooks comes to end during a 5–2 win over the Cardinals at Shea Stadium.

            During the streak, Brooks collected 33 hits and batted .398.

JUNE 4   With the number-one overall pick in the amateur draft, the Mets select outfielder Shawn Abner from Mechanicsburg High School in Mechanicsburg, Pennsylvania.

            The Mets sent Abner to the Padres in December 1986 in a deal that brought Kevin McReynolds to New York. Abner never came close to his billing as the number-one draft choice. He played in 392 major league games over six seasons beginning in 1987 and hit just .227 with 11 home runs in 840 at-bats.

JUNE 6   Dwight Gooden (nine innings), Doug Sisk (two innings) and Ton Gorman (two innings) combine to allow only four hits during a 13-inning, 2–1 win over the Pirates in Pittsburgh. Gooden had a no-hitter in progress until Doug Frobel led off the eighth inning with a single. Wally Backman scored the winning run on a wild pitch.

            The Mets were 11–1 in extra-inning games in 1984.

JUNE 13   Ed Lynch (six innings) and Doug Sisk (three innings) combine on a three-hitter to beat the Pirates 2–0 at Shea Stadium.

JUNE 14   The Mets score all six runs of a 6–0 win over the Cardinals in St. Louis in the sixth inning. Ron Darling pitched the shutout.

JUNE 15   On the combined effort of Walt Terrell (seven innings) and Jesse Orosco (two innings), the Mets record their third consecutive shutout by beating the Cardinals 5–0 in St. Louis.

JULY 1

George Foster records the 300th home run of his career during a 3–2 win over the Braves in the first game of a double-header at Shea Stadium. The milestone was struck in the fourth inning off ex-Met Pete Falcone. The Mets also won the opener 2–1.

Foster went 64 at-bats between his 299th home run on June 9 and number 300.

JULY 2

Dwight Gooden fans 12 batters in 8⅓ innings of a 4–2 victory over the Astros in Houston.

JULY 6

The Mets sweep the Reds 1–0 and 6–5 during a double-header at Shea Stadium. In the opener, Ron Darling pitched the shutout. Hubie Brooks provided the offense with a home run off Jeff Russell in the sixth inning. In the second tilt, Kelvin Chapman drove in the winning run with a walk-off single in the ninth.

JULY 7

The Mets score seven runs in the fourth inning and clobber the Reds 14–4 at Shea Stadium. Darryl Strawberry homered and singled during the seven-run rally. The victory lifted the Mets into first place.

JULY 10

At 19, Dwight Gooden becomes the youngest player ever to appear in an All-Star Game. At Candlestick Park in San Francisco, Gooden came into the contest in the fifth inning and fanned the first three batters he faced by setting down Lance Parrish, Chet Lemon and Alvin Davis. Fernando Valenzuela had struck out all three batters of the fourth, giving the National League six consecutive strikeouts. Gooden also pitched the sixth and didn't allow a run. The NL won 3–1.

JULY 12

The Mets score five runs in the ninth inning to defeat the Braves 8–6 in Atlanta. Keith Hernandez drove in the first two runs of the ninth with a single, and George Foster tied the score with another run-scoring single. With two out, Mike Fitzgerald broke the deadlock with a two-run double.

JULY 14

Bruce Berenyi (seven innings) and Tom Gorman (two innings) combine on a two-hitter to defeat the Braves 7–0 in Atlanta. The only hits by the Braves were singles by Chris Chambliss in the second inning and Claudell Washington in the sixth. The victory was the eighth in a row for the Mets.

JULY 16

The Mets collect 22 hits and thrash the Astros 13–3 in Houston.

JULY 23

A walk-off single by Wally Backman in the 12th inning beats the Cardinals 4–3 at Shea Stadium.

JULY 24

The Mets win with a walk-off single in extra innings for the second day in a row when Keith Hernandez delivers in the tenth to lift the club to a 9–8 victory over the Cardinals at Shea Stadium.

JULY 27

The Mets take a 4½-game lead in the NL East by beating the Cubs 4–1 at Shea Stadium.

The Mets had a record of 59–37 on July 27, but the lead in the pennant race didn't last long. The Mets began a losing streak the following day, which dropped the team behind the first-place Cubs. On August 6, the Mets traveled to Chicago for a four-game series against the Cubs, who were only one-half game *out of first. The Mets lost all four games during a contentious series in which the team exchanged beanballs. During the second game of a double-header on August 7, Keith Moreland of the Cubs rushed the mound and roll-blocked pitcher Ed Lynch, instigating a bench-clearing brawl. After pulling as close as 1^1/$_2$ games of the Cubs on August 17, the Mets couldn't battle their way back into the top spot in the NL East and finished second, 6^1/$_2$ games back of the Cubs. That the race developed into a two-team affair between the Mets and Cubs was a shocker. In 1983, the Cubs finished fifth in the six-team division and hadn't finished above .500 since 1972. The Mets were sixth in 1983, and the franchise hadn't enjoyed a winning season since 1976. The two teams had occupied the bottom two spots in the division every season from 1979 through 1983, and heading into 1984, there was little reason to expect that the same result wouldn't occur once more.*

AUGUST 17   Wally Backman hits a two-run homer off Mike Krukow in the tenth inning for the only two runs of a 2–0 victory over the Giants in San Francisco. Dwight Gooden (nine innings) and Jesse Orosco (one inning) combined on the shutout. Gooden struck out 12.

AUGUST 26   Kelvin Chapman hits a grand slam off Mark Davis in the sixth inning of an 11–6 win over the Giants at Shea Stadium.

AUGUST 27   Dwight Gooden strikes out 12 batters during a 5–1 win over the Dodgers at Shea Stadium.

AUGUST 29   Ron Darling strikes out 12 batters in seven innings of a 3–2 win over the Dodgers at Shea Stadium. Keith Hernandez drove in the winning run with a walk-off double in the ninth inning.

AUGUST 31   The Mets trade Gerald Young, Manuel Lee and Mitch Cook to the Astros for Ray Knight.

SEPTEMBER 7   Dwight Gooden pitches a one-hitter and strikes out 11 batters to beat the Cubs 10–0 at Shea Stadium. The only Chicago hit was an infield single by Keith Moreland on a slow roller up the third-base line in the fifth inning, which Ray Knight fielded but couldn't get out of his glove.

SEPTEMBER 12   Dwight Gooden strikes out 16 batters and beats the Pirates 2–0 with a five-hitter at Shea Stadium. Hubie Brooks drove in both runs with a homer off John Tudor in the fourth inning.

SEPTEMBER 17   Dwight Gooden strikes out 16 batters for the second game in a row, but loses 2–1 to the Phillies in Philadelphia. Gooden gave up the winning run on a balk in the eighth inning.

SEPTEMBER 25   The Mets score four runs in the ninth inning to beat the Phillies 6–4 at Shea Stadium. The Mets hit for the "cycle" during the ninth-inning rally with a double by Hubie Brooks, a pinch-hit triple from Mookie Wilson, a single by Ron Hodges and Rusty Staub's pinch-hit, walk-off, two-run homer.

Staub is one of only three players in major league history with a home run as a teenager and another after he turned 40. The other two are Ty Cobb and Gary Sheffield.

DECEMBER 7   A month after Ronald Reagan defeats Walter Mondale in the Presidential election, the Mets trade Walt Terrell to the Tigers for Howard Johnson.

Terrell was 47–32 for the Tigers from 1985 through 1987 and lasted in the majors until 1992, but the Mets came out way ahead in this transaction. Johnson's career started slowly. At the end of the 1986 seasons, he had spent five seasons in the majors, the last two with the Mets, and had a batting average of .252 with 40 home runs in 1,185 at-bats. Johnson was given the job as the Mets starting third baseman in 1987 and responded with 36 home runs. He made the All-Star team and ranked fifth in the MVP voting in both 1989 and 1991 and had three seasons of at least 30 homers and 30 stolen bases before injuries caused a premature decline. Among Mets players, Johnson ranks fifth all-time in games played (1,114), fifth in at-bats (3,968), second in runs (627), third in doubles (214), third in home runs (192), third in RBI (629), third in walks (556), third in stolen bases (202) and fourth in total bases (1,823).

DECEMBER 10   The Mets trade Hubie Brooks, Mike Fitzgerald, Herm Winningham and Floyd Youmans to the Expos for Gary Carter.

At the time he was acquired, Carter was 30 years old and had already played in eight All-Star Games. In 1984, he led the NL in RBI with 106. During the late 1970s and early 1980s, Carter was the best player on Montreal teams, which were almost always in contention but never reached the World Series. Many accused him of dividing the clubhouse by courting media attention for himself. Carter continued his high level of play in New York. He drove in 100 or more runs in both 1985 and 1986 and made four more All-Star teams in a Mets uniform. The trade for Carter was well worth the loss of four players, although Brooks had some excellent seasons in Montreal.

1985

Season in a Sentence

Behind a 24–4 season from Dwight Gooden and the addition of Gary Carter, the Mets win 98 games but fail to make the postseason by finishing three games behind the Cardinals.

Finish • Won • Lost • Pct • GB

Second   98   64   .605   3.0

Manager

Davey Johnson

Stats

Stats	Mets	AL	Rank
Batting Avg:	.257	.252	4
On-Base Pct:	.323	.319	5
Slugging Pct:	.385	.374	3
Home Runs:	134	3	
Stolen Bases:	117	7	
ERA:	3.11	3.59	3
Errors:	115	2	
Runs Scored:	695	3	
Runs Allowed:	568		1

Starting Lineup

Gary Carter, c
Keith Hernandez, 1b
Wally Backman, 2b
Howard Johnson, 3b
Rafael Santana, ss
George Foster, lf
Mookie Wilson, cf
Darryl Strawberry, rf
Danny Heep, lf-rf
Ray Knight, 3b
Lenny Dykstra, cf

Pitchers

Dwight Gooden, sp
Ron Darling, sp
Ed Lynch, sp
Sid Fernandez, sp
Rick Aguilera, sp
Roger McDowell, rp
Jesse Orosco, rp
Doug Sisk, rp

Attendance

2,761,601 (second in NL)

Club Leaders

Batting Avg:	Keith Hernandez	.309
On-Base Pct:	Darryl Strawberry	.389
Slugging Pct:	Darryl Strawberry	.557
Home Runs:	Gary Carter	32
RBI:	Gary Carter	100
Runs:	Keith Hernandez	87
Stolen Bases:	Wally Backman	30
Wins:	Dwight Gooden	24
Strikeouts:	Dwight Gooden	268
ERA:	Dwight Gooden	1 53
Saves:	Roger McDowell	17
	Jesse Orosco	17

JANUARY 18   As part of a three-team trade, the Mets deal Tim Leary to the Brewers and receive Frank Wills from the Royals.

MARCH 28   The April 1, 1985 issue of *Sports Illustrated* hits the newsstand, and with the help of the Mets, the publication plays an April Fool's joke on the public. An article by George Plympton reported that pitcher Sidd Finch was the sensation of the Mets training camp and could throw a fastball at 168 miles per hour, but couldn't decide whether or not to pursue a career in baseball or one playing the French horn. He also wore only one shoe—a heavy hiker's boot—while pitching. The Mets went along with the gag and "Finch" was shown in photographs with Lenny Dykstra and pitching coach Mel Stottlemyre. Joe Benton, a junior high school teacher from Oak Park, Illinois, posed as Finch in a Mets uniform provided by the club. Despite the obvious absurdity of the article, many believed that Finch was real. The April 8 issue of the magazine announced Finch's "retirement." In the April 15 issue, *Sports Illustrated* admitted it was a hoax.

APRIL 2   The Mets trade Jose Oquendo and Mark Davis to the Cardinals for Angel Salazar and John Young.

The Mets tried Oquendo as a starting shortstop in 1984, but at the age of 20, he was simply too young for the job. The Mets would regret the decision to trade him as Oquendo became a valuable member of the Cardinals for several seasons. In 1988, he played all nine positions during the season and was the club's starting second baseman in 1989 and 1990.

APRIL 9   The Mets open the season with a ten-inning, 6–5 win over the Cardinals before 46,781 at Shea Stadium. In his first game with the Mets, Gary Carter provided the game winner, with a walk-off homer off ex-Met Neil Allen. The Cards tied the score 5–5 in the ninth inning on a two-out, bases-loaded walk by Doug Sisk to Jack Clark. Keith Hernandez contributed three hits. Dwight Gooden was the starting pitcher and went six innings. Tom Gorman was the winning pitcher.

Carter batted .281 with 32 homers and 100 RBI in 1985.

APRIL 11   The Mets win in extra innings for the second game in a row, defeating the Cardinals 2–1 in 11 innings at Shea Stadium. Danny Heep drove in the winning run by drawing a bases-loaded walk in the 11th off Neil Allen. Roger McDowell was the winning pitcher in his major league debut.

McDowell was a starter in the minor leagues, but found a role out of the bullpen as a rookie with the Mets in 1985. By the end of the season, he had taken over as the club's closer, replacing Jesse Orosco. The two were tied for the team lead in saves with 17.

APRIL 12   A home run by Gary Carter off Mario Soto in the fourth inning provides the lone run of a 1–0 victory over the Reds at Shea Stadium. Bruce Berenyi (seven innings) and Doug Sisk (two innings) combined on the shutout.

APRIL 13   Darryl Strawberry hits a walk-off homer off John Franco in the ninth inning to defeat the Reds 2–1 at Shea Stadium.

The Mets opened the season with five straight wins. The first four were by one run, and three of those were walk-off victories.

APRIL 16   Ron Darling (seven innings) and Jesse Orosco (two innings) combine on a one-hitter to defeat the Pirates 2–1 at Three Rivers Stadium. The only Pittsburgh hit was a single by Johnny Ray leading off the first inning. The Pirates tied the score 1–1 in the eighth on three walks, two by Darling, and a ground out. The Mets won it in the ninth on Mookie Wilson's triple and a sacrifice fly by Keith Hernandez. John Candelaria fanned 14 Mets in eight innings.

APRIL 19   Keith Hernandez drives in a run with a single with two out in the ninth inning to down the Phillies 1–0 in Philadelphia. Dwight Gooden (eight innings) and Jesse Orosco (one inning) combined on the shutout.

At the age of 20, Gooden had one of the best seasons by a pitcher in major league history. He was 24–4 and led the NL in ERA (1.53), strikeouts (268), innings (276²/₃) and complete games (16). Gooden won the Cy Young Award by a unanimous vote among the 24 baseball writers in the poll. The earned run average is the second-lowest in baseball since 1920, trailing only Bob Gibson's

1.12 in 1968. Gooden currently has more wins (41) before his 21st birthday than any pitcher since the end of World War II. The last pitcher prior to Gooden to exceed that total was Bob Feller with 55 from 1936 through 1939. Gooden is also the only pitcher since Feller to win 100 games before turning 25. He was 100–39 at the end of the 1989 season. With a 132–53 record at the end of the 1991 season, Gooden is still the only post-World War II hurler with that many victories on his 27th birthday. But personal issues, including drug abuse, led to his decline, and he ended his career at 194–112 in 2000. Gooden never won as many as 20 games again after earning 24 victories as a 20-year-old. The $276^2/_3$ innings pitched and 16 complete games in 1985, and another 250 innings and 12 complete games in 1986, was also certainly a factor in his inability to fashion what seemed to be a clear path to the Hall of Fame. Few pitchers have survived such a workload at that age. No pitcher, at any age, has had as many as $276^2/_3$ innings pitched or 16 complete games since 1987. Through it all, Gooden is still second in franchise history in wins (153), first in winning percentage (.649), second in strikeouts (1,875), third in games started (303), third in complete games (67), third in innings ($2,169^2/_3$), fourth in shutouts (23) and fifth in ERA (3.10).

APRIL 26

Wally Backman collects five hits, including a double, in five at-bats during a 6–0 triumph over the Pirates at Shea Stadium. Ron Darling pitched the shutout.

On the same day, the Mets signed Joe Sambito, most recently with the Astros, as a free agent.

APRIL 28

The Mets outlast the Pirates 5–4 in 18 innings at Shea Stadium. Darryl Strawberry hit a grand slam with one out in the first inning to give the Mets a 4–0 lead, but the club didn't score again until the 18th. In fact, after Strawberry's homer, the Mets didn't collect another hit until Rafael Santana singled, leading off the 12th. Six Pirate pitchers combined to hold the Mets hitless for $10^2/_3$ innings from the first through the 11th. Pittsburgh couldn't dent the plate after the sixth on the combined efforts of Joe Sambito (one inning), Doug Sisk (one inning), Jesse Orosco (three innings) and Tom Gorman (seven innings). The Mets had the bases loaded and no one out in the 12th, and Pirate manager Chuck Tanner brought all three of his outfielders in to employ a seven-man infield. Pittsburgh got out of the jam. Pirate base runners were thrown at the plate in the ninth, tenth and 14th innings. With the Mets out of position players, Rusty Staub played the outfield for the first time since June 22, 1983, entering the game in the 12th inning. Staub played right field against right-handed batters and left field against left-handers. He switched positions 11 times with Clint Hurdle. With two out in the top of the 18th, Staub saved a run with a running catch off a fly ball by Rick Rhoden. It was Staub's only fielding chance of the season. He never played in the field again before his career ended at the end of the 1985 campaign. In the bottom half of the 18th, Gary Carter led off with a walk, went to second on Strawberry's single and crossed the plate when Clint Hurdle's grounder skipped through the legs of first baseman Jason Thompson. The contest lasted five hours and 21 minutes.

The Mets were 26–2 in extra inning games from June 9, 1983 through May 17, 1985.

MAY 3

Lenny Dykstra homers in the second at-bat of his major league debut, which results in a 9–4 win over the Reds in Cincinnati.

Dykstra didn't homer again until April 26, 1986, a span of 274 at-bats. In between the two homers, however, he established himself as a major leaguer with his pesky, feisty and scrappy play. Dykstra was the Mets starting center fielder from 1986 until a trade to the Phillies in May 1989.

MAY 4   The Reds erupt for ten runs in the sixth inning and thrash the Mets 14–2 in Cincinnati.

MAY 7   Gary Carter hits a grand slam off Bruce Sutter in the eighth inning of a 5–3 win over the Braves at Shea Stadium. Carter's slam broke a 1–1 tie.

MAY 8   Ed Lynch shuts out the Braves 4–0 at Shea Stadium.

MAY 10   Dwight Gooden strikes out 13 and pitches a three-hitter to defeat the Phillies 5–0 at Shea Stadium.

MAY 11   Sid Fernandez (six innings) and Roger McDowell (three innings) combine on a one-hitter to defeat the Phillies 4–0 at Shea Stadium. The only Philadelphia hit was a single by Von Hayes in the fourth inning. It was the third shutout in a row by Mets pitchers.

               During the game, Darryl Strawberry tore ligaments in his right thumb while diving for a fly ball in right field and missed seven weeks. Limited to 111 games, Strawberry batted .277 with 29 homers in 1985.

MAY 30   Dwight Gooden strikes out 14 batters during a 2–1 victory over the Giants in San Francisco.

JUNE 3   In the first round of the amateur draft, the Mets select shortstop Gregg Jefferies from Serra High School in San Mateo, California.

               Jefferies became the Mets starting second baseman at the age of 21 in 1988 and seemed destined for greatness. He never fully adjusted to the pressures of playing in New York, however, and was traded to the Royals in December 1991. Jefferies lasted in the majors until 2000 and finished his career with a .289 batting average and 126 homers in 1,465 games. Other future major leaguers drafted and signed by the Mets in 1985 were Scott Servais (second round), Tim Layana (fifth round) and Monty Fariss (seventh round).

JUNE 4   Dwight Gooden fans 12 batters during a 4–1 win over the Dodgers in Los Angeles.

JUNE 9   Terry Pendleton of the Cardinals hits an inside-the-park grand slam off Joe Sambito in the fifth inning of an 8–2 St. Louis win over the Mets in the second game of a double-header at Shea Stadium. The homer was the result of a collision between center fielder Terry Blocker and right fielder Danny Heep. The two crashed as Pendleton's drive hit Heep's glove. Before the Mets outfielders could recover, Pendleton had rounded the bases. The Cards also won the opener 6–1.

               Blocker didn't play in another major league game until 1988 when he was a member of the Braves.

JUNE 11   The Mets set a club record for most runs allowed in a game with a 26–7 trouncing at the hands of the Phillies at Veterans Stadium. Before the second inning was over, the score was 16–0 as Philadelphia scored nine runs in the first inning and seven in the second. Tom Gorman started for New York and surrendered six runs in one-third of an inning. He was relieved by Calvin Schiraldi, who gave up ten runs in $1\frac{1}{3}$ innings. Joe Sambito was on the mound in the fifth, sixth and seventh and allowed ten more runs. Von Hayes led off the first for the Phils and homered. Before the inning was over he batted again and belted a grand slam. Hayes thus became the first player in major league history to homer twice in the first inning. The Phillies collected 27 hits in all on the two homers by Hayes, a triple, nine doubles and 15 singles.

JUNE 12   A day after the Mets give up 27 hits, Ron Darling (seven innings), Jesse Orosco (two innings) and Rick Aguilera (two innings) combine on a three-hitter to beat the Phillies 7–3 in 11 innings in Philadelphia. Right fielder John Christensen capped the 11th-inning rally with a two-run homer.

JUNE 19   Dwight Gooden pitches the Mets to a 1–0 win over the Cubs at Shea Stadium.

JUNE 20   George Foster hits a grand slam off Ray Fontenot in the third inning of a 5–3 win over the Cubs at Shea Stadium.

After a 30–17 start, the Mets fell to 38–35 on July 1 and fell five games behind the first-place Cardinals.

JULY 4   The Mets defeat the Braves 16–13 in 19 innings in Atlanta in one of the most entertaining games in major league history. The promotion of a huge fireworks display after the game helped attract a crowd of 44,947 to Atlanta-Fulton County Stadium, the second-largest for a Braves home game all year. Rain delayed the start for an hour and 24 minutes to 9:04 p.m. More rain stopped play for 41 minutes in the third inning. The field was saturated with water, and players slipped on the wet surface all night. On a couple of occasions, balls hit puddles in the grass and stopped. The Mets had lead of 1–0 in the first inning, fell behind 3–1 and then scored four in the fourth for a 5–3 advantage. The lead stretched to 7–4 before Atlanta countered with four in the eighth. The Mets tied the contest with three consecutive singles with one out in the ninth. Howard Johnson belted a two-run homer in the 13th, but Terry Harper of the Braves countered with a two-run blast with two out and two strikes in the bottom half with the score 10–10. A sacrifice fly by Lenny Dykstra in the top of the 18th put the Mets up 11–10. The Mets blew a lead for the fourth time, however, and the second with two out and two strikes on the batter, in the bottom of the inning. Pitcher Rick Camp batted because the Braves were out of position players. Camp stepped to the plate with a .060 batting average and no home runs in 167 career at-bats. He promptly homered off Tom Gorman with two strikes to tie the score 11–11. The Mets came back with five runs off Camp in the 19th, three of them on a single by Danny Heep that brought Howard Johnson all the way around from first base. Ron Darling, in his only relief appearance between the start of his career in 1983 and 1990, gave up two runs in the bottom of the 19th before the game ended at 16–13. With over ten at-bats, Keith Hernandez hit for the cycle. He doubled in the first off Rick Mahler, tripled in the fourth against Jeff Dedmon, homered in the eighth facing Steve Shields and singled in the 12th versus Terry Forster. Gary Carter had five hits in nine at-bats. The Mets collected 28 hits in all. The game ended at 3:55 a.m with about 8,000 remaining in the stands. Playing time was six hours and ten minutes. As promised, the fireworks display went off as scheduled after the final out, beginning at 4:01 a.m., startling many Atlanta residents out of a sound sleep.

JULY 10	The Mets extend their winning streak to nine games with a 2–1 decision over the Reds in Cincinnati.
JULY 11	Pitching for the Astros, Nolan Ryan records his 4,000th career strikeout by fanning Danny Heep. The Mets lost 4–3 in 12 innings in Houston.
JULY 14	Dwight Gooden beats the Astros 1–0 in Houston.
JULY 16	Starting in right field in the All-Star Game, Darryl Strawberry singles, draws a walk and steals a base to help the National League to a 6–1 win at the Metrodome in Minneapolis.

> *On the same day, the Mets traded Dave Cochrane to the White Sox for Paciorek.*

| JULY 20 | Darryl Strawberry drives in seven runs during a 16–4 trouncing of the Braves at Shea Stadium. Strawberry belted a grand slam off Steve Bedrosian in the first inning and a three-run homer against Len Barker in the fourth. Strawberry also tripled in the sixth. The Mets had five homers in all, with Clint Hurdle, Danny Heep and Howard Johnson collecting the others. |
| JULY 21 | The Mets offense is in high gear for the second night in a row resulting in a 15–10 triumph over the Braves at Shea Stadium. |

> *After scoring 31 runs in back-to-back games, the Mets scored only three over the next three contests.*

| JULY 22 | Sid Fernandez strikes out 13 batters in $7\frac{1}{3}$ innings but gives up five runs, and the Mets lose 5–1 to the Reds at Shea Stadium. |
| JULY 27 | The Mets clobber the Astros 16–4 in the first game of a double-header at Shea Stadium. All 16 runs were unearned on the strength of five Houston errors. The Mets completed the sweep with a 7–3 victory in the nightcap. |

> *Amazingly, the Mets scored fewer runs than the league average in each of the first 23 seasons of the history of the franchise. The 1985 season was the first in which the club exceeded the league-wide average. The average NL squad that year scored 658 runs and the Mets accumulated 695. Despite playing in a ballpark that favored the pitchers, the Mets would lead the NL in runs scored in 1986, 1987, 1988 and 1990.*

| JULY 30 | George Foster drives in both runs of a 2–0 win over the Expos at Shea Stadium with singles in the sixth and eighth innings. Dwight Gooden pitched the shutout. |

> *Gooden had eight shutouts in 1985, but didn't lead the league. John Tudor of the Cardinals recorded ten shutouts, the most of any major league pitcher in a season between 1975 and the present.*

| AUGUST 3 | Howard Johnson homers in the tenth inning to defeat the Cubs 5–4 in Chicago. |

AUGUST 5   Darryl Strawberry hits three homers during a 7–2 win over the Cubs at Wrigley
                Field. Strawberry reached base all five times he stepped to the plate, scored four runs
                and drove in five. Facing Derek Botelho, he homered in the first and third innings
                and drew an intentional walk in the fifth. Strawberry walloped another home
                run in the seventh against Ron Meredith. In the ninth, Strawberry singled off
                Warren Brusstar.

AUGUST 6   The Mets game against the Expos in Montreal is postponed by a players' strike.
                The August 7 game between the two clubs was also called off. The strike ended on
                August 8, and both contests were made up with double-headers.

AUGUST 8   Keith Hernandez collects five hits, including a double, in six at-bats during a 14–7
                triumph over the Expos in Montreal. The Mets garnered 20 hits in all.

AUGUST 12   Sid Fernandez records 13 strikeouts in eight innings during a 4–3 win over the
                Phillies at Shea Stadium.

                *Fernandez was born in Honolulu and was proud of his Hawaiian roots. He wore
                uniform number 50 to represent Hawaii, which was the 50th state admitted to the
                Union in 1959. Ron Darling was also born in Honolulu to a Chinese-Hawaiian
                mother and a French-Canadian father. Growing up in a multi-lingual household,
                Darling spoke fluent Chinese and French. He grew up in Massachusetts, however,
                and attended Yale University. While in college, Darling hooked up with future
                Mets teammate Frank Viola in one of the greatest games in NCAA tournament
                history. On May 21, 1981, Darling held St. John's hitless through the first
                11 innings, but Viola and St. John's emerged with a 1–0 victory in the 12th.*

AUGUST 12   The Mets extend their winning streak to nine games with a 4–2 win over the Phillies
                at Shea Stadium.

AUGUST 19   Doubles by Danny Heep and Wally Backman in the eighth inning beat the Expos
                1–0 in Montreal. Ron Darling (seven innings) and Roger McDowell (two innings)
                combined on the shutout.

AUGUST 20   Dwight Gooden strikes out 16 batters during a 3–0 triumph over the Giants at
                Shea Stadium.

                *On the same day, the Mets signed Larry Bowa, most recently with the Cubs, as a
                free agent. Bowa would play the last 14 of his 2,247 big-league games as a Met.*

AUGUST 25   Dwight Gooden records his 14th win in a row, and 20th of the season, by beating
                the Padres 9–3 at Shea Stadium.

AUGUST 31   Dwight Gooden's 14-game winning streak comes to an end with a 3–2 defeat at the
                hands of the Giants in San Francisco.

SEPTEMBER 1   The Mets score three runs in the ninth inning to defeat the Giants 4–3 in San
                Francisco. Howard Johnson and Rusty Staub began the ninth with back-to-back
                doubles to pull the Mets within a run. Playing in his hometown, Keith Hernandez
                provided the game winner with a two-out homer.

SEPTEMBER 2   Keith Hernandez collects five hits, including a double, during a 12–4 victory over the Padres in San Diego. He also scored four runs and drove in three.

SEPTEMBER 3   Gary Carter garners three consecutive homers and drives in six runs during an 8–3 triumph over the Padres in San Diego. Carter homered in the first and fourth innings off Dave Dravecky and in the fifth against Luis DeLeon.

SEPTEMBER 4   Gary Carter hits two more homers during a 9–2 win over the Padres in San Diego. The five homers in consecutive games tied a major league record.

Carter hit eight homers over six games and 22 plate appearances from August 29 through September 4.

SEPTEMBER 6   The Mets defeat the Dodgers 2–0 in 13 innings in Los Angeles. Dwight Gooden (nine innings), Roger McDowell (two innings), Terry Leach (one-third of an inning) and Jesse Orosco (1²/₃ innings) combined on the shutout. Fernando Valenzuela started for the Dodgers and went eight innings. The two runs scored on a two-out double in the 13th by Darryl Strawberry off Tom Niedenfuer.

SEPTEMBER 8   Mookie Wilson leads off the 14th inning with a home run that beats the Dodgers 4–3 in Los Angeles.

Wilson hit exactly .276 in 1983, 1984 and 1985, following seasons of .271 in 1981 and .279 in 1982.

SEPTEMBER 10   Howard Johnson hits a grand slam off Danny Cox in the first inning of a 5–4 win over the Cardinals at Shea Stadium. Johnson's homer came after Danny Cox hit George Foster with a pitch that caused both benches to empty before order was restored. The win gave the Mets a one-game lead over St. Louis in the NL East race.

SEPTEMBER 11   The Cardinals beat the Mets 1–0 in ten innings on a home run by Cesar Cedeno off Jesse Orosco. John Tudor pitched a complete game three-hit shutout. Dwight Gooden hurled nine shutout innings. With the loss, the Mets dropped into a first-place tie with the Cards.

SEPTEMBER 12   The Mets capture first place again with a 7–6 win over the Cardinals at Shea Stadium. The Mets took a 6–0 lead in the second inning but allowed St. Louis to battle back and tie the score. Keith Hernandez drove in the game winner with a walk-off single.

SEPTEMBER 14   The Mets drop out of first place with a 5–1 loss to the Expos in Montreal.

Despite a 13–9 record the rest of the way, the Mets were never again able to reach first place in 1985.

SEPTEMBER 16   Dwight Gooden strikes out 11 and pitches a two-hitter to defeat the Phillies 9–0 at Shea Stadium. The only Philadelphia hits were a double by Mike Schmidt in the fourth inning and a single from Jeff Stone in the ninth.

Gooden pitched 31 consecutive scoreless innings over four starts from August 31 through September 16. From August 31 through October 2, he had a streak in which he went 49 innings and allowed only one run, and that one was unearned.

SEPTEMBER 19   Sid Fernandez strikes out 11 and allows only one hit in eight innings to defeat the Cubs 5–1 at Shea Stadium.

The Mets drew 2,671,601 fans in 1985, which was then a club record. It was nearly two million more than the Mets attracted in 1979.

SEPTEMBER 21   Dwight Gooden caps a seven-run first inning with a three-run homer and beats the Pirates 12–1 at Shea Stadium.

The homer was Gooden's first. He would hit eight of them in 731 career at-bats.

SEPTEMBER 24   Sid Fernandez pitches a two-hitter to defeat the Phillies 7–1 at Veterans Stadium. The only Philadelphia hits were a single by Rick Schu in the second inning and a homer by Luis Aquayo in the eighth.

SEPTEMBER 29   The Mets defeat the Pirates 9–7 in ten innings in Pittsburgh. Howard Johnson tied the score 7–7 with a home run in the ninth. Gary Carter clobbered a two-run homer in the tenth.

At the conclusion of the game, the Mets were three games behind with six contests left on the schedule. The next three were against the first–place Cardinals on October 1, 2 and 3 in St. Louis.

OCTOBER 1   Ron Darling (nine innings) and Jesse Orosco (two innings) combine to beat the Cardinals 1–0 in 11 innings in St. Louis. Darryl Strawberry won the game with a two-out homer off Ken Dayley with two out in the 11th.

OCTOBER 2   The Mets pull within a game of first place with a 5–2 victory over the Cardinals in St. Louis. Dwight Gooden earned his 24th win of the season.

OCTOBER 3   The Mets miss a chance to pull into a first-place tie with the Cardinals by losing 4–3 in St. Louis. Keith Hernandez collected five hits, including two doubles, in five at-bats.

The Mets closed out the season by losing two of three to the Expos at Shea Stadium while the Cards won the first two games of a three-game set versus the Cubs in Chicago to clinch the pennant.

NOVEMBER 13   The Mets trade Calvin Schiraldi, Wes Gardner, John Christensen and La Shelle Tarver to the Red Sox for Bobby Ojeda, Tom McCarthy, John Mitchell and Chris Bayer.

Schiraldi and Ojeda would have key roles in the 1986 World Series between the Mets and Red Sox. The Mets came out ahead in the transaction, as Ojeda was 18–5 with a 2.57 ERA during the 1986 campaign. Overall, he played five seasons in New York.

1986

Season in a Sentence

The Mets win a club record 108 regular season games, dispatch the pesky Astros in the NLCS, then come from behind to stun the Red Sox in a thrilling seven-game World Series.

Finish • Won • Lost • Pct • GB

First   108   54   .667   +21.5

National League Championship Series

The Mets defeated the Houston Astros four games to two.

World Series

The Mets defeated the Boston Red Sox four games to three.

Manager

Davey Johnson

Stats

Stats	Mets	AL	Rank
Batting Avg:	.263	.322	1
On-Base Pct:	.339	.322	1
Slugging Pct:	.401	.380	1
Home Runs:	148	3	
Stolen Bases:	118	10	
ERA:	3.11	3.72	1
Errors:	138	7	
Runs Scored:	783	1	
Runs Allowed:	578	2	

Starting Lineup

Gary Carter, c
Keith Hernandez, 1b
Wally Backman, 2b
Ray Knight, 3b
Rafael Santana, ss
Keith Mitchell, lf-rf-ss
Lenny Dykstra, cf
Darryl Strawberry, rf
Mookie Wilson, cf
Tim Teufel, 2b
George Foster, lf
Howard Johnson, 3b-ss
Danny Heep, lf

Pitchers

Dwight Gooden, sp
Bobby Ojeda, sp
Ron Darling, sp
Sid Fernandez, sp
Rick Aguilera, sp
Roger McDowell, rp
Jesse Orosco, rp
Doug Sisk, rp

Attendance

2,767,601 (second in NL)

Club Leaders

Batting Avg:	Keith Hernandez	.310
On-Base Pct:	Keith Hernandez	.413
Slugging Pct:	Darryl Strawberry	.507
Home Runs:	Darryl Strawberry	27
RBI:	Gary Carter	105
Runs:	Keith Hernandez	94
Stolen Bases:	Lenny Dykstra	31
Wins:	Dwight Gooden	17
Strikeouts:	Dwight Gooden	200
ERA:	Bobby Ojeda	2.57
Saves:	Roger McDowell	22

JANUARY 16   The Mets trade Billy Beane, Bill Latham and Joe Klink to the Twins for Tim Teufel and Pat Crosby.

MARCH 5   Six weeks after the space shuttle Challenger explodes, killing six astronauts and teacher Christa McAuliffe, Mookie Wilson is struck in the right eye by a ball thrown by Rafael Santana during a routine spring training rundown exercise. Wilson was out six weeks. His job as the starting center fielder was taken over by Lenny Dykstra, who batted a surprising .293 with eight home runs in 147 games.

APRIL 8   The Mets open the season with a 4–2 win over the Pirates in Pittsburgh. Dwight Gooden pitched a complete game.

> *Gooden was 17–6 with a 2.84 ERA and 200 strikeouts in 250 innings in 1986 after starting the season by winning his first five decisions. From May 30, 1985 through May 6, 1986, Gooden was as dominant as any pitcher in baseball history. Over that period, he had a record of 23–1 with an ERA of 1.32 in 252 1/3 innings and went at least nine innings in 19 of his 31 starts and eight innings in five others. Whether or not the workload contributed to his decline is open for speculation, but the numbers show his strikeouts dropped alarmingly from 11.4 per nine innings in 1984 to 7.2 in 1986, which is usually an indication of arm fatigue. Gooden's strikeout rate would fall to 6.3 per nine innings in 1988.*

APRIL 14   In the first home game of the season, the Mets lose 6–2 in 13 innings to the Cardinals before 47,752 at Shea Stadium.

> *The Mets irritated opposing players and fans with their perceived arrogance. Shea Stadium fans insisted on curtain calls after every homer, and the Mets responded in theatrical fashion. The club was involved in four on-field brawls between May 27 and July 22.*

APRIL 20   Sid Fernandez (eight innings) and Roger McDowell (one inning) combine on a two-hitter to defeat the Phillies 8–0 at Shea Stadium. The only Philadelphia hits were singles by Gary Redus leading off the first inning and Mike Schmidt in the fifth.

APRIL 21   The Mets score two runs in the ninth inning to down the Pirates 6–5 at Shea Stadium. Tim Teufel doubled in the first tally and crossed the plate on a walk-off single from Gary Carter.

> *Carter batted .255 with 24 homers and 105 RBI in 1986.*

APRIL 24   The Mets score two runs in the ninth inning and one in the tenth to defeat the Cardinals 5–4 in St. Louis. Howard Johnson tied the game 4–4 with a one-out, two-run homer. George Foster drove in the winning run with a single.

APRIL 30   The Mets extend their winning streak to 11 games with an 8–1 decision over the Braves in Atlanta. Darryl Strawberry collected five hits, including a home run and a double, in five at-bats.

> *Strawberry batted .259 with 27 home runs in 1986.*

MAY 6   Dwight Gooden pitches a two-hitter to defeat the Astros 4–0 at Shea Stadium. The only Houston hits were singles by Glenn Davis in the fifth inning and Craig Reynolds in the ninth.

> *On May 10, the Mets had a record of 20–4.*

MAY 12   A double by Ray Knight and a single from Tim Teufel in the ninth inning downs the Braves 1–0 at Shea Stadium. Sid Fernandez (seven innings) and Roger McDowell (two innings) combined on the shutout.

After batting .218 in 1985, Knight was nearly released. Davey Johnson pleaded with General Manager Frank Cashen to keep Knight for another year, and the move paid off. Ray walloped six home runs in the first 12 games of the season and finished the year with a .298 batting average and 11 homers in 137 games.

MAY 23   Mookie Wilson collects five hits, including a double and a triple, in five at-bats but the Mets lose 7–4 to the Padres in San Diego on a three-run, walk-off homer by Tony Gwynn off Jesse Orosco.

MAY 27   George Foster hits a grand slam off Tom Niedenfuer in the sixth inning, and Ron Darling strikes out 12 during an 8–1 win over the Dodgers at Shea Stadium.

After Foster's slam, Niedenfuer hit Ray Knight in the elbow with a pitch. Knight charged the mound and was tackled by the Dodger hurler. Both benches emptied, but no one was ejected.

JUNE 2   In the first round of the amateur draft, the Mets select outfielder Lee May, Jr. from Purcell-Marian High School in Cincinnati, Ohio.

Lee May, Sr. hit 354 major league home runs from 1965 through 1982 with the Reds, Astros, Orioles and Royals. Lee, Jr. never reached the majors and collected only eight homers with a .221 batting average in eight minor league seasons. Future major leaguers drafted and signed by the Mets in the June 1986 draft were Kip Gross (fourth round), Eddie Zosky (fifth round), Curtis Pride (tenth round) and Archie Corbin (16th round). John Olerud was chosen in the 27th round but elected to attend Washington State University instead of signing with the Mets. He was drafted by the Blue Jays in the third round in 1989. After eight season in Toronto, Olerud played for the Mets from 1997 through 1999.

JUNE 4   Bruce Berenyi (six innings) and Roger McDowell (three innings) combine on a two-hitter to defeat the Padres 4–2 at Shea Stadium. The San Diego runs crossed the plate on a two-run homer by Tony Gwynn in the third inning.

JUNE 6   A double-header against the Pirates at Three Rivers Stadium is marred by a brawl. In the opener, won 7–1 by Pittsburgh, the Mets accused opposing pitcher Rick Rhoden of doctoring the baseball. Rhoden and Mets first base coach, Bill Robinson, exchanged words, and soon they were swinging at each other. Kevin Mitchell grabbed Rhoden and Pirate catcher Tony Pena grabbed Mitchell. After order was restored, only Robinson was ejected. The Mets gained a measure of revenge by winning game two 10–4.

JUNE 10   Tim Teufel hits a walk-off, grand slam homer off Tom Hume in the 11th inning to defeat the Phillies 8–4 at Shea Stadium.

JUNE 13   Dwight Gooden strikes out 13 batters in eight innings, but the Mets need a run in the ninth inning to beat the Pirates 6–5 at Shea Stadium. Darryl Strawberry drove in the game winner with a walk-off single.

JUNE 30   The Mets trade Ed Lynch to the Cubs for Dave Liddell and Dave Lenderman.

JULY 3   After the Astros score two runs in the top of the tenth inning, the Mets respond with three tallies in their half to win 6–5 at Shea Stadium. Darryl Strawberry tied the score 5–5 with a two-run homer. Ray Knight won the contest with a two-out, walk-off homer.

JULY 4   The Mets extend their winning streak to eight games with a 2–1 decision over the Astros at Shea Stadium. The victory gave the Mets a record of 54–21.

JULY 11   Gary Carter drives in seven runs, and Sid Fernandez pitches a two-hitter to defeat the Braves 11–0 at Shea Stadium. Carter hit a three-run homer in the first inning and a grand slam in the third, both off David Palmer. The only Atlanta hits were a single by Terry Harper in the second inning and a double from Andreas Thomas in the third.

After Carter's first home run, he took a curtain call and raised his fist. On the next pitch, Palmer hit Darryl Strawberry in the back with a pitch. Without hesitation, Strawberry rushed the mound. Palmer threw his glove at the Mets outfielder and ducked away. Atlanta catcher Ozzie Virgil tackled Strawberry as both teams rushed onto the field. About two dozen players dove into a pile near the mound. No one was ejected.

JULY 13   Lenny Dykstra hits a home run and a triple and scores both runs of a 2–0 win over the Braves at Shea Stadium. Ron Darling pitched the shutout.

Rusty Staub was honored before the game. He played for the Mets from 1972 through 1975 and again from 1981 through 1985. About a dozen former teammates added a bit of levity by running onto the field sporting long, orange wigs in homage to Staub's nickname "Le Grande Orange," which was bestowed during his years with the Expos (1969–71) for the color of his hair.

JULY 15   At the Astrodome in Houston, Dwight Gooden is the National League starter in the All-Star Game and allows two runs in three innings. Sid Fernandez hurled the eighth and struck out three, but also walked two. The American League won 3–2.

JULY 17   Trailing 1–0, the Mets erupt for seven runs in the seventh inning, three in the eighth and three in the ninth to defeat the Astros 13–2 in Houston.

JULY 19   Tim Teufel, Ron Darling, Rick Aguilera and Bobby Ojeda are arrested following a scuffle with two off-duty policemen at a Houston nightclub, called Cooter's Executive Games and Burgers. The officers were hired as security personnel for the bar.

The four players were arrested at 2:00 a.m. and spent 11 hours in a holding cell before posting bail. Teufel and Darling were charged with aggravated assault on a police officer. Ojeda and Aguilera were charged with hindering an arrest. According to police, the incident unfolded after Teufel, who was celebrating the birth of his son, caused a disturbance and was asked to leave. The other three interceded on Teufel's behalf. Seven months later, Teufel and Darling were fined $200 and sentenced to a year's probation. The charges against Ojeda and Aguilera were dropped.

JULY 22   A tenth-inning brawl highlights a 14-inning, 6–3 win over the Reds at Riverfront Stadium. With two out in the ninth, Cincinnati leading 3–1 and two Mets on base, right fielder Dave Parker dropped a routine fly ball by Keith Hernandez, which tied the score 3–3. With one out in the bottom of the tenth, Eric Davis stole third on an aggressive pop-up slide and struck Ray Knight with an elbow. Knight responded by shoving Davis off the bag and belting him in the face with a right cross. The Knight-Davis match escalated into a bench-clearing melee that lasted for 16 minutes. Davey Johnson ran out of position players in the tenth and was forced to use Jesse Orosco and Roger McDowell in the outfield. The two pitchers played left field against left-handed batters, right field against right-handers and alternated between the outfield and the mound. Gary Carter played third base for the first of only two occasions during his 19-year career. Both Orosco and McDowell pitched in the 10th and 11th. Orosco took the mound in the 12th, and McDowell in the 13th and 14th. The two combined for five shutout innings in addition to their duties in the outfield. Howard Johnson won the game with a three-run homer in the 14th.

Hernandez hit .310 with 13 homers in 1986.

JULY 27   The Mets score all five of their runs of a 5–1 triumph over the Braves in Atlanta with three consecutive home runs off Rick Mahler. Gary Carter hit a three-run homer, which was followed by solo shots from Darryl Strawberry and Kevin Mitchell.

AUGUST 3   The Mets sign Lee Mazzilli following his release by the Pirates.

AUGUST 7   The Mets release George Foster.

A few days earlier, Foster intimated to a reporter that his lack of playing time was racially motivated. Foster was hitting only .227 with 13 homers in 233 at-bats at the time of his release and was a part-time outfielder while drawing the highest salary on the team ($2.8 million). He was signed by the White Sox on August 15 and played in 15 games in Chicago before ending his career.

AUGUST 9   The Mets come from behind to beat the Expos 10–8 at Olympic Stadium. Trailing 6–1, the Mets erupted for seven runs in the eighth inning for an 8–6 lead. Mookie Wilson capped the rally with a three-run homer. After Montreal tied the contest with two runs in the bottom of the eighth, the Mets added a pair in the ninth on three walks and a two-run single by Gary Carter off Jeff Reardon. The ten runs were accomplished with only seven hits.

AUGUST 26   The Mets collect 21 hits and beat the Padres 11–6 in San Diego.

AUGUST 27   The Mets end an 11-inning, 6–5 win over the Padres in San Diego with an unusual double play. Garry Templeton was the base runner on second with one out in the 11th when Tim Flannery lined a hit to center. Mookie Wilson grabbed the ball on one hop and fired home. Catcher John Gibbons took the thrown ball and hung on for the out after a collision with Templeton. Flannery tried to advance to third on the play and was out on a throw from Gibbons to Howard Johnson.

Gibbons had a peculiar two-year career in the majors. He batted .065 in 31 at-bats in 1984, spent all of 1985 in the minors and hit .444 in 18 at-bats in 1986.

SEPTEMBER 1   Sid Fernandez strikes out 14 batters in seven innings of a 5–2 win over the Giants at Shea Stadium.

SEPTEMBER 17   The Mets clinch the NL East by beating the Cubs 4–2 at Shea Stadium. Making his first major league start, Dave Magadan collected three hits. He was playing first base because Keith Hernandez was suffering from the flu. Hernandez entered the game in the seventh inning so he could be on the field for the clinching.

After the game, fans rushed the field and grabbed everything that wasn't nailed down, including the bases and home plate. Police were unable to control the mob. The field had to be re-sodded, and holes had to be filled in before the game the following evening.

SEPTEMBER 22   Dwight Gooden pitches a two-hitter to defeat the Cardinals 5–2 at Shea Stadium. The only St. Louis hits were singles by Ozzie Smith in the third inning and Andy Van Slyke in the fourth.

SEPTEMBER 25   The Mets earn their 100th victory of the season with a 6–5 decision over the Cubs in Chicago.

The 108 victories by the Mets in 1986 were 12 more than any other major league team that season.

SEPTEMBER 28   Darryl Strawberry hits a three-run homer in the 11th inning to beat the Pirates 4–1 in Pittsburgh.

OCTOBER 5   In the last game of the regular season, Darryl Strawberry hits a grand slam off Ray Krawczyk in the fifth inning of a 9–0 victory over the Pirates at Shea Stadium.

The Mets played the Houston Astros in the National League Championship. Managed by Hal Lanier, the Astros were 96–66 in 1986. It was the first postseason appearance by the Mets since 1973. The series was a best-of-seven affair, a change from a best-of-five format that existed in the NLCS from 1969 through 1984.

OCTOBER 8   The Astros open the Championship Series with a 1–0 win over the Mets in Houston. Mike Scott struck out 14 batters and pitched a five-hitter. The lone run scored on a home run by Glenn Davis in the second inning off Dwight Gooden, who pitched seven innings.

The series was telecast nationally over ABC. The announcers were Keith Jackson and Tim McCarver.

OCTOBER 9   The Mets even the series with a 5–1 victory over the Astros at the Astrodome. After Nolan Ryan retired the first ten batters to face him, the Mets scored two runs in the fourth inning and added three more in the fifth. Bobby Ojeda allowed ten hits, but only one run, while pitching a complete game.

OCTOBER 11   Lenny Dykstra hits a out-run, two-run, walk-off homer to beat the Astros 6–5 before 55,052 at Shea Stadium. Houston scored two runs in the first inning and two in the second for a 4–0 lead. The Mets finally broke through with four in the sixth, the last three on a home run by Darryl Strawberry. The Astros scored an unearned run in the seventh without a hit to lead 5–4. Wally Backman led off the ninth with a bunt single, just eluding the tag by first baseman Glenn Davis with a sweeping slide.

The play drew an argument by Astros manager, Hal Lanier, who claimed that Backman went out of the base line to avoid the tag. Backman moved to second on a passed ball before Dykstra homered off Dave Smith.

At the time, Dykstra had nine career homers in 667 regular-season at-bats. He would hit three homers during the 1986 postseason. During his career, Dykstra belted ten homers in 112 postseason at-bats, including six with the Phillies in 1993.

OCTOBER 12   Mike Scott once again beats the Mets 3–1 with a three-hitter before 55,038 at Shea Stadium. Alan Ashby gave the Astros a 2–0 lead with a two-run homer in the second inning.

OCTOBER 13   Rain postpones the fifth game of the series.

OCTOBER 14   The Mets move within one win of the World Series with a 12-inning, 2–1 win over the Astros before 54,986 at Shea Stadium. Because of the postponement the previous day, the contest began at noon on a Tuesday. Dwight Gooden went ten innings for the Mets. Nolan Ryan pitched nine innings for Houston and surrendered just two hits while striking out 12. Both teams scored in the fifth. Ryan had retired the first 13 batters to face him before Darryl Strawberry homered with one out in the fifth on a drive that barely cleared the right-field wall near the foul pole. With one out in the 12th, Wally Backman reached on a single and moved to second on Charlie Kerfeld's wild pick-off attempt. Gary Carter, mired in a 1-for-21 slump, drove Backman home with a walk-off single.

OCTOBER 15   The Mets win the National League pennant with a 16-inning, 7–6 win over the Astros in Houston. The Astros scored three runs in the first inning and held the advantage through eight innings behind the pitcher of Bob Knepper. The Mets went into the ninth inning down by three runs and facing the possibility of facing Mike Scott again in game seven. Lenny Dykstra led off the ninth with a triple and scored on Mookie Wilson's single. With one out, Keith Hernandez doubled home Wilson and Dave Smith replaced Knepper. Gary Carter and Darryl Strawberry walked to load the bases. Ray Knight's sacrifice fly tied the score. Roger McDowell entered the game in relief in the ninth and pitched five shutout innings. The Mets scored in the 14th on Wally Backman's RBI-single for a 4–3 lead, but Houston responded with a home run by Billy Hatcher in the bottom half off Jesse Orosco to tie the game 4–4. The Mets scored three in the 16th on Strawberry's double, a single from Ray Knight, two wild pitches, a walk and Dykstra's single. The Mets needed all three runs as Houston scored two in the bottom of the 16th against Orosco. The game ended on Orosco's strikeout of Kevin Bass with runners on first and second. It was Orosco's third win of the series. The game lasted four hours and 42 minutes.

The Mets played the Boston Red Sox in the World Series. Managed by John McNamara, the Sox were 95–66 during the regular season. Boston won the ALCS in dramatic fashion. They trailed the California Angels three games to one and were behind 5–2 heading into the ninth inning of game five in Anaheim. They rallied to win 7–6 in 11 innings, then won games six and seven at Fenway Park. The Sox hadn't won a World Series since 1918. Between that year and 1986, the franchise played in the Fall Classic in 1946, 1967 and 1975 and lost in the seventh game each time. The Mets were in the Series for the first time since 1973.

OCTOBER 18   The Mets open the 1986 World Series by losing 1–0 to the Red Sox before 55,076 at Shea Stadium. Bruce Hurst (eight innings) and Calvin Schiraldi (one inning) combined on the shutout. The lone run was unearned and scored in the seventh inning when second baseman Tim Teufel let a grounder roll through his legs for an error. Ron Darling (seven innings) and Roger McDowell (two innings) pitched for the Mets.

The Series was telecast nationally over NBC. The announcers were Vin Scully and Joe Garagiola.

OCTOBER 19   The Mets fall in a two-games-to-none hole by losing 9–3 to the Red Sox at Fenway Park. The contest figured to be a classic pitching match-up between Dwight Gooden and Roger Clemens, but it never materialized. The Mets managed three runs in $4^1/_3$ innings off Clemens, who was 24–4 in 1986. Red Sox relievers Steve Crawford and Bob Stanley pitched shutout ball. Gooden, who had a 41–10 record over the two previous seasons, surrendered six runs, five of them earned, in five innings. Crawford was the winning pitcher. He was 0–2 in 40 games during the regular season.

Gooden made eight postseason starts during his career with the Mets (1986 and 1988), Yankees (1997 and 2000) and Indians (1998). He was 0–4 with a 3.97 ERA in 59 innings.

OCTOBER 21   After losing the first two games at home, the Mets rebound to defeat the Red Sox 7–1 at Fenway Park in Boston. Lenny Dykstra was the batting star. He led the first inning with a home run off Oil Can Boyd on a 1–1 pitch, and before the inning was over, the Mets scored four times. Gary Carter drove in a run with a double. Danny Heep delivered a two-run single. Before the game ended, Dykstra added three more hits—all singles. Bobby Ojeda (seven innings) and Roger McDowell (two innings) pitched for New York.

The designated hitter was used during the three games in Boston, and it was the first time the Mets played in a World Series in which the DH rule was utilized. Danny Heep was the designated hitter in games three and four and Kevin Mitchell in game five.

OCTOBER 22   The Mets even the Series by beating the Red Sox 6–2 in Boston. Gary Carter started the scoring with a two-run homer in the fourth inning. Carter added a solo homer in the eighth. Lenny Dykstra homered in the seventh. Ron Darling was the New York starter and pitched seven shutout innings.

OCTOBER 23   The Red Sox move within one win of the world championship by winning game five 4–2 over the Mets at Fenway Park. Dwight Gooden struggled again, allowing four runs, three of them earned, in four innings. Bruce Hurst pitched his second complete game of the 1986 World Series. Tim Teufel homered in the losing cause.

OCTOBER 25   The Mets pull off one of the most incredible rallies in World Series history by scoring three runs in the tenth inning to beat the Red Sox 6–5 before 55,078 at Shea Stadium. The Red Sox took a 2–0 lead with singles runs in the first and second innings. The Mets deadlocked the contest with two tallies in the fifth. Boston scored in the seventh for a 3–2 lead. The Mets tied the game again in the eighth on a bases-loaded sacrifice fly by Gary Carter on a 3–0 pitch. The Red Sox scored two in the tenth off Rick Aguliera for a 5–3 advantage. Calvin Schiraldi retired the first two Mets hitters in the bottom of the tenth, but one of the most bizarre turnarounds in World Series history was about to take place. The Mets were one strike from losing on three separate pitches, two of them during Mookie Wilson's plate appearances. Gary Carter began the comeback by lining a 2–1 pitch to left field for a single. Pinch-hitter Kevin Mitchell drilled an 0–1 offering to center for another single, moving Carter to second. Schiraldi put Ray Knight in an 0–2 hole, and just one strike away from the Red Sox' first world championship since 1918, he allowed Knight to loop a single to center to score Carter. Mitchell advanced to third on the play. Bob Stanley replaced Schiraldi and ran Mookie Wilson to a 2–2 count. The Sox were again a strike away from winning when Wilson fouled off two pitches before Stanley threw a wild pitch to score Mitchell and move Knight to second. After fouling off another pitch, Wilson grounded over the first-base bag and through Bill Buckner's legs for an error. Knight scored, and the Mets had an unbelievable win.

> *After the second out, the right-field scoreboard briefly flashed the message: "Congratulations, Boston Red Sox, 1986 World Champions." In the press box, Bruce Hurst was announced as the MVP of the Series. In the Red Sox clubhouse, NBC-TV crews went to work setting up the staging for the victory celebration. Cameras were wheeled in, and plastic was taped to the fronts of the lockers to protect clothing from champagne stains. Twenty cases of Great Western were wheeled into the clubhouse. In New England, where it was past midnight, parents were waking their children so they could watch the Sox win a world championship that had eluded the region for 68 agonizing years.*

OCTOBER 26   Game seven is postponed by rain.

OCTOBER 27   The Mets claim the second world championship in franchise history with an 8–5 triumph over the Red Sox before 55,032 at Shea Stadium. The Red Sox scored three runs in the second inning off Ron Darling and held the advantage until the sixth. Sid Fernandez followed Darling to the mound and pitched $2^{1}/_{3}$ innings of shutout relief, fanning four. With one out in the sixth, the Mets loaded the bases on two singles and a walk. Keith Hernandez lined a single into left-center to score two runs. Gary Carter deadlocked the contest 3–3 with an RBI-single. Ray Knight broke the tie with a homer off Calvin Schiraldi leading off the seventh. Before the inning was over, the Mets added two more runs. The Red Sox narrow the gap to 6–5 with two runs off Roger McDowell before an out was recorded in the top of the eighth. Jesse Orosco relieved McDowell with a runner on second and retired three batters in a row. The Mets countered with two tallies in their half, the first on a home run by Darryl Strawberry. Orosco pitched the ninth and retired the Sox in order. The last out was a strikeout of Marty Barrett.

> *Ray Knight was the World Series MVP. He collected nine hits, including a homer and a double, and batted .391.*

NOVEMBER 12   President Ronald Reagan honors the Mets at the White House following the club's win in the World Series. Four front office officials, including President Fred Wilpon, 14 players and two coaches attended the event.

NOVEMBER 14   Nelson Doubleday, Jr. and Fred Wilpon purchase the Mets from the Doubleday Corporation, which bought the club in January 1980. The deal was tied to the purchase of the corporation by a West Germany communications firm. Previously, the corporation owned 95 percent of the stock and Wilpon five percent. In the new deal, Doubleday and Wilpon each owned 50 percent of the Mets franchise. Doubleday continued as chairman of the board. Wilpon, who had been team president, was now president and chief operating officer.

DECEMBER 11   In a trade involving four players named Kevin, the Mets send Kevin Mitchell, Kevin Brown, Kevin Armstrong, Shawn Abner and Stan Jefferson to the Padres for Kevin McReynolds, Gene Walter and Adam Ging.

The deal was essentially Mitchell for McReynolds. They were the only two players involved in the transaction who were ever big-league regulars. McReynolds gave the Mets five productive seasons, particularly in 1988 when he finished third in the MVP voting. Mitchell went to the Giants in a trade in 1989 and was the NL MVP in 1989. When healthy, Mitchell was a dominant force in the lineup, but injuries, weight issues and personal problems hampered his career. Mitchell played for six teams from 1991 through 1998. The Kevin Brown in the deal was not the All-Star pitcher but a career minor leaguer.

DECEMBER 13   Dwight Gooden is arrested with four friends in Tampa, Florida, after fighting with police after being stopped for a traffic citation. He was charged with assaulting an officer and resisting arrest. Witnesses stated that the Mets pitcher was beaten with nightsticks and a flashlight.

Police were cleared of misconduct in the arrest on February 20, 1987. A day earlier, riots had started in the College Hill neighborhood of Tampa following the death of an African-American youth who was in a police chokehold. The report clearing the officers in the Gooden arrest further inflamed the community, and the riots lasted three days. Gooden was sentenced to three years' probation and community service. During spring training in 1987, Gooden tested positive for cocaine. He entered a rehabilitation facility on April 1 and didn't make his first start until June 5.

DECEMBER 19   Michael Sergio is sentenced to 100 hours of community service and a $500 fine for criminal trespassing stemming from an incident during the 1986 World Series. A 37-year-old skydiver from Manhattan, Sergio landed on the Shea Stadium infield during the first inning of the sixth game carrying a banner from his parachute that read "Let's Go Mets." He was hustled off the field by New York City police and stadium personnel. Judge Phyllis Orilkoff Flug and her secretary wrote a 16-line poem called "Ode to a Criminal Trespasser" that was read to Sergio during his sentencing. The poem began with the lines, "'Twas game six of the Series when out of the sky/Flew Sergio's parachute a Met banner held high," and concluded with, "Community service and a fine you will pay/Happy holiday to all, and to all a good day."

1987

Season in a Sentence

The Mets follow their world championship season by falling 10½ games behind in July before a rally to overtake the Cardinals falls short.

Finish • Won • Lost • Pct • GB

Second 92 70 .556 3.0

Manager

Davey Johnson

Stats

Stats	Mets	AL	Rank
Batting Avg:	.268	.261	1
On-Base Pct:	.339	.328	2
Slugging Pct:	.434	.404	1
Home Runs:	192	3	
Stolen Bases:	159	6	
ERA:	3.84	4.08	3
Errors:	137	9	
Runs Scored:	823	1	
Runs Allowed:	698	5	

Starting Lineup

Gary Carter, c
Keith Hernandez, 1b
Wally Backman, 2b
Howard Johnson, 3b
Rafael Santana, ss
Kevin McReynolds, lf
Lenny Dykstra, cf
Darryl Strawberry, rf
Mookie Wilson, cf
Tim Teufel, 2b
Dave Magadan, 3b

Pitchers

Dwight Gooden, sp
Ron Darling, sp
Sid Fernandez, sp
Rick Aguilera, sp
David Cone, sp-rp
John Mitchell, sp
Roger McDowell, rp
Jesse Orosco, rp
Terry Leach, rp
Doug Sisk, rp
Randy Myers, rp

Attendance

3,034,129 (second in NL)

Club Leaders

Batting Avg:	Keith Hernandez	.290
On-Base Pct:	Darryl Strawberry	.398
Slugging Pct:	Darryl Strawberry	.583
Home Runs:	Darryl Strawberry	39
RBI:	Darryl Strawberry	104
Runs:	Darryl Strawberry	108
Stolen Bases:	Darryl Strawberry	36
Wins:	Dwight Gooden	15
Strikeouts:	Ron Darling	167
ERA:	Dwight Gooden	3.21
Saves:	Roger McDowell	25

FEBRUARY 12   Ray Knight signs with the Orioles as a free agent.

Mets fans were angry over the departure of Knight, who was the World Series MVP, but it proved to be a good move. Howard Johnson took over at third base for Knight and batted .265 with 36 homers and 32 stolen bases.

MARCH 27   The Mets trade Ed Hearn, Rick Anderson and Mauro Gozzo to the Royals for David Cone and Chris Jelic.

The Mets pulled off one of the greatest trades in club history in acquiring Cone. At the time of the transaction, he was 24 and had pitched in 11 major league games, all in relief. After a 5–6 record in 1987, Cone became a star in 1988 with 20 wins and only three defeats. He won 55 more games over the next four seasons for the Mets and led the NL in strikeouts in 1990 and 1991 before a trade to the Blue Jays in 1992.

APRIL 7   The Mets open the season with a 3–2 win over the Pirates before 46,102 at Shea Stadium. All three New York runs were provided by a home run from

Darryl Strawberry with two out in the first inning. Bobby Ojeda started for the Mets and allowed one run in seven innings. Before the game, the Mets received their World Series rings.

Strawberry homered in each of the first three games of the season. He finished the year with a .284 batting average, 39 home runs, 104 RBI and 36 stolen bases. Strawberry and Howard Johnson were the first pair of teammates in major league history with at least 30 homers and 30 steals in the same season. It didn't happen again until Dante Bichette and Ellis Burks accomplished the feat with the Rockies in 1996.

APRIL 9   Jesse Orosco retires all six batters he faces, four of them on strikeouts, to close out a 4–2 victory over the Pirates at Shea Stadium.

APRIL 12   Dion James of the Braves collects a bizarre double during a 12–4 Mets loss at Shea Stadium. What appeared to be a routine fly ball to left fielder Kevin McReynolds struck and killed a dove, allowing the ball to land safely. The bird was retrieved by shortstop Rafael Santana and handed to a reluctant, and visibly upset, ballgirl who was stationed along the third-base line.

APRIL 18   After the Mets score in the top of the tenth inning, the Cardinals rally with five tallies in their half, the last four on a two-out, walk-off grand slam by Tommy Herr off Jesse Orosco, to win 12–8 in St. Louis.

The road uniforms were modified in 1987, with "New York" written in script across the front instead of "Mets." The change lasted only one year. In 1998, "New York" appeared across the shirt fronts in block letters, and the uniform number was removed.

APRIL 19   On Easter Sunday, Cardinals pitcher John Tudor is injured in a freak accident during a 4–2 Mets loss in St. Louis. Mets catcher Barry Lyons ran into the Cardinal dugout in pursuit of a foul pop and landed on Tudor, breaking a bone below the pitcher's right kneecap. Ironically, Tudor was hurt in an attempt to protect Lyons. He could have gotten out of the way in time to avoid the collision but saw Lyons was going headfirst into the bench and tried to block his path. Tudor was out for three-and-a-half months.

APRIL 21   Some misguided base running contributes to a triple play, but the Mets survive to beat the Pirates 9–6 in Pittsburgh. With Darryl Strawberry on second base and Gary Carter on third, Wally Backman grounded out from second baseman Johnny Ray to first baseman Sid Bream. Carter broke for home but held up. Strawberry, seeing Carter on the run, attempted to move to third, then had to stop when Carter went back to the bag. Bream, noticing Strawberry off the base, fired to shortstop Denny Gonzalez, who tagged Strawberry for the second out. Carter broke for the plate once again and was out at home on a throw from Gonzalez to catcher Junior Ortiz.

APRIL 22   Kevin McReynolds collects a homer, two doubles and a single in five at-bats to lead the Mets to an 8–7 triumph over the Pirates in Pittsburgh.

MAY 1   Tim Teufel hits a pinch-hit, walk-off homer to beat the Expos 7–6 at Shea Stadium. Teufel was batting for Wally Backman.

MAY 27	The Mets score two runs in the ninth inning on back-to-back homers by Darryl Strawberry and Gary Carter to defeat the Giants 4–3 in San Francisco.
MAY 29	The Mets trade Scott Little and Al Pedrique to the Pirates for Bill Almon.
JUNE 2	In the first round of the amateur draft, the Mets select third baseman Chris Donnels from Loyola Marymount University.

Donnels reached the majors in 1991 and played two years with the Mets before a trade to the Astros. He played for five teams in all during an eight-season career and batted just .233 with 17 home runs in 798 at-bats. Other future major leaguers drafted and signed by the Mets in 1988 were Todd Hundley (second round), Pete Schourek (also in the second round), Tim Bogar (eighth round), Pat Howell (ninth round), Terry Bross (13th round), Eric Hillman (16th round), Danny Harriger (18th round), John Johnstone (20th round) and Anthony Young (38th round).

JUNE 5	Dwight Gooden makes his first start since his suspension for drug use (see December 13, 1986) and pitches 6²/₃ innings of a 5–1 win over the Pirates before 51,402 at Shea Stadium.

In 25 starts, Gooden had a 15–7 record and a 3.21 ERA in 1987.

JUNE 7	After the Pirates score in the top of the tenth inning, Lee Mazzilli hits a two-run, walk-off double in the bottom half for a 5–4 win in the first game of a double-header at Shea Stadium. Pittsburgh won the second tilt 10–9 despite five runs-batted-in from Mazzilli, who played left field, center field and first base during the twin bill.
JUNE 10	The Mets take an 8–0 lead after three innings and clobber the Cubs 13–2 in Chicago.
JUNE 12	Tim Teufel hits a grand slam off Bob Walk in the sixth inning of a 10–2 victory over the Pirates in Pittsburgh.
JUNE 18	The Mets use five home runs to power past the Expos 10–7 in Montreal. Darryl Strawberry hit two homers, and Gary Carter, Kevin McReynolds and Howard Johnson each hit one.
JUNE 22	Tom Seaver announces his retirement. Seaver had last pitched for the Red Sox in 1986 and at 42 decided to make a comeback with the Mets. After two weeks of workouts, he decided he didn't have enough left to pitch in a regular-season game. The Mets retired his number 41 in 1988.
JUNE 28	Ron Darling pitches no-hit ball through the first seven innings, but the Mets lose 5–4 to the Phillies at Veterans Stadium. The first Philadelphia hit was a triple by Greg Gross leading off the eighth with the Mets ahead 4–0. Before the inning ended, the Phils had three runs off Darling, Jesse Orosco and Roger McDowell. Two more Philadelphia runs off McDowell followed in the ninth.
JULY 2	Terry Leach pitches a two-hitter to defeat the Reds 5–0 at Riverfront Stadium. The only Cincinnati hits were singles by Ron Oester in the third inning and Bo Diaz in the eighth.

After spending most of the 1986 season in the minors, Leach made 32 relief appearances and 12 starts for the Mets in 1987. He was 33 years old that season, and it was his first full season in the majors. Leach wasn't even on the 40-man roster at the start of spring training. He had a 10–0 record before taking a loss on August 15. He finished the year 11–1 with a 3.22 ERA in 131 1/3 innings.

JULY 9   The Mets lose 4–3 to the Astros in Houston to fall 10 1/2 games behind the Cardinals in the NL East race.

The Mets had a record of 44–40 on July 9. A run of 19 victories in 25 games pulled the club to within 3 1/2 games of first by August 7.

JULY 14   Davey Johnson manages the National League to a 13-inning, 2–0 win in the All-Star Game at Oakland-Alameda County Coliseum in Oakland.

JULY 24   Dave Magadan collects five hits in five at-bats during a 7–4 win over the Astros in the second game of a double-header at Shea Stadium. He didn't play in the opener, which the Mets won 5–2.

JULY 29   Howard Johnson hits a two-run homer in the tenth inning to beat the Cardinals 6–4 in St. Louis.

AUGUST 1   Howard Johnson belts a grand slam off Randy St. Claire in the sixth inning of a 12–4 victory over the Expos in Montreal. The Mets scored 12 runs on only seven hits.

AUGUST 3   Keith Hernandez wallops a walk-off homer with two out in the 11th inning to defeat the Phillies 3–2 at Shea Stadium.

AUGUST 5   The Mets score six runs in the fifth inning and clobber the Phillies 13–3 at Shea Stadium.

AUGUST 16   The Mets set a club record for most runs scored in a game by winning a 23–10 slugfest with the Cubs at Wrigley Field. The 33 combined runs by the two teams are also tied for the most of any game involving the Mets. The record was set with a 26–7 loss to the Phillies on June 11, 1985. The Mets collected 21 hits. The 23 runs were accumulated with three in the first inning, one in the third, three in the fourth, three in the fifth, seven in the sixth, three in the seventh and three in the eighth. Darryl Strawberry was the offensive star with four extra base hits, five runs scored and five runs batted in in five at-bats. He had a homer, a triple and two doubles.

The Mets outscored the opposition by 125 runs (823–698) in 1987, the best run differential that season in the National League.

AUGUST 20   Barry Lyons hits a grand slam off Kelly Downs in the sixth inning of a 7–4 win over the Giants at Shea Stadium. The Mets trailed 4–3 at the time of Lyons's blast.

AUGUST 24   The Mets collect only three hits, but beat the Dodgers 1–0 at Shea Stadium. The only run scored on a double by Lenny Dykstra and a single from Keith Hernandez in the fourth inning. Rick Aguilera (7 2/3 innings), Randy Myers (one-third of an inning) and Roger McDowell (one inning) combined on the shutout.

AUGUST 26   During an unusual eighth inning at Shea Stadium, the Mets and Dodgers tie a major league record by combining to use eight pitchers, but only one run is scored. With the Mets leading 3–1 heading into the top of the eighth, the Davey Johnson utilized Ron Darling, Randy Myers and Roger McDowell. Darling allowed a run. In the bottom half, the Los Angeles hurlers were Tom Leary, Rick Honeycutt, Tim Crews, Matt Young and Brian Holton. Young failed to pitch to a complete batter. He was removed with an injury after throwing three pitches to Keith Hernandez. The Mets won 3–2.

AUGUST 30   Gary Carter hits a grand slam off Rick Reuschel in the first inning of a 5–3 win over the Giants in San Francisco.

AUGUST 31   Howard Johnson homers in the tenth inning to defeat the Padres 6–5 in San Diego.

SEPTEMBER 9   After being held to no runs and one hit through the first five innings, the Mets explode for seven runs in the sixth and beat the Phillies 11–5 at Shea Stadium. Mookie Wilson capped the rally with a three-run homer.

SEPTEMBER 11   The Mets blow a chance to move within one-half game of the first-place Cardinals by allowing three runs in the ninth inning and two in the tenth to lose 6–4 to the Cards at Shea Stadium. With two out and a runner on base in the ninth, Roger McDowell gave up a single to Willie McGee and a three-run homer to Terry Pendleton to tie the score 4–4. Jesse Orosco surrendered two runs in the tenth. The Mets also lost Ron Darling for the remainder of the season after he injured his thumb in the seventh inning diving for a bunt.

None of the Mets projected starters were in the rotation for the entire year. In addition to the injury to Darling, Gooden was suspended for two months for drug use. Bobby Ojeda started only four games because of elbow injuries, and Rick Aguilera also suffered damaged elbow ligaments. Sid Fernandez battled a strained knee, a sore shoulder and issues related to his increased waistline. In addition, closer Roger McDowell missed the first six weeks after undergoing hernia surgery.

SEPTEMBER 15   Keith Hernandez collects his 2,000th career hit during a 12–4 win over the Cubs at Shea Stadium. The milestone was a single off Jay Baller in the eighth inning.

On the same day, the Mets traded Jeff Richardson and Shane Young to the Angels for John Candelaria.

SEPTEMBER 16   Dwight Gooden pitches a three-hitter and strikes out 11 to beat the Expos 10–0 in Montreal. Lenny Dykstra hit a grand slam off Bob Sebra in the eighth inning.

After the win, the Mets were 1¹/₂ games behind the first-place Cardinals. The Expos were third at four games out.

SEPTEMBER 19   The Mets score all five runs of a 5–4 win over the Pirates in Pittsburgh in the fifth inning. With the Mets trailing 2–1, Keith Hernandez hit a grand slam off Vicente Palacios.

SEPTEMBER 21   Howard Johnson hits a grand slam off Ed Lynch in the eighth inning of a 7–1 victory over the Cubs in Chicago.

SEPTEMBER 27   The Mets draw 48,588 to the last game of the season at Shea Stadium, a 12–3 triumph over the Pirates. The figure allowed the Mets to surpass the three million mark in attendance for the first time.

SEPTEMBER 28   John Candelaria (five innings), Rick Aguilera (3¹/₃ innings) and Randy Myers (two-thirds of an inning) combine to shutout the Phillies 1–0 in Philadelphia. The lone run scored in the second inning on doubles by Kevin McReynolds and Howard Johnson.

                At the close of play, the Mets were two games behind the Cardinals with five contests left on the schedule. The Mets lost their next three and were eliminated from the pennant race.

DECEMBER 8   The Mets trade Doug Sisk to the Orioles for Blaine Beatty and Greg Talamantez.

DECEMBER 11   As part of a three-team trade, the Mets send Jesse Orosco to the Dodgers and receive Jack Savage from Los Angeles and Kevin Tapani and Wally Whitehurst from the Athletics. On the same day, the Mets traded Rafael Santana and Victor Garcia to the Yankees for Phil Lombardi, Darren Reed and Steve Frey.

                Orosco would last in the majors until 2003. It would still have been a positive deal for the Mets if the club had hung on to Tapani (see July 31, 1989).

1988

Season in a Sentence

The Mets win 100 games, the most in the National League, before losing to the underdog Dodgers in the Championship Series.

Finish • Won • Lost • Pct • GB

First   100   60   .625 +15.0

National League Championship Series

The Mets lost to the Los Angeles Dodgers four games to three.

Manager

Davey Johnson

Stats

Stats	Mets	AL	Rank
Batting Avg:	.256	.248	2
On-Base Pct:	.325	.310	1
Slugging Pct:	.396	.363	1
Home Runs:	152	1	
Stolen Bases:	140	5	
ERA:	2.91	3.45	1
Errors:	115	1	
Runs Scored:	703	1	
Runs Allowed:	532	1	

Starting Lineup

Gary Carter, c
Dave Magadan, 1b-3b
Wally Backman, 2b
Howard Johnson, 3b
Kevin Elster, ss
Kevin McReynolds, lf
Lenny Dykstra, cf
Darryl Strawberry, rf
Mookie Wilson, cf
Keith Hernandez, 1b
Tim Teufel, 2b

Pitchers

David Cone, sp
Dwight Gooden, sp
Ron Darling, sp
Sid Fernandez, sp
Bobby Ojeda, sp
Randy Myers, rp
Roger McDowell, rp
Terry Leach, rp

Attendance

3,055,445 (first in NL)

Club Leaders

Batting Avg:	Kevin McReynolds	.288
On-Base Pct:	Darryl Strawberry	.366
Slugging Pct:	Darryl Strawberry	.545
Home Runs:	Darryl Strawberry	39
RBI:	Darryl Strawberry	101
Runs:	Darryl Strawberry	101
Stolen Bases:	Lenny Dykstra	30
Wins:	David Cone	20
Strikeouts:	David Cone	213
ERA:	David Cone	2.22
Saves:	Randy Myers	26

JANUARY 15   John Candelaria signs with the Yankees as a free agent.

MARCH 21   The Mets trade Bill Almon to the Phillies for Shawn Barton and Vladimir Perez.

The Mets trained in Port St. Lucie, Florida, for the first time in 1988. St. Petersburg had been the club's spring training headquarters since 1962.

MARCH 26   The Mets trade Randy Milligan and Scott Henlon to the Pirates for Mackey Sasser and Tim Drummond.

APRIL 4   The Mets belt six home runs and beat the Expos 10–6 on Opening Day at Olympic Stadium. Darryl Strawberry was perfect in five plate appearances with two homers, two singles and a walk. Kevin McReynolds also had two home runs and two singles in five at-bats and drove in three runs. The other homers were provided by

Lenny Dykstra and Kevin Elster. Starting pitcher Dwight Gooden allowed four runs and 11 hits in five innings.

> *Strawberry's second homer was estimated to have traveled 525 feet. It crashed off a rim of lights high above right field just below the roof. By the end of the year, he led the NL in home runs (39) and slugging percentage (.545) in addition to batting .269 and stealing 29 bases.*

APRIL 12   In the home opener, the Mets defeat the Expos 3–0 before 48,719 at Shea Stadium. Ron Darling pitched the shutout and Darryl Strawberry homered.

APRIL 14   Both teams are held to two hits during a 1–0 Mets win over the Expos at Shea Stadium. The lone run scored on a sixth-inning homer by Lenny Dykstra off Dennis Martinez. Bobby Ojeda pitched a complete game for New York. The only Montreal hits were a double by Andres Galarraga in the second inning and a single from Mike Fitzgerald in the eighth.

APRIL 15   Dwight Gooden records the Mets' third consecutive shutout by beating the Cardinals 3–0 in a game at Shea Stadium shortened to six innings by rain.

APRIL 23   The Mets outslug the Cardinals 12–9 in St. Louis. The Mets broke a 7–7 tie with three runs in the eighth inning. Roger McDowell pitched 2 2/3 innings of relief and had an unusual day. He was credited with a blown save and a win in addition to hitting a two-run double in his lone plate appearance.

APRIL 26   Keith Hernandez drives in seven runs during a 13–4 trouncing of the Braves in Atlanta. He had a two-run homer off Tom Glavine in the fifth inning, brought home a run against Paul Assenmacher in the sixth and walloped a grand slam facing Charlie Puleo during the Mets seven-run eighth.

APRIL 27   The Mets score five runs in the ninth inning to beat the Braves 5–2 in Atlanta. Keith Hernandez tied the score with a two-run homer. After the Mets loaded the bases, Lenny Dykstra drew a walk to force home the winning run, and Mookie Wilson delivered a two-run single.

APRIL 30   Cincinnati manager Pete Rose shoves umpire Dave Pallone, and the Mets beat the Reds 6–5 on a wild night at Riverfront Stadium. The ruckus started with the score 5–5, two out in the ninth and Howard Johnson the New York base runner on second. Mookie Wilson grounded to shortstop Barry Larkin, whose throw to first baseman Nick Esasky was low. Pallone paused to make the call, and then ruled that Wilson was safe. Johnson took advantage of Pallone's indecision to score on the play. During the ensuing argument, Pallone poked Rose in the cheek, and Rose responded by shoving Pallone twice. The irate crowd of 33,463 showered the field with debris, causing a 14-minute delay. Pallone was removed from the field for his own safety, and the game finished with three umpires. Two days later, NL President Bart Giamatti suspended Rose for 30 days.

MAY 1   The Mets lambaste the Mets 11–0 in Cincinnati. In the fifth inning, Tim Teufel, Keith Hernandez and Darryl Strawberry hit consecutive homers. Dwight Gooden pitched the shutout.

MAY 3 — David Cone makes his first start of the season and beats the Braves 8–0 at Shea Stadium.

> *Cone began the year as a 25-year-old with a 5–6 career record. He pitched his first seven games of 1988 as a reliever and had a 3.63 ERA in 17$\frac{1}{3}$ innings. Cone ended the season with a 20–3 record and an earned run average of 2.22 with 213 strikeouts in 231$\frac{1}{3}$ innings.*

MAY 4 — Sid Fernandez (five innings) and Terry Leach (two innings) combine on a shutout to defeat the Braves 8–0 at Shea Stadium. Billy Hatcher collected both Houston hits with a double in the fourth inning off Fernandez and a single against Leach in the sixth. It was the Mets' third shutout in a span of four games, and it was accomplished against three different teams.

MAY 6 — The Mets come from behind to defeat the Reds 4–3 in ten innings at Shea Stadium. Cincinnati scored in the top of the tenth on a leadoff homer by Chris Sabo off Randy Myers. John Franco retired the first two New York batters in the bottom of the tenth, and then issued a walk to Keith Hernandez and a two-run, walk-off homer to Darryl Strawberry.

MAY 11 — The Mets score three runs in the ninth inning and one in the tenth to defeat the Astros 9–8 in Houston. Tim Teufel tied the score with a three-run double with one out in the ninth. Kevin McReynolds drove in the winning run in the tenth with a single. He entered the game as a pinch-hitter in the ninth and remained in the lineup in left field.

> *McReynolds finished third in the NL MVP balloting in 1988. He hit .288 with 27 home runs.*

MAY 16 — Gary Carter hits his 299th career home run during a 7–4 win over the Padres in San Diego.

> *Carter would go 230 at-bats and three months before hitting number 300 (see August 11, 1988).*

MAY 17 — David Cone (seven innings) and Randy Myers (two innings) combine to shut out the Padres 1–0 in San Diego. Cone struck out 12 batters and Myers fanned two. The lone run scored in the eighth when Keith Hernandez singled, stole second, moved to third on a ground out and scored on a wild pitch.

MAY 18 — Bobby Ojeda (8$\frac{1}{3}$ innings) and Roger McDowell (two-thirds of an inning) combine on a two-hitter to beat the Padres 5–2 at Jack Murphy Stadium. The only San Diego hits were a single by Keith Moreland in the fifth inning and a triple from Dickie Thon in the eighth.

MAY 21 — Dwight Gooden runs his season record to 8–0 with a 4–0 victory over the Dodgers in Los Angeles. During the game, Alfredo Griffin of the Dodgers had his hand broken by a pitch from Gooden in the fifth. Howard Johnson was the first New York batter in the fifth and was struck by an offering from Brian Holton in retaliation.

> *At the conclusion of the 8–0 start, Gooden had a career record of 81–26 and an earned run average of 2.49. He finished the season at 18–9 with an ERA of 3.19.*

MAY 22 | Tensions from the previous day spill over during a 5–2 win over the Dodgers in Los Angeles. David Cone hit Pedro Guerrero with a pitch in the sixth inning. The ball glanced off Guerrero's shoulder and struck him in the head. Guerrero threw his bat with both hands in Cone's direction. The bat landed near shortstop Kevin Elster. As Guerrero walked toward the mound, he was tackled by catcher Barry Lyons. Both benches emptied, but no punches were thrown. Guerrero was suspended for four days, which most observers believed was far too lenient.

At the conclusion of the game, the Mets had a record of 30–11.

MAY 31 | After the Dodgers score two runs in the top of the tenth, the Mets respond with two in the bottom half and 5–4 win in the 11th at Shea Stadium. Wally Backman and Keith Hernandez drove home the tenth-inning runs with singles. Kevin Elster provided a walk-off homer in the 11th.

JUNE 1 | In the first round of the amateur draft, the Mets select pitcher David Proctor from Allen County Community College in Iola, Kansas.

The 1988 draft was largely an exercise in futility for the Mets. Proctor never advanced beyond the Class AA level. The only future major leaguers drafted and signed by the club in 1988 were David Saunders (third round) and Kevin Baez (seventh round).

JUNE 2 | The Mets come from behind in extra innings for the second time in three days to defeat the Cubs 2–1 in 13 innings at Shea Stadium. After Damon Berryhill homered in the top of the tenth to break up a scoreless duel, the Mets responded with a run in the bottom half when Kevin McReynolds singled, stole second and crossed the plate on a pinch-hit single from Lee Mazzilli with two out. Howard Johnson led off the 13th with a walk-off homer. David Cone (ten innings), Roger McDowell (1^1/$_3$ innings) and Randy Myers(1^2/$_3$ innings) pitched for the Mets.

Johnson slumped most of the 1988 season and hit .230 with 24 homers.

JUNE 4 | For the third time in five days, the Mets come from behind in extra innings and win with a walk-off homer at Shea Stadium. After the Cubs scored in the top of the 11th, the Mets countered with a run in their half with two out. Kevin McReynolds contributed the walk-off home run in the 13th for a 6–5 victory.

JUNE 13 | David Cone (ten innings) and Roger McDowell (two innings) combine on a five-hitter to beat the Cardinals 2–1 in 12 innings at Shea Stadium. Lee Mazzilli drove in the winning run with a pinch-hit, walk-off single.

JUNE 18 | Extra-inning magic strikes again in the form of a 14-inning 3–2 win over the Phillies at Shea Stadium. After Philadelphia scored in the top of the 14th, the Mets came back with two in their half. Keith Miller drove in the winning run with a single. Miller entered the game as a third baseman during a double switch in the eighth.

JUNE 19 | David Cone pitches a two-hitter to defeat the Phillies 6–0 at Shea Stadium. Cone was four outs from a no-hitter when Steve Jeltz singled with two out in the eighth. Milt Thompson added another single in the ninth.

JUNE 21   Kevin McReynolds hits a grand slam off Doug Drabek in the sixth inning of a 9–0 win over the Pirates at Shea Stadium. Ron Darling pitched the shutout.

> *Darling had a 14–1 record at Shea Stadium in 1988. Overall, he was 17–9 with an ERA of 3.25. Combined, David Cone, Dwight Gooden and Darling were 55–21 during the season. The rest of the staff was 45–39.*

JUNE 29   The Mets defeat the Pirates 8–7 in 11 innings in Pittsburgh. Howard Johnson kept the Mets alive with a two-out homer in the ninth on a 1–2 pitch off Jim Gott. In the 11th, Roger McDowell doubled and scored on a single from Kevin McReynolds. McDowell also pitched three shutout innings.

JULY 3   Sid Fernandez pitches a two-hitter and strikes out 12 to defeat the Astros 5–0 at Shea Stadium. The only Houston hits were singles by Glenn Davis in the second inning and Rafael Ramirez in the third.

JULY 12   At Riverfront Stadium in Cincinnati, Dwight Gooden is the National League starter in the All-Star Game and allows a run and three hits. Gooden also started the 1986 Midsummer Classic. David Cone pitched a perfect fifth and struck out Paul Molitor. The American League won 2–1.

JULY 13   The Mets sign Bob McClure, most recently with the Expos, as a free agent.

JULY 14   Kevin McReynolds collects five hits, including a homer and two doubles, in six at-bats to lead the Mets to a 9–8 victory over the Braves in 11 innings in Atlanta.

> *At the close of play on July 21, the Mets held only a one-half game lead over the Pirates in the NL East race. The Mets were 44–23 over the remainder of the season to win the division by 15 games.*

JULY 24   The Mets retire Tom Seaver's number 41 prior to a 4–2 loss to the Braves at Shea Stadium.

JULY 27   Darryl Strawberry and Kevin McReynolds drive in all of the runs of a 10–2 triumph over the Phillies in Philadelphia. Each of them accounted for five RBI. McReynolds was 4-for-4 with a homer, a double and two singles.

JULY 29   Bobby Ojeda pitches a three-hitter to beat the Pirates 1–0 at Shea Stadium. John Smiley held the Mets to just one hit over the first 7$\frac{1}{3}$ innings before Kevin Elster homered for the lone run.

JULY 30   Sid Fernandez strikes out 12 batters in seven innings of a 3–0 victory over the Pirates at Shea Stadium.

AUGUST 8   While the Mets are losing 1–0 to the Pirates in Pittsburgh, the Cubs and the Phillies begin what is intended to be the first night game in Wrigley Field history. Phil Bradley of the Phillies led off the first inning with a homer, but play was stopped by rain with the Cubs leading 3–1 in the fourth inning. The game wasn't resumed, and since it failed to go the required five innings, it was not an official game.

| AUGUST 9 | In the first official night game at Wrigley Field, the Mets lose 6–4 to the Cubs. It was telecast nationally over NBC-TV on a Tuesday night. The contest was scoreless until the fifth inning when Lenny Dykstra hit the first official homer under the lights at Wrigley. |

AUGUST 11   The Mets score five runs in the ninth inning to beat the Cubs 9–6 in Chicago. Three singles produced the first run. After the Mets loaded the bases with two out, Kevin McReynolds delivered a grand slam off Goose Gossage. Facing Al Nipper in the second, Gary Carter hit his 300th career homer.

Carter finished his career in 1992 with 324 home runs.

AUGUST 12   David Cone strikes out 12 batters in eight innings, but the Mets lose 5–2 in 12 innings at Shea Stadium.

AUGUST 16   The Mets explode for nine runs in the first inning and defeat the Giants 13–6 in San Francisco. The nine runs were accomplished with eight hits (seven singles and a double), an error, an intentional walk and a balk.

AUGUST 17   David Cone strikes out 12 batters in seven innings, but the Mets lose 4–0 to the Giants in San Francisco. It was his second straight start with 12 strikeouts, but the Mets failed to win either game.

AUGUST 29   David Cone pitches a one-hitter to defeat the Padres 6–0 at Shea Stadium. The only San Diego hit was a single by Tony Gwynn in the fourth inning.

Gregg Jefferies, a 21-year-old rookie, helped the Mets during the stretch drive. Recalled on August 28, he collected 24 hits, including five homers, in his first 52 at-bats for an average of .462. He played both third base and second base. Overall, Jefferies batted .321 in 118 at-bats with six homers in 1988. Randy Myers was another star late in the year. In 12 relief appearances from August 23 through September 25, Myers pitched 16 1/3 shutout innings and allowed only three hits while striking out 18.

AUGUST 30   Bobby Ojeda pitches a complete game to beat the Padres 1–0 at Shea Stadium. The lone run scored on a double by Kevin McReynolds and a single from Gary Carter in the seventh inning.

SEPTEMBER 8   Howard Johnson collects five hits, including a homer and a double, in five at-bats to lead the Mets to a 13–6 win over the Cubs in Chicago. The Mets garnered 20 hits in all.

SEPTEMBER 11   Kevin McReynolds drives in all three runs of a 3–0 win over the Expos in Montreal. McReynolds had an RBI-single in the first inning and a two-run homer in the eighth. Bobby Ojeda pitched the shutout.

SEPTEMBER 12   Gary Carter hits a walk-off homer in the ninth inning to beat the Pirates 3–2 at Shea Stadium.

SEPTEMBER 17   Leading off the first inning, Lenny Dykstra concludes an 11-pitch at-bat against Bryn Smith with a home run sparking the Mets to a 6–2 win over the Expos at Shea Stadium. Dykstra fouled off six pitches, including five in a row.

SEPTEMBER 21 Bobby Ojeda accidentally severs the middle finger of his left hand using electric hedge clippers at his home. He underwent five hours of microsurgery to reattach the fingertip.

SEPTEMBER 22 The Mets clinch the NL East pennant with a 3–1 win over the Phillies at Shea Stadium. It was the club's eighth win in a row. Ron Darling pitched a complete game.

SEPTEMBER 24 The Mets thrash the Cardinals 14–1 in St. Louis.

SEPTEMBER 30 David Cone earns his 20th win of the season with a 4–2 decision over the Cardinals at Shea Stadium.

OCTOBER 2 The Mets achieve their 100th win of the season with a 7–5 decision over the Cardinals at Shea Stadium.

> *The Mets played the Los Angeles Dodgers in the National League Championship Series. Managed by Tommy Lasorda, the Dodgers were 94–67. During the regular season, the Mets were 10–1 against the Dodgers, including a 6–0 mark in Los Angeles. The series was telecast nationally over CBS. The announcers were Brent Musburger and Jerry Coleman.*

OCTOBER 4 The Mets open the Championship Series with a 3–2 win over the Dodgers in Los Angeles. The starting pitchers were Orel Hershiser and Dwight Gooden. Hershiser closed the regular season with a major league record 59 consecutive scoreless innings. Gooden pitched well, allowing two runs and four hits in seven innings while fanning ten, but Hershiser shut out the Mets over the first eight innings. The Dodger hurler entered the ninth without allowing a run over his last 67 innings on the mound. The spell was broken when rookie Gregg Jefferies singled and scored on a double from Darryl Strawberry. Hershiser was relieved by Jay Howell. Kevin McReynolds followed with a walk. The Mets were down their last strike when Gary Carter delivered a two-out double on an 0–2 pitch for a 3–2 lead. Center fielder John Shelby dived for Carter's drive, but could not make the catch. Shelby fired home, and McReynolds scored when he collided with catcher Mike Scioscia on a close play at the plate. Randy Myers retired all six batters he faced in the eighth and ninth.

> *David Cone enraged the Dodgers for comments he made in a column he wrote for the* New York Daily News. *Cone said that Howell reminded him of a "high school pitcher" and that Hershiser was lucky to shut out the Mets for eight innings. Cone was the starter in game two and riding an eight-game winning streak.*

OCTOBER 5 The Dodgers even the series by beating the Mets 6–3 in Los Angeles. Dodger hitters made quick work of David Cone with a run in the first inning and four in the second. "We wanted to make sure that Cone had time to meet his deadlines," scoffed Los Angeles second baseman Steve Sax.

> *Game two was moved from 3:07 p.m. Eastern Time to 10:08 p.m., so as not to conflict with the vice-presidential debate between Lloyd Bentsen and Dan Quayle. The following day Cone apologized to Howell and wrote no more newspaper columns.*

OCTOBER 7 Game three is postponed by heavy rainfall in New York City.

OCTOBER 8   The Mets score five runs in the eighth inning and beat the Dodgers 8–4 before 44,672 at Shea Stadium. Jay Howell began the eighth in relief of Orel Hershiser with the Dodgers leading 4–3. The Mets complained to umpire Joe West that Howell had a foreign substance on his glove. Crew chief Harry Wendelstedt checked the glove and ejected Howell. Three Dodger relievers combined to allow the five runs, all after two were out. Wally Backman tied the score with an RBI-single. Mookie Wilson broke the deadlock with another single. Darryl Strawberry capped the rally with a two-run double.

National League President Bart Giamatti suspended Howell for three games.

OCTOBER 9   On the brink of taking a three-games-to-one lead, the Mets allow two runs in the ninth inning and one in the 12th to lose 5–4 before 54,014 at Shea Stadium. The Mets trailed 2–0 when Kevin McReynolds and Darryl Strawberry hit back-to-back homers off John Tudor in the fourth to produce three runs. The Mets added another run in the sixth. Mike Scioscia hit a two-run homer in the ninth off Dwight Gooden to tie the score 4–4. Kirk Gibson's home run in the 12th against Roger McDowell won it for the Dodgers.

OCTOBER 10   The Dodgers move within one victory of a World Series berth by beating the Mets 7–4 before 52,069 on a Monday afternoon at Shea Stadium. Sid Fernandez allowed six runs in four innings. Lenny Dykstra hit a three-run homer in the losing cause.

OCTOBER 11   The Mets force a seventh game by defeating the Dodgers 5–1 in Los Angeles. Kevin McReynolds was the hitting star with four hits in four at-bats on a homer, a double and two singles. David Cone pitched a complete game.

OCTOBER 12   The Dodgers win the pennant by beating the Mets 6–0 in Los Angeles in game seven. Orel Hershiser continued his remarkable streak of pitching with a five-hit shutout. The Dodgers pummeled Ron Darling with a run in the first inning and five in the second.

The Dodgers went on to win the World Series four games to one over the heavily favored Oakland Athletics. Game one featured Kirk Gibson's dramatic walk-off homer off Dennis Eckersley. The loss left the Mets with an empty feeling of what might have been. The club was 488–320 from 1984 through 1988, a winning percentage of .604, yet reached the World Series only once. The 1988 Mets were 100–60. The cumulative age of the batters that season was the fifth youngest in the National League. The pitching staff was the second youngest. Those who were 27 or younger on Opening Day in 1989 included Dwight Gooden, Darryl Strawberry, Rick Aguilera, David Cone, Randy Myers, Kevin Tapani, Kevin Elster, Gregg Jefferies, Dave Magadan and Lenny Dykstra. It still appeared as though the Mets would remain on top for some time, but the franchise fell to 59–103 by 1993 with one of the oldest rosters in the league and failed to reach the postseason again until 2000.

DECEMBER 7   A month after George Bush beats Michael Dukakis in the Presidential election, the Mets trade Wally Backman and Mike Santiago to the Twins for Jeff Bumgarner, Steve Gasser and Toby Nivens.

1989

Season in a Sentence

The Mets fall far short of expectations with 87 wins and a second-place finish six games behind the Cubs.

Finish • Won • Lost • Pct • GB

| Finish | 87 | 75 | .537 | 6.0 |

Manager

Davey Johnson

Stats

Stats	Mets • AL • Rank		
Batting Avg:	.246	.246	7
On-Base Pct:	.311	.312	8
Slugging Pct:	.385	.365	3
Home Runs:	147	1	
Stolen Bases:	158	2	
ERA:	3.29	3.49	2
Errors:	144	9	
Runs Scored:	683	3	
Runs Allowed:	595	2	

Starting Lineup

Barry Lyons, c
Dave Magadan, 1b
Gregg Jefferies, 2b
Howard Johnson, 3b
Kevin Elster, ss
Kevin McReynolds, lf
Juan Samuel, cf
Darryl Strawberry, rf
Mookie Wilson, cf-lf
Tim Teufel, 2b-1b
Keith Hernandez, 1b

Pitchers

David Cone, sp
Sid Fernandez, sp
Ron Darling, sp
Bobby Ojeda, sp
Dwight Gooden, sp
Frank Viola, sp
Randy Myers, rp
Rick Aguilera, rp
Don Aase, rp

Attendance

2,918,710 (third in NL)

Club Leaders

Batting Avg:	Howard Johnson	.287
On-Base Pct:	Howard Johnson	.369
Slugging Pct:	Howard Johnson	.559
Home Runs:	Howard Johnson	36
RBI:	Howard Johnson	101
Runs:	Howard Johnson	104
Stolen Bases:	Howard Johnson	41
Wins:	Three tied with	14
Strikeouts:	Sid Fernandez	198
ERA:	Sid Fernandez	2.83
Saves:	Randy Myers	24

FEBRUARY 20   The Mets sign Don Aase, most recently with the Orioles, as a free agent.

APRIL 3   Ten days after the Exxon Valdez spills oil into Alaska's Prince William Sound, the Mets open the season with an 8–4 win over the Cardinals before 38,539 at Shea Stadium. It was the 11th year in a row in which the Mets won their home opener. Howard Johnson homered and drove in three runs. Darryl Strawberry collected three hits, two of them doubles, and stole two bases. Dwight Gooden was the starting pitcher and went seven innings.

Gary Cohen joined the Mets broadcasting team in 1989.

APRIL 14   The Mets break a 1–1 tie with seven runs in the fifth inning and beat the Cardinals 9–4 in St. Louis. Gregg Jefferies keyed the rally with a three-run double.

APRIL 17   During a span of four pitches in the third inning, Darryl Strawberry, Kevin McReynolds and Keith Hernandez hit consecutive homers off Dan Carman leading to a 5–2 win over the Phillies at Shea Stadium.

MAY 4   Howard Johnson hits a walk-off homer in the tenth inning to beat the Reds 3–2 at Shea Stadium.

Johnson led the Mets in nearly every offensive category in 1989 with a .287 average, 36 homers, 101 RBI, 104 runs, 41 doubles and 41 stolen bases.

MAY 19   With two out in the tenth inning and the score 2–2 against the Padres at Shea Stadium, Lenny Dykstra, Tim Teufel, Howard Johnson and Darryl Strawberry draw four consecutive walks off Craig Lefferts and Goose Gossage for a 3–2 victory.

JUNE 2   After the Pirates score a run in the top of the tenth, Dave Magadan hits a two-run, walk-off homer in the bottom half which results in a 3–2 win at Shea Stadium.

JUNE 5   In the first round of the amateur draft, the Mets select catcher Alan Zinter from the University of Arizona.

Zinter didn't play his first game in the majors until 2002 when he was with the Astros and was 34 years old. In 67 big-league games he hit .167. Other future major leaguers drafted and signed by the Mets in 1989 were Brook Fordyce (third round), Butch Huskey (seventh round), Mike Thomas (23rd round), Joe Vitko (24th round) and Dave Telgheder (31st round).

JUNE 6   The Mets pull off a triple play in the fifth inning of an 8–4 loss to the Cubs at Wrigley Field. The Chicago fifth began with five consecutive singles that produced three runs. With runners on first and second, Vern Law lined to first baseman Dave Magadan, who threw to shortstop Kevin Elster for a forceout at second base. Elster fired the ball back to Magadan for the completion of the 3–6–3 triple play.

JUNE 9   The Mets trade Terry Leach to the Royals for Aquedo Vasquez.

JUNE 15   Down 3–0, the Mets score a run in the eighth inning, two in the ninth and one in the 12th for a 4–3 win over the Cubs at Shea Stadium. Darryl Strawberry homered in the eighth. With two out and a runner on first base in the ninth, pinch-hitter Keith Miller doubled, Howard Johnson was intentionally walked to load the bases, and Dave Magadan delivered a two-run, game-tying single. Gregg Jefferies drove in the winning run with a walk-off single in the 12th.

JUNE 16   The Mets emerge with a 15–11 victory over the Phillies at Veterans Stadium. The Mets scored eight runs in the top of the first, but Philadelphia countered with five in the bottom half. By the end of the seventh, the Mets trailed 11–10. In the eighth, Mackey Sasser hit a two-run, pinch-hit double that put New York into the lead.

JUNE 17   Bobby Ojeda pitches a three-hit shutout to defeat the Phillies 1–0 in Philadelphia. The lone run scored on a double by Kevin McReynolds in the first inning.

JUNE 18   The Mets trade Lenny Dykstra, Roger McDowell and Tom Edens to the Phillies for Juan Samuel.

The failure to win the 1988 NLCS and the slow start in 1989 helped create a "win now" philosophy in the Mets organization, leading to several trades of young players for veterans. Most of them had a negative impact on the future of the franchise, including this one with the Phillies, which proved to be a disaster. Dykstra played in three All-Star Games in a Phillies uniform and was the runner-up to Barry Bonds in the 1993 MVP balloting. The 143 runs he scored that season were the most by a National Leaguer in any season between 1932 and 2000. Lenny led the NL in hits twice, and runs, on-base percentage and walks once each. McDowell was an effective reliever for the Phillies and Dodgers for five years after leaving New York. Samuel succeeded Dykstra as the Mets starting center fielder but hit only .228 with three homers in 86 games with the club. He went to the Dodgers in a trade after the close of the season. The Mets didn't have another player appear in 100 or more games in center field in back-to-back seasons until Jay Payton did it in 2000 and 2001.

JUNE 19   Dwight Gooden records his 100th career win with a 5–3 decision over the Expos at Shea Stadium.

                 Gooden reached the 100-win plateau with the second-fewest losses in major league history. He was 100–37. The pitcher with the fewest defeats and 100 victories is Whitey Ford, who was 100–36 with the Yankees from 1950 through 1958. At 24 years and eight months of age, Gooden is also the third youngest since 1899 to win 100 games. The two youngest are Bob Feller (22 years and nine months) with the Indians from 1936 through 1941, and Noodles Hahn (24 years and four months) with the Reds from 1899 and 1903.

JUNE 24   Ron Darling hits his first major league homer during a 4–2 victory over the Phillies at Shea Stadium.

JUNE 25   The Mets beat the Phillies 5–1 at Shea Stadium without a single assist. The 27 outs were recorded by Sid Fernandez (seven innings) and Rick Aguilera (two innings) on 13 strikeouts, 12 fly balls and two unassisted grounders to first baseman Dave Magadan.

JUNE 30   Ron Darling homers in his second straight start during an 11–1 triumph over the Reds in Cincinnati.

                 The homers by Darling on June 24 and June 30 were his only two over 526 at-bats during his career.

JULY 11   After drawing the starting assignment at third base, Howard Johnson drives in a run with a single during the All-Star Game in Anaheim. The American League won 5–3.

JULY 14   Sid Fernandez strikes out 16 batters without issuing a walk but loses 3–2 to the Braves in Atlanta by allowing a walk-off homer to Lonnie Smith leading off the ninth.

JULY 20   Rick Aguilera closes out a 4–1 win over the Braves at Shea Stadium with a spectacular relief performance. Aguilera retired all ten batters he faced, seven of them on strikeouts.

JULY 31   The Mets make three deals on deadline day. Rick Aguilera, Kevin Tapani, David West, Tim Drummond and Jack Savage were packaged in a deal with the Twins for Frank Viola. Mookie Wilson went to the Blue Jays for Mike Brady and Jeff Musselman. Lee Mazzilli also went to Toronto in a waiver deal.

In the long term, the deal with Minnesota was one of the worst in club history. Aguilera was the Twins closer until 1998 and lasted in the majors until 2000. Tapani was inconsistent throughout his career, but won 16 games for the Twins in 1991 and 1992 and 19 with the Cubs in 1998. Aguilera and Tapani were both key members of Minnesota's 1991 world championship club. Tapani recorded 141 big-league wins after leaving the Mets. The transaction did have some short-term benefits, however. A native of Long Island, who attended St. John's University, Viola won 93 games for the Twins over five seasons from 1984 through 1988. He was the AL Cy Young winner in 1988 with a 24–7 record. After posting a 5–5 record for the Mets over the remainder of 1989, Viola was 20–12 with the club in 1990. Following a 13–15 season in 1991, he departed to the Red Sox as a free agent.

AUGUST 1   Kevin McReynolds hits for the cycle, drives in six runs and scores four during an 11–0 thrashing of the Cardinals in St. Louis. Facing Scott Terry, McReynolds doubled in the first inning, grounded out in the fourth and hit a three-run homer in the sixth. McReynolds followed with a single off Dan Quisenberry in the eighth and a bases-loaded triple against Ricky Horton in the ninth.

AUGUST 6   A walk-off homer by Kevin McReynolds in the 14th inning beats the Expos 2–1 at Shea Stadium. Darryl Strawberry tied the score with a solo shot in the seventh. Sid Fernandez (eight innings), Randy Myers (1 1/3 innings), Jeff Innis (two-thirds of an inning), Don Aase (two innings) and Jeff Musselman (two innings) were the New York pitchers.

AUGUST 15   The Mets score two runs in the ninth inning on a homer by Kevin McReynolds, a single from Barry Lyons and Kevin Elster's double to beat the Padres 3–2 at Shea Stadium.

AUGUST 28   Frank Viola pitches a three-hitter to beat Orel Hershiser and the Dodgers 1–0 in Los Angeles. It was the first match-up of reigning Cy Young Award winners in major league history. The lone run was driven in with a single by Howard Johnson in the third inning. Both won the honor in 1988.

AUGUST 30   Kevin McReynolds hits a grand slam off Tim Crews in the seventh inning of a 9–3 victory over the Dodgers in Los Angeles.

            At the conclusion of the game, the Mets were 2 1/2 games behind the first-place Cubs, but lost 12 of their next 19 to drop out of the race.

SEPTEMBER 7   Gregg Jefferies ties a club record with four extra base hits during a 13–1 trouncing of the Cardinals at Shea Stadium. Jefferies hit two homers and two doubles in addition to driving in five runs.

SEPTEMBER 21 Sid Fernandez pitches a two-hitter and strikes out 13 without a walk to beat the Cardinals 6–1 at Busch Stadium. The only St. Louis hits were a triple by Terry Pendleton and a single from Todd Zeile in the fifth inning.

SEPTEMBER 23 The Mets score six runs in the fourth inning and rout the Expos 13–6 at Shea Stadium. Gregg Jefferies led off the first inning with a home run on the first pitch from Mark Langston.

SEPTEMBER 30   The Mets score five runs in the 11th inning to finish off the Pirates 7–2 in Pittsburgh.

NOVEMBER 14   A month after the San Francisco Bay area earthquake delays the World Series, the Mets release Gary Carter.

Carter hit only .183 in 50 games for the Mets in 1989. He played three more seasons with three clubs (Giants, Dodgers and Expos) before calling it a career. Carter was elected to the Hall of Fame in 2003.

DECEMBER 6   The Mets trade Randy Myers and Kip Gross to the Reds for John Franco and Don Brown.

A native of Brooklyn, Franco attended Lafayette High School and St. John's University. Lafayette also produced Sandy Koufax, Mets president Fred Wilpon, broadcaster Larry King, singer Vic Damone, sportswriter Larry Merchant, artist Peter Max and actor Paul Sorvino. When acquired by the Mets, Franco had played six seasons in Cincinnati and was named to two All-Star teams. He remained with the Mets until 2004 and led the NL in saves in 1990 and 1994. Franco is the club's all-time leader in games pitched (695) and saves (276). In all, he pitched in 1,119 big-league games and recorded 424 saves. Myers was the closer for the Cincinnati 1990 world champions. He would later lead his league in saves with the Cubs in 1993 and 1995 and the Orioles in 1997.

DECEMBER 7   Keith Hernandez signs with the Indians as a free agent.

Keith's days as an effective player were over. He hit only .200 with a single home run in 130 at-bats in Cleveland.

DECEMBER 20   The Mets trade Juan Samuel to the Dodgers for Mike Marshall and Alejandro Pena.

THE STATE OF THE METS

The Mets had a record of 666–466 from 1984 through 1990, the best in the majors over that seven-year period. Mets fans were left frustrated, however, because the club reached the postseason only in 1986 and 1988. The 1986 team won the World Series, but the 1988 squad lost the NLCS to the underdog Dodgers. Beginning in 1991, the franchise experienced six losing seasons in a row. The Mets finished above .500 five seasons in succession starting in 1997. Overall, the Mets were 767–786 during the 1990s, a winning percentage of .493. Of the 12 teams that were a part of the NL during the entire decade, the Mets ranked seventh. National League pennant winners during the 1990s were the Reds (1990), Braves (1991, 1992, 1995, 1996 and 1999), Phillies (1993), Marlins (1997) and Padres (1998). NL East champions were the Pirates (1990, 1991, 1992), Phillies (1993) and Braves (1995 through 1999). No, there were no pennant winners in 1994 because of the players' strike.

THE BEST TEAM

The 1999 Mets reached the playoffs as a wild card after beating the Reds in a one-game playoff and finished the regular season with a record of 97–66. The Mets reached the Championship Series before losing to the Braves.

THE WORST TEAM

The 1993 Mets bottomed out at 59–103, the worst record for the franchise between 1965 and the present.

THE BEST MOMENT

The Mets beat the Diamondbacks three games to one in the 1999 Division Series.

THE WORST MOMENT

Vince Coleman threw a firecracker out of a car window in 1993, injuring three people.

THE ALL-DECADE TEAM • YEARS W/METS

Todd Hundley, c	1990–98
Dave Magadan, 1b	1986–92
Edgardo Alfonso, 2b	1995–2002
Howard Johnson, 3b	1986–93
Rey Ordonez, ss	1996–2002
Bernard Gilkey, lf	1996–98
Lance Johnson, cf	1996–97
Bobby Bonilla, rf	1992–94
Rick Reed, p	1997–2001
Bobby Jones, p	1993–2000
Dwight Gooden, p	1984–94
John Franco, rp	1990–2001, 2003–04

Gooden was also on the 1980s All-Decade Team. Center field and right field were almost constant problems for the Mets during the 1990s. Other prominent Mets during the decade included first baseman John Olerud (1997–99), second baseman Gregg Jefferies (1987–91) and second baseman Jeff Kent (1992–96).

THE DECADE LEADERS

Batting Avg:	John Olerud	.315
On-Base Pct:	John Olerud	.425
Slugging Pct:	John Olerud	.501
Home Runs:	Todd Hundley	124
RBI:	Todd Hundley	397
Runs:	Edgardo Alfonso	363
Stolen Bases:	Vince Coleman	99
Wins:	Bobby Jones	63
Strikeouts:	Dwight Gooden	707
ERA:	John Franco	2.88
Saves:	John Franco	268

THE HOME FIELD

Shea Stadium was in its 27th season of existence in 1990. After drawing over three million in both 1987 and 1988, attendance was 2,732,745 in 1990, fell to 1,151,471 in the strike-shortened season of 1994 and rose again to 2,725,668 in 1999. There were few significant changes to the stadium. Huge dioramas were hung inside Shea in 1992 featuring action shots of memorable players and moments in franchise history. New seats were added behind home plate in 1999.

THE GAME YOU WISHED YOU HAD SEEN

Trailing the Braves 3–2 in the 15th inning in the 1999 NLCS on October 17, the Mets won 4–3 on Robin Ventura's "grand slam single."

THE WAY THE GAME WAS PLAYED

Baseball experienced one of its pivotal changes during the 1990s, as offensive numbers soared to new heights. Fueled by expansion to 30 teams, newer parks with fences closer to home plate and the use by some players of performance-enhancing substances, the average number of home runs in the NL increased from 114 per team in 1989 to 181 in 1999. The average number of runs per game increased from 7.9 in 1989 to 10.0 in 1999. The trend of the 1970s and 1980s toward the artificial turf ended as every new ballpark that opened or was on the drawing board featured a grass field. Most of the parks, beginning with Camden Yards in Baltimore in 1992, had "retro" features that tried to emulate the older, classic venues. Four new teams were added in Miami, Denver, St. Petersburg and Phoenix. Beginning in 1994, there were three divisions in each league, adding a new tier of playoffs. Inter-league play started in 1997, giving the Mets a chance to settle their rivalry with the Yankees on the field.

THE MANAGEMENT

Throughout the decade, Nelson Doubleday was the chairman of the board and Fred Wilpon was president. The Doubleday Corporation bought the Mets in 1980. Doubleday and Wilpon purchased the club from the corporation in 1986. There was considerable turnover in the front office. General managers were Frank Cashen (1980–91), Al Harazin (1991–93), Joe McIlvaine (1993–97) and Steve Phillips (1997–2003). This also led to several changes in the dugout. Field managers were Davey Johnson (1984–90), Bud Harrelson (1990–91), Mike Cubbage (interim 1991), Jeff Torborg (1992–93), Dallas Green (1993–96) and Bobby Valentine (1996–2002).

THE BEST PLAYER MOVE

The best player move was signing Edgardo Alfonso as an amateur free agent out of his native Venezuela in 1991. The best trade brought John Olerud to New York from the Blue Jays for Robert Person and cash in December 1996.

THE WORST PLAYER MOVE

The worst player move was the trade of Jeff Kent and Jose Vizcaino to the Indians for Carlos Baerga and Alvaro Espinoza in July 1996.

1990

Season in a Sentence

Davey Johnson is fired as manager in May but the change in managers fails to result in a pennant as the Mets finish second for the fifth time in seven years.

Finish • Won • Lost • Pct • GB

Second   91   71   .562   4.0

Managers

Davey Johnson (20–22) and Bud Harrelson (71–49)

Stats

Stats	Mets	AL	Rank
Batting Avg:	.256	.258	
On-Base Pct:	.323	.321	
Slugging Pct:	.408	.383	
Home Runs:	172	1	
Stolen Bases:	110	9	
ERA:	3.42	3.79	4
Errors:	132	9	
Runs Scored:	775	1	
Runs Allowed:	613	3	

Starting Lineup

Mackey Sasser, c
Dave Magadan, 1b
Gregg Jefferies, 2b
Howard Johnson, 3b-ss
Kevin Elster, ss
Kevin McReynolds, lf
Daryl Boston, cf
Darryl Strawberry, rf
Keith Miller, cf
Tom O'Malley, 3b

Pitchers

Frank Viola, sp
Dwight Gooden, sp
David Cone, sp
Sid Fernandez, sp
Ron Darling, sp-rp
John Franco, rp
Bobby Ojeda, rp-sp
Alejandro Pena, rp

Attendance

2,732,745 (second in NL)

Club Leaders

Club Leaders		
Batting Avg:	Dave Magadan	.328
On-Base Pct:	Dave Magadan	.417
Slugging Pct:	Darryl Strawberry	.518
Home Runs:	Darryl Strawberry	37
RBI:	Darryl Strawberry	108
Runs:	Gregg Jefferies	96
Stolen Bases:	Howard Johnson	34
Wins:	Frank Viola	20
Strikeouts:	David Cone	233
ERA:	Frank Viola	2.67
Saves:	John Franco	33

FEBRUARY 15   The owners lock the players out of spring training because of a lack of progress during negotiations for a new basic agreement.

FEBRUARY 20   Don Aase signs with the Dodgers as a free agent.

MARCH 18   The labor dispute between the players and owners is resolved.

Spring training camps opened on March 20. The season, scheduled to open on April 1, was delayed a week, with missed games made up with double-headers and by extending the close of the season by three days.

MARCH 26   The Mets sign D. J. Dozier as a free agent.

Dozier was an interesting experiment by the club. After starring as a running back at Penn State, Dozier was drafted in the first round (14th overall) by the Minnesota Vikings in 1987. After gaining just 631 yards in his first three seasons in the NFL, Dozier decided to give baseball a try as an outfielder. He played in 25 big-league games, all as an outfielder with the Mets in 1992, and batted .191 in 47 at-bats.

APRIL 9	The Pirates bury the Mets 12–3 before an Opening Day crowd of 47,919 at Shea Stadium. Dwight Gooden started and allowed five runs in $4^2/3$ innings. Howard Johnson and Barry Lyons homered in the losing cause.
APRIL 13	A two-run homer by Barry Lyons caps a three-run tenth inning that beats the Expos 4–1 in Montreal.
APRIL 22	Sid Fernandez pitches a two-hitter to defeat the Expos 5–0 at Shea Stadium. Tim Raines collected both Montreal hits with singles in the fourth and seventh innings.
APRIL 27	A home run by Mark Carreon off Mark Portugal in the fourth inning accounts for the lone run of a 1–0 win over the Astros in Houston. Frank Viola (five innings), Wally Whitehurst ($2^1/3$ innings) and John Franco ($1^2/3$ innings) combined on the shutout.

> *Viola won his first seven decisions in 1990 and finished the season 20–12 with an earned run average of 2.67. He led the NL in games started (35) and innings pitched ($249^2/3$).*

APRIL 30	David Cone allows two runs to score while arguing a call during a 7–4 loss to the Braves in Atlanta. With the Braves ahead 2–1 and two out in the fourth, Cone was facing Mark Lemke with Dale Murphy on second and Ernie Whitt on first. Second baseman Gregg Jefferies and first baseman Mike Marshall converged on a grounder, fielded by Jefferies. ? **Covered first,** and umpire Charlie Williams called Lemke safe. Cone ignored the runners on base and confronted Williams while still holding the ball. Teammates screamed at Cone while he continued the discussion with Williams, but Cone ignored the pleas and Murphy and Whitt both crossed the plate.

> *On the same day, the Mets purchased Daryl Boston from the White Sox. A former first round draft pick (seventh overall), Boston possessed a world of talent but was never able to hold a starting position in Chicago for very long. He played three seasons with the Mets as a platoon outfielder.*

MAY 6	A three-run, walk-off homer by Kevin McReynolds in the 11th inning beats the Astros 7–4 in the first game of a double-header at Shea Stadium. In the top of the 11th, Houston scored when John Franco loaded the bases with a single and two walks, then committed a balk. In the bottom half, Tim Teufel doubled in a run prior to the home run by McReynolds. In the second game, the Mets overcame a 6–2 deficit to win 7–6.
MAY 11	Dwight Gooden strikes out 15 batters in seven innings during a 9–4 win over the Dodgers at Shea Stadium. Gooden also delivered the key hit of the game with a three-run triple in the third inning.
MAY 21	The Mets score eight runs in the third inning and beat the Dodgers 12–3 in Los Angeles. Kevin McReynolds belted a grand slam off Mike Morgan.
MAY 22	Mike Marshall delivers six runs batted in during an 8–3 triumph over the Dodgers in Los Angeles. Marshall drove in the runs with a single and a sacrifice fly before walloping a grand slam off Mike Hartley in the sixth inning.

MAY 26   The Mets thrash the Padres 11–0 at Shea Stadium. Sid Fernandez (seven innings) and Alejandro Pena (two innings) combined on the shutout.

> *The Mets outscored the opposition 775 to 613 to lead the NL in run differential. It was the fifth consecutive season that the Mets had led the NL East in outscoring the opposition, and the fourth occasion during that period that the club led the league in the category, and yet the Mets won only two division titles and played on the World Series just once.*

MAY 29   With the club holding a record of 20–22, the Mets fire Davey Johnson as manager and replace him with 45-year-old Bud Harrelson.

> *In Johnson's six full years as manager, the Mets averaged 96 wins a season. But frustration had set in because the club made the postseason only twice and the World Series just once. Frank Cashen told reporters that he believed his team had been "underachieving." Johnson had been criticized for not being enough of a disciplinarian and a motivator. Harrelson played shortstop for the Mets from 1965 through 1977 before closing out his playing career with two seasons in Philadelphia. He had been a coach with the Mets in 1982, a broadcaster in 1983, a minor league manager in 1984 and a coach again from 1985 through 1990. Under Harrelson, the Mets lost four of their first five games to fall to 21–26, and then went on a 27–5 tear to vault into first place. The club finished at 91–71 and in second place, however, three games behind the Pirates. Harrelson was fired near the end of a losing season in 1991. Johnson later managed the Reds (1993–95), Orioles (1996–97) and Dodgers (1999–2000).*

JUNE 3   Playing in his only major league game, Dave Liddell singles in his lone plate appearance. Liddell came into the game as a pinch-hitter and remained in the lineup as a catcher. The Mets lost 8–3 to the Phillies in Philadelphia.

JUNE 4   David Cone strikes out 12 batters in $6^1/_3$ innings but also allows five runs, and the Mets lose 5–3 to the Expos at Shea Stadium.

> *On the same day, the Mets drafted outfielder Jeromy Burnitz from Oklahoma State University. Burnitz lived up to his billing as a first-round draft choice by fashioning a 14-year career in which he collected 315 homers. He hit only 53 of those home runs as a Met, however, in two separate stints in New York. The first was in 1993 and 1994 and the second in 2002 and 2003. The club let him go twice in trades for little or nothing in return. Overall, the Mets had one of the deepest drafts in franchise history. Other future major leaguers chosen and signed by the Mets in 1990 were Aaron Ledesma (second round), Micah Franklin (third round), Pete Walker (seventh round), Raul Casanova (eighth round), Fernando Vina (ninth round), Brian Daubach (17th round) and Ricky Otero (45th round). Like Burnitz, Vina and Daubach had long careers but were traded by the Mets before becoming big-league regulars.*

JUNE 5   Tom O'Malley hits a walk-off homer in the 11th inning that lifts the Mets to a 6–5 victory over the Expos at Shea Stadium. The home run was the first in the majors for O'Malley since 1987 when he was a member of the Rangers. He entered the game in the tenth and was the third individual to play first base, following Dave Magadan and Tim Teufel. It was the first time that O'Malley had ever played first base. He was then in the ninth, and last, year of his big-league career.

JUNE 12   The Mets erupt with 21 hits, 12 of them for extra bases, and rip the Cubs 19–8 at Wrigley Field. In seven plate appearances, Dave Magadan collected a home run, a triple, two singles, two walks and a sacrifice fly. He drove in six runs. Kevin McReynolds picked up two homers and scored four runs.

JUNE 13   The Mets' offense stays hot with 20 more hits during a 15–10 win over the Cubs in the first game of a double-header in Chicago. Five New York runs in the ninth inning broke a 10–10 tie. In the second tilt, the Mets had 16 more hits and won 9–6.

Over a 13–game period from June 12 through June 26, Magadan had 27 hits in 56 at-bats for an average of .482. He finished the year batting .328 with six home runs. The .328 average was the highest by a Met between 1969 (.340 by Cleon Jones) and 1996 (.333 by Lance Johnson).

JUNE 23   Dwight Gooden pitches a two-hitter to defeat the Phillies 3–0 at Shea Stadium. John Kruk garnered both Philadelphia hits with a double in the fifth inning and a single in the seventh.

JUNE 24   The Mets score three runs in the ninth inning to defeat the Phillies 6–5 at Shea Stadium. Three singles, the last by Gregg Jefferies, produced the first run. The game ended on a two-out, two-run pinch-hit single by Tim Teufel off Roger McDowell.

Jefferies hit .283 with 15 homers, 96 runs scored and a league-leading 40 doubles in 1990.

JUNE 29   The Mets extend their winning streak to 11 games with a 4–2 decision over the Reds at Shea Stadium.

JULY 3   The Mets rout the Astros 12–0 at Shea Stadium. Frank Viola pitched the shutout.

JULY 5   The Mets use five homers to slip past the Braves 9–8 in Atlanta. The five homers were struck by Dave Magadan, Darryl Strawberry, Mark Carreon, Kevin Elster and Orlando Mercado. Strawberry's three-run blast in the seventh turned a 7–5 deficit into an 8–7 lead.

Strawberry batted .277 with 37 home runs and 108 RBI in 1990.

JULY 10   At Wrigley Field in Chicago, Frank Viola and John Franco both pitch scoreless innings in the All-Star Game, but the National League loses 2–0.

JULY 20   Sid Fernandez strikes out seven batters in a row from the first through the third innings of a 6–1 win over the Braves at Shea Stadium. He fanned Ron Gant and Jim Presley in the first, Dale Murphy, Francisco Cabrera and Andreas Thomas in the second, and Greg Olson and Steve Avery in the third. Fernandez finished the game with ten strikeouts in 7²/₃ innings.

JULY 25   The Mets survive a six-run Philadelphia ninth inning to win 10–9 at Veterans Stadium. The Phillies began the rally with seven consecutive singles off Wally Whitehurst and Julio Machado.

JULY 27   The Mets trade Mike Marshall to the Red Sox for Ed Perozo, Greg Hansell and Paul Williams.

JULY 29   Mackey Sasser hits a grand slam off Jose DeLeon in the fifth inning of a 6–0 victory over the Cardinals at Shea Stadium. Dwight Gooden (seven innings) and Bobby Ojeda (two innings) combined on the shutout. The contest was the first regularly scheduled Sunday night game in Shea Stadium history. It was part of ESPN's television package.

AUGUST 1   The Mets score a run in the ninth inning and two in the tenth to defeat the Expos 6–4 in Montreal. Tim Teufel tied the score in the ninth with a two-out homer. Gregg Jefferies broke the 4–4 deadlock with a single.

AUGUST 3   A day after Iraq invades Kuwait and four days before Operation Desert Storm troops arrive in Saudi Arabia, the Mets score three runs in the ninth inning off Lee Smith to beat the Cardinals 5–4 in St. Louis. The Mets trailed 4–3 with two out in the inning before Dave Magadan and Gregg Jefferies delivered RBI-singles. The win gave the Mets a one-game lead over the Pirates in the NL East race.

AUGUST 18 David Cone strikes out 13 batters during a 9–2 triumph over the Giants in San Francisco.

AUGUST 19 Kevin McReynolds contributes two home runs and six runs batted in to a 10–9 victory over the Giants in San Francisco.

AUGUST 30 Darryl Strawberry hits a grand slam off Francisco Oliveras in the eighth inning of a 12–2 win over the Giants at Shea Stadium.

           On the same day, the Mets made several deals to bolster the roster for the stretch drive. Archie Corbin went to the Royals for Pat Tabler. Rocky Elli and Nikco Riesgo were traded to the Phillies for Tommy Herr. And Julio Machado and Kevin Brown were sent to the Brewers for Charlie O'Brien and Kevin Carmody.

AUGUST 31 The Mets score three runs in the ninth inning to defeat the Giants 4–3 at Shea Stadium. The first two New York batters in the ninth were retired. The three runs that produced the improbable victory were achieved with a single by Dave Magadan, a run-producing double by Gregg Jefferies, an intentional walk to Darryl Strawberry, and singles from Kevin McReynolds and Howard Johnson.

SEPTEMBER 4 The Mets drop out of first place with a 1–0 loss to the Cardinals in St. Louis.

           The defeat began a five-game losing streak over a four-day period in which the Mets scored only three runs and fell 3½ games behind the first-place Pirates. Three of the defeats came during a series against Pittsburgh at Three Rivers Stadium, two of them during a double-header on September 5.

SEPTEMBER 6   Bud Harrelson chooses to start 21–year-old Julio Valera during a crucial game against the Pirates in Pittsburgh. It was only Valera's second big-league start. He allowed four runs and eight hits in two innings, and the Mets lost 7–1.

Valera pitched only three more games, and one start, as a member of the Mets. He was traded to the Angels in 1992.

SEPTEMBER 7   David Cone strikes out 12 batters in $6^{1}/_{3}$ innings, but the Mets lose 4–1 to the Phillies in Philadelphia.

SEPTEMBER 8   The Mets break their five-game losing streak by walloping the Phillies 12–2 in Philadelphia.

SEPTEMBER 10   The Mets trade Nick Davis and Steve LaRose to the Astros for Dan Schatzeder.

SEPTEMBER 11   Darryl Strawberry hits a two-run, walk-off homer off Lee Smith to defeat the Cardinals 10–8 at Shea Stadium.

SEPTEMBER 14   Sid Fernandez strikes out 12 batters in $7^{1}/_{3}$ innings, but the Mets lose 4–1 to the Phillies at Shea Stadium.

SEPTEMBER 15   A 4–2 win over the Phillies at Shea Stadium pulls the Mets back to within one-half game of the first-place Pirates.

The Mets lost their next five to fall $3^{1}/_{2}$ games behind. After an 11–5 win over the Cubs in Chicago on September 22, the Mets were $2^{1}/_{2}$ games out with 11 to play, three of them against the Pirates, but were eliminated from the pennant race prior to that season-ending series in Pittsburgh.

OCTOBER 1   David Cone strikes out 12 batters and pitches a three-hitter to defeat the Pirates 4–1 in Pittsburgh.

Cone led the NL in strikeouts in 1990 with 233 in $211^{2}/_{3}$ innings.

OCTOBER 2   Pitching on three days' rest, Dwight Gooden fails in his attempt to win his 20th game of the season by dropping a 9–4 decision to the Pirates in Pittsburgh.

Gooden started the season with a 3–5 record, then won 16 of 17 decisions. His final won-lost ledger was 19–7, but he was helped greatly by his hitters. Gooden was the beneficiary of 6.8 runs per start. His ERA was 3.83, higher than the NL average that season of 3.79. At the end of the season, Gooden had a career record of 119–46, and he didn't turn 26 until November 16, 1990. The last prior pitcher with at least 119 wins before his 26th birthday was Noodles Hahn with the Reds from 1899 through 1905. With a 13–7 record in 1991, Gooden had more wins (132) at 27 than any pitcher since 1900. He underwent rotator cuff surgery on September 7, 1991, and was never the same afterward. Gooden finished his career in 2000 with a 194–112 record.

OCTOBER 3   Pitching on three days' rest, Frank Viola records his 20th win of the season with a 6–3 decision over the Pirates in Pittsburgh.

NOVEMBER 8   Darryl Strawberry signs with the Dodgers as a free agent.

> *Strawberry opted out of the pressure cooker atmosphere of New York to sign a five-year contract with his hometown Dodgers. He was 29 on Opening Day in 1991. The number one overall pick out of Crenshaw High School in Los Angeles in the 1980 amateur draft, Strawberry was compared to Ted Williams before he ever appeared in a major league game. Strawberry was named to seven All-Star teams as a Met, but no matter how well he played, he could never meet those lofty expectations. Strawberry and Los Angeles seemed like a perfect match. "His best years are ahead of him," said Dodgers general manager Fred Claire. "He's a premier player who can lead the Dodgers into the 1990s. There were warning signs, however, that Strawberry would cause a problem as a long-term investment. He was treated for alcoholism in February 1990, and there were rumors of drug use and domestic violence along with well-publicized battles with teammates and manager Davey Johnson. "We're a better franchise without him," said Mets general manager Frank Cashen. It was hoped that coming home would help Strawberry avoid his previous problems, but it failed to work. During his first year with the Dodgers, he missed 23 games with injuries and hit .265 with 28 homers, and then played in only 75 contests in 1992 and 1993 combined because of back problems. Strawberry started the 1994 season at the Betty Ford Clinic with a drug problem and was released by the Dodgers. Strawberry played for the Giants (1994) and Yankees (1995–99), but was never a regular again and often found himself embroiled in legal and health problems. He was indicted for tax evasion in 1994, started the 1995 season with a 60–day drug suspension, missed most of 1997 with a knee injury, underwent a successful recovery from colon cancer in 1998 and 1999, and was suspended for one year in 2000 for drug use, which ended his career.*

DECEMBER 4   Dan Schatzeder signs with the Royals as a free agent.

DECEMBER 5   Pat Tabler signs with the Blue Jays as a free agent. On the same day, the Mets signed Vince Coleman, most recently with the Cardinals, as a free agent.

> *Free agency became a reality in 1976, but for 14 years, the Mets steadfastly avoided signing high-profile free agents. The most prominent free agent acquired by the Mets prior to 1990 was Elliott Maddox in 1980. After making his major league debut in 1984, Coleman led the NL in steals in each of his first seasons in the majors with a total of 549 over that span, an average of 91.5 per year. He was 29 when signed by the Mets. But Coleman was a bust in New York, appearing in only 235 games over three seasons, while battling hamstring and rib injuries and hitting .270 with 99 steals. He complained that Shea Stadium's dirt infield was keeping him "out of the Hall of Fame" and had nasty run-ins with coach Mike Cubbage and manager Jeff Torborg. Coleman is best remembered by Mets fans for throwing firecrackers at fans in Los Angeles in 1993.*

DECEMBER 15   The Mets trade Bobby Ojeda and Greg Hansell to the Dodgers for Hubie Brooks.

The Phantom Dynasty

Mets fans will always savor 1986. The club won 108 regular season games, dispatched the Astros in a thrilling six-game NLCS and then beat the Red Sox in miraculous fashion in the World Series. But there remains a well-justified belief that the franchise should have followed that season with many more championships.

At the time Davey Johnson was hired by the Mets at the end of the 1983 season, the club had experienced seven consecutive seasons in which they failed to post a winning percentage above .420. They were 68–94 in 1983. There was little reason to think the Mets would be much better in 1984, but Johnson led the team to a 90–72 record and a second-place finish behind the Cubs. The 1984 Mets were an overachieving bunch that was outscored 676 runs to 652. The improvement continued in 1985 with 98 wins, the second best in the National League. Unfortunately, the Cardinals won 101 games that season in the same division.

Everything came together in 1986 and it appeared that the Mets would sustain the momentum for many years to come. But in 1987, the pitching staff was devastated by injuries, and Dwight Gooden missed two months with a suspension for drug use. The Mets won 92 games, again the second-best in the NL, but finished three games back of the Cardinals in the NL East. The Mets had a run differential that season plus 125, which was the best in the National league. The feeling remained that the Mets were a better team than the Cards, but had just run into bad luck.

The Mets came back in 1988 with a 100–60 record, which was the best in the league. The club came into the NLCS against a Dodgers club that was 94–67 and riddled with injuries. The Mets were heavy favorites but lost the series in seven games. In many ways, the franchise lost its way following the shocking defeat and never fully recovered.

The 1988 Mets were still among the youngest clubs in baseball. The club was built with a strong farm system that featured the likes of Dwight Gooden, Darryl Strawberry, Ron Darling, Sid Fernandez, Jesse Orosco, Lenny Dykstra and Roger McDowell. Trades brought Keith Hernandez and Gary Carter. The farm system was still producing,

but the loss to the Dodgers created a change in the mindset of the front office. Young players like Dykstra, McDowell, Rick Aguilera and Kevin Tapani were dealt for veterans during the 1989 season. The Mets were 87–75 that season and were second again, this time to the Cubs. For the fourth straight year, the Mets led the division in run differential, outscoring the opposition by 88 runs.

After a 20–22 start in 1990, Davey Johnson was fired because the front office thought he was too lax with the players. Johnson was replaced by Bud Harrelson, who was considered to be more of a disciplinarian.

The 1990 Mets led the NL in run differential, outscoring the opposition by 162 runs (775–613). It was the fourth time in five years that the Mets led the National League in the category, and the fifth straight season in which the team had the best run differential in the Eastern Division. Yet the result was another second-place finish, the fifth in a span of seven years. The Mets were 91–71 and finished three games behind the Pirates. From 1985 through 1991, 22 of the 28 division winners in the major leagues also led their division in run differential. The 1987, 1989 and 1990 Mets accounted for three of the half-dozen non-winners. (The others were the 1987 and 1990 Blue Jays and the 1987 Royals.)

The Mets had resolutely avoided the free agency market during the club's peak seasons when a few additional players could have filled holes in the roster and put the team over the top. Fans believed the team could well afford to delve into the free agent market because the franchise twice drew over three million to Shea Stadium and had a lucrative television and radio contract. The club front office changed tactics beginning with the 1990–91 offseason, and over the next two years signed free agents like Bobby Bonilla, Vince Coleman, Willie Randolph, Eddie Murray and Frank Tanana and traded for Bret Saberhagen and Tony Fernandez.

It only made matters worse. Tabbed by most as the favorites to win the division in 1991, the Mets stumbled to a 77–84 record. The club had the highest payroll in baseball in 1992 ($45 million), but the result was 72 wins and 90 defeats. John Klapisch and John Harper wrote a chronicle of that season titled *The Worst Team Money Could Buy*. But not even the authors could anticipate the complete meltdown of 1993 in which the Mets lost 103 games, the most of any Mets team since 1965.

In addition to being disappointments on the field, Coleman threw firecrackers at fans, Saberhagen sprayed bleach at reporters, and Bonilla threatened members of the media with physical violence. It was time to rebuild all over again.

1991

Season in a Sentence

The Mets are in second place just 2½ games out of first on July 13, but a 28–51 record the rest of the way results in the first losing record since 1983.

Finish • Won • Lost • Pct • GB

Fifth   77   84   .478   20.5

Managers

Bud Harrelson (74–80) and
Mike Cubbage (3–4)

Stats

Stats	Mets	AL	Rank
Batting Avg:	.244	.250	9
On-Base Pct:	.317	.317	9
Slugging Pct:	.365	.373	6
Home Runs:	117	7	
Stolen Bases:	153	4	
ERA:	3.56	3.58	4
Errors:	143	11	
Runs Scored:	640		8
Runs Allowed:	646	4	

Starting Lineup

Rick Cerone, c
Dave Magadan, 1b
Gregg Jefferies, 2b-3b
Howard Johnson, 3b
Kevin Elster, ss
Kevin McReynolds, lf
Vince Coleman, cf
Hubie Brooks, rf
Keith Miller, 2b
Daryl Boston, cf
Mark Carreon, lf
Mackey Sasser, c
Garry Templeton, ss-1b

Pitchers

David Cone, sp
Frank Viola, sp
Dwight Gooden, sp
Wally Whitehurst, sp
Ron Darling, sp
John Franco, rp
Pete Schourek, rp
Jeff Innis, rp
Alejandro Pena, rp
Doug Simons, rp

Attendance

2,284,484 (fifth in NL)

Club Leaders

Batting Avg:	Gregg Jefferies	.272
On-Base Pct:	Dave Magadan	.378
Slugging Pct:	Howard Johnson	.535
Home Runs:	Howard Johnson	38
RBI:	Howard Johnson	117
Runs:	Howard Johnson	108
Stolen Bases:	Vince Coleman	37
Wins:	David Cone	14
Strikeouts:	David Cone	241
ERA:	David Cone	3.29
Saves:	John Franco	30

JANUARY 21   Four days after the U.S. and its allies attack Iraq to start the Persian Gulf War, the Mets sign Rick Cerone, most recently with the Yankees, as a free agent.

APRIL 8   Six weeks after president George Bush orders a cease-fire to end the Persian Gulf War, the Mets open the season with a 2–1 win over the Phillies before 49,276 at Shea Stadium. Dwight Gooden (eight innings) and John Franco (one inning) combined on a six-hitter.

APRIL 9   The Mets use two late home runs to beat the Phillies 2–1 in ten innings at Shea Stadium. Rick Cerone homered in the ninth inning and Hubie Brooks in the tenth.

APRIL 14   Dwight Gooden strikes out 14 batters during a 5–3 win over the Expos at Shea Stadium. He threw 147 pitches.

APRIL 30   The game between the Mets and Padres at Shea Stadium is called because of fog in the bottom of the seventh inning with the Mets leading 6–3.

MAY 4   The Mets power their way past the Giants to win 6–4 in 12 innings at Shea Stadium. With the score 4–2 in favor of San Francisco, Mackey Sasser began the ninth by batting for Charlie O'Brien and belted a home run off Jeff Brantley. Mark Carreon followed Sasser as a pinch-hitter for Alejandro Pena and hit another homer to tie the score. Howard Johnson won the game with a two-run, walk-off home run in the 12th.

                 With a 30 stolen bases and a league-leading 38 homers, Johnson reached the 30–30 club for the third time in his career. He previously accomplished the feat in 1987 and 1989. Johnson also led the NL in RBI in 1991 with 117, scored 108 runs and batted .259.

MAY 14   Hubie Brooks hits a grand slam off Eric Nolte in the third inning of a 6–1 victory over the Padres in San Diego.

MAY 24   David Cone strikes out 12 batters and beats the Cardinals 4–2 at Shea Stadium.

MAY 31   The Mets trade Tim Teufel to the Padres for Garry Templeton.

JUNE 1   A broken-bat single in the tenth inning by Milt Thompson of the Cardinals ends a 6–5 loss in St. Louis. With Gerald Perry as the runner on third base, Thompson's bat splintered when he made contact with a John Franco pitch. The ball and half of Thompson's bat whizzed toward first baseman Dave Magadan at the same time. Magadan had to make a split-second decision. If he fielded the ball, he risked serious injury from being struck by the flying bat. If he ducked out of the way, Thompson's hit would win the game for the Cards. Magadan chose to duck, and Perry crossed the plate with the winning run.

JUNE 3   In the first round of the amateur draft, the Mets select outfielder Al Shipley from George Washington High School in Danville, Virginia.

                 Shipley never advanced beyond the Class AA level and hit just .213 during an eight-year minor league career. Future major leaguers drafted and signed by the Mets in 1991 were Bobby Jones (supplemental first-round choice), Mark Kroon (second round), Bill Pulsipher (also in the second round), Erik Hiljus (fourth round), Jason Jacome (12th round), Joe Crawford (17th round) and Jason Isringhausen (44th round).

JUNE 4   David Cone strikes out 13 batters in eight innings of a 4–2 win over the Reds in Cincinnati. He threw 147 pitches.

JUNE 7

Trailing 2–0, the Mets score six runs in the ninth inning and beat the Astros 6–3 in Houston. The six runs were accomplished with only two hits. The Astros used five pitchers during the ninth. They combined to walk seven batters, two of them intentionally.

JUNE 8

Howard Johnson homers in the 11th inning to down the Astros 4–3 in Houston.

JUNE 18

Howard Johnson hits a grand slam off Tom Browning in the third inning of a 7–5 win over the Reds at Shea Stadium.

JUNE 25

With the Mets down to their last strike, Kevin McReynolds hits a walk-off grand slam to beat the Expos 8–5 at Shea Stadium. The Mets loaded bases with a single and two walks, but two were out when McReynolds belted a 2–2 pitch off Scott Ruskin for his dramatic home run.

JULY 3

Ron Darling (eight innings) and Alejandro Pena (one inning) combine on a two-hitter to defeat the Expos 4–0 at Olympic Stadium. The only Montreal hits were singles by Dave Martinez in the second inning and Spike Owen in the eighth.

JULY 13

The Mets extend their winning to ten games with a 3–1 decision over the Padres at Shea Stadium. David Cone struck out 13 batters.

During the ten-game winning streak, the Mets gave up only 15 runS. The July 13 victory gave the Mets a record of 49–34 and a position in second place, 2½ games behind the first-place Pirates. Over the remainder of the season, the Mets were 28–51. It included a horrendous 2–17 stretch from July 30 through the first game of a double-header on August 21. Frank Viola mirrored the two halves of the season. He was 11–5 with a 2.76 ERA on July 12, and 2–10 with an earned run average of 5.75 afterward.

JULY 15

The Mets trade Ron Darling and Mike Thomas to the Expos for Tim Burke.

JULY 20

Mackey Sasser collects four hits, one of them a homer, and drives in five runs, but the Mets lose 11–7 to the Dodgers at Shea Stadium.

JULY 26

Making his first start in six weeks after being sidelined with a hamstring injury, Vince Coleman is ordered out of the batting cage for hitting with the wrong group. Coleman launched a profanity-filled tirade at coach Mike Cubbage and fired his helmet into the dugout. During the game, Coleman made an error and struck out three times as the Mets lost 8–2 in San Diego.

AUGUST 5

Bud Harrelson loses a great deal of credibility by having pitching coach Mel Stottlemyre make a pitching change during a 7–2 loss to the Cubs at Shea Stadium. Harrelson admitted later that he didn't go to the mound because he didn't want to get booed by the crowd.

AUGUST 21

The Mets extend their losing streak to 11 games with a 7–3 loss to the Cardinals in the first game of a double-header at Shea Stadium. The streak was snapped with an 8–0 victory in game two. Sid Fernandez (seven innings) and Alejandro Pena (two innings) combined on the shutout.

AUGUST 28   The Mets trade Alejandro Pena to the Braves for Tony Castillo and Joe Roa.

AUGUST 30   David Cone strikes out three batters on nine pitches in the fifth inning of a 3–2 win over the Reds in Cincinnati. Cone fanned Herm Winningham, Randy Myers and Mariano Duncan.

AUGUST 31   Howard Johnson hits homers from both sides of the plate during a ten-inning, 8–7 win over the Reds in Cincinnati. Johnson homered off Mo Sanford from the left side of the plate in the fourth inning and Norm Charlton from the right side in the seventh. Keith Miller won the contest with a homer in the tenth.

Johnson hit six homers during a six-game span from August 31 through September 6.

SEPTEMBER 10   Pete Schourek pitches a one-hitter to defeat the Expos 9–0 at Shea Stadium. The only Montreal hit was a single by Kenny Williams in the fifth inning.

It was Schourek's fourth major league start and his first win since May 4. He lasted in the majors until 2001 and made a total of 176 starts, but never pitched another shutout.

SEPTEMBER 13   Kevin McReynolds hits a two-run homer in the tenth to defeat the Cardinals 4–2 in St. Louis.

SEPTEMBER 14   David Cone (seven innings) and Jeff Innis (one inning) combine on a one-hitter, but the Mets lose 2–1 to the Cardinals in St. Louis. In the fifth inning, Cone walked two, threw a wild pitch and allowed a two-out, two-run single to Ray Lankford.

SEPTEMBER 20   David Cone hurls a one-hitter and strikes out 11 to beat the Cardinals 1–0 at Shea Stadium. Cone carried a no-hitter into the eighth before Felix Jose led off the inning with a double. The lone run scored on a single by Mark Carreon in the sixth inning.

In his last five starts in 1991, Cone allowed six runs and 15 hits in 39 innings and struck out 50.

SEPTEMBER 24   Daryl Boston hits a grand slam off Bob Walk in the fifth inning, but the Mets lose 10–8 to the Pirates at Shea Stadium.

SEPTEMBER 27   Frank Cashen, general manager of the Mets since 1980, retires at the age of 65. Cashen was replaced by longtime assistant Al Harazin, who was 48. The decline of the Mets continued unabated under Harazin. He was fired after a 59–103 season in 1993.

SEPTEMBER 29   The Mets fire Bud Harrelson as manager near the end of the club's first losing season in eight years. Coach Mike Cubbage served as interim manager for the final seven games of 1991. Harrelson never managed another major league team.

OCTOBER 2   In Pittsburgh, Kevin McReynolds breaks a 5–5 tie against the Pirates with a three-run homer in the 11th inning. Both teams scored an additional run, and the Mets emerged victorious 9–6.

OCTOBER 6   On the last game of the season, David Cone ties a Mets record with 19 strikeouts during a 7–0 win over the Phillies at Veterans Stadium. At the end of the sixth inning, Cone had 15 strikeouts and a chance at the existing major league record of 20 for a nine-inning game, set by Roger Clemens with the Red Sox in 1986, or the Mets' record of 19, established by Tom Seaver in 1970. Cone failed to fan a batter in the seventh, and then set two down on strikes in the eighth and the first two hitters in the ninth to run his total to 19. With a chance at strikeout number 20, Cone surrendered a double to Wes Chamberlain and retired Dale Murphy on a ground out.

Cone ended the year leading the NL in strikeouts for the second season in a row with 241 in 232²/₃ innings.

OCTOBER 10   The Mets hire 49–year-old Jeff Torborg as manager.

A native of nearby Plainfield, New Jersey, Torborg was a catcher in the majors from 1964 through 1973 with the Dodgers and Angels. He previously managed the Indians (1977–79) and White Sox (1989–1991) to a record of 407–436. Torborg led the Sox to a 94–68 record in 1990 and a surprising second-place finish. It was the club's first winning season since 1985. Torborg and the White Sox were 87–75 in 1991, but he was seldom in agreement with the policies of the owner, Jerry Reinsdorf, and the general manager, Ron Schueler, and was given permission to talk to the Mets. In New York, Torborg was 85–115 before being fired in May 1993.

NOVEMBER 27   The Mets sign Eddie Murray, most recently with the Dodgers, as a free agent.

Murray was 36 on Opening Day in 1992 and had 2,502 career hits and 398 home runs and had batted .330 as recently as 1990. His best days were behind him, but Murray gave the Mets two decent seasons with a .274 average, 43 homers and 193 RBI before departing to Cleveland as a free agent.

DECEMBER 2   The Mets sign Bobby Bonilla, most recently with the Pirates, as a free agent.

A native of the Bronx, Bonilla was 29 on Opening Day in 1992 and was one of the best players in baseball. He was an All-Star each season from 1998 through 1991 and was second in the MVP balloting in 1990 and third in 1991. The five-year contract at $29 million made Bonilla the highest-paid player in baseball. He got off on the wrong foot in New York while struggling to meet expectations and took the brunt of the blame when the club showed no improvement in 1992. Bonilla batted just .249 with 19 home runs that season. He would rebound with three good seasons in New York, but Mets fans never seemed to forgive him for underachieving in 1992 and his surly attitude failed to win over any converts. Bonilla hit 34 homers along with a .265 average in 1993, but the club lost 103 games. In the strike-shortened seasons of 1994 and 1995, Bonilla batted .306 with 38 home runs in 188 games for the Mets before being traded to the Orioles in a July 1995 deadline trade.

DECEMBER 10   The Mets trade Hubie Brooks to the Angels for Dave Gallagher.

DECEMBER 11   The Mets trade Gregg Jefferies, Kevin McReynolds and Keith Miller to the Royals for Bret Saberhagen and Bill Pecota.

Saberhagen was 27 and had won Cy Young Awards in 1985 and 1989. He had an exasperating habit of alternating good years with bad ones. In odd-numbered years, from his rookie year in 1984 through 1991, he was 74–30. In even-numbered seasons, he had a record of 36–48. Saberhagen had a problem with injuries during his first two seasons in New York and was 10–12 in 1992 and 1993 combined. Healthy in 1994, he was 14–4 when the strike was called in August. After a mediocre 1995, Saberhagen went to the Rockies in a trade. Following an unsuccessful year in Kansas City, Jefferies was an All-Star with the Cardinals in 1993 and 1994 before he went into a decline. McReynolds was never again a regular after leaving the Mets.

DECEMBER 20   The Mets sign Willie Randolph, most recently with the Brewers, as a free agent.

Randolph batted .327 for the Brewers in 127 games at the age of 36 in 1991, but it proved to be the last gasp of a stellar career. He hit just .252 in 90 games as a Met.

1992

Season in a Sentence

Adding Eddie Murray, Bobby Bonilla, Willie Randolph and Bret Saberhagen to the roster fails to work as the Mets post another losing season.

Finish • Won • Lost • Pct • GB

Fifth   72   90   .444   24.0

Manager

Jeff Torborg

Stats

Stats	Mets	AL	Rank
Batting Avg:	.235	.252	12
On-Base Pct:	.310	.315	10
Slugging Pct:	.342	.368	11
Home Runs:	93	11	
Stolen Bases:	129	5	
ERA:	3.66	3.50	10
Errors:	116	9	
Runs Scored:	599	9	
Runs Allowed:	653	10	

Starting Lineup

Todd Hundley, c
Eddie Murray, 1b
Willie Randolph, 2b
Dave Magadan, 3b
Dick Schofield, ss
Daryl Boston, lf
Howard Johnson, cf
Bobby Bonilla, rf
Bill Pecota, 2b-3b-ss
Vince Coleman, lf-cf
Chico Walker, 3b

Pitchers

Sid Fernandez, sp
David Cone, sp
Dwight Gooden, sp
Pete Schourek, sp
Bret Saberhagen, sp
Anthony Young, rp
Wally Whitehurst, rp
Jeff Innis, rp
Paul Gibson, rp
Lee Guetterman, rp

Attendance

1,779,534 (eighth in NL)

Club Leaders

Batting Avg:	Eddie Murray	.261
On-Base Pct:	Bobby Bonilla	.348
Slugging Pct:	Bobby Bonilla	.432
Home Runs:	Bobby Bonilla	19
RBI:	Eddie Murray	93
Runs:	Eddie Murray	64
Stolen Bases:	Vince Coleman	24
Wins:	Sid Fernandez	14
Strikeouts:	David Cone	214
ERA:	Sid Fernandez	2.73
Saves:	Anthony Young	15
	John Franco	15

JANUARY 2   Frank Viola signs with the Red Sox as a free agent.

FEBRUARY 12   Rick Cerone signs with the Expos as a free agent.

APRIL 3   The Mets play the first-ever game at Camden Yards in Baltimore and lost 5–3 to the
                 Orioles in an exhibition game. The first regular-season game at the new ballpark
                 took place on April 6 with the Orioles winning 2–0 over the Indians.

APRIL 6   Bobby Bonilla homers twice in his Mets debut to spark the club to a ten-inning, 4–2
                 victory over the Cardinals on Opening Day in St. Louis. Bonilla's first homer was
                 struck in the fourth inning. The Mets trailed 2–1 in the ninth before two singles and
                 a ground out tied the score. In the tenth, Bonilla homered again with a man aboard
                 to give the Mets the win. David Cone (eight innings), Jeff Innis (one inning) and John
                 Franco (one inning) were the New York pitchers.

                 Todd Kalas began a two-year stint as a radio announcer for the Mets in 1992.

APRIL 10   In the first home game of the season, the Mets lose 4–0 to the Expos before 47,218
                 at Shea Stadium.

APRIL 12   The Mets trade Julio Valera to the Angels for Dick Schofield and Julian Vasquez.

APRIL 22   Eddie Murray hits a walk-off homer in the tenth inning to beat the Cardinals 3–2 at
                 Shea Stadium. It was Murray's first home run with the club.

APRIL 23   The Mets outlast the Cardinals to win 1–0 in 13 innings at Shea Stadium. The
                 game ended when Daryl Boston was hit by a pitch from Juan Agosto with the bases
                 loaded. Bret Saberhagen (nine innings), Paul Gibson (two-thirds of an inning), Jeff
                 Innis ($1^1/_3$ innings) and John Franco (two innings) combined on the shutout.

APRIL 28   David Cone pitches a two-hitter to down the Astros 4–0 at Shea Stadium. Cone
                 had a no-hitter in progress until Benny Distefano singled with one out in the eighth
                 inning. Jeff Bagwell added another single leading off the ninth.

APRIL 29   Bret Saberhagen pitches a three-hitter to defeat the Astros 1–0 at Shea Stadium.
                 The lone run scored in the third inning on a double from Eddie Murray and Daryl
                 Boston's single.

APRIL 30   A day after riots begin in Los Angeles, which results in the death of 52 people,
                 Sid Fernandez strikes out 12 batters in $7^2/_3$ innings of a 4–3 victory over the Astros
                 at Shea Stadium. Mets pitchers allowed only eight hits during the three-game series
                 against Houston.

MAY 3   Eddie Murray collects his 400th career homer during a 7–0 win over the Braves in
                 Atlanta. The milestone was struck off Mark Freeman in the eighth inning.

MAY 6   Anthony Young is the losing pitcher in a 5–3 decision against the Reds in Cincinnati.

                 Young came into the game with a career record of 4–5 and was 2–0 in 1992.
                 The May 6 loss was the first of a major league record 27–game losing streak.
                 Young lost his last 14 decisions in 1992 and the first 13 in 1993. While compiling

the 0–27 record, Young pitched in 77 games, 17 of them starts, and had an ERA of 4.36 in 171^1/$_3$ innings. Given his earned run average, Young certainly didn't pitch badly enough to lose 27 straight. The NL average was 3.50 in 1992 and 4.04 in 1993. During the excruciating losing streak, Young actually recorded 16 saves.

MAY 8   In what proves to be his only at-bat as a member of the Mets, Rodney McCray singles during a 4–3 win over the Dodgers at Shea Stadium.

McCray had an unusual career. With the White Sox (1990–91) and Mets (1992), he played in 67 major league games, but had only 14 at-bats because he was used mainly as a pinch-runner. McCray made the highlight reel Hall of Fame in 1991 when he ran through an outfield wall in Portland, Oregon, while playing for Vancouver in the Pacific Coast League.

MAY 9   Dave Magadan hits a three-run, walk-off homer off Roger McDowell with two out in the ninth inning to lift the Mets to a 5–2 triumph over the Dodgers at Shea Stadium.

The Mets peaked on May 24 with a record of 25–20 and a position in third place, one game out of first.

JUNE 1   Bobby Bonilla reaches base five times in five plate appearances and drives in six runs during a 14–1 trouncing of the Giants at Shea Stadium. He walked twice, singled, doubled and belted a grand slam off John Burkett in the second inning. The Mets had scored only two runs in the previous four games.

On the same day, the Mets selected Preston Wilson from Bamberg Ehrhardt High School in Bamberg, South Carolina, in the first round of the amateur draft. Wilson was both the nephew and stepson of ex-Met Mookie Wilson. (Mookie's brother fathered Preston, and Mookie later married Preston's mother.) Preston made his major league debut in 1998, but played only eight games with the Mets before being sent to the Marlins in the Mike Piazza trade. Wilson was a regular for several years with the Marlins and Rockies, and led the NL in RBI in Colorado in 2003. At the end of his career in 2007, he had a .264 batting average and 189 home runs. The only other future major leaguer drafted and signed by the Mets in 1991 was 20th-round pick Allen McDill. The Mets also picked Darrin Erstad in the 13th round, but Erstad elected to attend the University of Nebraska rather turning professional. Erstad was drafted in the first round by the Angels in 1995.

JUNE 2   Eddie Murray breaks a scoreless tie with a grand slam off Trevor Wilson in the third inning, and the Mets go on to beat the Giants 4–3 at Shea Stadium.

JUNE 6   The Mets rout the Pirates 15–1 in Pittsburgh. The inconsistent New York offense was shut out in each of the next two games.

JUNE 8   A fifth-inning single by pitcher Anthony Young is the only Mets hit off Ken Hill during a 6–0 loss to the Expos in Montreal.

JUNE 10   The Mets commit six errors during an 8–2 loss to the Expos in Montreal.

JUNE 22   Bobby Bonilla charges the mound with his bat in his hand after being hit by a
               pitch from Shawn Boskie in the fourth inning of an 8–2 win over the Cubs at Shea
               Stadium. Both dugouts emptied, and Bonilla tried to charge through teammates
               and threw an umpire to the ground to get at Boskie. Bonilla was suspended for two
               games because of the incident.

JUNE 25   After the Cubs score seven runs in the first inning, Bobby Bonilla calls the Shea
               Stadium press box to complain to the official scorer about he error he receives during
               the rally. The Mets lost 9–2.

               *Bonilla was caught on television cameras talking on the phone during the top of
               the first inning while scowling and looking at the scoreboard. After the game he
               claimed that he was making the call to inquire about the health of Mets public
               relations director, Jay Hororwitz.*

JUNE 26   David Cone strikes out 12 batters in seven innings, and Vince Coleman steals four
               bases, but the Mets lose 4–3 to the Cardinals in St. Louis. Each of Coleman's stolen
               bases followed walks. He swiped second base in the first inning, second in the
               second inning, and second and third in the seventh. The fourth steal was the
               600th of his career.

JULY 10   The Mets score three runs in the ninth inning to defeat the Astros 7–6 in Houston.
               The Mets had runners on first and second and were trailing 6–4 with two out in
               the ninth when Howard Johnson walked on a 3–2 pitch. Eddie Murray followed
               Johnson, worked the count to 3–2, fouled off a pitch and then belted a three-run
               double to provide the winning margin.

JULY 14   In the fourth inning of the All-Star Game in San Diego, David Cone retires all
               three batters he faces, but the National League loses 13–6. Cone set down Roberto
               Alomar, Wade Boggs and Kirby Puckett.

JULY 17   David Cone strikes out 13 batters and beats the Giants 1–0 at Shea Stadium. Cone
               threw 166 pitches. The lone run scored on a double by Dave Magadan and a single
               from Howard Johnson in the first inning.

AUGUST 8   The Mets trade Rob Katzeroff to the Giants for Kevin Bass.

AUGUST 10   Vince Coleman sets a club record by drawing five walks, but the Mets lose 4–2 to the
               Pirates in 16 innings at Shea Stadium. Coleman drew the base on balls in eight plate
               appearances. Three of the walks were intentional.

AUGUST 20   Bobby Bonilla homers during an 11–4 win over the Dodgers in Los Angeles. Bonilla
               tied a club record by homering in four consecutive games from August 19 through
               August 23.

AUGUST 27   Three days after Hurricane Andrew hits South Florida, resulting in the death of
               65 people, the Mets trade David Cone to the Blue Jays for Jeff Kent and Ryan
               Thompson.

               *At the time of the transaction, Cone was 13–7 and leading the NL in strikeouts.
               After being dealt to Toronto, Cone lasted in the majors until 2003 and had a*

record of 114–78 with four clubs following the trade, which included seasons in 16–5 in 1994, 18–8 in 1995 and 20–7 in 1998. The Mets still would have come out ahead in the deal if they had kept Kent. He was the Mets regular second baseman for nearly four years before going to the Indians in a horrible trade in 1996.

AUGUST 28   The Mets sweep the Reds 4–3 and 12–1 in a double-header at Shea Stadium.

AUGUST 30   Bobby Bonilla hits a two-out, three-run walk-off homer off Rob Dibble to beat the Reds 4–3 at Shea Stadium. The game was nationally televised over ESPN, and each team wore vintage 1962 jerseys. After allowing three straight singles in the first inning, Cincinnati's Tim Belcher retired 23 batters in a row. Dibble relieved Belcher at the start of the ninth and walked two before Bonilla's homer. Dibble ripped his jersey to shreds after Bonilla's blast. A week later, the Mets billed the Reds $1,600 for damage that Dibble inflicted on the visitor's clubhouse.

SEPTEMBER 4   Eddie Murray hits a grand slam off Tom Belcher in the sixth inning of a 5–2 win over the Reds in Cincinnati. The score was 1–1 when Murray launched his blast.

SEPTEMBER 9   Bobby Bonilla's home run in the fifth inning is the only Mets hit off Curt Schilling during a 2–1 loss to the Phillies in Philadelphia.

SEPTEMBER 14   After falling behind 5–0 in the fifth inning, the Mets rally to win 10–8 over the Cubs in Chicago. The Mets were still down 8–7 with two out in the ninth and the bases loaded. Charlie O'Brien settled the issue with a three-run double.

SEPTEMBER 20   Sid Fernandez pitches the Mets to a 1–0 victory over the Expos at Shea Stadium. Ryan Thompson drove in the lone run with a single in the second inning.

SEPTEMBER 24   The Mets lose an unusual 14-inning, 4–3 decision to the Cardinals in St. Louis. The game was scoreless for the first 13 innings. Pitching shutout ball over that span for the Mets were Bret Saberhagen (eight innings), Anthony Young (two innings), Jeff Innis (two innings), Paul Gibson (one-third of an inning) and Mark Dewey (two-thirds of an inning). With two out in the top of the 14th, Jeff Kent walloped a three-run homer for a 3–0 lead. Dewey started the bottom of the 14th. He was relieved by Wally Whitehurst with one out, one run in and runners on first and second. Whitehurst allowed a walk to load the bases, a two-run single to Ozzie Smith, an intentional walk and a walk-off single to Todd Zeile to lose the game.

SEPTEMBER 26   The Pirates clobber the Mets 19–2 at Three Rivers Stadium. Pittsburgh led 19–2 at the end of the fourth inning. Bill Pecota became the first position player in Mets history to be used as a pitcher when he took the mound in the eighth. He gave up a run and a hit in one inning of work.

Pecota played five different positions in 1992, his only season with the Mets. During his nine-year career in the majors, he played all ten positions, including designated hitter.

SEPTEMBER 29   Anthony Young is the losing pitcher in a 5–3 defeat at the hands of the Phillies at Shea Stadium. It was his 14th loss in a row.

OCTOBER 26 The Mets trade Wally Whitehurst, D. J. Dozier and Raul Casanova to the Padres for Tony Fernandez.

> *The trade looked like a steal when it was announced. Fernandez played in his fifth All-Star Game in 1992 and filled a need at shortstop. But he played in just 48 games for the Mets and hit just .225 before going to Toronto in another deal in June 1993.*

NOVEMBER 17 Two weeks after Bill Clinton defeats George Bush in the Presidential election, the Mets lose Jose Martinez, John Johnstone and Chris Donnels to the Marlins in the expansion draft.

DECEMBER 8 Dave Magadan signs with the Marlins as a free agent.

DECEMBER 10 The Mets sign Frank Tanana, most recently with the Tigers, as a free agent.

> *Tanana came to the Mets with 233 career victories, but he was 39 years old. He was 7–15 in his lone season with the club.*

DECEMBER 18 The Mets sign Joe Orsulak, most recently with the Orioles, as a free agent.

DECEMBER 21 Daryl Boston signs with the Rockies as a free agent.

1993

Season in a Sentence

Despite the presence of two
first-year expansion teams,
the Mets lead the league in
defeats and immature behavior,
prompting the hiring of Dallas
Green.

Finish • Won • Lost • Pct • GB

Sixth   59   103   .364 38.0

Managers

Jeff Torborg (13–25) and
Dallas Green (46–78)

Stats

Stats	Mets	AL	Rank
Batting Avg:	.248	.264	13
On-Base Pct:	.305	.327	14
Slugging Pct:	.390	.399	10
Home Runs:	158	4	
Stolen Bases:	79	14	
ERA:	4.05	4.04	7
Errors:	156	10	
Runs Scored:	672	13	
Runs Allowed:	9		

Starting Lineup

Todd Hundley, c
Eddie Murray, 1b
Jeff Kent, 2b
Howard Johnson, 3b
Tim Bogar, ss
Vince Coleman, lf
Joe Orsulak, cf-lf
Bobby Bonilla, rf-3b
Ryan Thompson, cf
Jeromy Burnitz, rf
Chico Walker, 2b-3b

Pitchers

Dwight Gooden, sp
Frank Tanana, sp
Bret Saberhagen, sp
Sid Fernandez, sp
Eric Hillman, sp
Pete Schourek, rp-sp
Jeff Innis, rp
Mike Maddux, rp

Attendance

1,873,183 (11th in NL)

Club Leaders

Batting Avg:	Eddie Murray	.285
On-Base Pct:	Bobby Bonilla	.354
Slugging Pct:	Bobby Bonilla	.522
Home Runs:	Bobby Bonilla	34
RBI:	Eddie Murray	100
Runs:	Bobby Bonilla	81
Stolen Bases:	Vince Coleman	38
Wins:	Dwight Gooden	12
Strikeouts:	Dwight Gooden	149
ERA:	Dwight Gooden	3.45
Saves:	John Franco	10

JANUARY 5   Kevin Bass signs with the Astros as a free agent.

JANUARY 15   Dick Schofield signs with the Blue Jays as a free agent.

APRIL 5   Six weeks after a bomb explodes in the parking garage of the World Trade Center, killing six people, the Mets open the season with a 3–0 win over the Colorado Rockies before 53,127 at Shea Stadium. It was the first regular game in Rockies history. Eric Young was the first batter to represent Colorado and was out following a 2–1 pitch from Dwight Gooden on a bunt from catcher Todd Hundley to first baseman Eddie Murray. Gooden pitched a complete game four-hitter. The losing pitcher was David Nied. Bobby Bonilla homered on Opening Day for the second year in a row.

The Mets uniforms were altered slightly in 1993. An underline flourish was added under "Mets" on the home uniforms. "New York" was also in an underlined script form on the road jerseys. The underlining format lasted only two seasons.

APRIL 7   Bret Saberhagen (eight innings) and Mike Maddux (two innings) combine on a two-hitter to defeat the Rockies 6–1 at Shea Stadium. The only Colorado hits were a single by Jim Tatum in the sixth inning and a homer from Dante Bichette in the seventh.

APRIL 10   Bobby Bonilla and Eddie Murray threaten reporter Bob Klapisch of the *New York Daily News* in the clubhouse before a 6–3 loss to the Astros at Shea Stadium. Klapisch had co-authored a book with John Harper titled *The Worst Team That Money Could Buy,* which was critical of the players and management. Bonilla yelled, "I'll hurt you," and had to be physically restrained by teammates.

APRIL 13   The Mets play in Colorado for the first time and score six runs in the eighth inning to defeat the Rockies 8–4 at Mile High Stadium in Denver.

APRIL 16   The Mets start seven switch-hitters during a 3–1 win over the Reds in Cincinnati. The seven were Todd Hundley, Eddie Murray, Jeff McKnight, Howard Johnson, Vince Coleman and Bobby Bonilla.

           Hundley's father Randy was a catcher in the majors, mostly with the Cubs, from 1964 through 1977.

APRIL 20   The day after the siege of the Branch Davidian compound in Waco, Texas, which leaves more than 70 dead, Sid Fernandez strikes out 14 batters and allows only a run and three hits in eight innings, but the Mets wind up losing 4–1 to the Giants in 11 innings at Shea Stadium.

APRIL 21   The Mets rout the Giants 10–0 at Shea Stadium. Dwight Gooden (seven innings) and Mike Draper (two innings) combined on the shutout.

APRIL 23   Bobby Bonilla homers from both sides of the plate and drives in five runs during a 6–1 win over the Padres at Shea Stadium. Bonilla homered from the left side off Greg Harris in the first inning and from the right side against lefty Pat Gomez in the fourth.

APRIL 26   A few hours before a scheduled start against the Dodgers at Shea Stadium, Dwight Gooden is hit in the shoulder blade by a golf club. Vince Coleman had been trying out a new set of clubs at his locker, which was adjacent to Gooden's, and inadvertently hit the pitcher with his swing. Fortunately, Gooden suffered only a bruise. Pete Schourek started in Gooden's place, but the game was rained out after three innings of play. Gooden started the game the following day.

APRIL 27   Dwight Gooden (eight innings) and Jeff Innis (one inning) combine on a two-hitter, but the Mets lose 4–1 to the Dodgers at Shea Stadium. Los Angeles scored in the second inning on a home run by Mike Piazza. Gooden allowed three runs in the eighth on a single by Orel Hershiser, two walks and two errors.

MAY 7   The Mets play the Florida Marlins for the first time and win 4–0 at Shea Stadium. Dwight Gooden pitched the shutout.

MAY 10   Bret Saberhagen pitches a three-hitter to defeat the Marlins 1–0 at Shea Stadium. In the first inning, Vince Coleman led off with a single, stole second, went to third on a ground out and crossed the plate on a sacrifice fly from Eddie Murray. The Mets collected only three base hits off Ryan Bowen.

MAY 19   The Mets score three runs in the ninth inning and two in the tenth to defeat the Pirates 6–4 at Shea Stadium. Joe Orsulak tied the game in the ninth with a pinch-hit single. Bobby Bonilla ended the contest with a two-run homer.

After the game, the Mets dismissed Jeff Torborg as manager. The club had a record of 13–25 and had lost 18 of their last 23 games. Dallas Green was hired as Torborg's replacement. Green was 58 years old and played in the majors as a pitcher from 1960 through 1967, mostly with the Phillies. He became manager of the Phils with 30 games remaining in 1979; a year later he led the franchise to its first world championship. Green quit at the end of the 1981 season and was almost immediately hired as general manager of the Cubs. With a series of brilliant trades, Green took the Cubs from a 38–65 record in the strike-shortened season of 1981 to a 96–65 mark and an NL East title in 1984. The bubble burst quickly, however, and the Cubs returned to their losing ways. Green left Chicago in 1988 and managed the Yankees in 1989, but didn't mesh with George Steinbrenner and failed to last a full season. Green was known as a no-nonsense disciplinarian, and it was hoped that his approach would unite a fractured Mets clubhouse. At the end of the 103-loss 1993 season, most of the veterans were jettisoned and the Mets embarked on a youth program. Two more losing campaigns followed in 1994 and 1995, and Green was fired in August 1996. Overall, he 229–283 as Mets manager. Torborg later managed the Expos (2001) and Marlins (2002–03).

MAY 26   The Mets score four runs in the ninth inning to stun the Phillies 5–4 in Philadelphia. Dave Gallagher put the Mets within a run with a two-run single. With two out, two runners on a base and a 1–2 count, Charlie O'Brien smacked a two-run double to put New York into the lead.

JUNE 2   The Mets score seven runs in the fourth inning and defeat the Cubs 11–3 in Chicago. Chico Walker capped the rally with a three-run homer.

JUNE 3   With their first pick in the amateur draft, and the eighth overall, the Mets select pitcher Kirk Presley from Tupelo High School in Tupelo, Mississippi.

A distant cousin of Elvis, Presley failed to advance past Class A ball. Future major leaguers drafted and signed by the Mets in 1993 were Eric Ludwick (second round), Mike Welch (fourth round), Jerrod Patterson (20th round), Benny Agbayani (30th round) and Vance Wilson (44th round).

JUNE 10   Bobby Bonilla hits home runs from both sides of the plate, but the Mets lose 7–6 to the Phillies at Shea Stadium. Bonilla homered from the left side off Tommy Greene in the first inning and from the right side off Mark Davis in the fifth.

JUNE 11   The Mets trade Tony Fernandez to the Blue Jays for Darrin Jackson.

JUNE 22   Anthony Young loses his 23rd game in a row over two seasons with a 6–3 decision at the hands of the Expos at Shea Stadium. The first 14 losses took place in 1992. The 23 defeats tied a major league record set by Cliff Curtis of the Boston Braves in 1910 and 1911.

JUNE 27   By dropping a 5–3 decision to the Cardinals at Shea Stadium, Anthony Young loses his 24th game in a row to break the all-time record for consecutive defeats.

From April 24 through June 27, the Mets were 13–45.

JUNE 29   The Mets outlast the Marlins to win 10–9 in 12 innings in Miami. The Mets led 6–1 before allowing seven runs in the seventh. Three runs in the eighth produced a 9–8 lead, but Florida tied the contest with two out in the ninth. In the 12th, Jeromy Burnitz doubled, went to third on an error and crossed the plate on a sacrifice fly from Tim Bogar. It was the first time that the Mets played a regular season game in Florida.

JULY 7   Joe McIlvaine is hired as the new general manager of the Mets, replacing Al Harazin, who resigned on June 22. McIlvaine was 46 and had previously been the Mets scouting director (1981–85) and assistant general manager (1986–90). He left the organization to become general manager of the Padres before being fired earlier in the 1993 season. McIlvaine remained as general manager of the Mets until 1997.

On the same day, Bret Saberhagen threw a lit firecracker under a table near a group of reporters. He dismissed the incident as a "practical joke." Three weeks later, the pitcher sprayed bleach at the backs of a group of media representatives who were trying to interview Dwight Gooden.

JULY 8   Bobby Bonilla hits a three-run, walk-off homer in the tenth inning to beat the Dodgers 6–3 in the second game of a double-header at Shea Stadium. Los Angeles took the opener 11–8.

JULY 18   Dave Gallagher wallops a grand slam off Mike Jackson in the ninth inning of a 12–6 triumph over the Giants in San Francisco.

JULY 19   Charlie O'Brien leads off the tenth inning with a home run that lifts the Mets to a 2–1 victory over the Padres in San Diego.

JULY 22   The Mets score seven runs in the second inning and down the Dodgers 10–5 in Los Angeles. Eddie Murray homered twice, one of them a grand slam off Kevin Gross.

JULY 24   Anthony Young issues a bases-loaded walk to Dave Hansen to lose 5–4 to the Dodgers in Los Angeles. It was Young's 27th loss in a row. He lost his last 14 decisions in 1992 and the first 13 in 1993.

On the same day, Vince Coleman was arrested for throwing an M-80 firecracker out of a car window into a crowd of fans waiting for autographs in the Dodger Stadium parking lot. The car was driven by Dodgers outfielder Eric Davis. The explosion injured three people, including two-year-old Amanda Santos. Coleman was given a one-year suspended sentence, put on probation for three years, fined $1,000 and required to perform 200 hours of community service. He played only two more games as a member of the Mets before being placed on "administrative leave" by club president Fred Wilpon. Coleman was traded to the Royals the following January.

JULY 28

Anthony Young finally ends his 27–game losing streak with a 5–4 victory over the Marlins at Shea Stadium. Young entered the game in the ninth inning in relief with the score 3–3 and allowed a run to fall behind 4–3. A 28th consecutive defeat loomed, but the Mets scored twice in the bottom of the ninth. A single by Ryan Thompson tied the score. With two out, Eddie Murray lined a walk-off double for the victory.

Young lost his last three decisions in 1993 to finish with a 1–16 record despite a 3.77 ERA which was lower than the league average (4.03) that season. Young pitched for the Cubs in 1994 and 1995 and the Astros in 1996; he finished his career with a record of 15–48.

AUGUST 5

Jeromy Burnitz drives in seven runs during a 13–inning, 12–9 win over the Expos at Olympic Stadium. The Mets scored five runs in the fifth inning, four of them on a grand slam by Burnitz off Dennis Martinez, to take a 9–1 lead. But Montreal rallied with four in their half of the fifth and four more in the sixth to tie the score 9–9. Burnitz drove in two with a double during the three-run 12th.

AUGUST 14

Tim Bogar ties a club record with four extra base hits during a 9–5 victory over the Phillies in Philadelphia. In five at-bats, Bogar collected two homers and two doubles, drove in four runs and scored four times.

AUGUST 18

Joe Orsulak contributes a triple, two doubles and a single to a 12–2 pounding of the Reds in Cincinnati.

SEPTEMBER 2

Todd Hundley hits a grand slam off Jose Guzman in the third inning of an 8–3 win over the Cubs in Chicago.

SEPTEMBER 4

The Mets hit five home runs, but lose 9–8 to the Cubs in Chicago. Bobby Bonilla and Ryan Thompson each homered twice and Eddie Murray once.

Bonilla batted .265 with 34 home runs in 1993.

SEPTEMBER 8

Darryl Kile of the Astros pitches a no-hitter to beat the Mets 7–1 in Houston. The Mets scored in the fourth inning on a walk, an error and a wild pitch. Kile ended the game by striking out pinch-hitters Tito Navarro and Chico Walker.

SEPTEMBER 14

Major League Baseball announces its three-division alignment and an extra round of playoffs, including a wild-card team, to be put into effect for the 1994 season. The Mets were placed in the Eastern Division with the Braves, Marlins, Expos and Phillies.

SEPTEMBER 17

The Mets trade Frank Tanana to the Yankees for Kenny Greer.

SEPTEMBER 18

The Mets score two runs in the ninth inning and one in the tenth to defeat the Braves 3–2 in Atlanta. With the Mets trailing 2–0, Greg Maddux struck out the first two batters in the ninth before loading the bases on singles by Jeff McKnight and Ced Landrum and a walk to Ryan Thompson. Greg McMichael relieved Maddux and surrendered run-scoring singles to Todd Hundley and Dave Gallagher. Tito Navarro drove in the winning run with a pinch-hit single in the tenth.

The hit was the only one that Navarro collected in the majors. He played in 12 games and had 17 at-bats, all with the Mets in 1993. His career batting average was .059.

SEPTEMBER 20   The Mets lose their 100th game of the season by dropping a 6–2 decision to the Pirates in Pittsburgh.

The Mets won nine of their last 12 games to finish at 59–103.

SEPTEMBER 22   Charlie O'Brien breaks a 4–4 tie with a two-run homer in the tenth inning, and the Mets beat the Pirates 6–5 in Pittsburgh.

SEPTEMBER 26   Jeff Kent hits a grand slam off Ken Hill in the fifth inning of a 9–3 victory over the Expos at Shea Stadium.

SEPTEMBER 29   The Mets outlast the Cardinals to win 1–0 in 17 innings at Shea Stadium. The 17-inning shutout was spun by Bobby Jones (ten innings), Jeff Innis (three innings), Mauro Gozzo (three innings) and Kenny Greer (one inning). Jeff Kent drove in the winning run with a two-out double. Each team collected only six hits. Ryan Thompson struck out five times in seven plate appearances.

The game was Greer's major league debut, and he earned the victory. He never pitched another game for the Mets. Greer's next major league appearance was in 1995 with the Giants. The September 29, 1993 decision was his only win in the majors.

NOVEMBER 19   Howard Johnson signs with the Rockies as a free agent.

NOVEMBER 22   Sid Fernandez signs with the Orioles as a free agent.

NOVEMBER 26   Charlie O'Brien signs with the Braves as a free agent.

DECEMBER 2   Eddie Murray signs with the Indians as a free agent.

The Mets lost 103 games in 1993 with the oldest pitching staff in the NL and the second-oldest cumulative age among the batters. In an attempt to rebuild the club with a younger roster, the Mets made little attempt to retain Johnson, Fernandez, O'Brien and Murray during the free-agent signing period. None of them proved to be a loss, as all four were well past their prime.

1994

Season in a Sentence

The season is shortened by 49 games by the players' strike, but the Mets win two more games than the previous season.

Finish • Won • Lost • Pct • GB

Third   55   58   .487 18.5

Manager

Dallas Green

Stats

Stats	Mets	AL	Rank
Batting Avg:	.250	.267	13
On-Base Pct:	.316	.333	14
Slugging Pct:	.394	.415	13
Home Runs:	117	6	
Stolen Bases:	25	14	
ERA:	4.13	4.21	8
Errors:	89	9	
Runs Scored:	506	9	
Runs Allowed:	351	10	

Starting Lineup

Todd Hundley, c
David Segui, 1b
Jeff Kent, 2b
Bobby Bonilla, 3b
Jose Vizcaino, ss
Kevin McReynolds, lf
Ryan Thompson, cf
Joe Orsulak, rf
Kelly Stinnett, c
Jeromy Burnitz, rf

Pitchers

Bret Saberhagen, sp
Bobby Jones, sp
Pete Smith, sp
John Franco, rp
Roger Mason, rp
Josias Manzanillo, rp
Doug Linton, rp
Mauro Gozzo, rp-sp

Attendance

1,151,471 (13th in NL)

Club Leaders

Batting Avg:	Jeff Kent	.292
On-Base Pct:	Bobby Bonilla	.374
Slugging Pct:	Bobby Bonilla	.504
Home Runs:	Bobby Bonilla	20
RBI:	Bobby Bonilla	67
Runs:	Bobby Bonilla	60
Stolen Bases:	John Cangelosi	5
Wins:	Bret Saberhagen	14
Strikeouts:	Bret Saberhagen	143
ERA:	Bret Saberhagen	2.74
Saves:	John Franco	30

JANUARY 5   The Mets trade Vince Coleman to the Royals for Kevin McReynolds.

MARCH 27   The Mets trade Kevin Baez and Tom Wegmann to the Orioles for David Segui.

MARCH 30   The Mets trade Anthony Young and Ottis Smith to the Cubs for Jose Vizcaino.

MARCH 31   The Mets trade Alan Zinter to the Tigers for Rico Brogna.

Brogna was recalled from the minors in June and became a cult hero in New York by batting .351 with seven homers in 39 games before the strike. He hit 22 home runs for the Mets in 1995 before his career went into a premature decline. Brogna was traded to the Phillies prior to the start of the 1997 season.

APRIL 4   The Mets survive three homers from Cubs leadoff batter Tuffy Rhodes to win 12–8 on Opening Day at Wrigley Field. The home runs by Rhodes came consecutively off Dwight Gooden in the first, third and fifth innings. Rhodes came into the contest with five career homers in 280 at-bats. Gooden, who finished his career with a 28–4 lifetime record against the Cubs, was the winning pitcher despite giving up seven runs, five of them earned, and 11 hits in 5$^{1}/_{3}$ innings. The Mets broke a 2–2 tie with four runs in the fourth inning and never trailed afterward. Jose Vizcaino, Todd Hundley and Jeff Kent each homered for New York. It was Vizcaino's Mets debut. Kent also had a double and two singles.

Vizcaino attempted 12 stolen bases in 1994 and was successful on only one of them.

APRIL 11   In the home opener, the Mets lose 9–5 to the Cubs before 42,267 at Shea Stadium. Jeff Kent homered.

APRIL 14   Jeff Kent belts two homers and drives in five runs during a 10–9 win over the Cubs at Shea Stadium. The Mets led 8–3 before Chicago scored six times in the eighth to pull ahead 9–8. The Mets came back with two runs in the bottom half on Kent's second home run.

APRIL 27   The Mets edge the Padres 3–2 in 15 innings at Shea Stadium. Fernando Vina drove in the winning run with a walk-off single.

MAY 2   Following a two-out error by Jose Vizcaino, the Giants score nine unearned runs in the third inning and beat the Mets 10–3 at Shea Stadium. Nine straight San Francisco batters reached base off Bobby Jones on a home run, a triple, three singles, two walks and two errors.

MAY 3   Joe Orsulak hits a pinch-hit grand slam off Mike Jackson in the seventh inning to give the Mets a 5–4 lead, but the Giants score twice in the ninth to win 6–5 at Shea Stadium.

MAY 4   Bobby Bonilla homers from both sides of the plate during a 7–3 win over the Giants at Shea Stadium. Bonilla homered from the right side off Bryan Hickerson in the sixth inning and from the left side against Dave Burba in the seventh.

Bonilla batted .290 with 20 homers in 108 games in 1994.

MAY 7   Bobby Jones shuts out the Cardinals for a 1–0 victory in St. Louis. The lone run scored on a double by Kevin McReynolds in the sixth inning.

MAY 8   Mauro Gozzo (seven innings) and Josias Manzanillo (two innings) combine on a two-hitter for a 3–2 triumph over the Cardinals at Busch Stadium. The only St. Louis hits were a double by Gregg Jefferies and a single from Mark Whiten in the sixth inning. Gozzo received credit for the victory, his first in the majors since 1989 when he was a pitcher for the Blue Jays.

MAY 10   Joe Orsulak homers in the tenth inning to defeat the Expos 3–2 in Montreal.

MAY 14   Ryan Thompson hits a grand slam off John Smoltz in the fifth inning of an 11–4 win over the Braves at Shea Stadium.

MAY 17   The Mets score two runs in the ninth inning to defeat the Marlins 4–3 at Shea Stadium. The Mets trailed 3–2 with two out in the ninth and a runner on first when Jose Vizcaino and Joe McKnight walked to load the bases. Joe Orsulak fell behind 1–2, fouled off two pitches and then stroked a two-run single to win the game.

JUNE 2   With the first overall pick in the amateur draft, the Mets select pitcher Paul Wilson from Florida State University.

> *Wilson was 5–12 in his rookie season with the Mets in 1996. He was away from the majors for the next three years while battling elbow and shoulder injuries. Wilson later played for the Devil Rays and Reds from 2000 through 2005 and finished his career with a 40–58 record. First baseman Terrence Long from Stanhope Elmore High School in Millbrook, Alabama, was also chosen in the first round by the Mets with the 20th pick as compensation for losing Sid Fernandez in free agency. Long played three games with the Mets in 1998 before going to the Athletics in a trade. He had a seven-year career with a .269 batting average and 69 homers in 890 games. Other future major leaguers drafted and signed by the Mets in 1994 were Jay Payton (supplemental first round), Scott Sauerbeck (23rd round) and Brandon Villafuerte (66th round).*

JUNE 15   Bobby Jones (eight innings) and John Franco (one inning) combine forces to beat the Phillies 1–0 at Shea Stadium. Todd Hundley drove in the winning run with a single in the sixth inning.

JUNE 18   Todd Hundley hits home runs from both sides of the plate during an 11–3 win over the Marlins in Miami. Hundley homered from the right side off Pat Rapp in the third inning and from the left side against Jeff Mutis in the seventh.

JUNE 22   Pete Smith gives up homers to the first two batters he faces, but the Braves don't score again and the Mets win 5–2 in Atlanta. The pair of homers were surrendered to Roberto Kelly and Jeff Blauser, but Smith gave up only two more hits before being relieved after seven innings. Mauro Gozzo pitched the eighth and John Franco the ninth.

JUNE 27   The Mets score seven runs in the seventh inning for an 8–7 lead but wind up losing 9–8 to the Cardinals at Shea Stadium. The first two batters in the seventh were retired before the next eight reached base. Jeff Kent hit a three-run homer. With the Mets trailing 7–5, Jose Vizcaino delivered a three-run single. The terrific comeback vanished when the St. Louis scored twice in the ninth.

JUNE 28   Dwight Gooden is suspended for 60 days for violating baseball's aftercare drug program, to which he had been subjected since 1987. Gooden tested positive for cocaine in September during a three-week stay at the Betty Ford Clinic in Arizona. On November 4, Commissioner Bud Selig suspended Gooden for one year. A day later, Gooden was found by his wife, Monica, with a loaded gun to his head.

> *Gooden returned to baseball with the Yankees in 1996 and pitched a no-hitter on May 14. He had a 20–12 record with the Yanks over two seasons, and then pitched for the Indians in 1998 and 1999. Gooden's last season in the majors was in 2000 when he played for the Astros, Devil Rays and Yankees again. A string of arrests followed the end of his playing career. In 2002, Gooden was arrested for driving while intoxicated and having an open container of alcohol in his vehicle. In 2003, he was arrested for driving with a suspended license. In 2005, Gooden pulled away from a traffic stop in Tampa after being stopped for driving erratically. Three days later, he turned himself in to police.*

Gooden was arrested once more in 2006 for violating his probation for showing up at a meeting with his parole officer while intoxicated on cocaine. For that infraction he served seven months in prison.

JULY 4   All three runs of a ten-inning, 2–1 win over the Giants in San Francisco are scored on solo homers. Ryan Thompson put the Mets into the lead with a shot in the second inning. Barry Bonds tied the score in the eighth. Jim Lindeman provided the game winner in the tenth.

JULY 5   Bret Saberhagen (eight innings) and John Franco (one inning) combine on a two-hitter to defeat the Giants 4–2 at Candlestick Park. Both San Francisco hits came on home runs by Dave Martinez in the seventh inning and Darren Lewis in the eighth.

Saberhagen had a 14–4 record and a 2.74 ERA in 1994. He walked only 13 batters in 177$\frac{1}{3}$ innings. Number two starter Bobby Jones was 12–7 with an earned run average of 3.15. The rest of the starting pitchers combined for 15 wins, 29 losses and an ERA of 5.21.

JULY 7   In only his second major league start, Jason Jacome pitches a shutout to beat the Dodgers 3–0 in Los Angeles.

Jacome never pitched another shutout in the majors. When his career ended in 1998, Jacome's final numbers included a 10–18 record and a 5.34 ERA.

JULY 15   Bret Saberhagen pitches ten shutout innings, but the Mets lose 2–1 in 14 innings to the Padres in the second game of a double-header at Shea Stadium. The contest was scoreless until Mike Maddux gave up back-to-back homers to Tony Gwynn and Phil Plantier with one out in the 14th. The Mets scored in the bottom half in a rally that fell short.

JULY 22   Jeff Kent hits a grand slam off Bill Swift in the first inning of a 6–3 victory over the Giants at Shea Stadium.

JULY 25   Rico Brogna collects five hits, including two doubles, in five at-bats during a 7–1 win over the Cardinals in St. Louis.

JULY 26   Rico Brogna breaks an 8–8 tie with a two-run homer in the 11th inning as the Mets down the Cardinals 10–9 in St. Louis.

From July 22 through August 2, Brogna had 21 hits in 41 at-bats for an average of .521.

JULY 31   The Mets score four runs in the ninth inning to defeat the Pirates 6–4 in Pittsburgh. The four runs in the ninth were driven home by Todd Hundley, Kelly Stinnett, Jeromy Burnitz and Bobby Bonilla.

AUGUST 11   With the midnight strike deadline looming, the Mets lose 2–1 to the Phillies in 15 innings in Philadelphia.

AUGUST 12   With about 70 percent of the season completed, the major league players go on strike.

The strike, baseball's eighth interruption since 1972, had been anticipated all season. The owners wanted to put a lid on escalating payrolls by capping salaries and revising, if not eliminating, salary arbitration procedures. The players, who were not interested in these reforms, had only one weapon once talks broke down: a strike.

SEPTEMBER 14   The owners of the 28 major league clubs vote 28–2 to cancel the remainder of the season, including the playoffs and the World Series.

NOVEMBER 18   The Mets trade Jeromy Burnitz and Joe Roa to the Indians for Paul Byrd, Dave Mlicki, Jerry Dipoto and Jesus Azuaje.

Burnitz didn't pan out in Cleveland and was sent to the Brewers in another deal in 1996. He had some great years in Milwaukee, clouting 163 homers with 511 RBI over a five-year period beginning in 1997, which included a pair of All-Star appearances. Burnitz played for the Mets again in 2002 and 2003.

NOVEMBER 28   The Mets trade Juan Castillo and Todd Beckerman to the Astros for Pete Harnisch.

NOVEMBER 29   The Mets trade Quilvio Veras to the Marlins for Carl Everett.

Everett was 23 at the time of the trade and a former first-round draft pick. He lasted three years with the Mets, but never developed to the club's satisfaction before going to the Astros in a trade in 1997. Veras led the NL in stolen bases as a rookie in 1995 and had several good years as a starting second baseman for the Marlins and Padres.

NOVEMBER 30   Despite the strike, the Mets continue to make over the team by trading Fernando Vina and Javier Gonzalez to the Brewers for Doug Henry.

Henry had a 5–14 record in two seasons as a reliever for the Mets. In exchange, the Mets lost Vina, who was a starting second baseman with the Brewers and Cardinals for several years, played in the All-Star Game in 1998, won two Gold Gloves and batted over .300 three times.

1995

Season in a Sentence

The Mets complete their fifth consecutive losing season, but win 34 of their last 52 to provide some hope for the future.

Finish • Won • Lost • Pct • GB

Second   69   75   .479 21.0
(tie)

In the wild-card race, the Mets finished tied for fifth place, eight games behind.

Manager

Dallas Green

Stats

Stats	Mets	AL	Rank
Batting Avg:	.267	.263	5
On-Base Pct:	.330	.331	7
Slugging Pct:	.400	.408	7
Home Runs:	125	8	
Stolen Bases:	58	14	
ERA:	3.88	4.18	3
Errors:	115	9	
Runs Scored:	657	7	
Runs Allowed:	618	3	

Starting Lineup

Todd Hundley, c
Rico Brogna, 1b
Jeff Kent, 2b
Edgardo Alfonso, 3b
Jose Vizcaino, ss
Joe Orsulak, lf
Brett Butler, cf
Carl Everett, rf
Bobby Bonilla, 3b-lf
Ryan Thompson, cf-rf
Kelly Stinnett, c

Pitchers

Bobby Jones, sp
Dave Mlicki, sp
Jason Isringhausen, sp
Bill Pulsipher, sp
Bret Saberhagen, sp
Pete Harnisch, sp
John Franco, rp
Jerry Dipoto, rp
Doug Henry, rp

Attendance

1,273,183 (11th in NL)

Club Leaders

Batting Avg:	Brett Butler	.311
On-Base Pct:	Brett Butler	.381
Slugging Pct:	Rico Brogna	.385
Home Runs:	Rico Brogna	22
RBI:	Rico Brogna	76
Runs:	Rico Brogna	72
Stolen Bases:	Brett Butler	21
Wins:	Bobby Jones	10
Strikeouts:	Bobby Jones	127
ERA:	Bobby Jones	4.19
Saves:	John Franco	29

JANUARY 13   Major league owners vote to use replacement players during the 1995 season if the strike, which began on August 12, 1994, is not settled.

The Mets opened training camp in February at Port St. Lucie with replacement players and used them until the strike came to an end on April 2.

APRIL 2   The 234–day strike comes to an end.

The opening of the season, originally scheduled for April 3, was pushed back to April 26 with each team playing 144 games. The replacement players were either released or sent to the minors.

APRIL 11   The Mets sign Brett Butler, most recently with the Dodgers, as a free agent.

Butler was 37 but played in 111 of the Dodgers 114 games in 1994, batted .314 and led the NL in triples with nine. As a Met, he appeared in 90 games and hit .311 before going back to Los Angeles in an August trade.

APRIL 26   Seven days after 168 die in the bombing of a federal office building in Oklahoma City, the Mets participate in the first ever game at Coors Field in Denver and lose 11–9 to the Rockies in 14 innings in the strike-delayed season opener. The Mets scored in the top of the ninth to take a 7–6 advantage, but allowed Colorado to deadlock the contest in the bottom half. The Mets scored again with single runs in the 13th and 14th, but once more couldn't hold the lead. Mike Remingler gave up the Rockies run in the 13th and all three in the 14th. The game ended on a one-out, three-run homer by Dante Bichette. Bobby Jones was the New York starter and allowed five runs in $4^2/_3$ innings. Todd Hundley collected four hits, including a homer and a double, in six at-bats and drove in four runs. The home run was a grand slam off Bill Swift in the sixth inning. Rico Brogna also homered. Brett Butler scored three runs in his Mets debut.

            The underlining of the word "Mets," which had been part of the home uniforms in 1993 and 1994, was removed in 1995. "New York" appeared on the road jerseys in a fancy block format similar to the original 1962 jerseys.

APRIL 28   In the home opener, the Mets overcome a fifth-inning, 6–2 deficit to defeat the Cardinals 10–8 before 26,604 at Shea Stadium. Todd Hundley gave the Mets a 9–8 lead with a two-run double in the seventh. Rico Brogna, Bobby Bonilla and Carl Everett hit home runs.

MAY 4   Todd Hundley hits a pinch-hit grand slam off Bryan Eversgerd in the tenth inning to beat the Expos 5–1 in Montreal. It was only the fourth hit of the game for Mets batters.

            Hundley hit .280 with 15 homers in 90 games in 1995.

MAY 6   Just six outs from what seemed to be a certain victory, the Mets blow an 11–4 lead by allowing the Reds to score six runs in the eighth inning and three in the ninth, resulting in a 13–11 loss in Cincinnati. The game ended on a two-run homer by Jerome Walton.

            Edgardo Alfonso hit his first major league homer during the contest, and it was inside-the-park off Matt Grott in the fifth inning. On the all-time Mets career lists, Alfonso ranks fourth in hits (1,136), fourth in runs (614) and fourth in doubles (212).

MAY 11   The Mets trade Mike Remlinger to the Reds for Cobi Cradle.

MAY 12   Bobby Bonilla hits home runs from both sides of the plate during a 9–6 loss to the Expos at Shea Stadium. Bonilla homered from the right side of the plate off Jeff Fassero in the third inning and from the left side against Tim Scott in the ninth.

MAY 16   Bobby Jones (seven innings) and Doug Henry (two innings) combine on a three-hitter to defeat the Astros 1–0 at Shea Stadium. The lone run scored on a single from Brett Butler in the third inning.

MAY 31   After the Padres score in the top of the tenth inning, Chris Jones hits a three-run, pinch-hit homer off Trevor Hoffman in the bottom half for a 7–5 win at Shea Stadium.

JUNE 1

In the first round of the amateur draft, the Mets select shortstop Ryan Jaroncyk from Orange Glen High School in Escondido, California.

Jaroncyk never advanced beyond Class A ball. In fact, none of the first seven selections in 1995 reached the majors. The Mets picked up a gem in round eight in A. J. Burnett, but traded him to the Marlins before he made his big-league debut. The only other future major leaguers drafted and signed by the Mets in 1995 were Dan Murray (tenth round), Grant Roberts (11th round) and Nelson Figueroa (30th round).

JUNE 8

The Mets score seven runs in the top of the first inning and beat the Giants 9–6 in San Francisco.

On the same day, the Mets traded Diego Segui to the Expos for Reid Cornelius.

JUNE 15

The Mets score three runs in the ninth inning and one in the tenth to stun the Marlins 5–4 at Shea Stadium. The trio of runs in the ninth were driven home by Joe Orsulak, Jose Vizcaino and Rico Brogna. Orsulak also drove in the game-winning run with a walk-off single with one out in the tenth.

JULY 7

Trailing 8–3, the Mets score four runs in the seventh inning and two in the ninth to defeat the Pirates 9–8 in Pittsburgh. Todd Hundley drove in the pair of runs in the ninth with a one-out homer.

JULY 14

The Mets collect 20 hits and beat the Rockies 13–4 at Shea Stadium. It was the first 20–hit game for the Mets since they did so in back-to-back contests against the Cubs on June 12 and 13, 1990.

JULY 17

The Mets break a 2–2 tie with five runs in the ninth inning and defeat the Cubs 7–2 in Chicago. Brett Butler had three hits in five at-bats.

JULY 18

The Mets score seven runs in the fourth inning and down the Cubs 12–3 at Wrigley Field. Brett Butler collected four hits in five at-bats and scored four runs.

JULY 19

Bobby Bonilla homers in the tenth inning to beat the Cardinals 5–4 in St. Louis. Brett Butler garnered four hits, including two triples, in five at-bats.

JULY 20

Brett Butler collects four hits, including a home run, in five at-bats during an 8–6 loss to the Cardinals in St. Louis.

The outburst was Butler's third straight four-hit game and gave him 15 hits over a four-game span. The major league record for hits in four consecutive games is 16 by Milt Stock of the Brooklyn Dodgers, who had four games in a row of four hits in 1924.

JULY 21

The Mets erupt for eight runs in the eighth inning and rout the Rockies 12–1 in Denver.

JULY 28

The Mets trade Bobby Bonilla to the Orioles for Damon Buford, Alex Ochoa and Jimmy Williams.

At the time of the trade, Bonilla had a .315 batting average and 18 homers in 80 games. He led a nomadic existence between 1995 and the end of his career in 2001 by playing for six teams, including a return engagement with the Mets in 1999. Bonilla was the starting third baseman for the world champion Marlins in 1997. None of the three players acquired in the deal made a significant contribution while playing for the Mets.

JULY 29   Chris Jones hits a pinch-hit, walk-off homer in the ninth inning to beat the Pirates 2–1 at Shea Stadium. It was his second walk-off pinch-homer of the season (see May 31, 1995).

JULY 31   The Mets trade Bret Saberhagen to the Rockies for Juan Acevedo, Arnold Gooch and David Swanson.

After a 14–4 season in 1994, Saberhagen was 5–5 at the time of the trade. He continued to be frustratingly inconsistent until his career ended in 2001. Saberhagen gave the Red Sox a couple of solid seasons in 1998 and 1999 with a combined record of 25–14. His final career mark was 167–117. The Mets received next to nothing in return in the deal.

AUGUST 8   The Mets survive a four-run Phillies rally in the ninth inning to win 12–10 in Philadelphia.

AUGUST 16   Bill Pulsipher (eight innings) and John Franco (one inning) combine to defeat the Expos 1–0 at Shea Stadium.

AUGUST 18   The Mets trade Brett Butler to the Dodgers for Dwight Maness and Scott Hunter.

AUGUST 21   After the Giants score in the top of the 11th, the Mets respond with two runs in the bottom half to win 5–4 at Shea Stadium. The Mets were still down 4–3 with two out in the 11th when Joe Orsulak doubled in a run and crossed the plate on Jose Vizcaino's single.

AUGUST 24   The Mets score three times in the ninth inning to defeat the Padres 5–4 at Shea Stadium. Chris Jones drove in the game winner with a walk-off pinch-single.

AUGUST 25   Carl Everett hits a grand slam off Willie Blair in the fifth inning of a 10–5 triumph over the Padres at Shea Stadium.

AUGUST 26   The Mets survive a six-run Padres rally in the ninth inning to win 7–6 at Shea Stadium.

AUGUST 29   The Mets score two runs in the ninth inning to defeat the Dodgers 4–3 in Los Angeles. After the first two New York batters were retired, Jeff Kent homered. A walk and singles by Ryan Thompson and Butch Huskey produced another run.

Kent hit .278 with 20 homers in 1995.

SEPTEMBER 15   Jason Isringhausen allows 13 hits in 7⅓ innings, but hold the Phillies to a single run in a 4–1 victory at Shea Stadium.

As a 22–year-old rookie in 1995, Isringhausen had a 9–2 record and a 2.81 ERA.

SEPTEMBER 17   Rico Brogna hits a grand slam and a solo homer during an 8–2 victory over the Phillies at Shea Stadium. The slam was struck off Mike Williams in the third inning.

SEPTEMBER 23   Jose Vizcaino collects five hits, including a double, in five at-bats during a 4–3 loss to the Marlins in Miami.

OCTOBER 1   Two days before O. J. Simpson is found not guilty in the murders of his ex-wife and her companion, the Mets close the season with an 11-inning, 1–0 win over the Braves at Shea Stadium. Jason Isringhausen (eight innings), Doug Henry (two innings) and Pete Walker (one inning) combined on the shutout. The winning run scored on a bases-loaded walk to Tim Bogar.

                Walker was credited with his first big-league victory. He didn't win again in the majors until 2002 when he was a member of the Blue Jays.

DECEMBER 5   Joe Orsulak signs with the Marlins as a free agent.

DECEMBER 14   The Mets sign Lance Johnson, most recently with the White Sox, as a free agent.

                Johnson gave the Mets one tremendous season in 1996. He batted .333 along with 117 runs, 50 stolen bases and league-leading figures in hits (227) and triples (21). The hits and triples marks are Mets single-season records. Johnson was traded to the Cubs in August 1997.

1996

Season in a Sentence

Fielding the youngest team in the National League, the Mets lose 91 games and replace Dallas Green with Bobby Valentine.

Finish • Won • Lost • Pct • GB

Fourth   71   91   .438   25.0

In the wild-card race, the Mets finished in ninth place, 19 games behind.

Managers

Dallas Green (59–72) and Bobby Valentine (12–19)

Stats

Stats	Mets	AL	Rank
Batting Avg:	.270	.262	2
On-Base Pct:	.324	.330	10
Slugging Pct:	.412	.408	4
Home Runs:	147	9	
Stolen Bases:	97	13	
ERA:	4.22	4.21	7
Errors:	159	14	
Runs Scored:	746	10	
Runs Allowed:	779	9	

Starting Lineup

Todd Hundley, c
Butch Huskey, 1b
Jose Vizcaino, 2b
Jeff Kent, 3b
Rey Ordonez, ss
Bernard Gilkey, lf
Lance Johnson, cf
Alex Ochoa, rf
Edgardo Alfonso, 2b

Pitchers

Mark Clark, sp
Bobby Jones, sp
Pete Harnisch, sp
Jason Isringhausen, sp
Paul Wilson, sp
John Franco, rp
Dave Mlicki, rp
Jerry Dipoto, rp
Doug Henry, rp

Attendance

1,588,323 (12th in NL)

Club Leaders

Batting Avg:	Lance Johnson	.333
On-Base Pct:	Bernard Gilkey	.393
Slugging Pct:	Bernard Gilkey	.562
Home Runs:	Todd Hundley	41
RBI:	Bernard Gilkey	117
Runs:	Lance Johnson	117
Stolen Bases:	Lance Johnson	50
Wins:	Mark Clark	14
Strikeouts:	Mark Clark	142
ERA:	Mark Clark	3.43
Saves:	John Franco	28

JANUARY 22   The Mets trade Eric Ludwick, Erik Hiljus and Yudith Orozio to the Cardinals for Bernard Gilkey.

> *Gilkey was 29 at the time of the trade and teased the Cardinals with his potential but never quite became the star the club envisioned. For one year, he gave the Mets everything they could have asked for in return with a .317 batting average, 44 doubles, 30 homers and 117 RBI in 1996. Gilkey also led NL outfielders with 18 assists. His numbers fell dramatically afterward, however. In 1998, Gilkey batted .227 with four home runs in 264 at-bats for the club, prompting a trade to the Diamondbacks.*

MARCH 31   The Mets trade Ryan Thompson and Reid Cornelius to the Indians for Mark Clark.

> *The Mets went into the season expecting to improve on the 1995 record of 69–75 because of a starting rotation that included three of the top pitching prospects in baseball in 23-year-old Jason Isringhausen, 23-year-old Paul Wilson and 22-year-old Bill Pulsipher. But after a 9–2 rookie season in 1995,*

Isringhausen was 6–14 with a 4.77 ERA in 1996. The number-one overall draft choice in 1994, Wilson stumbled with 5 wins, 12 defeats and a 5.38 earned run average. Pulsipher missed the entire season because of injuries. Clark proved to be the staff's number-one starter with a 14–11 record and a 3.43 ERA.

APRIL 1   Before an Opening Day crowd of 42,060 at Shea Stadium, the Mets overcome a 6–0 deficit to defeat the Cardinals 7–6. Bobby Jones was the New York starting pitcher and allowed all six St. Louis runs in 3²/₃ innings. The Mets staged the comeback with two runs in the fourth inning, one in the sixth and four in the seventh. The 6–6 deadlock was broken on a double play. With one out in the seventh, Rico Brogna brought Lance Johnson across the plate with a sacrifice fly. Bernard Gilkey tried to advance from first to second on the play and was tagged out in a rundown. Gilkey and Todd Hundley homered. It was Gilkey's and Johnson's debut with the Mets. In his first game as a major leaguer, Rey Ordonez provided the defensive gem. In the seventh inning, Ordonez took a low relay from Gilkey in left field and, from his knees, threw out Royce Clayton at the plate.

Born in Havana, Cuba, Ordonez was signed by the Mets in 1993 as a 21-year-old after he defected to the United States. He was the club's starting shortstop from 1996 through 2002 and won three Gold Gloves. A debate raged almost constantly during those seven seasons in New York as to whether or not Ordonez's defensive brilliance outweighed his weaknesses as a hitter. In 916 games as a Met, Ordonez batted .245 with an on-base percentage of .290 and a .304 slugging percentage.

APRIL 4   The Mets score two runs with two out in the ninth inning off Dennis Eckersley to beat the Cardinals 10–9 at Shea Stadium. The Mets led 7–1 after four innings before falling behind 9–8. Brett Mayne drove in the winning run with a pinch-hit single.

APRIL 23   Chris Jones hits a two-run, walk-off homer in the tenth inning to defeat the Reds 8–6 at Shea Stadium. Jones entered the game as a right fielder during a double switch in the eighth inning.

APRIL 25   Trailing 3–1, the Mets erupt for eight runs in the seventh inning and beat the Cardinals 9–3 in St. Louis. Brett Mayne, Lance Johnson and Butch Huskey all homered during the rally.

MAY 11   On John Franco Day at Shea Stadium, the Mets beat the Cubs 7–6 in a game marked by a long and ugly brawl. There were nine ejections, including five Mets. In the fifth inning with New York leading 6–3, Cubs hurler Terry Adams threw a pitch behind Pete Harnisch, who then had words with Chicago catcher Scott Servais. Harnisch threw a punch at Servais, and both benches and bullpens emptied. The teams exchanged shoves, pushes and punches for 16 minutes before order was restored. The two teams even fought each other in the Cubs dugout. Franco, who was honored in pre-game ceremonies for recording his 300th career save on April 29, suffered a cut below his right eye in the brawl. Franco was also one of the five in a New York uniform ejected, along with Harnisch, Blas Minor, Todd Hundley and coach Steve Swisher. The Cubs came back to tie the score 6–6 before Rico Brogna hit a walk-off homer in the ninth. It was Rico's second home run of the game.

MAY 18   Todd Hundley drives in seven runs and homers from both sides of the plate during a 14–5 thrashing of the Giants in San Francisco. Hundley was hit by a pitch from

Will Van Landingham with the bases loaded in the second inning, belted a three-run homer off right-hander Jose Bautista in the fourth and struck another home run off lefty Doug Creek in the ninth.

MAY 26 A first-inning home run by Bernard Gilkey off Sean Bergman is all the Mets need to defeat the Padres 1–0 at Shea Stadium. Bobby Jones (eight innings) and John Franco (one inning) combined on the shutout.

Franco had one of the best seasons of his career in 1996 with a 1.83 ERA, a 4–3 record and 28 saves in 51 games and 54 innings.

MAY 30 Paul Wilson (eight innings) and John Franco (one inning) combine to shut out the Giants 1–0 at Shea Stadium. Jose Vizcaino drove in the winning run with a single in the eighth inning.

JUNE 4 In the first round of the amateur draft, the Mets select outfielder Robert Stratton from San Marcos High School in San Marcos, California.

Stratton hit 205 home runs in 2,980 minor league at-bats over 11 seasons, but failed to advance to the majors largely because of a low batting average (.243) and a high strikeout total (1,197). In all, he played for 13 minor league teams in six organizations. Future major leaguers drafted and signed by the Mets in 1996 were Ed Yarnall (third round), Dicky Gonzalez (16th round) and Tim Corcoran (44th round).

JUNE 10 Todd Hundley collects four hits, including two home runs, in four at-bats and drives in five runs during an 8–3 win over the Braves at Shea Stadium. The homers came from opposite sides of the plate. Hundley homered from the right side off Steve Avery in the second inning and from the left side against Mike Bielecki in the seventh.

JULY 3 Alex Ochoa hits for a cycle that includes two doubles during a 10–6 triumph over the Phillies in Philadelphia. Ochoa achieved the cycle in order. Facing Terry Mulholland, Ochoa singled in the second inning, doubled in the fourth and tripled in the sixth. With Ken Ryan on the mound, Ochoa homered in the eighth. He added icing on the cake with another double against Steve Frey in the ninth. The outburst came in only the 22nd game of Ochoa's big-league career. The triple was his first in the majors.

JULY 9 Batting leadoff for the National League, Lance Johnson collects three hits, including a double, in four at-bats in the All-Star Game at Veterans Stadium in Philadelphia. The NL won 6–0.

JULY 29 Two days after a bomb explodes in a park in Atlanta during the Olympics, the Mets trade Jeff Kent and Jose Vizcaino to the Indians for Carlos Baerga and Alvaro Espinoza.

In a swap involving four infielders, the Mets made one of the worst deals in club history. Baerga was an AL All-Star in 1992, 1993 and 1995, and was only 27 at the time he was acquired by the Mets. Often overweight, his skills deteriorated rapidly as his career went into a premature decline. Baerga was little more than a mediocre starting second baseman in New York through the end of the 1998 season before leaving the Big Apple as a free agent. Espinoza played in only 48 games for the Mets. Vizcaino lasted in the majors until 2006, played for the 2000 world champion Yankees and had a key hit in that year's World Series against the Mets. Kent was a huge loss. He was 28 at the time of the trade, eight months older than Baerga. Most thought the Mets made an excellent trade because Baerga was considered to be a better second baseman, both offensively and defensively, than Kent. The Indians dealt Kent to the Giants in a package to obtain Matt Williams in November 1996. Kent lasted in the majors until 2008 and, after leaving New York, played in five All-Star games. He was the league MVP in 2000, finished in the top ten in the MVP balloting in three other seasons and had eight years of 100 or more RBI. By the time his career concluded, Kent had 377 home runs, the most ever by a second baseman, and a .290 batting average.

JULY 30   The Mets sweep the Pirates 5–4 and 3–2 in a double-header at Shea Stadium. Todd Hundley won the second game with a walk-off homer in the 12th inning.

JULY 31   After the Pirates score in the top of the tenth inning, Chris Jones hits a walk-off homer in the bottom half to lift the Mets to a 3–2 victory at Shea Stadium. Jones entered the game in the fifth as a replacement for Carl Everett in center field.

               Jones played two seasons for the Mets (1995–96) and hit 12 homers. Four of the 12 were walk-off homers. Two came as a pinch-hitter and the other two after he entered the game defensively as a substitute.

AUGUST 8   Back-to-back homers by Bernard Gilkey and Todd Hundley off Kevin Brown in the eighth inning produce the only three runs of a 3–0 win over the Marlins in Miami. Gilkey's home run came with a man on base. Pete Harnisch (eight innings) and John Franco (one inning) combined on the shutout.

AUGUST 16   After falling behind 15–0, the Mets score three runs in the seventh inning and seven in the ninth before falling 15–10 to the Padres before 23,699 at Estadio de Beisbol in Monterrey, Mexico. Fernando Valenzuela, a native of Mexico, pitched six shutout innings before allowing the three runs in the seventh.

               The contest was the first of a three-game series in Monterrey as Major League Baseball eyed the expansion of its market south of the border. The Mets won 7–3 on August 17 and lost 8–0 on August 18. Todd Hundley came down with a case of food poisoning during the trip.

AUGUST 26   The Mets fire Dallas Green as manager and hire 46-year-old Bobby Valentine.

               Hired in May 1993, Green was never able to produce a winning record in New York. The club was in the midst of rebuilding, and the front office believed the crusty Green was using the wrong approach with the young players in his charge. Valentine was considered to be a star of the future when he made his major league debut with the Dodgers in 1969, but a series of injuries derailed a promising career. He lasted in the majors as a player until 1979, including a three-year stint with the Mets beginning in 1977. He was a third-base coach for the club until being hired by the Rangers as a manager in May 1985.

Valentine remained in Texas until 1992, but never won a division title. In 1994, he managed the Mets Class AAA farm team in Norfolk. The following year, Valentine became the first American to manage a team in Japan. He piloted the Chiba Lotte Marines to a 69–58 mark, and then returned to the States to manage at Norfolk again in 1996 until his promotion following the dismissal of Green. In 1997, Valentine managed the Mets to the first of five straight winning seasons, which included an appearance in the 1999 NCLS and a World Series berth in 2000. All was not rosy, however, even in the best of seasons. With his oversized ego, his outspokenness won him few friends, and there were only a handful of managers more disliked by opponents. Valentine frequently created clubhouse problems by publicly criticizing his players. With his vanity and arrogance, Valentine managed to make himself the center of attention in New York, no mean feat with a roster dotted with future Hall of Famers. He was fired following a 75–86 season in 2002. Green retired from baseball to his farm in Pennsylvania.

SEPTEMBER 1   After the Giants score in the top of the tenth inning, the Mets rally with two runs in their half to win 6–5 at Shea Stadium. Andy Tomberlin hit a pinch-hit double to tie the score and, two batters later, crossed the plate with the winning run on an infield grounder by Carl Everett.

SEPTEMBER 8   The Mets play at Atlanta-Fulton County Stadium for the last time and win 6–2 over the Braves.

SEPTEMBER 13   Reliever Derek Wallace strikes out four batters in the ninth inning of a 6–4 triumph over the Braves at Shea Stadium. It was just the 13th game of Wallace's career. He struck out Terry Pendleton to start the inning, but Pendleton reached first base on a passed ball by Todd Hundley. Before the ninth was over, Wallace fanned Chipper Jones, Ryan Klesko and Mike Mordecai.

SEPTEMBER 14   Down 5–0, the Mets score five runs in the seventh inning and one in the 12th to defeat the Braves 6–5 at Shea Stadium. The five runs in the seventh scored after two were out on a two-run double by Bernard Gilkey and a three-run homer from Todd Hundley. Lance Johnson singled home the winning run.

Hundley came into the season with 50 career homers over four seasons. He clubbed 41 home runs in 1996 along with 112 RBI and a .259 batting average. The 41 homers set a major league record for catchers. Johnny Bench hit 45 for the Reds in 1970, but 38 came while playing as a catcher. Hundley's record stood until Javy Lopez collected 42 homers for the Braves in 2003. The 41 homers by Hundley in 1996 also set a Mets record, since tied by Carlos Beltran in 2006.

NOVEMBER 25   Three weeks after Bill Clinton wins re-election as President in a race against Bob Dole, the Mets trade Paul Byrd and Andy Zwirchitz to the Braves for Greg McMichael.

McMichael gave the Mets one good year out of the bullpen before going to the Dodgers in a June 1998 trade. Byrd was plagued by inconsistency throughout his career, but won 15 games for the Phillies in 1999, 17 for the Royals in 2002 and 15 with the Indians in 2007.

NOVEMBER 27   The Mets trade Rico Brogna to the Phillies for Ricardo Jordan and Toby Borland.

DECEMBER 20   The Mets trade Robert Person to the Blue Jays for John Olerud.

> *Olerud batted a league-leading .363 with 24 homers as a 24-year-old first baseman for Toronto in 1993. Over the next three seasons, however, he was burdened with unrealistic expectations and failed to raise his average above .300. After batting .274 with 18 home runs in 1996, the Blue Jays were so happy to be rid of Olerud they were willing to pay a hefty portion of his salary. He turned his career around in New York. In three seasons with the Mets, Olerud batted .315 and belted 63 home runs in 476 games.*

1997

Season in a Sentence

In his first full season as manager, Bobby Valentine leads the Mets to their first winning year since 1990.

Finish • Won • Lost • Pct • GB

Third   88   74   .543   13.0

In the wild-card race, the Mets tied for second place, four games behind.

Manager

Bobby Valentine

Stats

Stats	Mets	AL	Rank
Batting Avg:	.262	.263	
On-Base Pct:	.332	.333	
Slugging Pct:	.405	.410	
Home Runs:	153		
Stolen Bases:	97		
ERA:	3.95	4.20	
Errors:	120	8	
Runs Scored:	777		
Runs Allowed:	709		

Starting Lineup

Todd Hundley, c
John Olerud, 1b
Carlos Baerga, 2b
Edgardo Alfonso, 3b
Rey Ordonez, ss
Bernard Gilkey, lf
Carl Everett, cf-rf
Butch Huskey, rf
Lance Johnson, cf
Alex Ochoa, rf
Matt Franco, 3b

Pitchers

Bobby Jones, sp
Rick Reed, sp
Dave Mlicki, sp
Mark Clark, sp
Brian Bohanon, sp
Armando Reynoso, sp
John Franco, rp
Greg McMichael, rp
Cory Lidle, rp

Attendance

1,766,174 (tenth in NL)

Club Leaders

Batting Avg:	Edgardo Alfonso	.315
On-Base Pct:	John Olerud	.400
Slugging Pct:	Todd Hundley	.549
Home Runs:	Todd Hundley	30
RBI:	John Olerud	102
Runs:	John Olerud	90
Stolen Bases:	Carl Everett	17
Wins:	Bobby Jones	15
Strikeouts:	Dave Mlicki	157
ERA:	Rick Reed	2.89
Saves:	John Franco	36

APRIL 1   In the season opener, the Mets lose 12–5 to the Padres in San Diego. The Mets led 4–0 before the Padres exploded for 11 runs in the sixth inning off Pete Harnisch, Yorkis Perez, Toby Borland and Barry Manuel. Todd Hundley homered in the losing cause.

> *The Mets opened the season with a nine-game road trip through San Diego, San Francisco and Los Angeles and went 3–6. Losses in the first three home games dropped the club to 3–9.*

APRIL 5   In his first game with the Mets, Rick Reed pitches seven shutout innings during a 2–0 loss to the Giants in San Francisco.

Reed turned 33 on April 16 and entered the season with a 9–15 record and a 4.63 ERA in the majors with four different teams. Reed was a replacement player for the Reds during the 1994–95 strike and played in four games for the club in July and August in 1995, during which he was shunned by his teammates. Reed spent the 1996 season in the minors with the Mets Class AAA farm club in Norfolk. Returning to the majors in 1997, Reed was 13–9 with an earned run average of 2.89. He played five seasons in New York and had an overall record of 59–36.

APRIL 12   The Mets scheduled home opener against the Giants is rained out.

APRIL 13   The Mets play their first games of 1997 at Shea Stadium with a double-header and lose 5–1 and 7–6 to the Giants before 21,981. John Olerud homered in the opener and Bernard Gilkey in game two.

An alternative home jersey was added in 1997. It was nearly identical to the regular uniform but without the pinstripes. For one season only, the Mets wore white caps for selected home games.

APRIL 15   During a 5–0 win over the Dodgers before 54,047 on a Tuesday night at Shea Stadium, Major League Baseball honors Jackie Robinson on the occasion of the 50th anniversary of his first major league game. Robinson died in 1972. Armando Reynoso (five innings) and Toby Borland (four innings) combined on the shutout.

Among those attending were Robinson's widow Rachel and their daughter Sharon, President Bill Clinton and many of Robinson's former teammates. Clinton was using two walking canes because of a knee injury. He was the first sitting President to attend a Mets game. Others in attendance included Larry Doby, who became the second African-American in the majors when he debuted for the Cleveland Indians in July 1947, and Branch Rickey III, the grandson of Branch Rickey, who signed Robinson to his first contract with the Dodgers. The ceremonies took place at the end of the fifth inning and lasted 35 minutes. Commissioner Bud Selig also addressed the sellout crowd and announced that Robinson's number 42 would be retired throughout baseball. Earlier on the same day, Governor George Pataki and Mayor Rudy Giuliani signed legislation that changed the name of the Interborough Parkway, which connected Brooklyn and Queens, to the Jackie Robinson Parkway.

APRIL 20   Carl Everett hits home runs from both sides of the plate during an 8–2 win over the Cubs in the first game of a double-header at Shea Stadium. Everett struck a grand slam from the left side off Steve Trachsel in the third inning and a solo shot against Steve Casian from the right side in the fourth. The loss dropped the Cubs to an 0–14 record in 1997. The Cubs ended that streak by defeating the Mets 4–3 in game two.

APRIL 23   Todd Hundley smacks two homers and drives in five runs during a 10–2 thrashing of the Reds at Shea Stadium.

Hundley hit 30 homers with a .273 batting average in 1997.

APRIL 28   The Mets score seven runs in the fifth inning and wallop the Reds 15–2 in Cincinnati.

MAY 5   Todd Hundley hits two homers, a double and a single in four at-bats and drives in five runs during a 6–1 victory over the Rockies in Denver. The home runs were struck from opposite sides of the plate. Hundley homered from the **left side** off Kevin Ritz in the third inning and from the **left side** against Mike Munoz in the eighth.

MAY 6   The Mets collect 20 hits, but lose 12–11 to the Rockies in Denver.

MAY 7   Butch Huskey breaks a 1–1 tie with a three-run homer in the ninth and the Mets defeat the Astros 4–1 in Houston.

MAY 11   The Mets score three runs in the ninth inning on back-to-back pinch-hit home runs off Dennis Eckersley to defeat the Cardinals 6–4 in St. Louis. Batting for Manny Alexander, Carl Everett gave the Mets a 5–4 lead with a two-run homer. Hitting in place of Cory Lidle, Butch Huskey followed with another home run.

MAY 14   Edgardo Alfonso ties a major league record for third baseman by participating in four double plays during a 1–0 loss to the Astros at Shea Stadium.

MAY 18   Trailing 4–2, the Mets erupt for eight runs in the eighth inning to defeat the Rockies 10–4 at Shea Stadium. Three Colorado pitchers (Mike Munoz, Bruce Ruffin and Mike DeJean) combined to walk five Mets batters in a row on 23 pitches. Three of them were with the bases loaded. In all, ten Mets reached base in succession on the five walks, four singles and a double.

MAY 19   John Olerud belts a two-run, walk-off homer with one out in the ninth inning to beat the Rockies 4–3 at Shea Stadium.

Olerud batted .294 with 22 homers and 102 RBI in 1997.

MAY 21   The Mets defeat the Marlins 2–1 in Miami with solo homers from Edgardo Alfonso in the fifth inning and Bernard Gilkey in the sixth.

MAY 22   The Mets break a 1–1 tie by scoring eight runs in the third inning off Curt Schilling and defeat the Phillies 10–3 in Philadelphia. John Olerud contributed a single and a three-run double to the rally.

JUNE 3   With the sixth overall pick in the first round of the amateur draft, the Mets select pitcher Geoff Goetz from Jesuit High School in Tampa, Florida.

Goetz never advanced beyond the Class AA level. Future major leaguers drafted and signed by the Mets in 1997 were Tyler Walker (second round), Cesar Crespo (third round), Eric Cammack (13th round), Jason Roach (20th round) and Jason Phillips (24th round).

JUNE 13   The Mets play their first regular season interleague game and lose 8–4 to the Red Sox at Shea Stadium. It was the first meaningful game between the two clubs since the 1986 World Series. The four Mets runs were achieved with four solo homers. Carl Everett homered on the first pitch of the first inning from Jeff Suppan, and cleared the fences with another drive in the seventh. Todd Hundley and Alex Ochoa also homered.

JUNE 16   The Mets play the Yankees in a regular season game for the first time, and win 6–0 at Yankee Stadium. The Mets scored three runs in the first inning, one of them on a double steal in which Todd Hundley stole home and Butch Huskey went to second. Dave Mlicki pitched the shutout.

The Mets lost the last two games of the three-game series 6–3 and 3–2 in ten innings. All three contests, played on a Monday, a Tuesday and a Wednesday, drew over 56,000. They were the second, third and fourth largest crowds at Yankee Stadium all year. The largest was on Opening Day. The Mets and Yankees played each other in just one series in 1997 and 1998. Beginning in 1999, the two clubs squared off in six games a year, with three in each ballpark.

JUNE 20   Bobby Jones ($8^2/_3$ innings) and John Franco (one-third of an inning) combine to defeat the Pirates 1–0 at Shea Stadium. The lone run scored in the sixth inning on a double by Butch Huskey and a single from Jason Hardtke.

The win gave Jones a 12–3 record and a 2.29 ERA. From that point through the end of the season, he was 3–6 with a 5.40 earned run average.

JUNE 22   Carl Everett hits a three-run, walk-off homer in the tenth inning to defeat the Pirates 12–9 at Shea Stadium.

JUNE 29   After falling behind 6–1 in the sixth inning, the Mets rally to defeat the Pirates 10–8 in Pittsburgh. The Mets hit five homers during the final three innings, which included three runs in the seventh inning, four in the eighth and two in the ninth. John Olerud homered twice, and Todd Hundley, Butch Huskey and Matt Franco added one each. Franco's blast came as a pinch-hitter. Luis Lopez broke a 7–7 tie in the eighth with a double that put the Mets into the lead for good.

JUNE 30   The Mets play the Tigers during the regular season for the first time, and lose 14–0 in Detroit. Bobby Higginson hit three homers and drove in seven runs.

JULY 10   The Mets play at Turner Field in Atlanta for the first time and rally from a fifth-inning, 5–1 deficit to defeat the Braves 10–7. Edgardo Alfonso extended his hitting streak to 20 games.

Alfonso collected 32 hits and batted .416 during the streak. He finished the season with a .315 average and ten home runs.

JULY 13   After the Braves score six runs in the first inning to take a 6–0 lead, the Mets rally to win 7–6 in ten innings in Atlanta. Bobby Jones gave up the six runs in the first, and then pitched six shutout innings. Greg McMichael hurled the eighth and ninth innings and John Franco the tenth. Alex Ochoa drove in the winning run with a homer in the tenth.

JULY 16   The Mets fire Joe McIlvaine as general manager and hire 34-year-old Steve Phillips.

McIlvaine was hired in the midst of the 103-loss season of 1993 and rebuilt the club. He was fired despite the fact the Mets had a 51–41 record in 1997 on the way to the club's first winning season since 1990. Even though the club had improved dramatically under McIlvaine's direction, co-owners Nelson

Doubleday and Fred Wilpon believed that he wasn't aggressive enough in making trades and moves in the free agent market and delegated too much authority to his subordinates. In addition, few of the selections made in the amateur drafts under McIlvaine's direction became big-league regulars, and he had a contentious relation with manager Bobby Valentine. Phillips helped bring the Mets back to the postseason in 1999 and the World Series in 2000. He was fired in June 2003 after the club stumbled to a 29–35 start.

JULY 20   Todd Hundley collects two homers, a double and a single in four at-bats and drives in five runs during a 10–1 win over the Reds at Shea Stadium. He also hit home runs from both sides of the plate. Hundley homered off Kent Mercker in the first inning and Felix Rodriguez in the eighth.

AUGUST 8   The Mets trade Lance Johnson, Mark Clark and Manny Alexander to the Cubs for Brian McRae, Turk Wendell and Mel Rojas.

               Wendell became a fan favorite during his five seasons as a Met with his exuberant personality, eccentric behavior and charitable contributions. Wearing number 99, Wendell jumped over the foul line to and from the mound, viciously threw down the rosin bag before delivering his first pitch, chewed black licorice while pitching, and brushed his teeth between innings. An avid hunter, he had a necklace made out of the teeth of the animals he had killed.

AUGUST 14   Edgardo Alfonso hits a grand slam off Donovan Osborne in the fifth inning of a 6–2 win over the Cardinals in St. Louis.

AUGUST 22   The Mets score three runs in the ninth inning and one in the 11th to defeat the Padres 9–8 at Shea Stadium. The Mets trailed 8–5 with two out and a runner on second base and Trevor Hoffman on the mound when John Olerud doubled in a run. Todd Hundley followed with a two-run homer. The winning run scored on a bases-loaded walk by Will Cunnane to Carlos Baerga.

AUGUST 23   Todd Hundley hits a grand slam off Sean Bergman in the seventh inning of a 9–5 triumph over the Padres at Shea Stadium.

AUGUST 27   The Mets score eight runs in the eighth inning and rout the Giants 15–6 at Shea Stadium. Edgardo Alfonso contributed four hits, including a double, in five at-bats and drove in five runs.

AUGUST 29   The Mets play the Orioles for the first time during the regular season and lose 4–3 in 12 innings in Baltimore.

AUGUST 30   The Mets collect 19 hits and trounce the Orioles 13–6 in Baltimore.

AUGUST 31   The Mets trade Pete Harnisch to the Brewers for Donny Moore.

               Harnisch missed much of the 1997 season while suffering from depression, brought on by his withdrawal from using chewing tobacco. Bobby Valentine's harsh handling of Harnisch blew up in an ugly confrontation and led to the trade. Harnisch pitched only four games for Milwaukee before going to the Reds. He had a 30–17 record for Cincinnati in 1998 and 1999. Harnisch was one of two Mets pitchers in 1997 who missed playing time because of clinical depression. The other was Bill Pulsipher, who only two years earlier was considered to be one of the top pitching prospects in baseball. Playing for four minor league teams in the Mets system in 1997, Pulsipher had a 1–9 record and a 5.60 ERA while walking 81 batters in 82 innings.

SEPTEMBER 1   The Mets play the Blue Jays during the regular season for the first time and win 3–0 at Shea Stadium. Jason Isringhausen (six innings), Greg McMichael (one inning), Mel Rojas (one inning) and John Franco (one inning) combined on a two-hitter. The only Toronto hits were singles by Tomas Perez in the second inning and Benito Santiago in the seventh.

SEPTEMBER 11   John Olerud hits for the cycle and drives in five runs during a 9–5 victory over the Expos at Shea Stadium. Facing Mike Johnson, Olerud doubled in the first inning and singled in the third. Olerud flied out versus Shayne Bennett in the fifth, and then hit a home run off Rick DeHart in the seventh and delivered a bases-loaded triple against Steve Kline in the eighth. The triple was the first for Olerud since July 31, 1994, a span of 1,410 at-bats.

SEPTEMBER 13   In one of the greatest comebacks in club history, the Mets score six runs in the ninth inning and three in the 11th to defeat the Expos 9–6 at Shea Stadium. During the ninth-inning rally, the Mets were down to their last strike three times. The Mets trailed 6–0 with two out in the ninth and runners on second and third when pinch-hitter Robert Petagine hit a two-run single. Luis Lopez and Matt Franco followed with singles to load the bases. On a 1–2 pitch against Ugueth Urbina, Carl Everett hit a grand slam. Bernard Gilkey ended the contest in the 11th with a three-run, walk-off homer. The hit by Petagine was his only one in the majors in 1997 in 15 at-bats.

                Butch Huskey extended his hitting streak to 20 games during the game. Over those 20 games, he had 29 hits and batted .363.

SEPTEMBER 14   A home run by Luis Lopez off Carlos Perez in the fifth inning accounts for the only run of a 1–0 win over the Expos at Shea Stadium. Dave Mlicki (8²/₃ innings) and Greg McMichael (one-third of an inning) combined on the shutout.

                The home run by Lopez was the only one he collected in 1997.

SEPTEMBER 15   The Mets score five runs in the tenth inning to defeat the Phillies 10–5 in the first game of a double-header at Veterans Stadium. The five runs during the first nine innings came on five solo homers. Butch Huskey and Bernard Gilkey each hit a pair, with Brian McRae adding the other one. During the five-run rally in the tenth, the Mets hit six consecutive singles. Philadelphia won the second game 2–1.

SEPTEMBER 17   The Braves score nine runs in the first inning, eight of them off Bobby Jones, and rout the Mets 10–2 in Atlanta.

SEPTEMBER 20   Brian McRae hits a grand slam off Alex Fernandez in the first inning of a 7–3 victory over the Marlins at Shea Stadium.

SEPTEMBER 24   John Olerud hits a grand slam off Chris Peters in the sixth inning of a 7–5 win over the Pirates at Shea Stadium.

NOVEMBER 18   The Mets lose Cory Lidle to the Diamondbacks and Carlos Mendoza to the Devil Rays in the expansion draft.

DECEMBER 22   The Mets trade Carl Everett to the Astros for John Hudek.

> *Everett was traded amid allegations that he abused his children. After leaving the Mets, he played nine more seasons in the majors and made two All-Star teams but was seldom far from controversy. During his career, which lasted from 1993 through 2006, Everett played for eight different teams.*

1998

Season in a Sentence

The Mets hold a one-game lead in the wild-card race with five games remaining, but lose all five to blow a chance at the postseason.

Finish • Won • Lost • Pct • GB

Second   88   74   .543   18.0

In the wild-card race, the Mets were in third place, two games behind.

Manager

Bobby Valentine

Stats

Stats	Mets	AL	Rank
Batting Avg:	.259	.262	9
On-Base Pct:	.330	.331	8
Slugging Pct:	.394	.410	11
Home Runs:	136	13	
Stolen Bases:	62	16	
ERA:	3.76	4.23	4
Errors:	101	3	
Runs Scored:	706	11	
Runs Allowed:	645	4	

Starting Lineup

Mike Piazza, c
John Olerud, 1b
Carlos Baerga, 2b
Edgardo Alfonso, 3b
Rey Ordonez, ss
Bernard Gilkey, lf
Brian McRae, cf
Butch Huskey, rf
Luis Lopez, 2b-ss
Matt Franco, 3b-lf-1b

Pitchers

Rick Reed, sp
Al Leiter, sp
Bobby Jones, sp
Masato Yoshii, sp
Armando Reynoso, sp
Hideo Nomo, sp
John Franco, rp
Turk Wendell, rp
Dennis Cook, rp
Mel Rojas, rp
Greg McMichael, rp

Attendance

2,287,948 (ninth in AL)

Club Leaders

Batting Avg:	John Olerud	.354
On-Base Pct:	John Olerud	.447
Slugging Pct:	John Olerud	.551
Home Runs:	Mike Piazza	23
RBI:	John Olerud	93
Runs:	Edgardo Alfonso	94
Stolen Bases:	Brian McRae	20
Wins:	Al Leiter	17
Strikeouts:	Al Leiter	174
ERA:	Al Leiter	2.47
Saves:	John Franco	38

FEBRUARY 6   The Mets trade A. J. Burnett, Jesus Sanchez and Robert Stratton to the Marlins for Al Leiter and Ralph Millard.

> *The final verdict on this trade is yet to be determined because Burnett was still active in 2010. But there's no doubt that Leiter was a success in New York and exceeded all expectations. He was 32 at the time of the trade, but was a mainstay*

in the Mets starting rotation until 2005. Leiter entered the 1998 season with a 60–53 lifetime record, but turned in the best season of his career that year with a 17–6 mark and a 2.47 ERA. Overall, Leiter was 95–67 in a Mets uniform. At the start of the 2011 season, Burnett was 34 years old and had a career record of 110–100.

MARCH 31   The Mets play 14 innings on Opening Day and defeat the Phillies 1–0 before 49,142 at Shea Stadium. The New York pitchers were Bobby Jones (six innings), Greg McMichael (1²/₃ innings), Dennis Cook (1¹/₃ innings), John Franco (one inning), Mel Rojas (two innings) and Turk Wendell (two innings). Curt Schilling started for Philadelphia and surrendered just two hits in eight innings. The Mets had only four hits through the first 13 innings. In the 14th, Matt Franco singled, Brian McRae drew a walk and Bernard Gilkey delivered a single to load the bases. With two out, Alberto Castillo pinch-hit for Wendell and singled in the winning run.

The game was the first ever played by the Mets during the regular season in the month of March. Despite the early start to the season, the temperature was 82 degrees under sunny skies.

APRIL 4   Down 6–2, the Mets rally with a run in the eighth inning, three in the ninth and one in the 13th to defeat the Pirates 7–6 at Shea Stadium. John Olerud contributed the key hit in the ninth with a two-run double to pull the Mets within a run. The tying run crossed the plate on a ground out by Butch Huskey. Rich Becker drove home the game winner with a bases-loaded single in the 13th.

Black was added to the blue and orange on the Mets uniforms as an official third color in 1998. The change included black caps, black shirts, black undershirts and black socks for many games. The Mets now had four uniforms styles: home pinstripe jersey, home "snow white" alternative jersey, road gray jersey and the black alternative jersey. The latter was worn both at home and on the road.

APRIL 5   In his major league debut, Masato Yoshii pitches seven shutout innings, and the Mets defeat the Pirates 7–0 at Shea Stadium.

APRIL 10   The Mets play the Brewers for the first time and lose 5–3 at County Stadium in Milwaukee.

The Brewers moved from the American League to the National League in 1998.

APRIL 15   The Mets and the Yankees play separate games at Shea Stadium on the same day. During the afternoon, the Yankees defeated the Anaheim Angels 6–3. In the evening, the Mets downed the Cubs 2–1. It marked the first time since 1900 that two regular-season games involving four teams were played in one stadium on the same day.

A 500-pound concrete-and-steel beam fell from beneath the lower deck of Yankees Stadium into empty seats below on April 13, necessitating the ballpark's temporary abandonment and full-scale inspection. The Yankees were forced to postpone the April 13 and 14 games against the Angels and play its Wednesday, April 15 game at Shea. The Yankees' weekend series on April 17, 18 and 19 against the Tigers was moved to Detroit, and their series the following weekend, scheduled for Detroit, was moved to the reopened Yankee Stadium. The incident reinforced George Steinbrenner's contention, encouraged by New York mayor Rudy Giuliani, that the Yankees needed a city-funded new ballpark. A new stadium to replace Shea was also seriously discussed for the first time in 1998. Plans were unveiled to model the new ballpark after Ebbets Field and build it next to Shea. The first models had a retractable roof with a grass field on a platform that could be rolled out into the parking lot to receive enough sunshine and moisture. Capacity would be 45,000 with 60,000 available for hockey and basketball. It was hoped that the Mets would be able to take occupancy by 2002.

APRIL 19   Bernard Gilkey ties a club record by scoring five runs during a 14–0 trashing of the Reds in Cincinnati. In six plate appearances, Gilkey reached base on two doubles, a single, a fielder's choice and a force-out.

APRIL 22   Jim Tatum hits a three-run, pinch-hit, walk-off homer to defeat the Astros 10–7 at Shea Stadium.

             The homer was the second of three that Tatum struck in 201 major league at-bats. The first was five years earlier on May 4, 1993 when he played for the Rockies. The third was struck five days later on April 27, 1998, also against the Astros.

MAY 4   The Mets play the Arizona Diamondbacks for the first time and lose 4–2 in 11 innings at Shea Stadium.

MAY 6   The Mets score seven runs in the eighth inning and beat the Diamondbacks 8–2 at Shea Stadium. Todd Pratt delivered a three-run triple during the rally. It was his only major league triple between June 29, 1994 and April 17, 2003.

             Todd Hundley underwent reconstructive elbow surgery in September 1997 and wasn't available at the start of the 1998 season. The injury left the club without a capable catcher, a situation that wasn't resolved until Mike Piazza was acquired (see May 22, 1998). The Mets used seven different starting catchers in the first 45 games of the season. Hundley returned in July and was tried in left field with disastrous results. The Mets used 15 players in left field during the season, 11 of them as a starters.

MAY 7   Masato Yoshii (seven innings), Greg McMichael (one inning) and John Franco (one inning) combine on a two-hitter to defeat the Cardinals 7–1 at Shea Stadium. The only St. Louis hits were a single by Mark McGwire in the first inning and a homer from Brian Jordan in the fourth.

MAY 22   The Mets play the Brewers at Shea Stadium for the first time and win 3–2.

             On the same day, the Mets traded Preston Wilson, Ed Yarnall and Geoff Goetz to the Marlins for Mike Piazza. Piazza rose from a lowly 62nd-round draft choice to become one of the best catchers in baseball history. Beginning with his rookie season in 1993, Piazza was a five-time All-Star with the Dodgers. He was traded to the Marlins on May 14, 1998 when negotiations for a contract extension stalled. Piazza lasted only eight days in Florida before going to the Mets. Piazza wasn't exactly welcomed by Mets fans—in fact, many were downright hostile. He was unfairly booed often during his first few weeks with *the club, but had a tremendous season nonetheless. Over the remainder of the 1998 season, Piazza batted .348 for the Mets and hit 23 homers in 394 at-bats. At the end of that season, the Mets signed him to a seven-year contract worth $91 million. In eight seasons with club, Piazza played in seven All-Star Games. Among Mets players all-time through the 2010 season, he is first in slugging percentage (.542), fourth in batting average (.296), fifth in on-base percentage (.373), second in home runs (220), second in RBI (655), fourth in total bases (1,885) and fifth in doubles (193).*

MAY 26   The Mets wipe out a 5–1 deficit by exploding for nine runs in the sixth inning and defeat the Marlins 10–6 in Miami. Butch Huskey contributed to the rally with five RBI on a pair of doubles. In his first at-bat in the sixth, Huskey drove in two with a two-bagger. With two out in the inning, he delivered a three-run double.

MAY 27   After the first two batters in the fifth inning are retired, the Mets erupt for six runs and beat the Marlins 8–2 in Miami.

MAY 29   The Mets bury the Phillies 11–0 in Philadelphia. Rick Reed (7$^1/_3$ innings) and John Hudek (1$^2/_3$ innings) combined on the shutout.

MAY 31   The Mets extend their winning streak to nine games with an 8–6 victory over the Phillies in Philadelphia.

JUNE 2   In the first round of the amateur draft, the Mets select outfielder Jason Tyner from Texas A&M University.

Tyner played only 13 games for the Mets before going to Tampa Bay in a 2000 trade. He had a .275 career batting average in the majors, but collected only one home run in 1,358 at-bats. Other future major leaguers drafted and signed by the Mets in 1998 were Pat Strange (second round), Craig Brazell (fifth round), Gil Velasquez (14th round), Ty Wiggington (17th round), Jaime Cerda (23rd round) and Earl Snyder (36th round).

JUNE 4   The Mets trade Greg McMichael and Brad Clontz to the Dodgers for Hideo Nomo.

Nomo became the first Japanese player to find success in the United States when he composed a 13–6 record and a 2.54 ERA and struck out a league-leading 236 batters in 191$^1/_3$ innings as a rookie with the Dodgers in 1995. The Dodgers traded him to the Mets after a 2–7 start in 1998. Nomo was still only 29, and the Mets hoped for a rebound. He was 4–5 along with a 4.84 earned run average for the club, however, and was released at the end of the season. Nomo played for six teams from 1999 through the end of his career in 2008 and won 16 games in both 2002 and 2003 in a return engagement with the Dodgers.

JUNE 5   The Mets play a regular season game at Fenway Park for the first time and beat the Red Sox 9–2.

JUNE 6   The Mets collect only two hits off Tim Wakefield and Tom Gordon, but beat the Red Sox 1–0 in Boston. The lone run scored in the sixth inning when Brian McRae walked, stole second, moved to third on a ground out and crossed the plate on a balk. Bobby Jones (eight innings) and John Franco (one inning) combined on the shutout.

JUNE 8	The Mets play the Devil Rays for the first time and win 3–0 at Shea Stadium. Rick Reed pitched a three-hit shutout and struck out ten.
JUNE 24	The Mets play the Orioles for the first at Shea Stadium during the regular season and win 6–3.
JUNE 26	The Mets play the Yankees for the first time at Shea Stadium during the regular season and lose 8–4.
JUNE 28	Masato Yoshii (seven innings) and Dennis Cook (two innings) combine on a two-hitter and fan 13 during a 2–1 win over the Yankees at Shea Stadium. The only Yankee hits were a single by Derek Jeter in the fifth inning and a homer from Scott Brosius in the seventh. The Mets were held hitless until the sixth by Orlando Hernandez when two singles and a wild pitch produced a run. In the ninth, Carlos Baerga doubled, went to third on a bunt and crossed the plate on a sacrifice fly from pinch-hitter Luis Lopez.

Each of the three games against the Yankees on June 26, 27 and 28 drew in excess of 53,000. They were the three largest crowds at Shea all year. The Mets lost two of the three games. The Yankees were dominant in 1998 with records of 114–48 during the regular season and 11–2 in the postseason.

JULY 3	The Mets trade John Hudek to the Reds for Lenny Harris.
JULY 10	The Mets trade Brian Bohannon to the Dodgers for Greg McMichael.

McMichael was traded to the Dodgers in June 4 in the Hideo Nomo trade. McMichael pitched 12 games for the Dodgers before heading back to New York.

JULY 11	John Olerud delivers two homers and two singles in four at-bats during an 8–4 win over the Expos at Shea Stadium.

Olerud batted .354 with a .447 on-base percentage in 1998, which are both Mets franchise records. He also contributed 22 home runs.

JULY 12	Hideo Nomo (5$\frac{1}{3}$ innings), Jeff Tam (1$\frac{2}{3}$ innings), Greg McMichael (one inning) and Dennis Cook (one inning) combine on a two-hitter to beat the Expos 5–2 at Shea Stadium. The only two Montreal hits were singles by Rondell White in the second inning and Javier Vasquez in the third. Nomo was relieved after walking seven batters, four of them in the sixth inning. The three relievers combined to retire all ten batters they faced.
JULY 31	The Mets trade Leo Estrella to the Blue Jays for Tony Phillips. On the same day, the Mets sent Bernard Gilkey and Nelson Figueroa to the Diamondbacks for Willie Blair and Jorge Fabregas.
AUGUST 1	The Mets score two runs in the ninth inning to defeat the Dodgers 2–1 at Shea Stadium. Matt Franco tied the score 1–1 with a pinch-hit homer. Edgardo Alfonso drove home the game winner with a two-out double.

AUGUST 5   The Mets pull off a triple play in the fifth inning of a 6–4 loss to the Giants at Shea Stadium. With Jeff Kent on first base and Bobby Bonds on third, J. T. Snow hit a grounder to first baseman John Olerud, who threw to shortstop Rey Ordonez at second base for the force. As Ordonez threw back to first to retire Snow, Bonds tried to score and was out from Olerud to catcher Todd Pratt.

AUGUST 9   John Olerud extends his hitting streak to 23 games during an 11–4 loss to the Rockies in Denver. During the 23-game streak, Olerud collected 40 hits and batted .449.

AUGUST 14   The Mets play in Phoenix for the first time and beat the Diamondbacks 3–2.

AUGUST 21   Armando Reynoso (seven innings), Turk Wendell (one inning) and John Franco (one inning) combine on a three-hitter to beat the Cardinals 1–0 in the second game of a double-header at Shea Stadium. The lone run scored on a home run by Edgardo Alfonso off Manny Aybar with one out in the first inning. St. Louis won the opener 10–5.

AUGUST 22   After the Diamondbacks score four runs in the top of the second, the Mets rally with six in their half and go on to win 9–4 at Shea Stadium. Mike Piazza capped the second-inning rally with a grand slam off Andy Benes.

AUGUST 29   The Mets score two runs in the ninth inning to defeat the Dodgers 4–3 in Los Angeles. The first two batters in the ninth were retired before Tony Phillips walked. Edgardo Alfonso gave the Mets the lead with a home run on a 2–2 pitch.

SEPTEMBER 1   Trailing 6–1, the Mets score seven runs in the top of the seventh inning, but allow three in the bottom half and lose 9–8 to the Padres in San Diego. Six of the seven runs in the seventh scored after two were out, three of them on a home run by Mike Piazza.

SEPTEMBER 8   On the day that Mark McGwire hits his 62nd home run of the season to break Roger Maris's single-season record, the Phillies use seven home runs to sink the Mets 16–4 in Philadelphia. The seven homers were allowed by Mel Rojas (three), Hideo Nomo (two), Willie Blair (one) and Brad Clontz (one) to Kevin Sefcik (two), Rico Brogna (two), Bobby Estalella (two) and Marlon Anderson (one).

SEPTEMBER 13   Willie Blair (7⅓ innings), Dennis Cook (two-thirds of an inning) and John Franco (one inning) combine forces to defeat the Expos 1–0 in Montreal. The lone run was driven home on a double by Brian McRae in the eighth inning.

SEPTEMBER 14   The Mets score two runs in the ninth inning and three in the 13th to defeat the Astros 7–4 in Houston. Brian McRae tied the score 4–4 with a two-run homer off Billy Wagner in the ninth. McRae then broke the deadlock with a two-run double in the 13th.

SEPTEMBER 16   The Mets take an exciting 11–inning, 4–3 win over the Astros in Houston. The Mets were held without a run until Mike Piazza hit a three-run homer with two out in the ninth inning for a 3–2 lead. Brad Ausmus homered in the bottom half, however, to tie the score. The deadlock was broken on a pinch-hit home run from Todd Hundley in the 11th.

John Olerud had an incredible streak over five games from September 15 through September 20 with 13 hits in a span of 14 at-bats. The last nine hits were in succession, one shy of the National League record. Included in the 13 hits were three homers and a double.

SEPTEMBER 20   The Mets take a one-game lead in the wild-card race with a 5–0 win over the Marlins at Shea Stadium. Al Leiter (eight innings) and Turk Wendell (one inning) combined on the shutout.

There were seven days left in the regular season, and the Mets had five games remaining. The one-game lead was over the Cubs. The Giants were still mathematically alive, four games out.

SEPTEMBER 22   The Mets drop into a tie with the Cubs for first place in the wild-card race by losing 5–3 to the Expos at Shea Stadium.

SEPTEMBER 25   The Mets extend their losing streak to three by dropping a 6–5 decision to the Braves in Atlanta. At the end of the day, there was a three-way tie for the lead in the wild-card race between the Mets, Cubs and Giants. Each team was 88–72.

SEPTEMBER 26   The Mets drop a game behind both the Cubs and Giants in the wild-card race by losing 4–0 to the Braves in Atlanta.

SEPTEMBER 27   The postseason hopes of the Mets are dashed with a 7–2 loss to the Braves in Atlanta. Both the Cubs and Giants lost to remain tied for first in the wild-card chase.

The following day, the Cubs won the wild-card berth with 5–3 win over the Giants in Chicago in a one-game playoff.

NOVEMBER 9   Lenny Harris signs with the Rockies as a free agent.

NOVEMBER 11   The Mets trade Mel Rojas to the Dodgers for Bobby Bonilla.

Bonilla was a disappointment when he previously played for the Mets from 1992 through 1995 (see December 2, 1991), and his return to New York was not a happy one. He began the year as the starting right fielder with a contract calling for him to be paid nearly $6 million, but ended he ended the year batting an abysmal .160 with four home runs in 119 at-bats. Bonilla also became a clubhouse distraction by sulking and whining after being benched. Fortunately, Rojas performed as badly. He pitched for three teams in 1999 and gave up 28 runs, all earned, in 14 innings over 13 games for an ERA of 18.00.

DECEMBER 1   The Mets sign Robin Ventura, most recently with the White Sox, as a free agent. On the same day, the Mets traded Todd Hundley and Arnold Gooch to the Dodgers for Charles Johnson and Roger Cedeno. Johnson was then dealt to the Orioles for Armando Benitez.

At the time he was signed, Ventura was 31 and had been a starting third baseman for the White Sox nine seasons. He gave the Mets one great year in 1999 with a .301 batting average, 32 homers and 120 RBI. In four seasons with the Mets, Ventura hit 104 home runs. Hundley was pushed out of a starting job in New York by an elbow injury, the trade for Mike Piazza and a .161 batting average in 124 at-bats in 1998. Hundley played five more years in the majors and hit 78 homers in 1,220 at-bats, but batted only .222. Supplanting John Franco, Benitez was the Mets closer from 1999 through July 2003 when he was traded to the Yankees. His 160 saves are the second best in Mets history behind Franco's 276. Cedeno proved to be a surprise in 1999 with a .313 batting average and a club-record 66 stolen bases.

DECEMBER 14   Tony Phillips signs with the Athletics as a free agent. On the same day, the Mets traded Butch Huskey to the Mariners for Leslie Brea.

DECEMBER 16   The Mets sign Rickey Henderson, most recently with the Athletics, as a free agent.

When signed, Henderson was nine days shy of his 40th birthday. Behind him were ten All-Star Game appearances, 12 seasons in which he led the AL in stolen bases, five in runs scored, four in base on balls and one in on-base percentage. Henderson gave the Mets a solid season in 1999 with a .315 batting average, 12 homers and 37 stolen bases in 121 games. After struggling with the club at the start of the 2000 season, Henderson was released by the club in May.

1999

Season in a Sentence

The Mets reach the postseason for the first time since 1988 by winning the wild-card berth in a one-game playoff with the Reds before losing in the Championship Series to the Braves.

Finish • Won • Lost • Pct • GB

Second   97   66   .595   6.5

In the wild-card race, the Mets finished in first place one game ahead.

National League Division Series

The Mets defeated the Arizona Diamondbacks three games to one.

National League Championship Series

The Mets lost to the Atlanta Braves four games to two.

Manager

Bobby Valentine

Stats

Stats	Mets	AL	Rank
Batting Avg:	.279	.266	2
On-Base Pct:	.363	.342	1
Slugging Pct:	.434	.429	5
Home Runs:	181	9	
Stolen Bases:	150	5	
ERA:	4.27	4.56	5
Errors:	68	1	
Runs Scored:	853	5	
Runs Allowed:	711	4	

Starting Lineup

Mike Piazza, c
John Olerud, 1b
Edgardo Alfonso, 2b
Robin Ventura, 3b
Rey Ordonez, ss
Rickey Henderson, lf
Brian McRae, cf
Roger Cedeno, rf
Benny Agbayani, rf-lf
Matt Franco, 3b-lf-1b

Pitchers

Al Leiter, sp
Orel Hershiser, sp
Masato Yoshii, sp
Rick Reed, sp
Octavio Dotel, sp
Kenny Rogers, sp
Armando Benitez, rp
John Franco, rp
Turk Wendell, rp
Dennis Cook, rp

Attendance

2,275,668 (seventh in NL)

Club Leaders

Batting Avg:	Rickey Henderson	.315
On-Base Pct:	Rickey Henderson	.423
Slugging Pct:	Mike Piazza	.575
Home Runs:	Mike Piazza	40
RBI:	Mike Piazza	124
Runs:	Edgardo Alfonso	123
Stolen Bases:	Roger Cedeno	66
Wins:	Al Leiter	13
	Orel Hershiser	13
Strikeouts:	Al Leiter	162
ERA:	Al Leiter	4.23
Saves:	Armando Benitez	22

JANUARY 27   Carlos Baerga signs with the Cardinals as a free agent.

FEBRUARY 3   Nine days before president Bill Clinton is acquitted in his impeachment trial, Tom Seaver replaces Tim McCarver in the Mets broadcast booth.

> *McCarver had been an analyst for the Mets on television since 1983, but was let go because many believed he was too critical of the team, particularly manager Bobby Valentine. McCarver maintained a national television presence over the FOX network. Seaver served as an announcer until 2005.*

MARCH 25   The Mets sign Orel Hershiser, most recently with the Giants, as a free agent.

APRIL 5 — The Mets open the season with a 6–2 loss to the Marlins in Miami. Al Leiter started and allowed five runs, four of them earned, in five innings. John Olerud homered in the losing cause.

> *The Mets set a major league record for fewest errors in a season in 1999 with just 68. The next lowest figure for an NL team that season was 100 for the Phillies. The key was the airtight infield of John Olerud, Edgardo Alfonso, Rey Ordonez and Robin Ventura. Alfonso moved from third base to second in 1999 and batted .304 with 27 homers and 108 RBI. The Mets' single-season errors record stood until 2003 when the Mariners committed only 65.*

APRIL 11 — John Olerud collects three doubles and a single in five at-bats during a 6–3 win over the Expos in Montreal.

APRIL 12 — In the home opener, the Mets triumph 8–1 over the Marlins before 52,052 at Shea Stadium. Bobby Jones not only allowed just one run in seven innings, but walloped his first, and only, career home run in 442 at-bats.

APRIL 28 — Mike Piazza hits a two-run, walk-off homer off Trevor Hoffman in the ninth inning to defeat the Padres 4–3 at Shea Stadium.

> *Piazza batted .303 with 40 homers and 120 RBI in 1999.*

MAY 1 — Brian McRae hits a grand slam off Jerry Spradlin in the seventh inning of a 9–4 victory over the Giants at Shea Stadium.

MAY 11 — Two pitchers named Bobby Jones are the starting pitchers in an 8–5 loss to the Rockies in Denver. Bobby J. Jones lasted $5\frac{1}{3}$ innings for the Mets and Bobby M. Jones went five innings for Colorado. It was the first time that two pitchers with the same first and last names started against each other in a major league game since Jack Taylor of the Reds squared off against Jack Taylor of the Cubs on April 16, 1899. Bobby J. Jones pitched for the Mets from 1993 through 2000. Bobby M. Jones played for the Mets in 2000 and again in 2002. During the 2000 season, the Mets had two Bobby Joneses on the pitching staff, but two pitchers with the same name wasn't a franchise first. The club had two Bob Millers in 1962.

MAY 20 — Playing the Brewers at Shea Stadium, Robin Ventura becomes the first (and to date, the only) player in major league history to hit grand slams in both ends of a double-header. Ventura hit his grand slam in the opener off Jim Abbott in the first inning, and the Mets went on to win 11–10. Benny Agbayani contributed two homers and two singles in four at-bats. In the second tilt, Ventura contributed to a 10–1 victory with a slam against Horacio Estrada in the fourth.

> *Ventura also hit two grand slams in a single game with the White Sox on September 4, 1995. He is one of only 12 players to accomplish that feat. During his career, Ventura batted .340 with 18 homers in 188 at-bats with the bases loaded.*

MAY 21 — Mike Piazza homers for the fourth game in a row during a 7–5 win over the Phillies at Shea Stadium.

MAY 23

The Mets score five runs in the ninth inning off Curt Schilling to stun the Phillies 5–4 at Shea Stadium. Mike Piazza led off the ninth with a single and scored on Robin Ventura's home run. The Mets added another run, but still trailed 4–3 with two out and runners on second and third. Edgardo Alfonso was hit by a pitch on a 1–2 count to load the bases. John Olerud lined a single to left-center to drive home the tying and winning runs.

JUNE 2

With their first pick in the amateur draft, the Mets select pitcher Neal Musser from Benton Central High School in Otterbein, Indiana.

The Mets lost their first pick to the White Sox by signing Robin Ventura as a free agent. It took Musser until 2007 to reach the majors when he was a member of the Royals, and he has yet to find success. Other future major leaguers drafted and signed by the Mets in 1999 include Jeremy Griffiths (third round), Angel Pagan (fourth round), Prentice Redman (tenth round) and Mike Jacobs (38th round).

JUNE 5

The Mets fire three coaches after losing their eighth straight game by dropping a 6–3 decision to the Yankees at Yankee Stadium. The three fired coaches were pitching coach Bob Apodaca, bullpen coach Randy Niemann and hitting coach Tom Robson. Replacing them were Al Jackson, John Stearns and Dave Wallace.

The loss dropped the Mets to a 27–28 record on the season.

JUNE 6

The Mets score seven runs off Roger Clemens in 2²/₃ innings and beat the Yankees 7–2 at Yankee Stadium. Clemens came into the game riding a 20–game winning streak over two seasons. The Mets went into the day with an eight-game losing streak.

JUNE 7

Benny Agbayani hits two homers during an 8–2 win over the Blue Jays at Shea Stadium.

Agbayani began the year in the minors and didn't play in his first game with the Mets in 1999 until May 11. In his first 75 at-bats through June 11, he had ten home runs and a batting average of .400. He soon cooled off, however, and ended the year with a .286 average and 14 homers in 276 at-bats.

JUNE 9

The Mets score three runs in the ninth inning and one in the 14th to defeat the Blue Jays 4–3 at Shea Stadium. David Wells went into the ninth with a shutout and had two out with a runner on first when Mike Piazza singled John Olerud to third and then stole second. Robin Ventura singled home both Olerud and Piazza. Bill Koch replaced Wells on the mound and surrendered a game-tying double to Brian McRae. Rey Ordonez drove in the winning run with a single. Pat Mahomes pitched three innings of relief for the win.

During the game, Bobby Valentine was ejected in the 12th inning for arguing a call. He later returned to the dugout wearing dark glasses and a lampblack mustache until the ruse was discovered by the umpires. Valentine was suspended for two days and fined $5,000 for the indiscretion.

JUNE 24

Mike Piazza runs his hitting streak to 24 games during an 8–2 triumph over the Marlins at Shea Stadium.

During the streak, Piazza had 36 hits and batted .353.

JUNE 28	Robin Ventura accounts for six runs batted in with a pair of three-run homers during a 10–4 rout of the Marlins in Miami.
JULY 1	The Mets score six runs in the third inning for a 6–0 lead and outslug the Marlins 12–8 in Miami.
JULY 2	The Mets collect only three hits and are walloped by the Braves 16–0 at Shea Stadium. Matt Franco was used as a pitcher and gave up a run and two hits in one-third of an inning.
JULY 4	Armando Benitez strikes out all three batters he faces in the ninth inning to close out a 7–6 victory over the Braves at Shea Stadium.

Benitez struck out 128 batters in 78 innings over 77 games and had an ERA of 1.85 in 1999. He fanned 14.8 batters per nine innings.

JULY 6	The Mets trounce the Marlins 10–0 at Shea Stadium. Orel Hershiser (five innings), Greg McMichael (one inning) and Jason Isringhausen (three innings) combined on the shutout.
JULY 10	Trailing 8–7 with two out in the ninth inning, Matt Franco delivers a two-run, walk-off, pinch-single to defeat the Yankees 9–8 at Shea Stadium.

From 1997 through 2000, Franco played in 438 games for the Mets, but had only 681 plate appearances. He played in 271 games as a pinch-hitter over those four seasons.

JULY 15	The Mets play a regular season game in St. Petersburg for the first time and defeat the Devil Rays 8–7 in ten innings.
JULY 23	The Mets trade Terrence Long and Leo Vasquez to the Athletics for Kenny Rogers.
JULY 27	The Mets lose 5–1 to the Pirates on "Turn Ahead the Clock Night" at Shea Stadium.

To mark the end of the century, Major League Baseball staged several games with teams wearing futuristic uniforms. The home team was dubbed the "Mercury Mets" and wore black and silver jerseys. The Pirates donned red and yellow. According to the New York Times, the "threads looked like a cross between softball uniforms and something a 1980s band would wear on stage." The futuristic theme was carried on throughout the night with the scoreboard flashing computerized photos of each player as he came to bat. Rickey Henderson, for example, was given three eyes and pointy ears and played "left quadrant." When Henderson first saw the photo leading off the first inning, he was laughing so hard he had to step out of the batter's box to compose himself before lining out.

JULY 28	The Mets break a 2–2 tie with seven runs in the eighth inning and beat the Pirates 9–2 at Shea Stadium.
JULY 30	After falling behind 7–2 in the second inning, the Mets rally to defeat the Cubs 10–9 at Wrigley Field. New York scored in seven of the nine innings.

JULY 31
Robin Ventura drives in six runs with two homers, a double and a single, but it's not enough to prevent a 17–10 loss to the Cubs in Chicago.

On the same day, the Mets made three transactions. The club traded Jason Isringhausen and Greg McMichael to the Athletics for Billy Taylor and dealt Brian McRae, Rigo Beltran and Thomas Johnson to the Rockies for Darryl Hamilton and Chuck McElroy. In a third deal, Craig Paquette was sent to the Cardinals for Shawon Dunston. The Oakland trade was the only one of the three that would have long-lasting implications. The A's converted Isringhausen from a starter to a reliever, and he developed into one of the best closers in the game. Isringhausen recorded 30 or more saves in seven different seasons, with two in Oakland and five in St. Louis. In exchange, Taylor pitched in only 18 games with the Mets and had an ERA of 8.10.

AUGUST 1
Al Leiter strikes out 15 batters in seven innings of a 13-inning, 5–4 victory over the Cubs in Chicago.

AUGUST 8
Matt Franco is used as a pitcher for the second time in 1999, this time during a 14–3 loss to the Dodgers at Shea Stadium. Franco gave up a run and a hit and walked three in one inning.

AUGUST 15
The Mets play at Candlestick Park for the last time and beat the Giants 12–5. Robin Ventura hit a grand slam off Livan Hernandez in the fifth inning.

AUGUST 16
Edgardo Alfonso homers in the tenth inning to beat the Padres 4–3 in San Diego. Octavio Dotel had a no-hitter in progress until the seventh inning when he walked two and gave up a three-run homer to Phil Nevin. Turk Wendell, Dennis Cook and Armando Benitez each hurled an inning in relief of Dotel to close out the win. Mike Piazza homered for the fourth game in succession.

On the same day, the Mets signed 16-year-old shortstop Jose Reyes out of the Dominican Republic as an undrafted free agent.

AUGUST 21
Armando Benitez strikes out all three batters he faces in the ninth inning to close out a 7–4 victory over the Cardinals at Shea Stadium.

AUGUST 22
During a double-header at Shea Stadium, the Mets win the opener 8–7, but lose the nightcap 7–5. In the first game, the Mets trailed 6–1 in the eighth when John Olerud smacked a grand slam off Rick Croushire. Two pitches later, Mike Piazza homered to deadlock the contest at 6–6. After St. Louis scored in the top of the ninth, the Mets rallied for two in their half for the win. Rickey Henderson drove in the tying run with a double, and Edgrado Alfonso delivered a walk-off single for the victory.

Mark McGwire hit his 49th and 50th home runs of the season in the first game. Number 49 was struck off Octavio Dotel and hit the scoreboard about halfway up in right-center, shattering a light blub. It was estimated to have traveled 502 feet.

AUGUST 30
Edgardo Alfonso has the greatest single day by a hitter in Mets history during a 17–1 victory over the Astros in Houston. Alfonso had six hits, including three homers and a double, in six at-bats. He tied a major league record (as well as making a club record) with six runs scored in addition to five runs batted in. Facing Shane Reynolds,

Alfonso homered in the first inning and singled in the second. Alfonso homered against Brian Williams in the fourth inning and Bergman in the sixth. With a chance at the major league record-tying fourth home run, Alfonso added a single off Bergman in the eighth and a double versus Trever Miller in the ninth. The Mets had 21 hits in all. Mike Piazza and Darryl Hamilton also homered.

Alfonso was the fifth player to combine six hits and three homers in the same day. The first four were Guy Hecker with the Louisville Colonels in 1886, Ty Cobb with the Tigers in 1925, Jimmie Foxx with the Philadelphia Athletics in 1930 and Walker Cooper for the Reds in 1949. Shawn Green had a six-hit, four-home run contest as a Dodger in 2002.

SEPTEMBER 1   The Mets play at the Astrodome for the last time and beat the Astros 9–5.

SEPTEMBER 5   Darryl Hamilton hits a grand slam off Darryl Kile in the fifth inning of a 6–2 triumph over the Rockies at Shea Stadium.

SEPTEMBER 9   Orel Hershiser (eight innings) and Armando Benitez (one inning) combine on a two-hitter to defeat the Dodgers 3–1 at Dodger Stadium. The only Los Angeles hits were a home run by Gary Sheffield in the first inning and a single from Mark Grudzielanek in the fourth.

SEPTEMBER 18   Rey Ordonez hits a grand slam off Carlton Loewer in the sixth inning of an 11–1 trouncing of the Phillies at Shea Stadium.

The home run was the only one that Ordonez collected between September 15, 1998 and July 21, 2001.

SEPTEMBER 19   The Mets pull within one game of the first-place Braves with an 8–6 victory over the Phillies at Shea Stadium.

The following day, the Mets began a seven-game losing streak. At the end of the streak on September 28, the Mets were eight games behind the Braves and were eliminated from the NL East race. In the wild-card chase, the Mets were 1¹/₂ games behind the Astros with five games remaining.

SEPTEMBER 29   The Mets score seven runs in the fourth inning and break a seven-game losing streak with a 9–2 triumph over the Braves at Shea Stadium. John Olerud hit a grand slam off Greg Maddux.

SEPTEMBER 30   The postseason dreams of the Mets receive a setback with an 11-inning, 4–3 loss to the Braves at Shea Stadium.

With three games remaining, the Mets were two games back in the wild-card race. The Reds and Astros were tied for first in the NL Central race.

OCTOBER 1   Robin Ventura hits a walk-off single in the 11th inning to beat the Pirates 3–2 at Shea Stadium. Pat Mahomes was the winning pitcher, and the decision gave him an 8–0 record on the season after spending all of 1998 playing in Japan. The Reds and Astros both lost, which put the Mets one game out of a playoff spot with two contests left.

OCTOBER 2   Rick Reed strikes out 12 batters without a walk and pitches a complete game three-hitter to defeat the Pirates 7–0 at Shea Stadium. The Astros won 3–0 over the Dodgers in Houston while the Reds lost 10–6 to the Brewers in Milwaukee. With one game left, Houston led Cincinnati by one game in the NL Central, and the Mets and Reds were tied in the wild-card race.

OCTOBER 3   Melvin Mora scores from third base on a wild pitch in the ninth inning to give the Mets a 2–1 win over the Pirates at Shea Stadium.

The contest ended at 4:47 p.m. Eastern Time, and the Mets had to await the outcomes of two games to determine their opponent in the Division Series. At 5:51 p.m. Eastern Time, the Astros wrapped up a 9–4 victory over the Dodgers to claim the NL Central crown. If the Reds defeated the Brewers in Milwaukee, it would force a playoff game between the Reds and Mets the following day in Cincinnati for the wild-card berth. If the Reds lost, the Mets would claim the wild card and begin a playoff series against the Diamondbacks in Phoenix on October 5. Steady rain in Milwaukee delayed the start of the Reds-Brewers game until 9:52 p.m. Eastern Time. The Mets boarded a plane not knowing whether or not it would land in Cincinnati or Phoenix. The club was in a holding pattern over the Greater Cincinnati Airport, awaiting the outcome of the Reds-Brewers game, which ended at 12:28 a.m. with a 7–1 Cincinnati victory. The playoff game was originally scheduled for 2:05 p.m., but was moved back to 7:05 p.m. because of the late start in Milwaukee.

OCTOBER 4   The Mets clinch a playoff berth with a 5–0 win over the Reds at Cinergy Field in Cincinnati. Al Leiter pitched a two-hitter. The only Cincinnati hits were a single by Jeffrey Hammonds in the second inning and a double from Pokey Reese in the ninth. The Mets had a 2–0 lead two batters into the game on a single by Rickey Henderson and a homer from Edgardo Alfonso. Henderson later added a home run of his own.

The Mets met the Arizona Diamondbacks in the Division Series. Managed by Buck Showalter, Arizona had a 65–97 record in 1998 as a first-year expansion team. The Diamondbacks improved to 100–62 in 1999 to win the NL West.

OCTOBER 5   The Mets score four runs in the ninth inning, three of them off Randy Johnson, to win game one of the Division Series over the Diamondbacks by an 8–4 score in Phoenix. The Mets took a 4–1 lead in the fourth inning with the help of home runs from Edgardo Alfonso and John Olerud, but allowed Arizona to come back and tie the contest 4–4 in the sixth. In the ninth, Johnson loaded the bases on two singles and a walk before he was relieved. With two out, Alfonso delivered the game winner with a grand slam just inside the left-field foul pole off Bobby Chouinard.

Games one and two were televised on ESPN, game three on NBC and game four on ESPN2. The announcers were Chris Berman, Ray Knight and Buck Martinez over ESPN and ESPN2, and Bob Costas and Joe Morgan on NBC.

OCTOBER 6   The Diamondbacks even the series with a 7–1 win over the Mets in Phoenix.

OCTOBER 8   In game three, the Mets score six runs in the sixth inning and defeat the Diamondbacks 9–2 before 56,180 at Shea Stadium. John Olerud drove in three runs, and Rickey Henderson collected three hits.

Henderson stole six bases during the four-game series.

OCTOBER 9   The Mets advance to the Championship Series on Todd Pratt's walk-off homer off Matt Mantei in the tenth inning, which lifts the club to a 4–3 victory over the Diamondbacks before 56,177 at Shea Stadium. Pratt was the starting catcher in place of Mike Piazza, who was out with an injured thumb. Edgardo Alfonso started the scoring with a solo homer in the fourth inning, but the Mets trailed 3–2 heading into the bottom of the eighth. Roger Cedeno tied the score 3–3 with a sacrifice fly. John Franco was the winning pitcher. It was his first victory since September 13, 1997. During the 1998 and 1999 regular seasons combined, Franco had a record of 0–10.

The Mets played the Atlanta Braves in the National League Championship Series. managed by Bobby Cox, the Braves had a record of 103–59 in 1999. The Braves were looking for their fifth World Series appearance of the 1990s. The club had previously reached the Fall Classic in 1991, 1992, 1995 and 1996, winning in 1995.

OCTOBER 12   The Mets open the NLCS with a 4–2 loss to the Braves at Turner Field in Atlanta. Greg Maddux started for the Braves and allowed only a run in seven innings.

The series was telecast nationally by NBC. The announcers were Bob Costas and Joe Morgan.

OCTOBER 13   The Braves take game two 4–3 in Atlanta. The Mets took a 2–0 lead in the fifth inning on a solo homer by Melvin Mora, who replaced Rickey Henderson in left field in the third inning. But in the sixth, Kenny Rogers gave up two-run homers to both Brian Jordan and Eddie Perez to put the Mets behind 4–2.

Entering the game, Mora had only 32 big-league at-bats, including one in the Division Series against the Diamondbacks, and had failed to hit a home run. Playing as a pinch-hitter and at all three outfield positions, Mora collected six hits in 14 at-bats during the NLCS for a batting average of .429.

OCTOBER 15   The Braves take a three-games-to-none lead in the NLCS by beating the Mets 1–0 before 55,911 at Shea Stadium. The Braves scored an unearned run in the first inning with the help of errors by pitcher Al Leiter and catcher Mike Piazza. It was the first time all season that the Mets made two errors in an inning. A three-hitter by Leiter (seven innings), John Franco (one-third of an inning) and Armando Benitez (1²/₃ innings) was wasted because the Mets couldn't score off of Tom Glavine (seven innings), Mike Remlinger (one inning) and John Rocker (one inning). Rocker had saves in each of the first three games of the series.

OCTOBER 16   The Mets stay alive in the NLCS by beating the Braves 3–2 before 55,872 at Shea Stadium. John Olerud broke a scoreless deadlock with a solo homer against John Smoltz in the sixth. Rick Reed carried a one-hitter and that 1–0 lead into the eighth before giving up back-to-back homers to Brian Jordan and Ryan Klesko. Roger Cedeno led off the eighth with a single off Smoltz, and after two batters were retired, reliever Mike Remlinger walked Melvin Mora. Cedeno and Mora moved to second and third with a double steal, and John Rocker replaced Remlinger. Olerud gave the Mets the lead with a two-run single.

OCTOBER 17   The Mets' win gave five over the Braves 4–3 in 15 innings before 55,723 at Shea Stadium on Robin Ventura's famous "grand slam single." The Mets scored two in the first inning on a two-run homer by John Olerud off Greg Maddux. The Braves countered with two tallies in the fourth off Masato Yoshii. There was no more scoring until the top of the 15th when Kevin Lockhart delivered a run-scoring triple against Octavio Dotel, who was the ninth New York pitcher in the game. In the bottom half, the Mets loaded the bases with one out on a single, a walk, a bunt to advance both runners, and an intentional walk. Todd Pratt tied the score by drawing a walk from Kevin McGlinchy. Robin Ventura followed by driving a McGlinchy pitch over the wall for an apparent grand slam. But the Mets rushed the field to congratulate Ventura, and he was not able to complete his trip around the bases. Officially, Ventura was credited with a single and the Mets with a 4–3 win.

OCTOBER 18   The Yankees win the American League Championship Series over the Red Sox to set up the possibility of an all-New York Subway Series if the Mets could win games six and seven in Atlanta.

OCTOBER 19   The Braves win the National League pennant by defeating the Mets 10–9 in 11 innings in Atlanta in game six. The Braves took a 5–0 lead in the first inning off Al Leiter and Pat Mahomes. At the end of the sixth, the score was 7–3. The Mets tied the contest with four tallies in the seventh, the last two on a homer by Mike Piazza. The Mets took an 8–7 lead in the eighth inning and a 9–8 advantage in the tenth, but on both occasions, the Braves rallied to tie the score. Kenny Rogers, the eighth Mets pitcher, started the 11th. He gave up a double, a sacrifice bunt, two intentional walks and a single to Andruw Jones to lose the game. The Braves went on to lose the World Series four games to none against the Yankees.

Braves reliever John Rocker was quoted in a January 2000 issue of Sports Illustrated *expressing his disdain for New Yorkers and a host of minority groups, including immigrants and gays. Commissioner Bud Selig suspended Rocker for the first 14 games of the 2000 season for the remarks and ordered him to undergo sensitivity training (see June 29, 2000).*

DECEMBER 10   The Mets trade Chuck McElroy to the Orioles for Jesse Orosco.

Orosco previously played for the Mets from in 1979 and again from 1981 through 1987 and is best remembered for throwing the last pitch of the 1986 World Series. He began spring training in 2000 with the Mets but didn't finish it. Orosco was traded to the Cardinals for Joe McEwing on March 18.

DECEMBER 11   The Mets sign Todd Zeile, most recently with the Rangers, as a free agent.

Zeile played for 11 clubs during his career from 1989 through 2004, and he hit at least five home runs for each one of them. He was the Mets starting first baseman in 2000 and 2001 and again in 2004. He had mainly been a third basemen before arriving in New York and had played in only 76 games at first base heading into 2000.

DECEMBER 15   John Olerud signs with the Mariners as a free agent.

The Mets would regret the failure to sign Olerud. He was a starting first baseman in Seattle for four seasons.

DECEMBER 17   Orel Hershiser signs with the Dodgers as a free agent.

Hershiser gave the Mets a 13–12 season with a 4.58 ERA in 1999. After pitching in just 24²/₃ innings over ten games, with a 13.14 ERA for the Dodgers in 2000, he called it a career.

DECEMBER 23   The Mets trade Roger Cedeno, Octavio Dotel and Kyle Kessel to the Astros for Mike Hampton and Derek Bell.

Hampton was 22–4 with Houston in 1999. He gave the Mets one solid season with a 15–10 record and a 3.14 ERA in 2000 before leaving for the Rockies as a free agent.

DECEMBER 29   Kenny Rogers signs with the Rangers as a free agent.

After being acquired from the Athletics in a July 23, 1999 trade, Rogers was 5–1 in 12 games with the Mets. He still had several years of excellent pitching ahead of him and was named to the All-Star team in 2004, 2005 and 2006.

THE STATE OF THE METS

The decade was one of peaks and valleys for the Mets and their fans. It began with an all-New York World Series against the Yankees in 2000. There were three consecutive losing seasons beginning in 2002 and four straight winning years starting in 2005. The second of two postseason appearances, and the only division title, occurred in 2006. The 2007 and 2008 teams blew what appeared to be certain playoffs seasons with meltdowns in the final weeks of the regular season. The 2009 outfit won only 70 games followed by another losing season in 2010. Overall, the Mets were 815–803 during the decade from 2000 through 2009, for a winning percentage of .504. NL championships during the 2000s were the Mets (2000), Diamondbacks (2001), Giants (2002), Marlins (2003), Cardinals (2004 and 2006), Astros (2005), Rockies (2007), Phillies (2008 and 2009) and Giants (2010). NL East pennant winners were the Braves (2000 through 2005), Mets (2006) and Phillies (2007 through 2010).

THE BEST TEAM

The 2006 Mets were 97–65 and won nine more games than any other NL team. But in the postseason, the Mets lost the NLCS to the Cardinals.

THE WORST TEAM

In Art Howe's first season as manager, the Mets sank to a 66–95 record, the second worst in the NL that season.

THE BEST MOMENT

The long-awaited opening of Citi Field occurred in 2009. The first baseball game was a collegiate match-up between St. John's and Georgetown on March 29. The Mets played their first game on April 3 with an exhibition against the Red Sox. The first regular season contest was on April 13 with the Padres as the opponent.

THE WORST MOMENT

The Mets had a seven-game lead in the NL East, with the best record in the National League with 17 games remaining in 2007, but wound up sitting out the postseason by losing 12 of those 17 games.

THE ALL-DECADE TEAM (2000–10) • YEARS W/METS

Mike Piazza, c	1998–2005
Carlos Delgado, 1b	2006–09
Edgardo Alfonso, 2b	1995–2002
David Wright, 3b	2004–10
Jose Reyes, ss	2003–10
Cliff Floyd, lf	2003–06
Carlos Beltran, cf	2005–10
Timo Perez, rf	2000–03
Al Leiter, p	1998–2004
Tom Glavine, p	2003–07
Steve Trachsel, p	2001–06
Armando Benitez, p	1999–2003

Alfonso was also on the 1990s All-Decade Team as a third baseman. Right field has been a merry-go-round for more than 20 years. The last individual to play in at least 100 games in right in two or more consecutive seasons was Darryl Strawberry from 1983 through 1991. In addition, few starting pitchers remained in the starting rotation for very long. The only three pitchers to log more than 510 innings during the decade were Leiter, Glavine and Trachsel. Third baseman Robin Ventura (1999–2001) was another prominent Mets player during the decade.

THE DECADE LEADERS (2000–10)

Batting Avg:	David Wright	.305
On-Base Pct:	David Wright	.383
Slugging Pct:	Mike Piazza	.525
Home Runs:	David Wright	169
RBI:	David Wright	664
Runs:	David Wright	639
Stolen Bases:	Jose Reyes	331
Wins:	Al Leiter	65
Strikeouts:	Al Leiter	770
ERA:	Al Leiter	3.43
Saves:	Armando Benitez	138

THE HOME FIELD

Mets bid a fond farewell to Shea Stadium in 2008. During the final season, the club led the NL in attendance for the first time since 1988. Attendance bottomed out in 2003 and 2004, when the Mets ranked 11th among the 16 NL franchises. There were no significant changes to Shea during the last ten years of its existence. Citi Field opened a year later.

THE GAME YOU WISHED YOU HAD SEEN

On September 21, 2001, in the first game following the September 11 terrorist attacks, the Mets beat the Braves 3–2.

THE WAY THE GAME WAS PLAYED

The offensive explosion experienced during the 1990s continued into the 2000s, as did the trend toward new baseball-only parks with grass fields. About mid-decade, allegations of the use of performance-enhancing drugs became a hot topic, with many of the sport's greatest sluggers admitting to the use of the substances. Major League Baseball instituted much harsher penalties for players using steroids as the decade progressed.

THE MANAGEMENT

At the start of the decade, Nelson Doubleday was chairman of the board, and Fred Wilpon was president and CEO. The Doubleday Corporation bought the club in 1980. Doubleday and Wilpon purchased the franchise from the corporation in 1986. Doubleday sold his stake in the Mets to Wilpon in 2002. Wilpon was elevated to chairman of the board in 2003. General managers were Steve Phillips (1998–2003), Jim Duquette (2004) and Omar Minaya (2005–2010). Field managers were Bobby Valentine (1996–2002), Art Howe (2003–04), Willie Randolph (2005–08) and Jerry Manuel (2008–2010).

THE BEST PLAYER MOVE

The best player move was the selection of David Wright in the 2001 amateur draft.

THE WORST PLAYER MOVE

On July 28, 2000, the Mets traded Melvin Mora and three others to the Orioles for Mike Bordick.

2000

Season in a Sentence

The Mets enter the playoffs as a wild card and advance all the way to the World Series before losing to the Yankees in five games.

Finish • Won • Lost • Pct • GB

Second   94   68   .580   1.0

In the wild-card race, the Mets finished in first place, eight games ahead.

National League Division Series

The Mets defeated the San Francisco Giants three games to one.

National League Championship Series

The Mets defeated the St. Louis Cardinals four games to one.

World Series

The Mets lost to the New York Yankees four games to one.

Manager

Bobby Valentine

Stats

Stats	Mets	AL	Rank
Batting Avg:	.263	.266	10
On-Base Pct:	.346	.342	5
Slugging Pct:	.430	.432	8
Home Runs:	198	6	
Stolen Bases:	66	15	
ERA:	4.16	4.63	3
Errors:	118	8	
Runs Scored:	807	7	
Runs Allowed:	738	3	

Starting Lineup

Mike Piazza, c
Todd Zeile, 1b
Edgardo Alfonso, 2b
Robin Ventura, 3b
Mike Bordick, ss
Benny Agbayani, lf
Jay Payton, cf
Derek Bell, rf
Melvin Mora, ss
Joe McEwing, lf-cf-3b-2b
Matt Franco, 1b-3b

Pitchers

Al Leiter, sp
Mike Hampton, sp
Glendon Rusch, sp
Rick Reed, sp
Bobby Jones, sp
Armando Benitez, rp
Pat Mahomes, rp
Turk Wendell, rp
John Franco, rp
Dennis Cook, rp

Attendance

2,800,221 (eighth in NL)

Club Leaders

Batting Avg:	Mike Piazza	.324
	Edgardo Alfonso	.324
On-Base Pct:	Edgardo Alfonso	.425
Slugging Pct:	Mike Piazza	.614
Home Runs:	Mike Piazza	38
RBI:	Mike Piazza	113
Runs:	Edgardo Alfonso	109
Stolen Bases:	Derek Bell	8
	Lenny Harris	8
Wins:	Al Leiter	16
Strikeouts:	Al Leiter	200
ERA:	Mike Hampton	3.14
Saves:	Armando Benitez	41

FEBRUARY 3   A month after the celebrations marking the beginning of the 21st century and the end of worries about Y2K computer glitches, Shawon Dunston signs with the Cardinals as a free agent.

MARCH 18   The Mets trade Jesse Orosco to the Cardinals for Joe McEwing.

MARCH 27   The Mets purchase Timo Perez from the Hiroshima Toyo Carp of the Japanese Central League.

MARCH 29   The Mets open the 2000 season with a regular-season game against the Cubs in Tokyo and lose 5–3 before 55,000 at the Tokyo Dome. It was the first regular-season game ever played outside of North America and the first of a two-game series in Japan. The game began at 7:06 p.m. Tokyo time, which was 5:06 a.m. in New York City. Mike Hampton was the Mets starter, making his debut with the club. He walked nine batters and allowed two runs and four hits in five innings. Mike Piazza homered in the losing cause.

MARCH 30   Benny Agbayani hits a pinch-hit grand slam off Danny Young in the 11th inning to lift the Mets to a 5–1 victory over the Cubs in Tokyo.

APRIL 3   In the home opener, the Mets defeat the Padres 2–1 before 52,308 at Shea Stadium. Derek Bell, playing in his first game at Shea as a Met, broke a 1–1 tie with a home run in the eighth inning.

APRIL 14   Mike Piazza collects five hits, including a home run and two doubles, in six at-bats to lead the Mets to a 12–inning, 8–5 victory over the Pirates in Pittsburgh. The Mets collected 20 hits in all. Piazza's homer capped a four-run Mets rally in the 12th.

Piazza finished third in the MVP voting in 2000 after batting .324 with 38 home runs and 113 RBI.

APRIL 16   Robin Ventura drives in six runs during a 12–9 triumph over the Pirates in Pittsburgh.

APRIL 18   Robin Ventura wallops a grand slam off Jaime Navarro in the fourth inning of a 10–7 victory over the Brewers at Shea Stadium.

APRIL 20   Melvin Mora hits a walk-off homer in the tenth inning to defeat the Brewers 5–4 at Shea Stadium.

APRIL 23   The Mets break a 3–3 tie with seven runs in the fourth inning and beat the Cubs 15–8 at Shea Stadium.

APRIL 24   The Mets score in the ninth inning on a double by Robin Ventura and a single from Matt Franco to defeat the Dodgers 1–0 at Shea Stadium. Pat Mahomes ($5^2/_3$ innings), Dennis Cook (one-third of an inning), Turk Wendell (two innings) and Armando Benitez (one inning) combined on the shutout.

APRIL 25   The Mets extend their winning streak to nine games with a 6–5 decision over the Reds at Shea Stadium.

APRIL 29   The Mets collect 23 hits and beat the Rockies 13–6 in Denver.

APRIL 30   The Mets outslug the Rockies 14–11 in Denver on an afternoon in which the game-time temperature is 43 degrees.

Edgardo Alfonso collected 15 hits in 22 at-bats during a five-game stretch from April 27 through May 1. He finished the season with a .324 batting average, 25 homers and 109 runs scored.

MAY 1   The Mets play at AT&T Park in San Francisco for the first time and lose 10–3 to the Giants.

MAY 9   The Mets use back-to-back homers by Derek Bell and Edgardo Alfonso off Kris Benson in the third inning to defeat the Pirates 2–0 in Pittsburgh. Mike Hampton (8 1/3 innings) and Armando Benitez (two-thirds of an inning) combined on the shutout.

MAY 11   The Mets play at Three Rivers Stadium in Pittsburgh for the last time and defeat the Pirates 3–2.

MAY 13   The Mets release Rickey Henderson.

               Henderson started 29 of the Mets' first 38 games as a leadoff hitter, but hit only .217. He would end the season as the club leader in games started batting leadoff, as the Mets used 12 different players to top the batting order. The others were Jon Nunnally, Melvin Mora, Benny Agbayani, Joe McEwing, Derek Bell, Jason Tyner, Jay Payton, Lenny Harris, Mike Bordick, Darryl Hamilton and Timo Perez. With the absence of Henderson, the left-field position was also in a state of flux in 2000. The Mets used 14 different left fielders that season, 12 of them as starters. Henderson played for the Mariners, Padres, Red Sox and Dodgers before ending his career in 2003 as the all-time leader in runs scored (2,295) and stolen bases (1,440). He was elected to the Hall of Fame on the first ballot in 2009.

MAY 14   Mike Piazza hits a grand slam off Brad Penny in the fifth inning of a 5–1 victory over the Marlins at Shea Stadium.

               On May 16, the Mets had a 20–20 record and were seven games behind the Braves.

MAY 23   Mike Piazza hits a two-run homer in the tenth inning to down the Padres 5–3 in San Diego.

MAY 27   Todd Zeile hits a grand slam off Andy Benes in the first inning and a solo shot against Dave Veres in the eighth to lead the Mets to a 12–8 triumph over the Cardinals in St. Louis.

MAY 30   The Mets score six runs in the ninth inning to defeat the Dodgers 10–5 in Los Angeles. Todd Pratt capped the rally with a pinch-hit grand slam off Terry Adams.

JUNE 3   The Mets edge the Devil Rays 1–0 at Shea Stadium. The lone run scored in the third inning on doubles by Todd Zeile and Edgardo Alfonso. Al Leiter (6 2/3 innings), Dennis Cook (one-third of an inning), John Franco (one inning) and Armando Benitez (one inning) combined on the shutout.

JUNE 5   With the first pick in the amateur draft, the Mets select pitcher Billy Traber from Loyola Marymount University.

               Traber was traded to the Indians before making his big-league debut in 2003 and has struggled in the majors. Other future major leaguers drafted and signed by the Mets in 2000 include Bobby Keppel (supplemental first round), Chris Basak (sixth round) and Jeff Duncan (seventh round).

June 8	Shortstop Kurt Abbott hits a walk-off homer in the tenth inning to defeat the Orioles 8–7 at Shea Stadium.
June 9	The Mets pummel the Yankees 12–2 at Yankee Stadium.
June 18	The Mets play at County Stadium in Milwaukee for the last time and win 7–3 over the Brewers.
June 23	The Mets score nine runs in the third inning and wallop the Pirates 12–2 at Shea Stadium. Mike Piazza hit a three-run homer during the rally, and Melvin Mora contributed a three-run double.
June 25	The Mets use five home runs to defeat the Marlins 10–5 at Shea Stadium. Benny Agbayani homered twice, and Mark Johnson, Melvin Mora and Jay Payton added one each. The homer by Johnson, which came in a pinch-hit role, was his first in the majors since 1997 when he was a member of the Pirates.
June 29	Amid heightened security, Braves pitcher John Rocker makes his first appearance at Shea Stadium following his derogatory comments about New York City during a *Sports Illustrated* interview the previous offseason. The game attracted 46,987 fans. Over 700 police officers were summoned (above the usual 60), and 300 press passes were given out. A limit on beer sales was imposed. A special protective cover was erected over the Braves' bullpen in left field. During batting practice, fans were barred from sitting in the first four rows behind the Braves' dugout. A videotaped apology from Rocket was shown on Shea's 26-foot-tall screen in left-center before the game. The video was loudly booed, and hostile signs could be seen throughout the stadium. In the eighth inning, Rocker replaced Jason Marquis, and some fans threw objects onto the field. Rocket retired all three batters to face him, and the Braves won 6–4. Rocker left the stadium a half-hour after the rest of the team in a black van trailed by three security vehicles.
	Rocker's major league career went into a steep decline after 2000 and ended in 2003. He played in 23 games for the Long Island Ducks, an independent club based in Central Islip, New York, in the Atlantic League in 2005. At that time he asked New Yorkers to "bury the hatchet," but was released after posting an ERA of 6.50.
June 30	Trailing 8–1, the Mets erupt for ten runs in the eighth inning to shock the Braves 11–8 at Shea Stadium. Nine of the runs scored after two were out as eight straight Mets batters reached base. Back-to-back singles by Todd Zeile and Jay Payton and four consecutive walks to Benny Agbayani, Mark Johnson, Melvin Mora and Derek Bell, the last three with the bases loaded, made the score 8–6. A two-run single from Edgardo Alfonso deadlocked the contest at 8–8. Mike Piazza broke the tie with a three-run homer.
	Piazza drove in runs in 15 consecutive games, two shy of the major league record, from June 14 through July 2. He collected 28 RBI during those 15 games and hit eight home runs. Piazza also had a 21-game hitting streak from June 7 through July 3.

JULY 1   Al Leiter strikes out 12 batters in seven innings of a 9–1 win over the Braves at Shea Stadium.

JULY 5   During an 11–2 thrashing of the Marlins in Miami, Mets pitcher Eric Cammack triples in his only big-league at-bat. Cammack played in eight games, each of them in 2000.

JULY 8   The Mets and the Yankees play a unique double-header with one game at Shea Stadium at 1:15 p.m. and a second clash at Yankee Stadium beginning at 8:05 p.m. It was the first such instance in the majors since September 7, 1903, when the Giants and Dodgers played a game in Brooklyn at Washington Park and another in Manhattan at the Polo Grounds. Major League Baseball scheduled the unique twin bill because one game of the three-game series between the Mets and Yankees at Yankee Stadium in June was rained out. The Yanks won both tilts 4–2. The second game featured a controversial incident when Roger Clemens beaned Mike Piazza with a pitch in the second inning. Fortunately, Piazza suffered only a concussion and was playing again five days later.

JULY 18   Mike Piazza collects his third grand slam of the season with a blast off Chris Carpenter in the fifth inning of an 11–7 victory over the Blue Jays in Toronto.

JULY 27   After falling behind the Expos 7–2 in the second inning, the Mets rally to win 9–8 in the first game of a double-header at Shea Stadium. The Mets pulled ahead with a pair of two-out, run-scoring singles from Todd Zeile and Matt Franco in the eighth. The Mets completed the sweep with a 4–3 victory in the second tilt.

JULY 28   The Mets trade Melvin Mora, Mike Kinkade, Lesli Brea and Pat Gorman to the Orioles for Mike Bordick.

             Bordick was acquired to fill a hole at shortstop following a season-ending injury (broken forearm) to Rey Ordonez in May. Bordick was an All-Star with the Orioles in 2000, but played no where near that level with the Mets. Mora had been filling in for Ordonez at short, and the Mets didn't believe they would miss him. He was 28 at the time of the trade, and hit just .248 with six home runs in 246 big-league at-bats. But Mora would go on to become a regular for the Orioles for a decade, mostly as a third baseman. He made the All-Star team in both 2003 and 2005 and batted .340 with 27 home runs in 2004.

JULY 29   On the first pitch of his first plate appearance with the Mets, Mike Bordick homers to spark the club to a 4–3 triumph over the Cardinals at Shea Stadium.

AUGUST 7   The Mets play at Minute Maid Park in Houston for the first time and defeat the Astros 6–5 in 11 innings. Former Astro Derek Bell tied the score 5–5 with a two-run homer in the ninth. Kurt Abbott delivered the game-winner by clobbering a home run in the 11th.

AUGUST 12   The Mets prevail 3–2 over the Giants at Shea Stadium despite a boneheaded play by left fielder Benny Agbayani. In the Giants' half of the fourth inning, with the Mets leading 1–0 and the bases loaded with one out, Agbayani caught a fly ball from Bobby Estalella near the foul line. Believing it was the third out, Agbayani handed the ball to a fan and began to trot to the dugout. Recognizing his mistake,

Agbayani pulled the ball back from the fan and fired toward home plate. Since the ball left the field of play, the play was ruled dead, and two Giants runners were waved across the plate to give San Francisco a 2–1 lead. The Mets came back with two tallies in the seventh to win the game.

Agbayani wore number 50 in honor of his native Hawaii, the 50th state.

AUGUST 13   Al Leiter (eight innings) and John Franco (one inning) combine on a two-hitter to defeat the Giants 2–0 at Shea Stadium. Leiter also struck out 12. The only San Francisco hits were singles by Ramon Martinez in the first inning and Jeff Kent in the seventh. Robin Ventura had a hand in both New York runs in the eighth by doubling in a run and crossing the plate on a single from Mike Bordick.

AUGUST 22   Derek Bell pitches the eighth inning of a 16–1 loss to the Padres in San Diego. Bell gave up five runs, four of them earned, after walking three and surrendering three hits.

AUGUST 23   Al Leiter and Armando Benitez combine to strike out 15 batters during a 4–1 victory over the Padres in San Diego. Leiter fanned 12 in eight innings. Benitez struck out all three hitters he faced in the ninth.

AUGUST 25   The Mets bury the Diamondbacks 13–3 at Shea Stadium.

AUGUST 30   Rick Reed (seven innings), Turk Wendell (one inning) and Armando Benitez (one inning) combine on a three-hitter to defeat the Astros 1–0 at Shea Stadium. Benitez struck out all three batters he faced in the ninth.

At the close of play on August 30, the Mets were tied for first place with the Braves. The Mets held sole possession of first on August 31 and September 1 before dropping back to second on September 2, where the club remained for the rest of the season. The Mets maintained a comfortable lead in the wild-card race throughout September, however.

SEPTEMBER 5   Todd Zeile homers in the tenth inning to defeat the Reds 3–2 in Cincinnati.

SEPTEMBER 13   Jay Payton smacks a three-run, walk-off homer in the tenth inning to defeat the Brewers 4–1 at Shea Stadium. Robin Ventura tied the score 1–1 with a two-out, RBI-double in the ninth.

SEPTEMBER 19   The Mets are all but eliminated in the NL East pennant race with a 12–4 loss to the Braves in Atlanta. The defeat left the Mets five games back with 11 to play.

The Mets won nine of their last 11 to pull within one game of the Braves at the end of the season.

SEPTEMBER 24   Timo Perez accounts for his first major league homer with an inside-the-park drive in the third inning of a 3–2 victory over the Phillies in Philadelphia.

SEPTEMBER 27   The Mets clinch a wild-card berth with a 6–2 victory over the Braves at Shea Stadium.

SEPTEMBER 29   Jay Payton hits a grand slam off Mike Thurman in the first inning of an 11–2 win over the Expos at Shea Stadium.

OCTOBER 1   In the last regular-season game, the Mets use 25 players to defeat the Expos 3–2 in 13 innings at Shea Stadium.

The Mets played the Giants in the Division Series. Managed by Dusty Baker, the Giants were 97–65 in 2000 and had the best record in the National League.

OCTOBER 4   The Mets open the Division Series with a 5–1 loss to the Giants in San Francisco. The Giants broke a 1–1 tie with four runs in the third inning off Mike Hampton, the last three on a homer by Ellis Burks.

The series was telecast by ESPN (games one and four) and FOX (games two and three). The announcers were Jon Miller and Joe Morgan (games one and four), Thom Brennaman and Bob Brenly (game two) and Joe Buck and Tim McCarver (game three).

OCTOBER 5   The Mets even the series with a ten-inning, 5–4 win over the Giants in San Francisco. The Mets took a 4–1 lead in the top of the ninth on a two-run homer by Edgardo Alfonso. But in the bottom half of the inning, pinch-hitter J. T. Snow tied the score with a three-run home run against Armando Benitez. With two out in the tenth, Darryl Hamilton doubled and Jay Payton singled to drive home the winning run.

OCTOBER 7   The Mets take a two-games-to-one lead in the series with a 3–2 win in 13 innings over the Giants before 56,270 at Shea Stadium. The Giants took a 2–0 advantage in the fourth, but didn't score again off Rick Reed, Dennis Cook, Turk Wendell, John Franco, Armando Benitez and Rick White. Russ Ortiz held New York hitless until the sixth. The Mets tied the game with single runs in the sixth and eighth. Benny Agbayani won the contest with a walk-off homer into the left-field bleachers off Aaron Fultz.

OCTOBER 8   The Mets win the series with a 4–0 triumph over the Giants before 52,888 at Shea Stadium on a brilliant one-hitter by Bobby Jones. Robin Ventura gave the Mets a 2–0 lead with a homer in the first inning. Jones retired the first 12 batters to face him before Jeff Kent doubled leading off the fifth on a drive that ticked off the top of the leaping Ventura at third base. Jones loaded the bases in the fifth with two walks before pitching out of the jam. He retired the last 13 San Francisco hitters.

The Mets faced the Cardinals in the Championship Series. Managed by Tony LaRussa, St. Louis was 94–68 during the regular season and swept the Braves three straight in the Division Series.

OCTOBER 11   The Mets open the NLCS with a 6–2 win over the Cardinals in St. Louis. Todd Zeile and Jay Payton homered for the Mets. Mike Hampton was the starting pitcher and hurled seven shutout innings.

The series was telecast by FOX with Joe Buck and Tim McCarver serving as announcers.

OCTOBER 12   The Mets take game two with a 6–5 decision over the Cardinals in St. Louis. New York allowed the Cards to come back and tie the contest twice after holding a 3–1 lead in the fifth inning and a 5–3 advantage in the eighth. With the score 5–5, Jay Payton singled home the game winner in the ninth. Mike Piazza homered in the third.

OCTOBER 14   The road team wins for the third time in a row as the Cardinals defeat the Mets 8–2 before 55,693 at Shea Stadium. Rick Reed started and gave up five runs, four of them earned, in 3^1/$_3$ innings.

OCTOBER 15   The Mets move within one win of the World Series with a 10–6 decision over the Cardinals at Shea Stadium. After St. Louis scored two in the first, the Mets responded with four in their half and three more in the second for a 7–2 lead. Timo Perez, Edgardo Alfonso, Mike Piazza and Robin Ventura started the first inning with four consecutive doubles off Darryl Kile. Benny Agbayani added another double with one out in the first. Ventura drove in three runs during the game, and Piazza added a home run.

OCTOBER 16   The Mets win the National League pennant with a 7–0 decision over the Cardinals before 55,695 at Shea Stadium. Mike Hampton pitched a three-hit shutout. Todd Zeile drove in three runs.

OCTOBER 17   The Yankees win the American League pennant by defeating the Seattle Mariners 9–7 at Yankee Stadium. The Yankees beat the Mariners four games to two.

Managed by Joe Torre, the Yankees were 87–74 in 2000 after losing 15 of their last 18 regular-season games to finish with the fifth-best record in the AL. The Yanks won the World Series in 1996, 1998 and 1999. The clash between the Mets and the Yankees was the 14th all-New York World Series in the modern era, but it was the first involving the Mets. The previous Subway Series were between the Yankees and the New York Giants in 1921, 1922, 1923, 1936, 1937 and 1951 and the Yankees and the Brooklyn Dodgers in 1941, 1947, 1949, 1952, 1953, 1955 and 1956. The American Association Dodgers and the National League pennant-winning Giants also played in a World Series in 1889. It was technically not an all-New York World Series, however, because Brooklyn was a separate city until 1898. It was also not a Subway Series because New York's subway didn't open until 1904. The Dodgers joined the National League in 1890.

OCTOBER 21   The Mets open the World Series with a 12-inning, 4–3 loss to the Yankees at Yankee Stadium. The Yanks scored twice in the sixth for a 2–0 lead, but the Mets rebounded with three tallies in the seventh, the first two on a bases-loaded, pinch-hit single by Bubba Trammell. Armando Benitez took the mound in the ninth with a 3–2 lead and a lifetime record of five blown saves in eight postseason save opportunities with the Orioles and Mets. He would blow his sixth save by allowing the Yankees to tie the score 3–3. Ex-Met Jose Vizcaino drove in the game winner with a walk-off single against Turk Wendell. Vizcaino hadn't started any of the Yankees' 11 postseason games against the Athletics and Mariners, but Joe Torre gave him the start at second base because Vizcaino was 10-for-19 during his career against Mets starter Al Leiter. Vizcaino collected four hits in six at-bats.

The series was telecast by FOX with Joe Buck, Tim McCarver and Bob Brenly serving as announcers.

OCTOBER 22   The Mets score five runs in the ninth inning, but lose 6–5 to the Yankees at Yankee Stadium. Most of the headlines centered around an incident in the first inning. Mike Piazza hit a foul ball facing Roger Clemens and shattered his bat. Not knowing the ball was foul, Piazza ran toward first, and Clemens tossed the jagged barrel end of the bat toward Piazza, narrowly missing the Mets catcher. The two had a history: Clemens had beaned Piazza earlier in the season (see July 8, 2000). Piazza glared at Clemens, and the two exchanged words as both benches emptied. Clemens pitched eight shutout innings and allowed only two hits before being relieved. The Mets scored their five runs in the ninth on a two-run homer by Mike Piazza off Jeff Nelson and a three-run blast by Jay Payton against Mariano Rivera.

Clemens was later fined $50,000 for his actions.

OCTOBER 24   The Mets defeat the Yankees 4–2 before 55,299 at Shea Stadium. The Mets managed to touch up Orlando Hernandez for four runs in 7$\frac{1}{3}$ innings despite his 12 strikeouts. Benny Agbayani broke a 2–2 tie in the eighth with an RBI-double before the Mets added an insurance run. Rick Reed started for the Mets and surrendered two runs in six innings. John Franco, playing in his first World Series at the age of 40, was the winning pitcher.

The Yankees entered the contest with a 14–game winning streak in the World Series, having taken the last four games of a six-games series against the Braves in 1996, all four against the Padres in 1998 and the Braves in 1999, and the first two versus the Mets in 2000.

OCTOBER 25   The Yankees move within a victory of the world championship with a 3–2 win over the Mets before 55,290 at Shea Stadium. The Yanks took a 3–0 lead with single runs in the first, second and third innings prior to Mike Piazza's two-run homer in the bottom of the third.

OCTOBER 26   The Yankees win their third consecutive world championship by beating the Mets 4–2 before 55,292 at Shea Stadium. The Mets took a 2–1 lead in the second inning, but the Yankees tied the contest with a run in the sixth, and then shattered the 2–2 tie with two in the ninth.

DECEMBER 10   Derek Bell signs with the Pirates as a free agent.

DECEMBER 11   The Mets sign Kevin Appier, most recently with the Royals, as a free agent.

DECEMBER 12   On the day that the Supreme Court declares George Bush the winner in the controversial presidential election against Al Gore, Mike Hampton signs with the Rockies as a free agent.

DECEMBER 14   The Mets sign Steve Trachsel, most recently with the Blue Jays, as a free agent.

Trachsel spent six seasons in the Mets starting rotation and posted a record of 66–59.

DECEMBER 20   Mike Bordick signs with the Orioles as a free agent.

2001

Season in a Sentence

In the weeks before and after the September 11 terrorists attacks, the Mets make a run at the postseason with a stretch of 25 wins in 31 games but fall short.

Finish • Won • Lost • Pct • GB

Third   82   80   .506   6.0

In the wild-card race, the Mets finished in sixth place, eight games behind.

Manager

Bobby Valentine

Stats

Stats	Mets	AL	Rank
Batting Avg:	.249	.261	15
On-Base Pct:	.323	.331	12
Slugging Pct:	.387	.425	16
Home Runs:	147	15	
Stolen Bases:	66	13	
ERA:	4.07	4.36	5
Errors:	101		4
Runs Scored:	642	16	
Runs Allowed:	713	5	

Starting Lineup

Mike Piazza, c
Todd Zeile, 1b
Edgardo Alfonso, 2b
Robin Ventura, 3b
Rey Ordonez, ss
Benny Agbayani, lf
Tsuyoshi Shinjo, cf-lf-rf
Timo Perez, rf
Jay Payton, lf
Joe McEwing, lf-rf-3b
Desi Relaford, 2b-ss-3b
Lenny Harris, 1b-3b

Pitchers

Kevin Appier, sp
Al Leiter, sp
Steve Trachsel, sp
Glendon Rusch, sp
Rick Reed, sp
Armando Benitez, rp
Rick White, rp
John Franco, rp
Turk Wendell, rp

Attendance

2,658,330 (tenth in NL)

Club Leaders

Batting Avg:	Mike Piazza	.300
On-Base Pct:	Mike Piazza	.384
Slugging Pct:	Mike Piazza	.573
Home Runs:	Mike Piazza	36
RBIs:	Mike Piazza	94
Runs:	Mike Piazza	81
Stolen Bases:	Desi Relaford	13
Wins:	Three tied with	11
Strikeouts:	Kevin Appier	172
ERA:	Al Leiter	3.31
Saves:	Armando Benitez	43

FEBRUARY 15   Bobby Jones signs with the Padres as a free agent.

MARCH 31   Outfielder Brian Cole, one of the Mets' top prospects, dies in an auto accident while driving from Port St. Lucie, Florida, to his home in Meridian, Mississippi. He was 22. The accident occurred near Panama City, Florida, when Cole's Ford Explorer drifted into the grass median, and then flipped over.

APRIL 3   The Mets open the season with a 6–4 victory in ten innings over the Braves at Turner Field. Mike Piazza put the Mets into the lead in the first inning with a two-run homer, before the Braves battled back to tie the score 2–2. Robin Ventura broke the tie in the eight inning with a two-run homer off John Rocker to give the Mets a 4–2 lead, but Atlanta countered with two in their half. Ventura stepped to the plate again in the tenth with the contest still deadlocked at 4–4 and walloped another two-run homer against Kerry Ligtenberg. Al Leiter started for the Mets and allowed two runs in seven innings.

APRIL 9   In the home opener, Mike Piazza hits two homers and drives in five runs to lead the Mets to a 9–4 triumph over the Braves before 53,640 at Shea Stadium. In his first game with the Mets at Shea, Tsuyoshi Shinjo also homered.

Piazza hit .300 with 36 home runs in 2001.

APRIL 12   The Mets need ten innings to outlast the Braves 1–0 at Shea Stadium. Rey Ordonez drove in the winning run with a single. Glendon Rusch (seven innings), John Franco (one inning) and Armando Benitez (two innings) combined on the shutout.

In 2001, Shea Stadium was the National League's third-oldest venue behind Wrigley Field (1914) and Dodger Stadium (1962). The only older ballparks in the AL were Fenway Park (1912) and Yankee Stadium (opened in 1923 and extensively remodeled in 1976).

APRIL 24   The Mets play at Miller Park in Milwaukee for the first time and lose 6–4 to the Brewers.

APRIL 28   The Mets score three runs in the ninth inning and one in the 11th to defeat the Cardinals 6–5 in St. Louis. The Mets scored their three runs in the ninth before a batter was retired on a single by Jay Payton, Joe McEwing's home run, and back-to-back doubles from Rey Ordonez and Edgardo Alfonso. In the 11th, Desi Relaford singled, stole second and crossed the plate on a single by Benny Agbayani.

MAY 1   With the Mets trailing 5–3 in the seventh inning, Robin Ventura delivers a grand slam off Jay Powell to lift the club to a 7–5 win over the Astros at Shea Stadium.

MAY 7   The Mets score seven runs in the third inning for a 9–0 lead and hang on to defeat the Rockies 10–9 in Denver. The first six batters in the third reached base on six consecutive singles by Benny Agbayani, Edgardo Alfonso, Mike Piazza, Todd Zeile, Robin Ventura and Jay Payton. A double from Tsuyoshi Shinjo made it seven hits in a row. Holding a 10–5 lead, Armando Benitez allowed four runs in the ninth before closing out the victory.

MAY 15   Rick Reed (eight innings) and Armando Benitez (one inning) combine to defeat the Padres 1–0 at Shea Stadium. Rey Ordonez drove in the lone run with a single in the fifth inning.

MAY 17   The Padres wallop the Mets 15–3 at Shea Stadium. Steve Trachsel tied a major league record by giving up four home runs in the third inning to Alex Arias, Rickey Henderson, Ryan Klesko and Bubba Trammell. Desi Relaford pitched the ninth and retired all three batters he faced. Relaford's fastball was timed at 91 miles per hour.

After the beating, Trachsel was sent to the minors with an 8.24 ERA in $39^1/_3$ innings. After three starts at Norfolk, he returned to the Mets. Trachsel rebounded from a 1–9 start to fashion a 10–4 record after June 29.

JUNE 5   With their first pick in the amateur draft, the Mets select pitcher Aaron Heilman from the University of Notre Dame.

Heilman pitched six seasons for the Mets from 2003 through 2008, first as a starter, and then as a reliever. He pitched in over 70 games in 2006, 2007 and 2008, with a peak of 81 in 2007. The Mets made a brilliant choice in the supplemental first round (38th overall), by drafting David Wright from Hickory High School in Chesapeake, Virginia. Wright made his major league debut in 2004 at the age of 21 and has already established himself as the best third baseman in club history. The Mets received the supplemental pick as a result of losing Mike Hampton to the Rockies in free agency. Other future major leaguers drafted and signed by the Mets in 2001 include Lenny DiNardo (third round), Danny Garcia (fifth round), Joe Hietpas (16th round) and Randy Wells (44th round).

JUNE 10   The Mets trounce the Devil Rays 10–0 in St. Petersburg. Kevin Appier (seven innings), Dennis Cook (one inning) and Armando Benitez (one inning) combined on the shutout.

JUNE 13   After falling behind 6–0, the Mets score a run in the seventh inning, two in the eighth, three in the ninth and one in the tenth to defeat the Orioles 7–6 in Baltimore. With the bases loaded and one out in the ninth, Mark Johnson delivered a two-run, pinch-hit single. Lenny Harris tied the score 6–6 with another pinch-single. In the tenth, Mike Piazza doubled, and Tsuyoshi Shinjo singled to account for the winning run.

JUNE 17   Trailing 7–2, the Mets erupt for six runs in the eighth inning to beat the Yankees 8–7 at Shea Stadium. With two out in the eighth, Mike Piazza walloped a two-run homer to put the Mets into the lead.

JULY 7   The Mets score three runs in the tenth inning to down the Yankees 3–0 at Yankee Stadium. The three runs scored with two out on three consecutive RBI-singles from Mike Piazza, Timo Perez and Todd Zeile off Mariano Rivera. Kevin Appier (eight innings), John Franco (one inning) and Armando Benitez (one inning) combined on the shutout.

JULY 13   Mike Piazza collects his 300th career homer during a 3–1 loss to the Red Sox at Shea Stadium. The milestone was struck off Derek Lowe in the ninth inning.

JULY 14   Glendon Rusch (eight innings) and Armando Benitez (one inning) combine on a one-hitter to defeat the Red Sox 2–0 at Shea Stadium. The only Boston hit was a single by Trot Nixon with one out in the first inning. Mark Johnson drove in both runs with a homer in the second inning off Bronson Arroyo and a ground out in the seventh.

JULY 17   Al Leiter (seven innings), Turk Wendell (one-third of an inning), Dennis Cook (two-thirds of an inning) and Armando Benitez (one inning) combine on a ten-hit shutout to defeat the Blue Jays 1–0 at Shea Stadium. Mike Piazza drove in the lone run with a single in the first inning.

JULY 21   Armando Benitez strikes out all three batters he faces in the ninth inning on just 11 pitches to close out a 6–3 win over the Phillies in Philadelphia.

JULY 24   In his only plate appearance as a member of the Mets, Gary Bennett singles during a 4–3 loss to the Marlins in Miami.

JULY 25   The Mets leave 16 men on base but beat the Marlins 5–2 in Miami.

JULY 27   The Mets trade Turk Wendell and Dennis Cook to the Phillies for Bruce Chen and Adam Walker.

JULY 28   A day after being traded, Turk Wendell gives up a walk-off homer to Robin Ventura in the ninth inning to give the Mets a 4–3 win over the Phillies at Shea Stadium.

JULY 29   The Mets win with a walk-off homer for the second day in a row when Mike Piazza goes deep off Rheal Cormier with one out in the ninth to give the Mets a 6–5 win over the Phillies at Shea Stadium.

                 The Mets finished last in the National League in runs scored in 2001. Excluding pitchers, Bobby Valentine used 143 different batting orders.

JULY 30   The Mets trade Rick Reed to the Twins for Matt Lawton.

AUGUST 1   The Mets score six runs in the tenth inning, three of them on a homer by Edgardo Alfonso, to defeat the Astros 8–2 in Houston. In his first game with the Mets, Bruce Chen allowed two runs and two hits in six innings.

AUGUST 7   Bruce Chen (seven innings), John Franco (one inning) and Armando Benitez (one inning) combine on a two-hitter to beat the Brewers 3–0 at Shea Stadium. The only Milwaukee hits were back-to-back singles by Richie Sexson and Jeromy Burnitz in the fourth inning.

AUGUST 17   The Mets extend their losing streak to seven games by dropping an 8–3 decision to the Dodgers. The defeat gave the Mets a 54–68 record and left the club 13 games out of first.

AUGUST 22   Kevin Appier (seven innings), Rick White (one inning) and Armando Benitez (one inning) combine on a two-hitter to defeat the Rockies 2–1 at Shea Stadium. The only Colorado hits were a home run by Todd Helton in the second inning and a single from Jeff Cirillo in the ninth.

SEPTEMBER 3   The Mets score five runs in the ninth inning to defeat the Phillies 10–7 in Philadelphia.

SEPTEMBER 8   The Mets score three runs in the ninth inning to down the Marlins 9–7 in Miami. Matt Lawton put the Mets into the lead with a two-run double.

SEPTEMBER 11   Two hijacked commercial airliners strike and destroy the twin towers of the World Trade Center in New York City in the worst terrorist attack ever on American soil. A third hijacked plane destroyed a portion of the Pentagon in northern Virginia just outside Washington D.C., and a fourth crashed in rural Pennsylvania. Some 3,000 were killed, including about 2,800 at the World Trade Center.

                 Almost immediately, commissioner Bud Selig canceled the slate of games for the day, including the Mets-Pirates match-up in Pittsburgh. Later in the week, Selig announced that all games through Sunday, September 16, would be postponed. The contests were made up by extending the regular season by a week. Shea Stadium served as a relief center following the unspeakable horror in lower Manhattan. Most of the gate area and parking lots at Shea were filled with food, supplies and makeshift lodging for the massive relief effort. Supplies and food were brought into the city by the truckloads. The Mets series against the Pirates, scheduled for Shea on September 17, 18 and 19, was transferred to Pittsburgh. When play resumed, an air of heightened security and patriotism imbued every game. Fans endured close scrutiny by stadium personnel. "God Bless America" replaced "Take Me Out to the Ball Game" as the song of choice during the seventh-inning stretch.

SEPTEMBER 17   In the first game following the September 11 terrorists attacks, the Mets score three runs in the ninth inning to defeat the Pirates 4–1 in Pittsburgh. It was also the first time the Mets played at PNC Park.

SEPTEMBER 21   In the first baseball game played in New York City following the September 11 terrorist attacks, Mike Piazza hits a two-run homer in the eighth inning to lift the Mets to a 3–2 win over the Braves before 41,325 at Shea Stadium. Piazza had already doubled twice prior to his soaring drive over the center-field fence.

The victims of the collapse of the Twin Towers of the World Trade Center were honored in pre-game ceremonies. Among those taking part were Mayor Rudy Giuliani, Liza Minelli and Diana Ross. Giuliani received the biggest ovation of the night in a ballpark where he was previously routinely booed because he was an avid Yankees fan. The umpires and the Mets both wore caps representing the city's police, fire and emergency personnel.

SEPTEMBER 23   The Mets blow a golden opportunity to move within 2½ games of the first-place Braves by allowing three runs in the ninth inning and one in the 11th to lose 5–4 at Shea Stadium. Armando Benitez was one out away from a 4–1 win over Atlanta when he gave up a two-run homer to Brian Jordan. A walk and two singles produced another run. Jordan hit another homer, this one off Jerrod Riggan, in the 11th.

SEPTEMBER 27   After trailing 6–2 at the end of the fifth inning, the Mets rally to beat the Expos 12–6 in Montreal. The Mets set a club record with ten doubles. Matt Lawton, Desi Relaford and Jay Payton each had two and Edgardo Alfonso, Robin Ventura, Mark Johnson and Mike Piazza collected one each.

At the end of the day, the Mets were in third place in the NL East, three games behind the first-place Braves with nine to play. The Phillies were second with one game out.

SEPTEMBER 28   With a chance to move two games behind the Braves, the Mets lose 5–3 to the Atlanta club at Turner Field.

SEPTEMBER 29   The Mets are all but eliminated from postseason consideration by allowing seven runs in the ninth inning to lose 8–5 to the Braves in Atlanta. For the second time in seven days, Armando Benitez failed to hold a lead of three or more runs in the ninth inning. He turned a 5–1 lead into a nailbiter by allowing three runs and was relieved by John Franco with the score 5–4, two out and runners on first and second. Franco walked Wes Helms to load the bases, then gave up a walk-off grand slam to Brian Jordan, the hero of the Braves comeback win over the Mets six days earlier.

The Braves went on to win the NL East by two games over the Phillies.

OCTOBER 3 Four days before the United States launches a sustained air campaign in Afghanistan against al-Qaeda, Steve Trachsel pitches a two-hitter to defeat the Pirates 3–0 at Shea Stadium. The only Pittsburgh hits were singles by Aramis Ramirez in the first inning and Adam Hyzdu in the eighth.

DECEMBER 7 The Mets trade Robin Ventura to the Yankees for David Justice.

DECEMBER 11 The Mets trade Matt Lawton, Alex Escobar, Jerrod Riggan, Earl Snyder and Billy Traber to the Indians for Roberto Alomar and Mike Bacsik.

> *Alomar was 34 on Opening Day in 2002 and made 12 consecutive All-Star teams from 1990 through 2001. He finished in the top six in the MVP voting in 1991, 1992 and 1993 with the Blue Jays and 1999 and 2001 with Cleveland. Alomar also owned ten Gold Gloves. In 2001, he batted .336 with 20 home runs and 100 RBI. Unfortunately, age caught up with Alomar after he arrived in New York and in 853 at-bats as a Met over two seasons, he hit .265 with 13 home runs.*

DECEMBER 13 The Mets sign David Weathers, most recently with the Brewers, as a free agent.

DECEMBER 14 The Mets trade David Justice to the Athletics for Mark Guthrie and Tyler Yates.

DECEMBER 16 The Mets trade Desi Relaford and Tsuyoshi Shinjo to the Giants for Shawn Estes.

DECEMBER 17 The Mets sign Roger Cedeno, most recently with the Tigers, as a free agent.

DECEMBER 27 The Mets trade Kevin Appier to the Angels for Mo Vaughn.

> *For a six-year period, from 1993 through 1998, Vaughn was one of the most feared hitters in the game, averaging 36 homers and 111 RBI per season while batting .315. He went to the Angels as a free agent after the 1998 season, but posted ordinary numbers in Anaheim while battling injuries. Vaughn missed the entire 2001 season after surgery to repair a torn biceps tendon in his left arm. The Mets gambled he would return to form, but over two seasons with the club, Vaughn hit only .249 with 29 home runs in 654 at-bats. Appier had one good season left in his arm and pitched for the Angels in the 2002 World Series.*

DECEMBER 28 The Mets purchase Gary Matthews, Jr. from the Pirates.

2002

Season in a Sentence

An aging roster and an unproductive farm system results in the first losing season since 1996 and the dismissal of Bobby Valentine.

Finish • Won • Lost • Pct • GB

Fifth   75   86   .466   26.5

In the wild-card race, the Mets finished in eighth place, 20 games behind.

Manager

Bobby Valentine

Stats	Mets	AL	Rank
Batting Avg:	.253	.259	11
On-Base Pct:	.330	.331	10
Slugging Pct:	.408	.410	9
Home Runs:	160	10	
Stolen Bases:	87	10	
ERA:	3.89	4.11	5
Errors:	144	16	
Runs Scored:	690	13	
Runs Allowed:	703	7	

Starting Lineup

Mike Piazza, c
Mo Vaughn, 1b
Roberto Alomar, 2b
Edgardo Alfonso, 3b
Rey Ordonez, ss
Roger Cedeno, lf
Timo Perez, cf
Jeromy Burnitz, rf
Jay Payton, cf
John Valentin, ss-1b-3b
Joe McEwing, rf-ss-1b

Pitchers

Al Leiter, sp
Pedro Astacio, sp
Steve Trachsel, sp
Jeff D'Amico, sp
Shawn Estes, sp
Armando Benitez, rp
Dave Weathers, rp
Steve Reed, rp
Scott Strickland, rp
Mark Guthrie, rp

Attendance

2,804,838 (fifth in NL)

Club Leaders

Batting Avg:	Edgardo Alfonso	.308
On-Base Pct:	Edgardo Alfonso	.391
Slugging Pct:	Mike Piazza	.544
Home Runs:	Mike Piazza	33
RBIs:	Mike Piazza	98
Runs:	Edgardo Alfonso	78
Stolen Bases:	Roger Cedeno	25
Wins:	Al Leiter	13
Strikeouts:	Al Leiter	172
ERA:	Al Leiter	3.48
Saves:	Armando Benitez	33

JANUARY 16   The Mets sign Pedro Astacio, most recently with the Astros, as a free agent.

JANUARY 21   The Mets trade Alex Ochoa, Glendon Rusch and Lenny Harris to the Brewers for Jeromy Burnitz, Jeff D'Amico, Lou Collier and Mark Sweeney. The Mets also sent Todd Zeile and Benny Agbayani to the Rockies for Ross Gload and Craig House.

Burnitz was the key player in the seven-player deal with the Brewers. He had previously played for the Mets in 1993 and 1994. In the five seasons prior to the trade, Burnitz belted 163 homers for Milwaukee, but was a bust in his return to New York. Burnitz's numbers in 2002 included a .215 batting average and 19 home runs.

JANUARY 30   The Mets sign John Valentin, most recently with the Red Sox, as a free agent.

MARCH 28   Angry over being hit by a pitch in the seventh inning of an exhibition game, Mike Piazza confronts Dodgers pitcher Guillermo Mota. A few moments later, Mota walked off the field while Piazza approached him. Piazza than grabbed Mota by the collar with both hands before eventually letting go and walking away (see March 12, 2003).

APRIL 1   The Mets win the season opener 6–2 over the Pirates before 53,734 at Shea Stadium. Al Leiter was the starting pitcher and went six innings, allowing just one run. Jay Payton homered and Edgardo Alfonso contributed three hits.

Keith Hernandez became one of the Mets' television broadcasters in 2002.

APRIL 3   The Mets trade Gary Matthews, Jr. to the Orioles for John Bale.

APRIL 6   The Mets break a 2–2 tie with nine runs in the ninth inning to defeat the Braves 11–2 in Atlanta. Seven of the runs scored after two were out, three of them on a bases-loaded double by Rey Ordonez.

APRIL 14   Prior to a 6–4 win over the Expos at Shea Stadium, the Mets hold a 40th birthday party for the mascot Mr. Met. Attending were several other costumed mascots from around Major League Baseball.

APRIL 15   The Mets come from behind to win 7–6 in 12 innings over the Braves at Shea Stadium. The Mets tied the contest 6–6 with five runs in the seventh inning, the final two on John Valentin's first home run as a Met. Edgardo Alfonso drove in the winning run with a single. Grant Roberts pitched the sixth and seventh innings and struck out five of the seven batters he faced.

APRIL 18   Al Leiter pitches a two-hitter to beat the Expos 1–0 at Olympic Stadium. The only Montreal hits were doubles by Michael Barrett in the fifth inning and Jose Vidro in the sixth. Mike Piazza drove in the lone run with a double in the fourth.

APRIL 25   Armando Benitez strikes out all three batters he faces in the ninth inning to close out a 7–6 win over the Cardinals at Shea Stadium. The Mets came back from a 5–1 deficit in the fifth inning.

APRIL 26   Shawn Estes pitches a one-hitter to defeat the Brewers 1–0 at Shea Stadium. Estes held Milwaukee hitless until Eric Young led off the seventh with a single. The lone run scored on a home run by Jay Payton off ex-Met Glendon Rusch. It was one of three New York hits.

APRIL 27   Pedro Astacio carries a no-hitter into the seventh inning of a 2–1 victory over the Brewers at Shea Stadium. The first of three Milwaukee hits was a single by Geoff Jenkins.

APRIL 30   Mike Piazza hits two homers and drives in six runs during a 10–1 win over the Diamondbacks in Phoenix.

Piazza batted .280 with 33 home runs in 2002.

MAY 14   Pedro Astacio pitches a two-hitter to defeat the Dodgers 3–0 at Dodger Stadium. The only Los Angeles hits were a double by Hiram Bocachica in the fourth inning and a single from Cesar Izturis in the sixth.

MAY 15   The Mets record a two-hit, complete-game shutout for the second game in a row, this time from Jeff D'Amico to defeat the Dodgers 2–0 at Dodger Stadium. The only Los Angeles hits were singles by Paul LoDuca and Mark Grudzielanek, both in the second inning.

MAY 17   A triple play and an eight-run seventh inning highlight a 13–4 triumph over the Giants in San Francisco. The triple play occurred in the fifth inning on an around-the-horn grounder that went from third baseman Edgardo Alfonso to second baseman Roberto Alomar and to first baseman Mo Vaughn.

MAY 23   A double by pinch-hitter Mark Johnson in the ninth inning drives in the lone run of a 1–0 victory over the Phillies in Philadelphia. Steve Trachsel (six innings), Scott Strickland (two innings) and Armando Benitez (one inning) combined on the shutout.

MAY 26   Mike Piazza has a hand in all three runs of a 3–0 win over the Marlins at Shea Stadium. In the first inning, Piazza doubled in two runs and crossed the plate on a single from Mo Vaughn. Jeff D'Amico (seven innings), Mark Guthrie (one inning) and Scott Strickland (one inning) combined on the shutout.

> *Guthrie didn't allow a run over 33 consecutive appearances covering 27 innings from May 25 to August 3.*

MAY 31   A home run by Rey Ordonez in the tenth inning beats the Marlins 6–5 in Miami. It was the only home run of the year for Ordonez in 460 at-bats.

JUNE 4   With their first pick in the amateur draft, and the 15th overall, the Mets select pitcher Scott Kazmir from Cypress Falls High School in Houston, Texas.

> *Kazmir was considered to be one of the best prospects in the draft, but fell to the Mets at number 15 because of his bonus demands. The Mets traded Kazmir to the Devil Rays in 2004 before he appeared in a major league game. Other future major leaguers drafted and signed by the Mets in 2002 include Matt Lindstrom (tenth round).*

JUNE 7   The Mets play the Indians for the first time during the regular season and win 4–3 in Cleveland.

JUNE 8   The Mets overcome a three-run deficit with seven runs in the seventh inning and defeat the Indians 8–6 in Cleveland. Six of the runs in the seventh scored after two were out, three of them on a home run by Mike Piazza.

JUNE 10   The Mets play the White Sox for the first time during the regular season and win 3–1 in Chicago.

JUNE 15   Shawn Estes hits a home run off Roger Clemens, in addition to pitching seven shutout innings and striking out 11 during an 8–0 victory over the Yankees at Shea Stadium.

JUNE 18   The Mets play the Twins for the first time during the regular season and lose 6–1 at Shea Stadium.

JUNE 21   The Mets play the Royals for the first time during the regular season and win 4–3 at
               Shea Stadium.

JULY 3   Mike Piazza hits two homers and drives in six runs, but the Mets lose 8–7 to the
               Phillies at Philadelphia.

JULY 11   The Mets break a 1–1 tie with eight runs in the eighth inning and win 9–1 over
               the Phillies at Shea Stadium. The big blow of the rally was a three-run double by
               Timo Perez.

JULY 19   Armando Benitez strikes out all three batters he faces to close out a 4–2 win over
               the Reds in Cincinnati.

JULY 21   The Mets play at Cinergy Field in Cincinnati for the last time and lose 9–1 to the Reds.

JULY 26   Roberto Alomar collects his 2,500th career hit during a 3–2 win over the Reds at
               Shea Stadium. The milestone was a single in the first inning off Elmer Dessens.

JULY 31   The Mets score seven runs in the first inning and three in the second to trounce the
               Astros 10–0 at Shea Stadium. Shawn Estes (seven inning) and Mike Bacsik (two
               innings) combined on a two-hitter. The only Houston hits were doubles by Lance
               Berkman in the fourth inning and Jose Vizcaino in the seventh.

               *On the same day, the Mets traded Jay Payton and Mark Corey to the Rockies
               for John Thomson and Mark Little.*

AUGUST 4   In his first major league start, Ty Wiggington collects four hits, including a home run
               and a double, in five at-bats of a 12–7 loss to the Diamondbacks at Shea Stadium.

AUGUST 13   Fred Wilpon buys out Nelson Doubleday, Jr. Each had owned 50 percent of the stock
               in the franchise, an arrangement that had been in force since 1986. Animosity had
               simmered between the two for years, much of it centered around stadium issues. Wilpon
               wanted a brand-new ballpark for the Mets. Doubleday desired to renovate Shea.

AUGUST 23   The Mets' losing streak reaches 12 games with a 10–4 defeat at the hands of the
               Rockies in Denver.

               During the 12 games, the Mets were outscored 64–24.

AUGUST 24   The Mets break their 12-game losing streak with four runs in the ninth inning to
               defeat the Rockies 5–2 in Denver. After the first two batters in the ninth were retired,
               a single by Joe McEwing and a homer from Timo Perez put the Mets into the lead.
               A pair of insurance runs were added on a double by Roberto Alomar.

               *McEwing started games at seven different positions in 2002. He was a starter for
               15 games in right field, ten at shortstop, five as a third baseman, four at second
               base, four in left field, two at first base and one in center field.*

SEPTEMBER 3   The Mets extend their National League record home losing steak to 15 games
               with a 3–2 loss to the Marlins in 12 innings in the first game of a double-header

at Shea Stadium. The Mets ended the streak with an 11–5 victory in game two. Mike Piazza hit a three-run pinch-homer.

SEPTEMBER 9   Trailing 4–0, the Mets score six runs in the seventh inning to defeat the Phillies 6–4 in Philadelphia. Mike Piazza put the Mets into the lead with a grand slam off Jose Santiago.

SEPTEMBER 10   Roger Cedeno hits the first pitch of the first inning for a home run off Damian Moss, but the Mets lose 12–6 to the Braves in Atlanta.

SEPTEMBER 13   Mo Vaughn collects two homers and two singles in four at-bats in addition to scoring four runs and driving in four, but the Mets lose 11–8 to the Expos in Montreal.

SEPTEMBER 17   A two-run, walk-off homer by Jeromy Burnitz in the ninth inning downs the Cubs 3–1 at Shea Stadium.

After setting a major league record with only 68 errors in 1999, the Mets led the National League in the category in 2002 with 144 miscues.

SEPTEMBER 21   A three-run, walk-off homer by Esix Snead in the 11th inning defeats the Expos 6–3 at Shea Stadium. Snead entered the game in the eighth as a pinch-hitter and remained in the lineup as a right fielder. The game was tied 3–3 in the ninth on a two-out Montreal error.

Snead had only 13 major league at-bats and collected four hits. The home run was his only one as a major leaguer and accounted for his only three RBI.

OCTOBER 1   The Mets fire Bobby Valentine as manager.

After taking over as manager in 1996 in the midst of the club's sixth consecutive losing season, Valentine led the Mets to five straight years over .500, from 1997 through 2001, including the appearance in the World Series in 2000. But because of his massive ego and inability to get along with General Manager Steve Phillips, there was almost constant turmoil during the Valentine regime. A losing season in 2002 sealed his fate. Valentine returned to Japan and managed the Chiba Lotte Marines until being fired in a dispute with the team's owner. He led the Marines to the Japanese championship in 2005.

OCTOBER 28   The Mets hire 55-year-old Art Howe as manager.

Howe was hired after the Mets initially pursued Lou Piniella and Dusty Baker. Howe had previously managed the Astros (1989–93) and Athletics (1996–2002). The last three years in Oakland were highly successful. With a limited budget, Howe posted records of 91–71 in 2000, 101–61 in 2001 and 103–59 in 2003. Howe didn't see eye-to-eye with General Manager Billy Beane, however, and each of those three seasons ended with disappointing defeats in the playoffs. Howe was allowed to depart despite one year remaining on his deal with the A's. His laid-back approach wasn't an ideal fit with the Mets, a team composed largely of underachieving veterans. Howe lasted two seasons in New York with records of 66–95 in 2003 and 71–91 in 2004.

DECEMBER 5   The Mets sign Tom Glavine, most recently with the Braves, as a free agent.

Glavine came to the Mets with a 242–143 lifetime record, Cy Young Awards in 1991 and 1998, and five seasons of 20 or more victories. He was 37 on Opening Day in 2003, but was coming off of a 2002 season in which he was 18–11 with a 2.96 ERA. Glavine had an unspectacular but steady five seasons with the Mets, compiling a record of 61–56.

DECEMBER 15   Edgardo Alfonso signs with the Giants as a free agent. On the same day, the Mets traded Rey Ordonez to the Devil Rays for Russ Johnson and Josh Pressley.

Only 29 when he signed with the Giants, Alfonso went into a steep decline after a 2002 season in which he batted .308 with 16 homers. Much of the problem stemmed from chronic back problems. Alfonso's career ended in 2006.

DECEMBER 19   The Mets sign Mike Stanton, most recently with the Yankees, as a free agent.

DECEMBER 31   The Mets sign Rey Sanchez, most recently with the Red Sox, as a free agent.

2 0 0 3

Season in a Sentence

In Art Howe's first year as manager, the Mets jettison high-salaried veterans in mid-season and lose 95 games.

Finish • Won • Lost • Pct • GB

Fifth   66   95   .410   34.5

In the wild-card race, the Mets finished in 12th place, 24$\frac{1}{2}$ games behind.

Manager

Art Howe

Stats

Stats	Mets	AL	Rank
Batting Avg:	.247	.262	14
On-Base Pct:	.314	.332	15
Slugging Pct:	.374	.417	15
Home Runs:	124	15	
Stolen Bases:	70	12	
ERA:	4.50	4.28	10
Errors:	118	12	
Runs Scored:	642	15	
Runs Allowed:	754	10	

Starting Lineup

Vance Wilson, c
Jason Phillips, 1b
Roberto Alomar, 2b
Ty Wiggington, 3b
Jose Reyes, ss
Cliff Floyd, lf
Timo Perez, cf-lf
Roger Cedeno, rf
Joe McEwing, 2b-ss
Tony Clark, 1b
Mike Piazza, c
Jeromy Burnitz, rf
Raul Gonzalez, lf-cf-rf

Starting Lineup

Al Leiter, sp
Steve Trachsel, sp
Jae Weong Seo, sp
Tom Glavine, sp
Armando Benitez, rp
David Weathers, rp
Mike Stanton, rp

Attendance

2,140,599 (11th in NL)

Club Leaders

Batting Avg:	Jason Phillips	.298
On-Base Pct:	Jason Phillips	.373
Slugging Pct:	Cliff Floyd	.518
Home Runs:	Cliff Floyd	18
	Jeromy Burnitz	18
RBIs:	Ty Wiggington	71
Runs:	Ty Wiggington	73
Stolen Bases:	Roger Cedeno	14
Wins:	Al Leiter	15
Strikeouts:	Al Leiter	139
ERA:	Steve Trachsel	3.78
Saves:	Armando Benitez	21

JANUARY 9   The Mets sign Cliff Floyd, most recently with the Red Sox, as a free agent.

Floyd spent four seasons as a starter in the outfield for the Mets. His best season was 2005, when he clouted 34 home runs.

JANUARY 20   The Mets sign Tony Clark, most recently with the Red Sox, as a free agent.

FEBRUARY 11   The Mets sign Jay Bell, most recently with the Diamondbacks, as a free agent.

FEBRUARY 13   The Mets sign David Cone as a free agent.

Cone missed all of 2002 with injuries. He pitched only five games in 2003 before retiring with a record of 194–126.

MARCH 12   Mike Piazza and Guillermo Mots battle again during a 13–6 exhibition game loss to the Dodgers at Port St. Lucie, Florida. The pair had a previous confrontation during spring training a year earlier (see March 28, 2002). Round two started when Mota nailed Piazza with a pitch in the sixth inning. The Mets catcher charged the mound with his fist clenched. Mota threw his glove at Piazza and backpedaled away. As Piazza gave chase, the Dodger pitcher ran into the outfield. Piazza was intercepted and tackled to the ground by Los Angeles players Brian Jordan, Adrian Beltre and Larry Barnes. As Piazza tried to struggle free, Jeromy Burnitz took up the chase of Mota, who ran into the dugout and escaped to the locker room. Piazza got into his car, drove to the other side of the ballpark and entered the Dodger clubhouse. He searched every nook and cranny looking for Mota, who had left about ten minutes earlier. Both Mota and Piazza were suspended for the first four regular-season games.

MARCH 31   Twelve days after the start of the Iraq War, the Mets open the season with a 15–2 thrashing at the hands of the Cubs before 53,586 at Shea Stadium. In his Mets debut, Tom Glavine gave up five runs in $3^2/_3$ innings.

APRIL 11   In the Expos' first home game in San Juan, Puerto Rico, the Mets lose 10–0 at Hiram Bithorn Stadium.

The Montreal Expos played 22 games in San Juan in 2003 and another 21 in 2004 before moving to Washington in 2005, where the franchise was renamed the Nationals.

MAY 4   Cliff Floyd hits a grand slam off Matt Kinney in the fifth inning of a 5–3 win over the Brewers in Milwaukee.

MAY 10   A two-run, walk-off homer by Mike Piazza in the tenth inning downs the Padres 4–2 at Shea Stadium.

MAY 23   Jeromy Burnitz wallops a grand slam off Russ Ortiz in the sixth inning of a 6–5 victory over the Braves in Atlanta.

MAY 30   In his first regular-season game since 2001 after missing a full season with Tommy John surgery, John Franco hurls a shutout inning during a 5–2 loss to the Braves at Shea Stadium. It was the 999th appearance of Franco's career.

JUNE 1   Down 4–2, the Mets erupt for eight runs in the sixth inning and win 10–4 over the Braves at Shea Stadium. Jeromy Burnitz started the rally with a double and capped it with a three-run homer.

JUNE 3   With their first pick in the amateur draft, the Mets select Lastings Milledge from Lakewood Ranch High School in Bradenton, Florida.

After the Mets drafted Milledge, it was reported that as an 18-year-old he had gotten into trouble over a sexual relationship with a 15-year-old girl. He was also kicked out of a St. Petersburg High School when he was 16 for sexual contact with 12- and 13-year-old girls. Milledge avoided prosecution by completing a juvenile program. He reached the majors as a 21-year-old in 2006 and was traded by the Mets to the Nationals in 2008. Other future major leaguers drafted and signed by the Mets in 2003 include Brian Bannister (seventh round) and Carlos Muniz (13th round).

JUNE 6   The Mets play the Mariners for the first time and win 3–2 at Shea Stadium.

JUNE 10	The Mets play the Rangers for the first time and lose 9–7 in Arlington.
JUNE 12	The Mets clobber the Rangers 11–0 in Arlington. Al Leiter (six innings), Graeme Lloyd (two innings) and John Franco (one inning) combined on an 11-hit shutout.

> *On the same day, the Mets fired Steve Phillips as general manager. Hired in 1997, Phillips added many of the pieces that led to the club's appearance in the 2000 World Series, but the Mets declined afterward with 82 wins in 2001, 75 in 2002 and a slow start in 2003 that led to only 66 victories. Phillips was replaced by Jim Duquette, who had been his top assistant. Duquette lasted as the Mets general manager until after the end of the 2004 season when Omar Minaya succeeded him.*

JUNE 13	The Mets play the Angels for the first time and win 7–3 in Anaheim.
JUNE 15	Steve Trachsel pitches a one-hitter to defeat the Angels 1–0 in Anaheim. The only hit off Trachsel was a single by David Eckstein in the sixth inning. Playing in his sixth major league game, 20-year-old Jose Reyes accounted for his first home run with a grand slam off Jerrod Washburn in the second inning. Reyes became the youngest player in the majors with a grand slam since Tony Conigliaro struck one for the Red Sox at 19 in 1964.
JUNE 16	After flying coast to coast, the Mets are the victims of a one-hitter by Dontrelle Willis and lose 1–0 to the Marlins in Miami.
JUNE 17	The Mets participate in a one-hitter for the third game in a row, beating the Marlins 5–0 in Miami. Jae Weong Seo (6 2/3 innings), David Weathers (1 1/3 innings) and Armando Benitez (one inning) combined on the gem while facing the minimum 27 hitters. Juan Encarnacion was the lone Florida base runner with a single in the fifth inning. He was subsequently caught stealing.
JUNE 28	For the second time, the Mets and the Yankees play in two different ballparks in a single day. The first instance was on July 8, 2000. The 2003 double-header was created by a rainout at Shea Stadium on June 21. The Mets lost the afternoon tilt 7–1 at Yankee Stadium. Later that evening at Shea, the Mets lost again 9–8 after falling behind 9–0 in the sixth inning.
JULY 1	The Mets trade Roberto Alomar to the White Sox for Royce Ring and Andrew Salvo.
JULY 4	The Mets play at Great American Ballpark in Cincinnati for the first time and win 7–2 over the Reds.
JULY 8	Mets pitcher Jason Roach collects a pair of singles in what proves to be his only two big-league plate appearances during a 5–3 loss to the Braves at Shea Stadium. He allowed five runs in six innings on the mound. Roach appeared in one previous contest, on June 14, and did not bat. He never played in the majors again after July 8, 2003, and as a pitcher had an 0–2 record with a 12.00 ERA in nine innings.
JULY 13	The 1973 National League champion Mets are honored prior to a 4–3 win over the Phillies at Shea Stadium. Tug McGraw, suffering from terminal brain cancer, threw out the ceremonial first pitch. He passed away on January 5, 2004.

JULY 14   The Mets trade Jeromy Burnitz to the Dodgers for Kole Strayhorn, Jose Diaz and Victor Diaz.

JULY 16   The Mets trade Armando Benitez to the Yankees for Jason Anderson, Ryan Bicondoa and Andrew Garcia.

JULY 29   The Mets trade Rey Sanchez to the Mariners for Kenny Kelly.

AUGUST 3   Tony Clark homers from both sides of the plate and drives in five runs during a 13–5 triumph over the Cardinals at Shea Stadium. He homered from the left side of the plate off Garrett Stephenson in the sixth inning and from the left side against Pedro Borbon, Jr. in the eighth.

AUGUST 5   The Mets score seven runs in the fifth inning of a 10–1 victory over the Astros in Houston. The rally was capped by a home run from Vance Wilson.

AUGUST 14   A blackout cancels the game between the Mets and the Giants at Shea Stadium.

               The power failure spread rapidly through Ohio, Michigan and the Northeast, as well as eastern Canada. Some 50 million people in eight states and the province of Ontario were left without electricity for as long as two days.

AUGUST 15   Tom Glavine earns his 250th career victory with a 5–0 decision over the Rockies at Shea Stadium. Glavine pitched six innings.

               A former draft pick of the Los Angeles Kings, Glavine was invited to a ten-day tryout with the New York Rangers following the 2003 baseball season. He was a high school hockey star at Billerica High School in Billerica, Massachusetts.

AUGUST 17   Cliff Floyd collects four hits in four at-bats during a 6–4 win over the Rockies at Shea Stadium.

               Floyd garnered 10 hits in 11 at-bats over three games on August 15, 16 and 17. His last game in 2003 was on August 18 before his season ended with surgery on his right Achilles tendon.

AUGUST 18   Steve Trachsel pitches a one-hitter to defeat the Rockies 8–0 at Shea Stadium. The lone Colorado hit was a double by opposing pitcher Chin-hui Tsao in the sixth inning. It was the first of only two hits that Tsao would collect during his big-league career.

AUGUST 21   The Mets play at Qualcomm Stadium in San Diego for the last time and defeat the Padres 5–1.

AUGUST 24   Tom Glavine (seven innings), Grant Roberts (1⅔ innings) and John Franco (one-third of an inning) combine on a two-hitter to defeat the Dodgers 2–1 at Dodger Stadium. The only Los Angeles hits were a double by Jolbert Cabrera and a triple from Cesar Izturis, both in the fifth inning.

AUGUST 28   At 20, Jose Reyes becomes the youngest player in major league history to hit switch homers in a game in addition to driving in all three runs of a 3–1 victory over the

Braves in Atlanta. Reyes homered from the right side of the plate off Mike Hampton in the fifth inning and from the left side against Trey Hodges in the ninth.

SEPTEMBER 7   The Mets play at Veterans Stadium in Philadelphia for the last time and lose 5–4 in 11 innings to the Phillies.

SEPTEMBER 14   Tom Glavine's brother Mike makes his big-league debut as a pinch-hitter for the Mets during a 7–3 loss to the Expos in Montreal. Mike Glavine was 30 and spent nine years in the minors as an outfielder. Mike appeared in six games in the majors, all with the Mets in 2003, and had one hit in seven at-bats. Tom and Mike were the first pair of brothers to play for the Mets at the same time.

SEPTEMBER 23   Al Leiter pitches the Mets to a 1–0 win over the Pirates at Shea Stadium.

SEPTEMBER 25   Bob Murphy makes his last broadcast, a 3–1 loss to the Pirates at Shea Stadium.

Murphy had been a broadcaster with the Mets since the club's inception in 1962. He died of cancer at the age of 79 on August 3, 2004.

SEPTEMBER 27   The Mets score seven runs in the seventh inning of a 9–3 win over the Marlins in Miami.

NOVEMBER 18   Bill Singer is fired by the Mets only 12 days after being hired as an assistant to general manager Jim Duquette. Singer was dismissed after making racially insensitive remarks to the Dodger's Assistant General Manager Kim Ng regarding her Chinese-American heritage. Singer blamed his diet and state of inebriation for his actions. Ironically, Singer was hired in 2006 by the Washington Nationals to head scouting operations in Asia.

DECEMBER 10   The Mets sign Kaz Matsui, most recently with the Seibu Lions of the Japanese Pacific League, as a free agent.

Matsui was only 28 when he was signed after starring in Japan, but he never came close to fulfilling expectations in New York. He was traded to the Rockies in 2006.

DECEMBER 23   The Mets sign Mike Cameron, most recently with the Mariners, as a free agent.

2004

Season in a Sentence

A second straight losing season leads to the hiring of Omar Minaya as general manager and Willie Randolph as field manager and the free agent acquisitions of Pedro Martinez and Carlos Beltran.

Finish • Won • Lost • Pct • GB

Fourth   71   91   .438   25.0

In the wild-card race, the Mets finished in ninth place, 21 games behind.

Manager

Art Howe

Stats

Stats	Mets	AL	Rank
Batting Avg:	.249	.263	14
On-Base Pct:	.317	.333	14
Slugging Pct:	.409	.423	11
Home Runs:	185	8	
Stolen Bases:	107	4	
ERA:	4.09	4.30	7
Errors:	137	15	
Runs Scored:	684	12	
Runs Allowed:	731	8	

Starting Lineup

Jason Phillips, c
Mike Piazza, 1b-c
Jose Reyes, 2b
Todd Zeile, 3b-1b
Kaz Matsui, ss
Cliff Floyd, lf
Mike Cameron, cf
Richard Hidalgo, rf
Ty Wiggington, 3b
Eric Valent, lf-1b-rf
David Wright, 3b

Pitchers

Tom Glavine, sp
Steve Trachsel, sp
Al Leiter, sp
Jae Weong Seo, sp
Braden Looper, rp
Mike Stanton, rp
Ricky Bottalico, rp
Mike DeJean, rp
John Franco, rp

Attendance

2,318,321 (11th in NL)

Club Leaders

Batting Avg:	Kaz Matsui	.272
On-Base Pct:	Mike Piazza	.362
Slugging Pct:	Mike Cameron	.479
Home Runs:	Mike Cameron	30
RBI:	Mike Cameron	76
Runs:	Mike Cameron	76
Stolen Bases:	Mike Cameron	22
Wins:	Steve Trachsel	12
Strikeouts:	Al Leiter	117
	Steve Trachsel	117
ERA:	Tom Glavine	3.60
Saves:	Braden Looper	29

JANUARY 6   The Mets sign Braden Looper, most recently with the Marlins, as a free agent.

JANUARY 12   Tony Clark signs with the Yankees as a free agent.

FEBRUARY 3   Scott Erickson signs with the Mets as a free agent.

FEBRUARY 8   The Mets sign Todd Zeile, most recently with the Expos, as a free agent. Zeile played previously with the Mets in 2000 and 2001.

MARCH 27   The Mets trade Timo Perez to the White Sox for Matt Ginter.

APRIL 3   The Mets trade Roger Cedeno to the Cardinals for Chris Widger and Wilson Delgado.

APRIL 6   The Mets open the season with a 7–2 victory over the Braves at Turner Field. Kaz Matsui made an immediate impact in his Mets debut. Leading off the first inning against Atlanta pitcher Russ Ortiz, Matsui homered on the first pitch he saw as an American major leaguer. Matsui reached base five times in five plate appearances on the home run, two doubles and two walks. Mike Piazza also homered. Tom Glavine pitched six innings and allowed two runs.

APRIL 7   Mike Piazza collects five hits, including two homers and a double, in five at-bats, but the Mets lose 18–10 to the Braves at Turner Field. The Mets led 6–0 before Atlanta erupted with three runs in the third inning and 11 in the fourth off Steve Trachsel, Grant Roberts and Dan Wheeler.

Two games into the season, Piazza already had three homers, but age and injuries began to slow him down in 2004. He batted .266 with 20 home runs. Piazza played 50 games as a catcher and 66 at first base.

APRIL 12   In the home opener, the Mets defeat the Braves 10–6 before 53,666 at Shea Stadium.

APRIL 30   The Mets play at Petco Park in San Diego for the first time and lose 7–6 to the Padres.

MAY 5   Mike Piazza passes Carlton Fisk to become the all-time leader in home runs by a catcher during an 8–2 triumph over the Giants at Shea Stadium. It was Piazza's 352nd homer as a catcher and his 363rd overall. He finished his career in 2007 with 427 home runs, 396 of them while playing as a catcher.

MAY 6   The Mets beat the Giants 2–1 in 11 innings at Shea Stadium with a pair of solo homers. Karim Garcia tied the score 11–1 with a home run in the seventh inning. Mike Piazza won it with a walk-off blast in the 11th.

MAY 10   Ty Wiggington collects five hits, including a double, but the Mets lose 12–8 to the Diamondbacks in Phoenix.

MAY 12   Kaz Matsui leads off the first inning with a home run off Randy Johnson, and it holds up for a 1–0 win over the Diamondbacks in Phoenix. The blast came on a 1–0 pitch. Each team collected only three hits in a match-up of future 300-game winners. Tom Glavine ($7^2/_3$ innings) and Braden Looper ($1^1/_3$ innings) combined on the shutout.

MAY 14   Cliff Floyd hits a grand slam off Roy Oswalt in the third inning of an 8–3 win over the Astros in Houston.

MAY 16   The Mets score two runs in the ninth inning and one in the 13th to defeat the Astros 3–2 in Houston. The score was tied 2–2 on a dramatic homer by Mike Piazza on a 1–2 pitch with two out in the ninth inning. Jason Phillips drove in the game winner in the 13th with a home run. Phillips entered the game as a catcher during a double switch in the tenth inning. Piazza played first base.

MAY 18   Two runs in the ninth inning after two are out beats the Cardinals 5–4 at Shea Stadium. Kaz Matsui drove in the tying run and Cliff Floyd the game winner, both with singles.

MAY 22   Kaz Matsui leads off the first inning with a home run off Aaron Cook, and the Mets down the Rockies 5–4 at Shea Stadium.

MAY 23   Kaz Matsui connects with a leadoff homer for the second game in a row and Tom Glavine pitches a one-hitter for a 4–0 win over the Rockies at Shea Stadium. Matsui's homer was struck off Shawn Estes. Glavine was four outs from a no-hitter when Kit Pellow doubled with two out in the eighth.

Each of Matsui's first five home runs as a major leaguer led off the first inning.

MAY 31   The Mets play at Citizens Bank Park in Philadelphia for the first time and beat the Phillies 5–3.

JUNE 1   A two-run pinch-homer by Vance Wilson caps a three-run, tenth-inning rally that beat the Phillies 4–1 in Philadelphia.

JUNE 2   The Mets win in the tenth inning for the second game in a row, defeating the Phillies 5–3 in Philadelphia. Todd Zeile broke the 3–3 tie with a two-run homer in the tenth.

JUNE 7   In the first round of the amateur draft, the Mets select pitcher Philip Humber from Rice University. Humber was taken with the third overall pick.

Humber made his major league debut with the Mets in 2006 and was traded to the Twins in 2008. He has yet to make much of an impact in the majors. Other future major leaguers drafted and signed by the Mets in 2004 include Nick Evans (fifth round) and Mike Carp (ninth round).

JUNE 8   The Mets play in Minnesota for the first time and lose 2–1 to the Twins.

JUNE 11   The Mets play in Kansas City for the first time and lose 7–5 to the Royals.

JUNE 15   The Mets play the Indians at Shea Stadium for the first time and win 7–2.

JUNE 17   The Mets trade David Weathers and Jeremy Griffiths to the Astros for Richard Hidalgo.

JUNE 18   The Mets play the Tigers at Shea Stadium for the first time and win 3–2. The game was won on a walk-off homer by Mike Cameron with two out in the ninth inning.

JUNE 19   Mike Cameron delivers a walk-off hit for the second game in a row, this time with a single in the tenth inning, which defeats the Tigers 4–3 at Shea Stadium.

JUNE 22   Braden Looper strikes out all three batters he faces in the ninth inning of a 7–4 win over the Reds at Shea Stadium.

JULY 2   Kaz Matsui collects two homers and drives in five runs during an 11–2 win over the Yankees at Shea Stadium.

Richard Hidalgo set a Mets record by homering in five consecutive games from July 1 through July 5.

JULY 7   The Mets rout the Phillies 10–1 in Philadelphia.

At the close of the day, the Mets were one game out of first in the NL East with a 43–40 record. The club was 28–51 the rest of the way.

JULY 13   In a somewhat bizarre pairing given their past history (see July 8, 2000 and October 22, 2000), Roger Clemens and Mike Piazza are the National League's starting battery for the All-Star Game. Clemens was then a member of the Astros, and the game was played at Minute Maid Park in his hometown of Houston. Clemens gave up six runs in the first inning, three of them earned, and the NL lost 9–4.

JULY 21   David Wright makes his major league debut at the age of 21 and is hitless in four at-bats of a 5–4 win over the Expos at Shea Stadium.

JULY 26   Todd Zeile pitches the eighth inning of a 19–10 loss to the Expos in Montreal. Zeile allowed five runs in the inning on four hits and two walks.

JULY 29   Eric Valent hits for the cycle during a 10–1 trouncing of the Expos in Montreal. Valent singled in the second inning and tripled in the third off Rocky Biddle, homered in the fifth against Sun-Woo Kim and tripled in the seventh facing Roy Corcoran.

Valent is one of the most obscure players ever to hit for the cycle in the major leagues. He played five seasons in the majors (2001–05) with three teams and had a .234 batting average in 205 games and 406 at-bats. During the 2004 season with the Mets, he hit .267 with 13 home runs. Those were the only 13 homers he collected as a big leaguer.

JULY 30   The Mets trade Ty Wiggington, Jose Batista and Matt Peterson to the Pirates for Kris Benson and Jeff Keppinger. On the same day, the club traded Scott Kazmir and Jose Diaz to the Devil Rays for Victor Zambrano and Bartolome Fortunato.

How the trade with the Devil Rays will rank on the all-time list of the worst deals ever made by the Mets won't be known until the end of Kazmir's career. At the end of the 2010 season, Kazmir was 26 with a record of 66–61. Zambrano pitched in only three games for the Mets in 2004 prior to a season-ending injury and was 7–12 with the club in 2005 and 1–2 in 2006. A former overall number-one pick in the amateur draft by the Pirates in 1996, Benson was 14–12 over two seasons with the Mets in 2004 and 2005. His wife Anna, a former model, created headlines by saying she would sleep with the entire Mets team if her husband ever cheated on her. She also entered the 2005 World Series of Poker in Las Vegas under the nickname "Gold Digger" and outlasted 70 percent of the field. Benson was traded to the Orioles in January 2006 after Anna told reporters that Mets General Manager Omar Minaya was trying to put together an "all Latino team."

JULY 31   The Mets trade Scott Erickson to the Rangers for Josh Hoffpauir.

AUGUST 3   Mike Stanton strikes out four batters in the eighth inning of a 12–3 win over the Brewers in Milwaukee. The four-strikeout performance was made possible when Scott Podsednik swung and missed at a wild pitch with two strikes and reached first base. Stanton also fanned Gary Bennett, Trent Durrington and Wes Helms.

AUGUST 5   David Wright drives in six runs on a home run and two doubles during an 11–6 triumph over the Brewers in Milwaukee.

The game was Wright's 14th as a major leaguer. As a rookie in 2004, he batted .293 with 14 home runs in 69 games.

AUGUST 10   Tom Glavine loses two of his front teeth and suffers a split lower lip in an auto accident while riding in a taxi. The accident happened on the way from LaGuardia Airport to Shea Stadium. Glavine missed 11 days because of his injuries. Ironically, Glavine, a standout in both baseball and hockey in high school, said he chose baseball over hockey as a professional career because "I have all of my teeth and I plan to keep it that way."

AUGUST 12   Victor Zambrano (seven innings), Ricky Bottalico (two-thirds of an inning), Mike Stanton (one-third of an inning) and Braden Looper (one inning) combine on a two-hitter to defeat the Astros 2–1 at Shea Stadium. The only Houston hits were singles by Jose Vizcaino in the fifth inning and Lance Berkman in the sixth.

AUGUST 21   The Mets outlast the Giants 11–9 in 12 innings in San Francisco. David Wright led the offense with two doubles and a single in six at-bats.

After the win, the Mets lose 19 of their next 21 games.

SEPTEMBER 8   The Mets lose their 11th game in a row with a 3–0 decision at the hands of the Marlins in Miami.

SEPTEMBER 11   The Mets and the Phillies combine to use 18 pitchers during an 11–9 Philadelphia win in 13 innings at Shea Stadium. The Phillies utilized ten hurlers—a major league record.

SEPTEMBER 15   The Mets announce that Art Howe will not be returning as manager in 2005. He finished out the remainder of the season, however.

Hired at the end of the 2002 season, Howe became the scapegoat for a considerable amount of front office bungling. The Mets rosters in 2003 and 2004 were filled with expensive, injury-plagued veterans like Mo Vaughn, Roberto Alomar and Jeromy Burnitz, who were on the downsides of their careers.

SEPTEMBER 16   The Mets score seven runs in the first inning and defeat the Braves 9–4 at Shea Stadium. The highlight of the rally was back-to-back homers from Richard Hidalgo and Todd Zeile.

SEPTEMBER 18   The Mets score six runs in the top of the first inning, but need ten innings to beat the Pirates 8–7 in Pittsburgh. Todd Zeile started as a catcher for the first time since 1990, when he was a member of the Cardinals. Zeile broke into the majors in 1989 as a catcher before moving to third base in 1991.

SEPTEMBER 19   Todd Zeile collects his 2,000th career hit with a single off Jose Mesa in the ninth inning of a 1–0 loss to the Pirates in the first game of a double-header at PNC Park. It was one of only three New York hits. Aaron Heilman (seven innings) and Ricky Bottalico (one inning) combined on a two-hitter. Both Pittsburgh hits were by Humberto Cota, one of them a third-inning home run. The Mets also lost the second tilt 6–1.

SEPTEMBER 23   The Mets play in Montreal for the last time and defeat the Expos 4–2.

SEPTEMBER 25   The Mets score three runs in the ninth inning and one in the 11th to defeat the Cubs
                 4–3 at Shea Stadium. Heading into the contest, the Cubs held a 1¹/₂–game lead over
                 the Giants in the wild-card race. Down 3–0 in the ninth, two Mets reached base on
                 walks by Ryan Dempster before Victor Diaz hit a three-run homer with two out on a
                 2–2 pitch from LaTroy Hawkins. Craig Brazell won the game with a walk-off homer
                 in the 11th. Neither Diaz nor Brazell were in the starting lineup. Diaz entered the
                 contest in the seventh in a double switch as a right fielder. Brazell came into the game
                 in the top of the 11th in another double switch as a first baseman.

                 *Both Diaz and Brazell were rookies in 2004. It was only the eighth game of
                 Diaz's career and his second home run. It was the only homer in the majors for
                 Brazell in 38 career at-bats.*

SEPTEMBER 28   The Mets use a pair of solo homers to defeat the Braves 2–1 in the first game of a
                 double-header at Turner Field. Gerald Williams homered in the third inning and
                 Eric Valent in the fifth. Atlanta won the second tilt 5–2.

                 *On the same day, the Mets hired Omar Minaya as general manager, replacing
                 Jim Duquette. Minaya was born in the Dominican Republic and moved to the
                 United States with his family when he was eight. He grew up in Queens. Minaya
                 was the assistant general manager of the Mets from 1997 through 2002, and
                 the general manager of the Expos in 2003 and 2004. At the time, Major League
                 Baseball was operating the Expos franchise, and Minaya oversaw what proved
                 to be its demise. The club moved to Washington just after the close of the 2004
                 season. During a productive 2004–05 offseason, Minaya hired Willie Randolph
                 as manager and signed free agents Pedro Martinez and Carlos Beltran. With his
                 proactive approach and a generous budget provided by owner, Fred Wilpon,
                 Minaya helped turn a club that was 71–91 in 2004 to one that would win 97
                 games in 2006. But a slide followed with September collapses that cost the Mets
                 a chance at the postseason in both 2007 and 2008 and losing seasons in 2009
                 and 2010. Minaya was fired at the end of the 2010 season.*

OCTOBER 3   Todd Zeile hits a home run in his last major league at-bat, during an 8–1 win over
                 the Expos at Shea Stadium. Zeile started the game as a catcher for only the second
                 time since 1990 (see September 18, 2004). It was also the last game for the Montreal
                 Expos franchise.

NOVEMBER 3   The day after George Bush defeats John Kerry in the Presidential election, the Mets
                 hire 50-year-old Willie Randolph as manager.

                 *The first African-American manager in Mets history, Randolph was a second
                 baseman in the majors from 1975 through 1992. He was named to six All-Star
                 teams and played in three World Series. Randolph played most of his career as
                 a Yankee from 1976 through 1988. He also appeared in 90 games for the Mets
                 in 1992. After his playing career ended, Randolph hooked up with the Yankees
                 again as a coach from 1994 through 2004, a period in which the club played in
                 six World Series and won four of them. Despite his long association with the
                 Yankees, Randolph grew up in Brooklyn as a diehard Mets fan. He helped bring
                 the Mets back to respectability as the club posted the best record in the NL in*

2006 before losing in the NLCS to the Cardinals. A late-season collapse in 2007 and a slow start the following season led to his dismissal in June 2008.

DECEMBER 3   The Mets trade Mike Stanton to the Yankees for Felix Heredia.

DECEMBER 8   Al Leiter signs with the Marlins as a free agent.

DECEMBER 10   Richard Hidalgo signs with the Rangers as a free agent.

DECEMBER 16   The Mets sign Pedro Martinez, most recently with the Red Sox, as a free agent.

Considered to be the second-best player available on the free agent market during the 2004–05 offseason, behind Carlos Beltran (see January 11, 2005), Martinez came to the Mets as a 33-year-old with a 182–76 lifetime record and three Cy Young Awards. He had led his league in ERA five times and in strikeouts three. Martinez was coming off a 16–9 season for Boston in 2004, helping the franchise to its first world championship since 1918. But there were alarm signs as his earned run average ballooned from 2.22 in 2003 to 3.90 in 2004. Martinez gave the Mets one good season with 15–8 mark and a 2.82 ERA in 2005, but afterward was largely ineffective or out of action with injuries before his contract with the club ended at the close of the 2008 season.

2005

Season in a Sentence

In Willie Randolph's first year with the Mets, the club improves from a 71–91 record in 2004 to 83–79 in 2005. Then Randolph bolsters the roster with another round of offseason acquisitions.

Finish • Won • Lost • Pct • GB

Third (tie)   83   79   .512   7.0

In the wild-card race, the Mets finished tied for third place, six games behind.

Manager

Willie Randolph

Stats	Mets	AL	Rank
Batting Avg:	.258	.262	11
On-Base Pct:	.322	.330	12
Slugging Pct:	.416	.414	8
Home Runs:	175	5	
Stolen Bases:	153	1	
ERA:	3.77	4.22	3
Errors:	106	12	
Runs Scored:	722	7	
Runs Allowed:	648	3	

Starting Lineup

Mike Piazza, c
Doug Mientiewicz, 1b
Miguel Cairo, 2b
David Wright, 3b
Jose Reyes, ss
Cliff Floyd, lf
Carlos Beltran, cf
Mike Cameron, rf
Victor Diaz, rf
Kaz Matsui, 2b
Marlon Anderson, 1b-2b
Ramon Castro, c

Pitchers

Pedro Martinez, sp
Tom Glavine, sp
Kris Benson, sp
Victor Zambrano, sp
Kazuhisa Ishii, sp
Jae Weong Seo, sp
Braden Looper, rp
Aaron Heilman, rp
Roberto Hernandez, rp
Heath Bell, rp

Attendance

2,829,929 (sixth in NL)

Club Leaders

Batting Avg:	David Wright	.306
On-Base Pct:	David Wright	.388
Slugging Pct:	David Wright	.523
Home Runs:	Cliff Floyd	34
RBIs:	David Wright	104
Runs:	David Wright	99
	Jose Reyes	99
Stolen Bases:	Jose Reyes	60
Wins:	Pedro Martinez	15
Strikeouts:	Pedro Martinez	208
ERA:	Pedro Martinez	2.82
Saves:	Braden Looper	28

JANUARY 10   The Mets sign Miguel Cairo, most recently with the Yankees, as a free agent.

JANUARY 13   The Mets sign Carlos Beltran, most recently with the Astros, as a free agent.

Only 28 on Opening Day in 2005, Beltran was considered to be the top free agent available during the 2004–05 offseason. He was coming off a 2004 postseason in which he hit eight home runs in 12 games for the Astros. Beltran was a disappointment in his first season with the Mets, batting only .266 with 16 home runs, but rebounded with a 41-home run season in 2006, the first of three straight seasons of 100 or more RBI.

JANUARY 17   The Mets sign Roberto Hernandez, most recently with the Phillies, as a free agent.

JANUARY 27   The Mets trade Ian Bladergroen to the Red Sox for Doug Mientiewicz.

APRIL 4   On Opening Day, the Reds score three runs in the ninth inning to beat the Mets 7–6 in Cincinnati. Pedro Martinez made his Mets debut and allowed three runs and three hits in six innings while striking out 12. Carlos Beltran, also in his first game as a Met, contributed three hits, including a home run. Cliff Floyd had three hits, one of them a homer. Jose Reyes was another New York batter with three hits. Kaz Matsui hit a first-inning homer on Opening Day for the second year in a row. But in the ninth inning, Braden Looper blew a save opportunity by allowing a single to Austin Kearns and back-to-back homers to Adam Dunn and Joe Randa.

The Mets lost their first five games in 2005.

APRIL 10   Pedro Martinez pitches a two-hitter to beat the Braves 6–1 at Turner Field. The only Atlanta hits were a triple by Andruw Jones in the second inning and a double from Johnny Estrada in the fifth.

APRIL 11   A Shea Stadium crowd of 53,663 watches the Mets win the home opener 8–4 over the Astros. The Mets trailed 4–3 before scoring five times in the eighth inning.

APRIL 13   The Mets win 1–0 over the Astros in 11 innings at Shea Stadium. Kazuhisa Ishii (seven innings), Roberto Hernandez (one inning), Braden Looper (two innings) and Mike DeJean (one inning) combined on a four-hitter. The Mets also collected only four hits, two of them off Roger Clemens, in the first seven innings. Jose Reyes drove in the game winner with a single.

APRIL 15   Aaron Heilman pitches a one-hitter to defeat the Marlins 1–0 at Shea Stadium. The only Florida hit was a single by Luis Castillo in the fourth inning.

APRIL 19   The Mets use seven home runs to power past the Phillies 16–4 in Philadelphia. Jose Reyes and Victor Diaz each homered twice. The others were by Mike Piazza, David Wright and Doug Mientiewicz. Wright's home run was a grand slam off Gavin Floyd in the sixth inning.

APRIL 21   The Mets score seven runs in the second inning of a 10–1 win over the Marlins in Miami. Doug Mientiewicz hit a grand slam off Al Leiter, who played the previous seven seasons with the Mets.

APRIL 29   The Mets play in Washington for the first time and lose 5–1 to the Nationals at RFK Stadium.

MAY 4   Cliff Floyd runs his hitting streak to 20 games during a 3–2 win over the Phillies in Philadelphia.

Floyd collected 30 hits and batted .395 during the 20-game streak.

MAY 6   The Mets homer four times during a 7–4 victory over the Brewers in Milwaukee. Mike Piazza hit two home runs, and David Wright and Mike Cameron added the others.

MAY 7   The Mets hit four home runs for the second game in a row and down the Brewers 7–5 at Miller Park. Carlos Beltran led the way with two homers, and David Wright and Doug Mientkiewicz added the others.

MAY 13	Cliff Floyd hits two solo homers for the only runs of a 2–0 victory over the Cardinals at Shea Stadium. Both were struck off Jason Marquis in the second and seventh innings. Tom Glavine (seven innings), Roberto Hernandez (one inning) and Braden Looper (one inning) combined on the shutout.
MAY 26	Jose Reyes hits two triples during a 12–4 triumph over the Marlins in Miami. The 12-run eruption came after the Mets were shut out in the previous two games.

> *Reyes hit seven triples in a ten-game span from May 16 through May 26. He finished the season with league-leading figures in triples (17) and stolen bases (60).*

MAY 27	The Mets edge the Marlins 1–0 in Miami. Pedro Martinez (eight innings) and Braden Looper (one inning) combined on the shutout. The lone run scored in the fourth inning on back-to-back doubles by Cliff Floyd and Mike Cameron.
JUNE 5	The Mets score in six of eight turns at bat and clobber the Giants 12–1 in the second game of a double-header at Shea Stadium. San Francisco won the opener 6–1.
JUNE 7	Pedro Martinez pitches a two-hitter and strikes out 12 batters to defeat the Astros 3–1 at Shea Stadium. Martinez had a no-hitter in progress until Chris Burke homered with one out in the seventh inning. Two batters later, Lance Berkman hit a single.

> *On the same day, the Mets selected pitcher Mike Pelfrey from Wichita State University in the first round of the amateur draft. Pelfrey reached the majors in 2006 and became a part of the Mets starting rotation in 2008. Other future big leaguers drafted and signed by the Mets in 2005 include Jonathan Niese (seventh round), Bobby Parnell (ninth round) and Josh Thole (13th round).*

JUNE 8	The Mets sign Jose Offerman, most recently with the Phillies, as a free agent.
JUNE 10	The Mets play the Angels at Shea Stadium for the first time and lose 12–2.
JUNE 11	The Mets put together a thrilling comeback to beat the Angels 5–3 in ten innings at Shea Stadium. The Mets tied the score 2–2 with one out in the ninth on an inside-the-park homer by Marlon Anderson. The Angels scored in the top of the tenth for a 3–2 advantage. With two out and two on base in the bottom half, Cliff Floyd hit a three-run, walk-off homer on a 3–2 pitch from Brendan Donnelly for the win. It was the ninth pitch of the at-bat. Floyd fouled off the previous three pitches.

> *On the same day, the Mets signed Danny Graves, most recently with the Reds, as a free agent.*

JUNE 14	The Mets play the Athletics for the first time during the regular season and lose 5–0 in Oakland.
JUNE 16	The Mets score seven runs in the fifth inning and defeat the Athletics 9–6 in Oakland. Carlos Beltran and Ramon Castro both hit three-run homers.
JUNE 17	The Mets play the Mariners in Seattle for the first time and lose 5–0.

JUNE 24   The Mets tie a major league record with three sacrifice flies in an inning during a 6–4 victory over the Yankees at Yankee Stadium. The record was made possible because Jose Reyes was credited with a sacrifice fly when center fielder Bernie Williams dropped his fly ball for an error with a runner on third base. The two other sacrifice flies were by Ramon Castro and Mike Cameron.

JULY 19   A two-run, walk-off, pinch-homer by Chris Woodward in the 11th beats the Padres 3–1 at Shea Stadium.

JULY 21   The Mets score seven runs in the sixth inning and trounce the Padres 12–0 at Shea Stadium.

AUGUST 7   Jose Reyes runs his hitting streak to 20 games during a 6–1 win over the Cubs at Shea Stadium.

           Reyes collected 34 hits and batted .374 during the 20-game hitting streak.

AUGUST 10 David Wright drives in six runs with a homer, a double and two singles during a 9–1 win over the Padres in San Diego.

AUGUST 11 Right fielder Mike Cameron and center fielder Carlos Beltran are involved in a horrible collision during a 2–1 loss to the Padres in San Diego. With one out in the seventh inning, David Ross lifted a fly ball into shallow left-center. Both dived headlong toward the ball at precisely the same time and collided head-to-head in mid-air and crumpled together. The force was so great that Cameron's sunglasses flew into center field. Ross wound up with a triple after second baseman Kaz Matsui retrieved the ball. Beltran hobbled to the clubhouse with help from his teammates. Cameron was bleeding from the mouth and was on the field for ten minutes before being carried off on a stretcher. He missed the rest of the season with a concussion, temporary loss of vision, and two broken cheekbones.

AUGUST 14 Pedro Martinez is five outs from a no-hitter, but winds up losing 2–1 to the Dodgers in Los Angeles. With one out in the eighth inning, and holding a 1–0 lead, Martinez gave up a triple to Antonio Perez. Jayson Werth followed with a home run to account for the two Los Angeles runs.

AUGUST 19 The Mets win 1–0 over the Nationals at Shea Stadium. Jae Weong Seo (eight innings) and Braden Looper (one inning) combined on the shutout. The lone run scored in the seventh inning on a double by Ramon Castro and a single from Victor Diaz.

AUGUST 20 The Mets win 9–8 in ten innings over the Nationals in a nail-biter at Shea Stadium. New York led 8–0 before Washington scored six runs in the seventh inning and two in the ninth. Chris Woodward drove in the winning run with a walk-off, pinch-single in the tenth.

AUGUST 21 In his first major league plate appearance, Mike Jacobs hits a three-run pinch-homer in the fifth inning of a 7–4 victory over the Nationals at Shea Stadium.

AUGUST 23 David Wright scores four runs during a 14–1 hammering of the Diamondbacks in Phoenix.

AUGUST 24   The Mets collect 20 hits and rout the Diamondbacks again 18–4 in Phoenix. In just his fourth major league game, Mike Jacobs hit two home runs, a double and a single and scored five runs. Dave Wright added two homers, a double and a single and crossed the plate four times. It was his second consecutive four-run game. Jose Reyes also homered.

After his first four major league games, Jacobs had four homers among his seven hits in 13 at-bats and scored eight runs. He finished his rookie year with 11 home runs and a .310 batting average in 100 at-bats. Jacobs was traded to the Marlins the following November in a package to obtain Carlos Delgado.

AUGUST 26   Steve Trachsel (eight innings) and Braden Looper (one inning) combine on a three-hitter to beat the Giants 1–0 in San Francisco. It was Trachsel's first appearance of the season after five months on the disabled list with injuries. The lone run scored on a home run by David Wright off Kevin Correia in the second inning.

At the end of the day, the Mets were 68–60 and were 1 1/2 games behind in the wild-card race. Any hopes for a postseason berth were dashed with 15 defeats in the next 18 games.

SEPTEMBER 11   Two weeks after Hurricane Katrina strikes the Gulf Coast and causes massive flooding in New Orleans, the Mets play for the last time at the second of three St. Louis ballparks named Busch Stadium and beat the Cardinals 7–2.

SEPTEMBER 15   Cliff Floyd hits a grand slam off Livan Hernandez in the fifth inning of a ten-inning, 6–5 loss to the Nationals at Shea Stadium.

SEPTEMBER 23   A three-run homer by Carlos Beltran in the tenth inning downs the Nationals 5–2 at RFK Stadium. Washington tied the score 2–2 on a two-run homer with two out in the ninth by Carlos Baerga off Roberto Hernandez.

SEPTEMBER 24   A five-run rally in the first inning holds up for a 5–2 win over the Nationals in Washington. David Wright hits a grand slam off Livan Hernandez.

Wright batted .306 with 99 runs, 42 doubles, 27 homers and 102 RBI in 2005.

SEPTEMBER 27   Jose Reyes collects a triple, two doubles and a single during a 3–2 win over the Phillies in Philadelphia.

SEPTEMBER 29   Tom Glavine pitches a two-hitter with 11 strikeouts to defeat the Rockies 11–0 at Shea Stadium. The only Colorado hits were singles by Choo Freeman in the third inning and Matt Holliday in the seventh.

OCTOBER 2   On the final day of the season, Mike Piazza is cheered by Mets fans during an 11–3 loss to the Rockies at Shea Stadium. It was known that he wouldn't be returning to the club in 2006. Willie Randolph removed Piazza from the game in the eighth inning, and play was halted during an eight-minute standing ovation. The ballpark's video screen displayed highlights of Piazza's eight-year, 972-games career with the Mets.

NOVEMBER 18   The Mets trade Mike Cameron to the Padres for Xavier Nady.

NOVEMBER 24   The Mets trade Mike Jacobs, Yusmeiro Petit and Grant Psomas to the Marlins for Carlos Delgado. On the same day, the Mets signed Billy Wagner, most recently with the Phillies, as a free agent.

Delgado made an immediate splash in New York in 2006 with 38 home runs, 114 RBI and a .265 batting average. He also hit 38 homers in 2008 before a hip injury wrecked his 2009 and 2010 seasons. At the close of the 2010 season, it appeared that the hip injury had prematurely ended Delgado's career. Wagner gave the club three great years as a closer. As a Met, he collected 101 saves and had a 2.37 ERA and 230 strikeouts in 183 games and 189²/₃ innings.

DECEMBER 5   The Mets trade Gaby Hernandez and Dante Brinkley to the Marlins for Paul Lo Duca.

Lo Duca was the Mets starting catcher for two seasons. In 2006, he was the National League's starter in the All-Star Game and batted .318 with five homers in 124 games.

DECEMBER 12   The Mets sign Jose Valentin, most recently with the Dodgers, as a free agent. On the same day, the Mets also signed Julio Franco, most recently with the Braves, as a free agent.

Valentin hit 25 or more homers for the Cubs in every season from 2000 through 2004 as a shortstop and third baseman. The Mets obtained him after he batted .170 in 56 games for the Dodgers in 2005. At the age of 36, Valentin hit .271 with 18 homers in 137 contests for the Mets in 2006. He also appeared in 94 games at second base, a position he hadn't played since 1994. Franco was 47 when signed and entered the season with a .299 batting average in 2,377 major league games. He made his major league debut with the Phillies 1982 and spent his peak years as a shortstop and a second baseman with the Indians and Rangers. Franco was a three-time All-Star and won the AL batting title in Texas in 1991. A native of the Dominican Republic, Franco also played professionally in Japan (1995 and 1997), Mexico (1999 and 2001) and Korea (2000). He spent five seasons with the Braves from 2001 through 2005 as a first baseman and pinch-hitter. Franco also filled that role in two seasons with the Mets, batting .256 with three home runs in 215 at-bats.

DECEMBER 15   Roberto Hernandez signs with the Phillies as a free agent.

DECEMBER 16   Doug Mientkiewicz signs with the Royals as a free agent.

DECEMBER 22   Braden Looper signs with the Cardinals as a free agent.

2006

Season in a Sentence

The Mets record 97 regular season wins, nine more than any other NL team, but lose the NLCS in seven games to the Cardinals.

Finish • Won • Lost • Pct • GB

First   97   65   .599   +12.0

National League Division Series

The Mets defeated the Los Angeles Dodgers three games to none.

National League Championship Series

The Mets lost four games to three to the St. Louis Cardinals.

Manager

Willie Randolph

Stats

Stats	Mets	AL	Rank
Batting Avg:	.264	.265	8
On-Base Pct:	.334	.334	8
Slugging Pct:	.445	.427	3
Home Runs:	200	4	
Stolen Bases:	146	1	
ERA:	4.14	4.49	3
Errors:	104	7	
Runs Scored:	834	3	
Runs Allowed:	673	3	

Starting Lineup

Paul Lo Duca, c
Carlos Delgado, 1b
Jose Valentin, 2b
David Wright, 3b
Jose Reyes, ss
Cliff Floyd, rf
Carlos Beltran, cf
Endy Chavez, rf-cf-lf
Xavier Nady, rf
Chris Woodward, 2b

Pitchers

Tom Glavine, sp
Steve Trachsel, sp
Pedro Martinez, sp
Orlando Hernandez, sp
John Maine, sp
Billy Wagner, rp
Aaron Heilman, rp
Chad Bradford, rp
Pedro Feliciano, rp
Duaner Sanchez, rp
Darren Oliver, rp

Attendance

3,379,535 (third in NL)

Club Leaders

Batting Avg:	Paul Lo Duca	.318
On-Base Pct:	David Wright	.381
Slugging Pct:	Carlos Delgado	.548
Home Runs:	Carlos Beltran	41
RBI:	Carlos Beltran	116
	David Wright	116
Runs:	Carlos Beltran	127
Stolen Bases:	Jose Reyes	64
Wins:	Tom Glavine	15
	Steve Trachsel	15
Strikeouts:	Pedro Martinez	137
ERA:	Tom Glavine	3.82
Saves:	Billy Wagner	40

JANUARY 6   Miguel Cairo signs as a free agent with the Yankees.

JANUARY 19   The Mets sign Darren Oliver, most recently with the Astros, as a free agent.

JANUARY 22   The Mets trade Kris Benson to the Orioles for John Maine and Julio Jorge.

FEBRUARY 6   Mike Piazza signs with the Padres as a free agent.

> *Piazza gave San Diego a solid season in 2006, with 22 home runs and a .283 batting average. He finished his career as a DH with the Athletics in 2007.*

APRIL 3   The Mets win the season opener 3–2 over the Nationals before 54,371 at Shea Stadium. In his Mets debut, Xavier Nady collected four hits, including two doubles, in four at-bats. David Wright homered. Tom Glavine started and allowed a run in six innings.

In the second game of the season, on April 5, Nady made it five hits in his first five at-bats as a Met with a home run in his first plate appearance. The Mets lost 9–5 to the Nationals in ten innings at Shea Stadium.

APRIL 13   The Mets score four runs in the first inning on the way to a 13–4 win over the Nationals in Washington.

Ron Darling became one of the Mets television broadcasters in 2006, replacing Tom Seaver.

APRIL 20   At 47, Julio Franco becomes the oldest player in major league history to hit a home run. Franco homered as a pinch-hitter with a man on base in the eighth inning of a 7–2 win over the Padres in San Diego. The previous record holder was 46-year-old Joe Quinn, a pitcher with the Philadelphia Athletics in 1930.

Franco hit two more home runs as a major leaguer. The last one was as a 48-year-old with the Mets in 2007.

APRIL 26   Julio Franco becomes the second-oldest player in major league history with a stolen base during an 11-inning, 9–7 victory over the Giants in San Francisco. The oldest individual with a stolen base is Arlie Latham, who swiped one for the New York Giants at the age of 54 in 1909. But Latham, then a coach with the Giants, was in that game only as a publicity stunt.

Franco stole six bases in 2006 and two more in 2007 before retiring.

APRIL 29   Paul Lo Duca homers off John Thomson in the sixth inning for the lone run of a 1–0 victory over the Braves in Atlanta. Tom Glavine (seven innings), Aaron Heilman (one inning) and Billy Wagner (one inning) combined on the shutout.

MAY 3   Carlos Delgado hits a walkoff homer in the 12th inning to defeat the Pirates 4–3 at Shea Stadium.

MAY 5   Jose Reyes collects five hits, including a triple, during a 14-inning, 8–7 win over the Braves at Shea Stadium. Both teams score in the 11th on solo home runs, with Wilson Betimet delivering for Atlanta in the top half and Cliff Floyd for New York in the bottom half. David Wright drove in the game winner with a double in the 14th.

Reyes hit .300 with 19 homers, 122 runs and league-leading figures in triples (17) and stolen bases (64) in 2006.

MAY 10   A six-run third inning gives the Mets a 10–0 lead and leads to a 13–4 crushing of the Phillies in Philadelphia.

MAY 16   The Mets play at the new Busch Stadium for the first time and win 8–3 over the Cardinals.

MAY 23	Carlos Beltran hits a walk-off homer in the 16th inning to defeat the Phillies 9–8 at Shea Stadium. Darren Oliver, the eighth Mets pitcher, hurled four shutout innings. *Beltran tied a club record with 41 homers in 2006, a mark previously set by Todd Hundley in 1996. Beltran also drove in 116 runs, scored 127 and batted .275.*
MAY 24	The Mets trade Jorge Julio to the Diamondbacks for Orlando Hernandez.
MAY 26	Pedro Martinez injures his hip in the first inning of a 5–1 loss against the Marlins in Miami. Martinez was ordered by the umpires to change his long black undershirt, and in his haste to get to the clubhouse, the Mets pitcher slipped and fell on his hip on the concrete runway. The injury affected him for the rest of the season. After June 5, he was 4–7 with a 7.10 ERA.
MAY 31	The Mets outlast the Diamondbacks 1–0 in 13 innings at Shea Stadium. The winning run scored on a double by Jose Valentin and a single from Endy Chavez. Pedro Martinez (eight innings), Billy Wagner (two innings) and Duaner Sanchez (three innings) combined on the shutout.
JUNE 4	The Mets lose 7–6 to the Giants in 12 innings at Shea Stadium despite tenth-inning homers from Jose Valentin and Lastings Milledge off Armando Benitez after San Francisco scores two in the top of the inning. The homer by Milledge was the first of his career.
JUNE 6	In the second round of the amateur draft, the Mets select pitcher Kevin Mulvey from Villanova University. The Mets lost their first-round choice by signing Billy Wagner as a free agent. Mulvey was dealt to the Twins in February 2008 in the Johan Santana trade. Other future major leaguers drafted by the Mets in 2006 include Joe Smith (second round), Dan Murphy (13th round) and Tobi Stoner (16th round).
JUNE 9	Carlos Beltran hits two homers, a double and a single and scores four runs during a 10–6 win over the Diamondbacks in Phoenix. Carlos Delgado also struck two homers and David Wright belted one. *On the same day, the Mets traded Kaz Matsui to the Rockies for Eli Marrero.*
JUNE 10	Alay Soler pitches a two-hitter to beat the Diamondbacks 5–0 in Phoenix. The only Arizona hits were doubles by Orlando Hudson in the third inning and Jeff DaVanon in the eighth. *Soler was a 26-year-old in his first professional season in the United States after defecting from Cuba. The two-hitter came in his fourth major league start. He never won another game and finished his career with a 2–3 record and a 6.00 ERA in 45 innings over eight games, all of them starts.*
JUNE 11	The Mets score six runs in the fifth inning for a 13–0 lead and demolish the Diamondbacks 15–2 in Phoenix.
JUNE 15	The Mets run their winning streak to eight games with a 5–4 decision over the Phillies in Philadelphia.

JUNE 18   David Wright hits a grand slam off Adam Loewen in the fifth inning of a 9–4 win over the Orioles at Shea Stadium.

JUNE 22   The Mets move ten games in front in the NL East race with a 6–2 win over the Reds at Shea Stadium.

The victory gave the Mets a 45–27 record. The club maintained their double-digit lead for the rest of the season. The Mets were the first NL East team other than the Braves to end the season in first place since 1994. Atlanta won 11 Eastern Division titles in a row.

JULY 5   The Mets beat the Pirates 5–0 at Shea Stadium. All five New York runs and each of the four hits were collected in the first inning. Orlando Hernandez (seven innings), Chad Bradford (one inning) and Duaner Sanchez (one inning) combined on the shutout.

JULY 8   Jose Valentin drives in seven runs in the first two innings of a 17–3 thrashing of the Marlins in the second game of a double-header at Shea Stadium. Valentin hit a grand slam in the first inning and a bases-loaded triple in the second, both off Ricky Nolasco. Florida won the opener 3–2.

JULY 11   Four Mets are in the starting lineup at the All-Star Game at PNC Park in Pittsburgh. Paul Lo Duca was the catcher, David Wright the third baseman, Jose Reyes the shortstop and Carlos Beltran the center fielder. Wright homered off Kenny Rogers in the second inning. Beltran collected two hits, including a double. Despite the contributions of Wright and Beltran, the NL lost 3–2.

Wright batted .311 with 40 doubles, 26 homers and 116 RBI in 2006.

JULY 16   After falling behind 5–0, the Mets score single runs in the fourth and fifth innings, then erupt for 11 runs in the sixth and defeat the Cubs 13–7 in Chicago. Cliff Floyd and Carlos Beltran both hit grand slams during the 11-run rally. Floyd cleared the bases with a drive off Sean Marshall, while Beltran delivered against Roberto Novoa. David Wright hit the third New York home run of the inning with a two-run shot. The Mets collected five homers in all. Floyd hit an earlier one in the fourth inning, and Chris Woodward struck one in the fifth.

This was only the seventh instance in major league history in which a team hit two grand slams in an inning. It was the first time for the Mets. The Astros accomplished the feat against the Mets on July 30, 1969.

JULY 18   Carlos Beltran hits a grand slam for the second game in a row with a blast off Eric Milton in the seventh inning of an 8–3 triumph over the Reds in Cincinnati.

Beltran is the only Mets batter with grand slams in consecutive games.

JULY 21   Jose Valentin hits a grand slam off Taylor Buchholz in the second inning of a 7–0 victory over the Astros at Shea Stadium. John Maine pitched a complete game shutout.

JULY 26   A two-out run in the tenth inning beats the Cubs 1–0 at Shea Stadium. The run scored on a double by Carlos Delgado and a walk-off single from Jose Valentin.

John Maine (seven innings), Duaner Sanchez (one inning) and Aaron Heilman (one inning) combined on the shutout.

JULY 29   The Mets score seven runs in the sixth inning of an 11–3 win over the Braves in Atlanta. Carlos Beltran hit two homers in the contest. Julio Franco recorded another age-related achievement by becoming the oldest pinch-runner in major league history. Franco went into the game as a pinch-runner for Carlos Delgado in the third inning after Delgado was hit by a pitch. Franco remained in the game, succeeding Delgado at first base.

JULY 30   Carlos Beltran hits two home runs for the second consecutive game and records his third grand slam of the month of July during a 10–6 triumph over the Braves in Atlanta. The slam was struck off Chris James in the second inning.

JULY 31   The Mets trade Xavier Nady to the Pirates for Roberto Hernandez and Oliver Perez. The Mets made the deal for the two pitchers because of a traffic accident involving Duaner Sanchez. Just after midnight on July 31, Sanchez was riding in the backseat of a taxi in Miami heading for a Dominican restaurant when it was broadsided by a Ford Crown Victoria, which crossed three lanes of I-95. The taxi slammed into a concrete median. Sanchez suffered a separated shoulder, which put him out of action for the rest of the year. The Mets kept the accident out of the media until they could complete the deal with the Pirates. Sanchez didn't pitch in a regular season game again until 2008.

AUGUST 6   The Mets score seven runs in the fourth inning of an 8–1 win over the Phillies at Shea Stadium. Jose Reyes hit a grand slam off Scott Mathieson.

AUGUST 15   Jose Reyes hits three homers, but the Mets lose 11–4 to the Phillies at Citizens Bank Park. Reyes led off the first inning with a home run off Randy Wolf and added another against Wolf in the third. After a walk in the fifth, Reyes walloped his third home run against Brian Sanches in the eighth. The switch-hitting Mets shortstop also homered from both sides of the plate, connecting off Wolf from the right side and Sanchez batting left-handed. Orlando Hernandez tied a Mets record for most runs allowed by a pitcher in a game, surrendering all 11 Philadelphia tallies in four innings.

AUGUST 20   Solo homers by Carlos Beltran and Carlos Delgado beat the Rockies 2–0 at Shea Stadium. Orlando Hernandez (six innings), Chad Bradford (one inning), Aaron Heilman (one inning) and Billy Wagner (one inning) combined on the shutout.

AUGUST 22   A two-run, walk-off homer by Carlos Beltran in the ninth inning beats the Cardinals 8–7 at Shea Stadium. Earlier, Carlos Delgado hit the 399th and 400th homers of his career. Number 400 was a grand slam off Jeff Weaver in the fifth inning.

   On the same day, the Mets traded Evan McLane to the Diamondbacks for Shawn Green.

AUGUST 26   The Mets explode for seven runs in the seventh inning and beat the Phillies 11–5 at Shea Stadium.

AUGUST 30   David Wright hits a grand slam off Josh Fogg in the first inning of an 11–3 win over the Rockies in Denver.

SEPTEMBER 3   Orlando Hernandez ($5^2/_3$ innings), Roberto Hernandez (one inning), Darren Oliver (two-thirds of an inning) and Guillermo Mota (one inning) combine on a one-hitter, but the Mets lose 2–1 to the Astros at Minute Maid Park. The only Houston hit was a single by Aubrey Huff in the second inning. The Astros scored runs in the sixth and seventh innings without the benefit of a hit. The four New York pitchers combined to walk nine batters.

SEPTEMBER 6   Jose Reyes hits the first pitch of the first inning from Kyle Davies for a home run to spark the Mets to an 8–0 victory over the Braves in the second game of a double-header at Shea Stadium. Oliver Perez pitched a complete game shutout. The Mets also won the opener 4–1.

SEPTEMBER 13   The Mets score a run in the ninth inning and three in the 11th to defeat the Marlins 7–4 in Miami. Carlos Delgado tied the score 4–4 with a two-out, solo homer in the ninth.

SEPTEMBER 18   The Mets clinch the NL East pennant with a 4–0 triumph over the Marlins at Shea Stadium. Steve Trachsel ($6^1/_3$ innings), Guillermo Mota (two-thirds of an inning), Aaron Heilman (one inning) and Billy Wagner (one inning) combined on the shutout.

SEPTEMBER 19   Julio Franco plays third base for the first time since his rookie season with the Phillies in 1982. He was the starter at third and batted clean-up during the Mets 3–2 win over the Marlins at Shea Stadium.

SEPTEMBER 30   The Mets use five homers to power past the Nationals in Washington. The home runs were struck by David Wright, Endy Chavez, Shawn Green, Ramon Castro and Julio Franco. Tom Glavine (six innings), Darren Oliver (one inning) and Royce Ring (two innings) combined on the shutout.

The Mets played the Los Angeles Dodgers in the National League Division Series. Managed by Grady Little, the Dodgers were 88–74 in 2006 and qualified for the playoffs as a wild card.

OCTOBER 4   The Mets open the playoffs with a 6–5 win over the Dodgers before 56,979 at Shea Stadium. John Maine was the New York starter because Pedro Martinez and Orlando Hernandez were out with injuries. A strange play took place in the second inning in which two Dodgers were tagged out at the plate. Jeff Kent was on second base and J. D. Drew on first when Russell Martin lashed a drive into right field. Shawn Green played the ball off the wall and relayed to second baseman Jose Valentin, who threw home to catcher Paul Lo Duca. Kent got a terrible read on the ball, started late and was tagged out at the plate. Drew, running right behind Kent, was also tagged out. To add to the bizarre nature of the play, Green, Valentin and Lo Duca all played for the Dodgers as recently as 2004. Carlos Delgado and Cliff Floyd homered in the fourth for a 2–1 lead, but the Dodgers came back to tie the contest 4–4 in the top of the seventh. In the bottom half, the Mets scored twice on an RBI-single by Delgado and a run-scoring double from David Wright. Delgado collected four hits in the contest, and Wright drove in three runs.

The series was telecast by ESPN (game one) and FOX (games two and three). The announcers for game one were Gary Thorne, Joe Morgan and Steve Phillips. Thom Brennaman and Steve Lyons announced game two, and Brennaman and Tim McCarver announced game three.

OCTOBER 5	The Mets take a two-games-to-none lead in the best-of-five series by beating the Dodgers 4–1 before 57,029 at Shea Stadium. Tom Glavine pitched six shutout innings.
OCTOBER 7	The Mets complete the sweep of the Dodgers with a 9–5 win in Los Angeles. The Mets scored three runs in the first inning off Greg Maddux but trailed 5–4 at the end of the fifth. A three-run sixth put the Mets into the lead as Jose Reyes, Paul Lo Duca and Carlos Beltran delivered three consecutive RBI-singles. Shawn Green contributed three hits, including two doubles.

> *The Mets played the St. Louis Cardinals in the National League Championship Series. Managed by Tony LaRussa, the Cards won a weak NL Central with an 83–78 record, the fifth best in the NL. It was the third straight division title for St. Louis. The club won 105 games and played in the World Series in 2004 and had 100 victories in 2005.*

OCTOBER 11	The first game of the NLCS is postponed by rain.
OCTOBER 12	The Mets win the opener with a 2–0 decision over the Cardinals before 56,311 at Shea Stadium. Carlos Beltran drove in both runs with a home run off Jeff Weaver in the sixth inning. Tom Glavine (seven innings), Guillermo Mota (one inning) and Billy Wagner (one inning) pitched the shutout.
OCTOBER 13	The Cardinals even the series with a 9–6 win over the Mets in front of a crowd of 56,349 at Shea Stadium. The Mets led 6–4 after six innings, but the Cards scored two runs in the seventh inning and three in the ninth. Carlos Delgado hit two homers and drove in three runs. Jose Reyes had three hits, including a double.
OCTOBER 14	In game three, the Mets lose 5–0 to the Cardinals in St. Louis. Jeff Suppan pitched eight shutout innings and hit a home run.
OCTOBER 15	The Mets even the series at two games apiece with a 12–5 triumph over the Cardinals in St. Louis. The Mets blew the game open with six runs in the sixth inning, the last three on a double by Jose Valentin. There were seven home runs in the game. Carlos Beltran hit two homers, and Carlos Delgado and David Wright one each for the Mets. The St. Louis home runs were by David Eckstein, Jim Edmonds and Yadier Molina. Delgado drove in five runs and Beltran scored four.
OCTOBER 16	Game five is postponed by rain.
OCTOBER 17	The Mets fall behind three games to two with a 4–2 loss in St. Louis. The Mets had a 2–0 lead in the fourth inning, but the Cards rebounded with two runs in the bottom of the fourth, one in the fifth and another in the sixth.
OCTOBER 18	Facing elimination, the Mets force a game seven by beating the Cardinals 4–2 before 56,334 at Shea Stadium. John Maine started for the Mets and allowed no runs in $5^2/_3$ innings. Jose Reyes led off the first inning with a homer off Chris Carpenter and later added two singles and two stolen bases.
OCTOBER 19	The Cardinals advance to the World Series by beating the Mets 3–1 in game seven before 56,357 at Shea Stadium. With the score 1–1 in the top of the seventh inning and a runner on base, Scott Rolen hit a drive that cleared the left-field fence.

Endy Chavez grabbed it and brought it back with a snow cone catch, landed on the warning track and threw out Jim Edmonds at first base. The score was still 1–1 in the ninth when Yadier Molina hit a two-run homer off Aaron Heilman. The Mets loaded the bases in the bottom of the ninth, but Adam Wainright struck out Carlos Beltran to end the game.

The Cardinals won the World Series by defeating the Tigers in five games.

NOVEMBER 13   The Mets award the naming rights for their new ballpark, scheduled to open in 2009, to Citigroup, Inc. The agreement called for Citigroup to pay $20 million per year for 20 years to call the facility Citi Field, plus the purchase of commercial time on the club's radio and television broadcasts. The arrangement was criticized following the financial crisis that beset the country beginning in 2008, however. A total of $45 billion in taxpayer funds was allocated to Citigroup by the U.S. Federal Government in two separate rescue packages.

NOVEMBER 15   The Mets trade Heath Bell and Royce Ring to the Padres for Jon Adkins and Ben Johnson.

Bell was 29 when traded and posted a 6.40 ERA for the Mets in 37 innings in 2006. He suddenly found his form in San Diego, however, and led the NL in saves in 2009 with 42.

NOVEMBER 17   The Mets sign Damion Easley, most recently with the Diamondbacks, as a free agent.

NOVEMBER 21   The Mets sign Moises Alou, most recently with the Giants, as a free agent.

Alou was 40 years old when signed by the Mets. He played brilliantly in New York when healthy, but unfortunately, that wasn't very often. In two seasons with the club, Alou batted .342 with 13 homers in 414 at-bats.

DECEMBER 2   Roberto Hernandez signs with the Indians as a free agent.

2 0 0 7

Season in a Sentence

In a meltdown of historic proportions, the Mets miss the playoffs after blowing a seven-game lead in the NL East.

Finish • Won • Lost • Pct • GB

First   88   74   .543   1.0

In the wild-card race, the Mets finished in second place, 1 1/2 games behind.

Manager

Willie Randolph

Stats

Stats	Mets	AL	Rank
Batting Avg:	.275	.266	2
On-Base Pct:	.342	.334	3
Slugging Pct:	.432	.423	7
Home Runs:	177	5	
Stolen Bases:	200	1	
ERA:	4.26	4.43	7
Errors:	101	8	
Runs Scored:	804	4	
Runs Allowed:	750	7	

Starting Lineup

Paul Lo Duca, c
Carlos Delgado, 1b
Luis Castillo, 2b
David Wright, 3b
Jose Reyes, ss
Moises Alou, lf
Carlos Beltran, cf
Shawn Green, rf
Damion Easley, 2b
Ruben Gotay, 2b

Pitchers

John Maine, sp
Oliver Perez, sp
Tom Glavine, sp
Orlando Hernandez, sp
Billy Wagner, rp
Aaron Heilman, rp
Pedro Feliciano, rp
Scott Schoeneweis, rp
Joe Smith, rp
Jorge Sosa, rp-sp
Guillermo Mota, rp

Attendance

3,853,955 (second in NL)

Club Leaders

Batting Avg:	David Wright	.325
On-Base Pct:	David Wright	.416
Slugging Pct:	David Wright	.546
Home Runs:	Carlos Beltran	33
RBI:	Carlos Beltran	112
Runs:	Jose Reyes	119
Stolen Bases:	Jose Reyes	78
Wins:	John Maine	15
	Oliver Perez	15
Strikeouts:	John Maine	180
ERA:	Oliver Perez	3.56
Saves:	Billy Wagner	34

FEBRUARY 1   Cliff Floyd signs with the Cubs as a free agent.

FEBRUARY 13   The Mets sign Chan Ho Park, most recently with the Padres, as a free agent.

MARCH 1   The Mets sign Aaron Sele, most recently with the Dodgers, as a free agent.

MARCH 23   The Mets sign Fernando Tatis as a free agent. On the same day, Steve Trachsel signed with the Orioles as a free agent.

APRIL 1   In a rematch of the 2006 National League Championship Series, the Mets open the season with a 6–1 triumph over the Cardinals in St. Louis in a contest televised nationally on Sunday night over ESPN. Tom Glavine pitched six innings and gave up one run. Paul Lo Duca contributed three RBI.

APRIL 4   John Maine (seven innings), Ambiorix Burgos (one inning) and Aaron Sele (one inning) combine on a two-hitter to defeat the Cardinals 10–0 at Busch Stadium. The only St. Louis hits were a single by Scott Rolen in the fifth inning and a double from Chris Duncan in the ninth.

APRIL 6   The Mets wallop the Braves 11–1 in Atlanta.

               *The Mets began the season with four straight victories in which they outscored
               their opponents 31–3.*

APRIL 9   In the home opener, the Mets trail 5–4 before erupting for seven runs in the eighth
               inning and beat the Phillies 11–5 before 56,227 at Shea Stadium.

APRIL 19   Three days after 27 students and five faculty members are shot to death on the
               campus of Virginia Tech University, David Wright runs his hitting streak to 26
               games over two seasons during an 11–3 win over the Marlins in Miami. Wright had
               a hit in the last 14 games of 2006 and the first 12 of 2007.

               *Wright batted .325 with 113 runs, 196 hits, 42 doubles, 30 home runs and
               107 RBI in 2007 in addition to winning a Gold Glove.*

APRIL 24   The Mets edge the Rockies 2–1 in 12 innings at Shea Stadium. The game was
               scoreless through nine innings. Both clubs scored a run in the tenth. In the bottom
               half, pinch-hitter Damion Easley tied the score 1–1 by clubbing a home run with
               two out on a 2–2 pitch. A squeeze bunt with two out in the 12th by Endy Chavez
               brought Shawn Green across the plate with the winning run.

APRIL 29   A home run by Carlos Beltran off Jay Bergmann in the sixth inning is the only run
               of a 1–0 victory over the Nationals in Washington. John Maine (seven innings),
               Aaron Heilman (two-thirds of an inning), Scott Schoeneweis (one-third of an inning)
               and Billy Wagner (one inning) combined on the shutout.

MAY 3   The Mets score six runs in the ninth inning to defeat the Diamondbacks 9–4 in
               Phoenix. The rally was achieved with a pair of three-run homers from Damion
               Easley and David Wright.

MAY 16   Jorge Sosa (seven innings), Joe Smith (one inning) and Billy Wagner (one inning)
               combine on a two-hitter to defeat the Cubs 8–1 at Shea Stadium. The only Chicago
               hits were singles by Cesar Izturis in the third inning and Cliff Floyd in the eighth.

MAY 17   The Mets score five runs in the ninth inning to shock the Cubs 6–5 at Shea Stadium.
               With one out and the bases loaded, Endy Chavez walked to make the score 5–2.
               Consecutive one-run singles from Ruben Gotay and David Wright pulled the Mets
               within a run. Carlos Delgado drove in the tying and winning runs with another
               single. Wright's hit came in a rare role as a pinch-hitter. Julio Franco played at third
               base for the fifth, and last, time of his 23-year major league career.

MAY 19   In five plate appearances, David Wright hits two homers and draws three intentional
               walks during a 10–7 triumph over the Yankees at Shea Stadium.

MAY 26   Carlos Delgado delivers two homers and drives in five runs during a 7–2 win over the
               Marlins in Miami.

MAY 29   After the Giants score in the top of the tenth, Carlos Delgado belts a two-run,
               walk-off homer against Armando Benitez in the bottom half to lift the Mets to a
               5–4 victory at Shea Stadium.

JUNE 7   The only three runs of a ten-inning, 6–3 loss to the Phillies at Shea Stadium come in the sixth inning on consecutive home runs by Carlos Delgado, David Wright and Paul Lo Duca. Cole Hamels surrendered all three home runs in a span of nine pitches.

On the same day, the Mets selected pitcher Eddie Kunz from Oregon State University with their first pick in the amateur draft. Kunz was chosen in the supplemental phase of the first round. The Mets lost their pick in the regular phase of the first round for signing Moises Alou. Kunz made his major league debut with four games in 2008, and then he spent all of the 2009 and 2010 seasons in the minors. Other future major leaguers drafted and signed by the Mets in 2007 include Lucas Duda (7th round) and Dillon Gee (21st round).

JUNE 8   The Mets play at Comerica Park in Detroit for the first time and beat the Tigers 3–0. Jorge Sosa (eight innings) and Billy Wagner (one inning) combined on the shutout.

JUNE 15   Jose Reyes drives in both runs of a 2–0 win over the Yankees at Yankee Stadium. Reyes delivered a run-scoring single in the third inning and a home run in the fifth, both off Roger Clemens. Reyes also stole three bases. Oliver Perez (7⅓ innings), Pedro Feliciano (one-third of an inning), Joe Smith (one-third of an inning) and Billy Wagner (one inning) combined on the shutout.

Reyes led the NL in stolen bases with 78 in 2007 in addition to 112 runs scored, 12 homers and a .280 batting average.

JUNE 22   The Mets play the Athletics at Shea Stadium for the first time during the regular season and win 9–1.

JUNE 23   Doubles by Ruben Castro and David Wright in the ninth inning beat the Athletics 1–0 at Shea Stadium. Orlando Hernandez (seven innings), Pedro Feliciano (one-third of an inning), Aaron Heilman (two-thirds of an inning) and Billy Wagner (one inning) combined on the shutout.

JUNE 25   A walk-off homer by Shawn Green in the 11th inning beats the Cardinals 2–1 at Shea Stadium. It was only the third Mets hit of the game.

JUNE 29   Billy Wagner strikes out all three batters he faces in the ninth inning to close out a 6–5 victory over the Phillies in the first game of a double-header in Philadelphia. The Mets were also victorious in the second tilt 5–2 behind two homers from Carlos Beltran.

JUNE 30   Carlos Beltran hits two homers for the second game in a row to lead the Mets past the Phillies 8–3 in Philadelphia.

Beltran batted .276 with 33 homers and 112 RBIs in 2007.

JULY 7   The Mets outlast the Astros 5–3 in 17 innings in Houston. The Mets tied the contest 3–3 with a run in the seventh. There was no scoring from the eighth through the 16th. Carlos Beltran saves the Mets with an amazing catch with two on base and two outs in the 14th. Luke Scott crushed a pitch that traveled more than 430 feet before Beltran tracked it down after scaling Minute Maid Park's incline in center field. In the 17th, Jose Reyes walks and moves to third on a single by Ruben Gotay.

Beltran provides the heroics again with a go-ahead single. Another single from David Wright provides an insurance tally. Eight Mets pitchers (Tom Glavine, Aaron Heilman, Pedro Feliciano, Guillermo Mota, Scott Schoeneweis, Joe Smith, Aaron Sele and Bill Wagner) kept Houston from crossing the plate over the final 13 innings.

JULY 10   Mets batters collect five hits in ten a-bats in the All-Star Game but the National League loses 5–4 at AT&T Park in San Francisco. Billy Wagner contributed to the defeat by allowing a two-run homer to Victor Martinez in the eighth inning that turned a 4–3 lead into a 5–4 deficit. Jose Reyes collected three hits, including a double, and a stolen base. Carlos Beltran garnered a triple and David Wright a single.

JULY 14   Tom Glavine (eight innings) and Billy Wagner (one inning) combine on a two-hitter to beat the Reds 2–1 at Shea Stadium. The only Cincinnati hits were a home run by Brandon Phillips in the second inning and a single from Ken Griffey, Jr. in the seventh.

JULY 19   The Mets score six runs in the first inning on the way to a 13–9 win over the Dodgers in Los Angeles.

JULY 25   Tom Glavine records his 299th career win with a 6–3 decision over the Pirates at Shea Stadium. Glavine allowed three runs in six innings.

JULY 30   The Mets trade Travis Bowyer and Scott Tyler to the Twins for Luis Castillo.

JULY 31   In his quest for his 300th career win, Tom Glavine allows only a run and two hits in six innings and leaves with a 2–1 lead against the Brewers in Milwaukee, but the bullpen blows the slim advantage, and the Mets lose 4–2 in 13 innings.

AUGUST 5   Tom Glavine records his 300th career win with an 8–3 decision over the Cubs in Chicago. Glavine allowed two runs in 6²/₃ innings.

AUGUST 15   The Mets score five runs in the top of the ninth inning for a 10–4 lead, then survive a four-run Pirate rally in the bottom half to win 10–8 in Pittsburgh.

AUGUST 20   The Mets trade Jose Castro and Sean Henry to the Reds for Jeff Conine.

SEPTEMBER 1   Mike Pelfrey (six innings), Guillermo Mota (one inning) and Pedro Feliciano (two innings) combine on a two-hitter to defeat the Braves 5–1 at Turner Field. Feliciano struck out five of the six batters he faced. The only Atlanta hits were singles by Mark Teixeira in the fourth inning and Jeff Francoeur in the seventh.

SEPTEMBER 3   In his first appearance of the 2007 season, Pedro Martinez records his 3,000th career strikeout during a 10–4 triumph over the Reds in Cincinnati. The victim of the milestone was Aaron Harang in the second inning. Martinez missed most of the 2007 campaign because of a torn rotator cuff.

SEPTEMBER 12 The Mets take a seven-game lead over the Phillies in the NL East race by beating the Braves 4–3 at Shea Stadium.

> *With the victory, the Mets had a record of 83–62, which was the best in the National League, one game ahead of the Diamondbacks. The Mets chances of reaching the playoffs were calculated by baseball statisticians at 99.8 percent.*

SEPTEMBER 18   The Mets drop a 9–8 decision to the Nationals in Washington for their fifth straight loss.

> *The five-game losing streak, which included three defeats at the hands of the Phillies at Shea Stadium on September 14, 15 and 16, cut the Mets' lead in the NL East to 1¹/₂ games.*

SEPTEMBER 20   The Mets score four runs in the top of the ninth inning for a 7–4 lead, but allow three in the bottom half and one in the tenth to lose 8–7 to the Marlins in Miami.

SEPTEMBER 23   The Mets outlast the Marlins to win 7–6 in 11 innings in Miami. David Wright drove in the winning run with a single.

> *The win gave the Mets a 2¹/₂–game lead over the Phillies in the NL East race, three up in the loss column, with seven to play. The Mets were also just one-half game back of the Diamondbacks in the race for home field advantage throughout the playoffs.*

SEPTEMBER 25   A six-run rally in the ninth inning falls short, and the Mets lose 10–9 to the Nationals at Shea Stadium. A three-run homer by Jose Reyes made the score 10–6. Moises Alou added a three-run double with one out, but the Mets couldn't bring him across the plate.

SEPTEMBER 27   The Mets fall into a tie for first place with the Phillies as a result of a 3–0 loss to the Cardinals at Shea Stadium. The Cards came to New York for a one-game series because of a rainout on June 28.

> *With three games remaining, the Mets and the Phillies both had records of 87–72. The Mets had a three-game series at Shea against the Marlins. The Phils traveled to Washington for three against the Nationals.*

SEPTEMBER 28   The Mets drop into second place with a 7–4 loss to the Marlins at Shea Stadium. The club was also one game behind the Padres in the wild-card race. The Mets had been in first place since May 15.

SEPTEMBER 29   The Mets move back into a tie for first place with a 13–0 thrashing of the Marlins at Shea Stadium while the Phillies lose 4–2 to the Nationals in Washington. John Maine had a no-hitter in progress with 14 strikeouts when Paul Hoover singled with two out in the eighth inning. It was only Hoover's eighth hit as a major leaguer. Willie Collazo (one-third of an inning) and Carlos Muniz (one inning) completed the one-hitter.

SEPTEMBER 30   The Mets miss out on the playoffs with an 8–1 loss to the Marlins at Shea Stadium while the Phillies defeat the Nationals 6–1 in Washington. The suspense was over early, as Tom Glavine allowed seven runs in the first inning while retiring only one batter.

> *The Mets let the seven-game advantage of September 12 slip away by going 5–12 while the Phillies posted a record of 13–4.*

NOVEMBER 18   Tom Glavine signs with the Braves as a free agent.

Glavine was 2–4 with a 5.54 ERA for the Braves in 2008 in what proved to be his last year in the majors. He finished his career with a record of 305–203.

DECEMBER 10   Paul Lo Duca signs with the Nationals as a free agent.

2008

Season in a Sentence

In the last season at Shea Stadium, the Mets blow a chance for the playoffs on the last game of the season for the second year in a row with a loss to the Marlins.

Finish • Won • Lost • Pct • GB

Second   89   73   .549   3.0

In the wild-card race, the Mets finished in second place, one game behind.

Managers

Willie Randolph (34–35) and Jerry Manuel (55–38)

Starting Lineup

Brian Schneider, c
Carlos Delgado, 1b
Luis Castillo, 2b
David Wright, 3b
Jose Reyes, ss
Fernando Tatis, lf
Carlos Beltran, cf
Ryan Church, rf
Damion Easley, 2b
Endy Chavez, rf-lf

Pitchers

Johan Santana, sp
Mike Pelfrey, sp
Oliver Perez, sp
John Maine, sp
Pedro Martinez, sp
Billy Wagner, rp
Aaron Heilman, rp
Joe Smith, rp
Scott Schoeneweis, rp
Pedro Martinez, rp
Duaner Sanchez, rp

Attendance

4,042,045 (first in NL)

Club Leaders

Batting Avg:	David Wright	.302
On-Base Pct:	David Wright	.390
Slugging Pct:	David Wright	.534
Home Runs:	Carlos Delgado	38
RBI:	David Wright	124
Runs:	Carlos Beltran	116
Stolen Bases:	Jose Reyes	56
Wins:	Johan Santana	16
Strikeouts:	Johan Santana	202
ERA:	Johan Santana	2.53
Saves:	Billy Wagner	27

JANUARY 5   The Mets trade Ryan Meyers and Corey Coles to the Cubs for Angel Pagan.

FEBRUARY 2   The Mets trade Carlos Gomez, Philip Humber, Kevin Mulvey and Deolis Garcia to the Twins for Johan Santana.

Santana came to the Mets as a 30-year-old with a 93–44 career record and Cy Young Awards in 2004 and 2006. In his first season in New York, Santana led the NL in ERA (2.53) and innings pitched (234^1/$_3$) while striking out 202 batters and posting a 16–7 record. He was 13–9 in 2009 and 11–9 in 2010 in seasons plagued by injures.

MARCH 31   The Mets open the season with a 7–2 win over the Marlins in Miami. A six-run New York fourth inning broke a scoreless tie. David Wright drove in three runs with a pair of doubles. Johan Santana, in his Mets debut, pitched seven innings and allowed two runs and three hits with eight strikeouts.

Wayne Hagin became part of the Mets radio broadcasting team in 2008.

APRIL 2   The Mets maul the Marlins 13–0 in Miami. Oliver Perez (three innings), Nelson Figueroa (one inning), Pedro Feliciano (one inning) and Billy Wagner (one inning) combined on the shutout.

APRIL 8   In the home opener, the Mets lose 5–2 to the Phillies before 56,350 at Shea Stadium. Carlos Delgado homered in the losing cause.

APRIL 11   Nelson Figueroa (six innings), Joe Smith (one inning), Aaron Heilman (one inning) and Billy Wagner (one inning) combine on a two-hitter to defeat the Brewers 4–2 at Shea Stadium. The only Milwaukee hits were doubles by J. J. Hardy in the fifth inning and Prince Fielder in the sixth. It was Figueroa's first major league win since 2003 when he was a member of the Pirates.

APRIL 15   David Wright hits a home run, two doubles and a single and drives in five runs during a 6–0 triumph over the Nationals at Shea Stadium. Mike Pelfrey (seven innings), Aaron Heilman (one inning) and Duaner Sanchez (one inning) combined on the shutout.

Wright batted .302 with 115 runs, 42 doubles, 33 homers and 124 RBIs in 2008.

APRIL 17   The Mets edge the Nationals 3–2 in 14 innings at Shea Stadium. The winning run crossed the plate on a bases-loaded wild pitch by Joel Hanrahan in the 14th.

APRIL 18   David Wright contributes a triple, two doubles and a single in four at-bats during a 6–4 victory over the Phillies in Philadelphia.

APRIL 23   The Mets play at Nationals Park in Washington for the first time and win 7–2.

MAY 2   Jose Reyes delivers two triples, a double and a single to lead the Mets to a 7–2 win over the Diamondbacks in Phoenix.

Reyes batted .297 with 16 homers and 56 stolen bases in addition to league leading figures in hits (204) and triples (19) in 2008.

MAY 6   At the age of 41, Moises Alou steals home in the third inning of a 5–4 loss to the Dodgers in Los Angeles. It was accomplished as part of a double steal, with Angel Pagan swiping second.

MAY 7   The Mets score six runs in the fifth inning and crush the Dodgers 12–1 in Los Angeles.

MAY 14   Mike Pelfrey holds the Nationals hitless through six innings, but winds up losing 1–0 at Shea Stadium. The first of four Washington hits was a single by Aaron Boone leading off the seventh.

MAY 24   In his first major league game, left fielder Nick Evans collects three doubles in four at-bats to help the Mets to a 9–2 victory over the Rockies in Denver.

MAY 28   After the Marlins score in the top of the 12th, Fernando Tatis belts a two-run, walk-off double in the bottom half to lift the Mets to a 7–6 victory at Shea Stadium. Florida collected only five hits in the game, but four of them were home runs.

           The 2008 Mets were the first in the majors since 1968 to have four players appear in at least 159 games. The four were Carlos Beltran (161), David Wright (160), Carlos Delgado (159) and Jose Reyes (159).

JUNE 3   The Mets break a 1–1 tie with eight runs in the fifth inning and defeat the Giants 9–6 in San Francisco.

JUNE 5   In the first round of the amateur draft, the Mets select first baseman Ike Davis from Arizona State University.

           Davis is the son of Ron Davis, who pitched in the majors from 1978 through 1988 with the Yankees, Twins, Cubs, Dodgers and Giants. Ike made his major league debut two weeks into the 2010 season and appeared in 147 of the club's last 150 games. He finished his rookie campaign with a .264 batting average and 19 home runs.

JUNE 11   A two-run, walk-off homer by Carlos Beltran with two out in the ninth inning beats the Diamondbacks 5–3 at Shea Stadium.

           Beltran batted .284 with 40 doubles, 27 homers, 116 runs and 112 RBIs in 2008.

JUNE 13   The Mets play the Rangers for the first time at Shea Stadium and win 7–1.

           On the same day, the Mets purchased Trot Nixon from the Diamondbacks.

JUNE 17   With the club holding a record of 34–35, the Mets fire Willie Randolph as manager following a 9–6 win over the Angels in Anaheim. Also fired were coaches Rick Peterson and Tom Nieto. Randolph was replaced by bench coach Jerry Manuel. The dismissal was announced at 3:12 a.m. Eastern Time. Omar Minaya flew coast to coast on the first day of a West Coast road trip to deliver the bad news to Randolph. The Mets' front office was pilloried in the media for the embarrassingly unprofessional nature of the firing. Randolph had angered club ownership during the previous few weeks by suggesting in newspaper interviews that some of the criticism directed at him was racially motivated and that the Mets television announcers went out of their way to portray him in a negative light. Manuel was 54 years old. He was a second baseman in the majors from 1975 through 1982 with three clubs and hit only .150 in 96 games and 127 at-bats. He was a coach with the Expos from 1991 through 1996 and was Jim Leyland's bench coach on the 1997 world champion Marlins. A stint as manager for the White Sox followed from 1998 through 2003 to a record of 500–471. Manuel's club in 2000 posted the best record in the AL, but lost in the first round of the playoffs. He had been a coach with the Mets since 2005. Under Manuel in 2008, the club went 55–38 and took a 3½–game lead with 17 contests remaining, only to finish second to the Phillies. Following losing seasons in both 2009 and 2010, Manuel was fired.

JUNE 18   A home run by Damion Easley in the tenth inning downs the Angels 5–4 in Anaheim. David Wright tied the score 4–4 with a two-out single in the ninth.

JUNE 23   Felix Hernandez of the Mariners becomes the first American League pitcher since 1971 to hit a grand slam when he delivers one off Johan Santana in the second inning of a 5–2 Seattle win over the Mets at Shea Stadium.

JUNE 27   The Mets and Yankees play two games in two different ballparks in a single day for the third time in history. The previous two were in 2000 and 2003. The double-header was scheduled because of a rainout at Yankee Stadium on May 16. In the afternoon at Yankee Stadium, Carlos Delgado set a Mets record with nine runs batted in during a 15–6 win. Delgado was in the lineup as a designated hitter. He hit a two-run double in the fifth inning off Edwar Ramirez, a grand slam against Ross Ohlendorf in the sixth, and a three-run homer facing LaTroy Hawkins in the eighth. The game began at 2:10 p.m. and ended at 6:04 p.m. Under the lights at Shea Stadium in an 8:10 p.m. start, the Mets lost 9–0.

JULY 3   The Mets score six runs in the third inning for a 9–0 lead and clobber the Cardinals 11–1 in St. Louis.

JULY 6   A two-run homer by Fernando Tatis in the 12th inning beats the Phillies 4–2 at Citizens Bank Park. Philadelphia tied the score 2–2 on a two-run homer by Jayson Werth off Billy Wagner on a 1–2 pitch with two out in the ninth.

Tatis was a pleasant surprise in 2008. He was signed by the Mets in 2007 and spent the entire year at the club's Triple A farm club in New Orleans. After starting the 2008 campaign in New Orleans, Tatis was called up in May. At the time, he was 33 and had played in only 28 big-league games since 2003. Tatis didn't play professional baseball at all in 2004 and 2005, spending those two years helping raise money to build a church in his native Dominican Republic. Tatis wound up batting .297 for the Mets in 2008 with 11 home runs in 273 at-bats. He also had to learn a new position, moving to left field after playing at third base for most of his career.

JULY 7   After taking a 10–1 lead in the sixth inning, the Mets survive to beat the Phillies 10–9 in Philadelphia.

JULY 12   Five Mets pitchers combine on a one-hitter to defeat the Rockies 3–0 at Shea Stadium. The one-hitter was achieved by Pedro Martinez (four innings), Carlos Muniz (two innings), Aaron Heilman (one inning), Scott Schoeneweis (one inning) and Billy Wagner (one inning). The only Colorado hit was a single by Brad Hawpe in the fourth inning.

During a six-game span from July 8 through July 13, the Mets allowed only four runs and 20 hits. The club also became the first in major league history to allow three hits or less in five straight games, which was accomplished from July 8 through July 12.

JULY 17   The Mets score four runs in the ninth inning to beat the Reds 10–8 in HERE Cincinnati. David Wright tied the score with a two-run homer. Three consecutive singles by Carlos Beltran, Damion Easley and Carlos Delgado and a double from Fernando Tatis produced two more runs.

JULY 20   Billy Wagner strikes out all three batters he faces in the tenth inning to close out a 7–5 win over the Reds in Cincinnati.

JULY 24   Mike Pelfrey strikes out 12 batters in $7^2/_3$ innings of a 3–1 victory over the Phillies at Shea Stadium.

JULY 26   Skip Schumaker of the Cardinals collects six hits in seven at-bats during a 14-inning, 10–8 win over the Mets at Shea Stadium.

> The Mets drew a franchise record 4,042,045 fans in 2008. The club also led the National League in attendance for the first time since 1988. Unless the capacity of Citi Field is increased, the record will stand for all time. Even if the Mets sell out all 81 home games at the new ballpark, they will fall short of 4,000,000.

AUGUST 8   Oliver Perez (seven innings) and Aaron Heilman (two innings) combine on a two-hitter to defeat the Marlins 3–0 at Shea Stadium. The only Florida hits were a double by Wes Helms in the second inning and a single from Cody Ross in the seventh.

AUGUST 13   The Mets score eight runs in the third inning of a 12–0 trouncing of the Nationals in Washington. John Maine (five innings) and Brian Stokes (four innings) combined on the shutout.

> Dan Murphy made his debut on August 2 and went on a tear during his first two weeks in the majors. He collected 14 hits, including two home runs, in his first 30 at-bats for an average of .467.

AUGUST 21   Carlos Delgado collects five hits, including a double, in five at-bats during a 5–4 victory over the Braves at Shea Stadium.

AUGUST 25   Carlos Delgado collects six RBIs on a pair of three-run homers in the first and seventh innings of a 9–1 win over the Astros at Shea Stadium.

> Delgado finished the season with a .271 batting average, 38 home runs and 115 RBIs.

AUGUST 29   A grand slam by Carlos Beltran in the top of the ninth inning off Kevin Gregg gives the Mets a 5–2 lead over the Marlins in Miami, and the club survives a two-run Florida rally in the bottom half to win 5–4.

SEPTEMBER 3   The Mets score six runs in the first inning and beat the Brewers 9–2 in Milwaukee. Ryan Church belted a grand slam off David Bush.

SEPTEMBER 10   The Mets outslug the Nationals 13–10 at Shea Stadium. David Wright led the offense with a home run, a double, two singles and four runs scored.

> The win gave the Mets an 82–63 record and a $3^1/_2$–game lead over the Phillies in the NL East race with 17 contests left on the schedule.

SEPTEMBER 16   The Mets blow their 3½–game advantage in just six days and drop out of first place with a 1–0 loss to the Nationals in Washington.

SEPTEMBER 19   The Mets regain first place with a 9–5 triumph over the Braves in Atlanta.

SEPTEMBER 20   The Mets' hold on first place lasts just one day as the club loses 4–2 to the Braves in Atlanta.

                 The Mets were one-half game behind the Phillies in the NL East race with eight games left to play, but were 2½ games ahead of the Brewers in the wild-card race.

SEPTEMBER 24   The Mets squander a 5–1, third-inning lead and lose 9–8 to the Cubs in ten innings at Shea Stadium.

                 With four games left, the Mets were 1½ games behind the Phillies in the NL East and tied with the Brewers at the head of the wild-card standings.

SEPTEMBER 25   The Mets maintain a tie for first place in the wild card chase with a 7–6 win over the Cubs at Shea Stadium. The winning run scored in the ninth inning on a single by Jose Reyes, a stolen base and another single from David Wright.

                 For the second straight year, the Mets closed the season with a three-game series against the Marlins at Shea Stadium with their postseason dreams on the line.

SEPTEMBER 26   The Mets fall one game behind in the wild-card race and two games out in the NL East by losing 6–1 to the Marlins at Shea Stadium. There were two games left to play.

SEPTEMBER 27   The Mets are eliminated from the NL East pennant race because of a victory by the Phillies, but move into a first-place tie in the wild-card race by beating the Marlins 2–0 at Shea Stadium. The Brewers lost 7–3 to the Cubs in Milwaukee. Johan Santana pitched a three-hit shutout for the Mets on three days' rest.

SEPTEMBER 28   In the last game ever played at Shea Stadium, the Mets are eliminated from postseason contention by losing 4–2 to the Marlins. The Brewers captured the wild card by beating the Cubs 3–1 in Milwaukee. Carlos Beltran tied the score 2–2 with a two-run homer in the sixth inning, but Florida scored twice in the eighth. The last pitch at Shea was delivered by Matt Lindstrom and resulted in a fly ball by Ryan Church to center fielder Cameron Maybin.

                 After the game, farewell ceremonies at Shea Stadium were held. What should have been a celebration of Shea's illustrious past was dampened considerably by the Mets second straight late-season collapse. Former players were introduced one by one, entering the field from behind the outfield wall. The last two to be presented were Tom Seaver and Mike Piazza. Others included Lenny Dykstra, Wally Backman, Jerry Koosman, Ed Charles, Dwight Gooden, Darryl Strawberry, Keith Hernandez, Ron Darling, Bud Harrelson, Robin Ventura, Ed Kranepool, Jesse Orosco, Sid Fernandez, Bobby Ojeda and Willie Mays. Seaver delivered one last pitch to Piazza before the players disappeared behind the center-field wall.

OCTOBER 14   Demolition work on Shea Stadium begins.

Stadium fragments and memorabilia were sold to fans. Seats went for $869 each. Other pieces marketed were the foul poles, dugouts, stadium signage and the giant letters that spelled out "SHEA" in front of the facility.

DECEMBER 9   Five weeks after Barack Obama defeats John McCain in the presidential election, the Mets sign Francisco Rodriguez, most recently with the Angels, as a free agent.

Rodriguez was signed at the age of 27 after a season in which he posted a major league-record 62 saves for the Angels. At the time of his signing, Rodriguez had a 2.35 career ERA in 451^2/$_3$ innings. After a so-so season as a closer with the Mets in 2009, Rodriguez was brilliant in 2010 before his season came to an end in mid-August after being arrested in a domestic dispute (see August 11, 2010).

DECEMBER 11   The Mets trade Aaron Heilman, Endy Chavez, Jason Vargas, Mike Carp, Joe Smith and Maikel Cleto to the Mariners for J. J. Putz, Sean Green and Jeremy Reed.

On the same day, investment manager Bernie Madoff was arrested on charges he defrauded clients of tens of billions of dollars in a massive Ponzi scheme. Among Madoff's clients was Mets owner, Fred Wilpon. Reports of Wilpon's losses vary, and some claim he actually made money in his dealings with the notorious Madoff, who was convicted and sentenced to 150 years in jail in 2009.

2009

Season in a Sentence

Possessing the highest payroll in the NL in the first year at Citi Field, an injury-riddled roster wins only 70 games.

Finish • Won • Lost • Pct • GB

Fourth   70   92   .432   23.0

In the wild-card race, the Mets finished tied for tenth place, 22 games behind.

Manager

Jerry Manuel

Stats	Mets	AL	Rank
Batting Avg:	.270	.259	1
On-Base Pct:	.335	.331	7
Slugging Pct:	.394	.409	12
Home Runs:	95	16	
Stolen Bases:	122	1	
ERA:	4.45	4.19	12
Errors:	97	11	
Runs Scored:	671	12	
Runs Allowed:	757	9	

Starting Lineup

Omir Santos, c
Dan Murphy, 1b
Luis Castillo, 2b
David Wright, 3b
Alex Cora, ss
Gary Sheffield, lf
Angel Pagan, cf
Jeff Francoeur, rf
Fernando Tatis, 1b-3b-lf
Carlos Beltran, cf
Ryan Church, rf

Pitchers

Johan Santana, sp
Mike Pelfrey, sp
Livan Hernandez, sp
John Maine, sp
Tim Redding, sp
Francisco Rodriguez, rp
Bobby Parnell, rp
Brian Stokes, rp
Sean Green, rp
Pedro Feliciano, rp

Attendance

3,168,571 (fifth in NL)

Club Leaders

Batting Avg:	David Wright	.307
On-Base Pct:	David Wright	.390
Slugging Pct:	David Wright	.440
Home Runs:	Dan Murphy	12
RBI:	David Wright	72
Runs:	David Wright	88
Stolen Bases:	David Wright	27
Wins:	Johan Santana	13
Strikeouts:	Johan Santana	146
ERA:	Johan Santana	3.13
Saves:	Francisco Rodriguez	35

JANUARY 22   The Mets sign Alex Cora, most recently with the Red Sox, as a free agent.

JANUARY 31   Fans are allowed to say good-bye one last time to Shea Stadium with an open invitation to the demolition site. Only a small portion of the lower stands remained when a crowd of 100 came to pay their last respects.

FEBRUARY 14   The Mets sign Livan Hernandez, most recently with the Rockies, as a free agent.

FEBRUARY 18   The last remaining sections of Shea Stadium are demolished. Later, the locations of home plate, the pitcher's mound and the bases were marked in the parking lot of Citi Field.

MARCH 29   In the first event staged at Citi Field, St. John's defeats Georgetown 6–4 in a college baseball game before a crowd of 22,697. St. John's alum and former Mets reliever John Franco threw out the ceremonial first pitch.

APRIL 3   The Mets play at Citi Field for the first time and defeat the Red Sox 4–3 before 37,652. The game was delayed an hour and seven minutes by rain.

APRIL 4   In the second of two exhibition games against the Red Sox, the Mets lose 9–3 at Citi Field. Jed Lowrie hit the first home run by a major leaguer at the new facility with a blast off Oliver Perez during Boston's six-run first inning. The temperature was 48 degrees with a 21-miles-per-hour wind blowing out to right field.

APRIL 5   The Mets sign Gary Sheffield, most recently with the Tigers, as a free agent.

> *Sheffield was 40 when signed, had 499 career home runs and was coming off a season in Detroit in which he hit .225 along with 19 homers in 418 at-bats. In 100 games and 268 at-bats in 2009, he batted .276 and hit ten home runs.*

APRIL 6   The Mets open the season with a 2–1 win over the Reds in Cincinnati. Dan Murphy drove in both runs with a home run in the fifth inning and a sacrifice fly in the sixth. Johan Santana (5 2/3 innings), Sean Green (1 1/3 innings), J. J. Putz (one inning) and Francisco Rodriguez (one inning) combined on a three hitter.

APRIL 12   Johan Santana strikes out 13 batters in seven innings, but the Mets lose 2–1 to the Marlins in Miami.

APRIL 13   In the first regular-season game at Citi Field, the Mets lose 6–5 to the Padres before 41,944. The temperature at game time was 54 degrees with a 13-miles-per-hour wind blowing out to center field. San Diego leadoff batter Judy Gerut homered on the third pitch of the game from Mike Pelfrey. It was the first time in major league history that the first batter in a new ballpark hit a home run. David Wright struck the first Mets homer at Citi Field with a three-run shot in the fifth that tied the score 5–5. The Padres broke the deadlock in the sixth on a balk by Pedro Feliciano that brought a runner home from third base.

> *The ceremonial pitch mimicked the last one at Shea Stadium (see September 28, 2008). Tom Seaver and Mike Piazza, each wearing Mets uniforms, emerged from the center-field fence and walked to the diamond. Seaver threw a strike to Piazza and pumped his fist in the air.*

APRIL 15   In the second game at Citi Field, the Mets record their first regular-season win at the ballpark with a 7–2 decision over the Padres.

> *Before the contest, the Jackie Robinson Rotunda was formally dedicated. It was the 62nd anniversary of Robinson's first major league game. The 160-foot diameter rotunda with 70-foot arched windows contained photographs of Robinson and an eight-foot-high statue of his number 42. His widow, Rachel Robinson, spoke to the crowd. In honor of Robinson, every player in the major leagues wore number 42 during the day.*

APRIL 17   During a 5–4 win over the Brewers at Citi Field, Gary Sheffield records his 500th career home run. It was also his first as a member of the Mets and was struck as a pinch-hitter off Mitch Stetter in the seventh inning.

APRIL 18   Johan Santana (seven innings), J. J. Putz (one inning) and Francisco Rodriguez (one inning) join forces on a shutout to defeat the Brewers 1–0 at Citi Field.

APRIL 27   John Maine (six innings), Sean Green (one inning), J. J. Putz (one inning) and Francisco Rodriguez (one inning) combine on a two-hitter to beat the Marlins 7–1 at Shea Stadium. The only Florida hits were singles by Jorge Cantu in the first inning and Emilio Bonifacio in the eighth. Omir Santos hit a grand slam off Anibal Sanchez in the six-run first inning.

Citi Field

Shea Stadium was considered to be a state-of-the-art facility when it opened in 1964. It was constructed during a period in which cities were designing multi-purpose stadiums for both baseball and football, and the tenants at Shea were the Mets and the Jets. Other municipalities building the hybrid stadiums included Washington, St. Louis, Atlanta, Oakland, San Diego, Cincinnati, Pittsburgh and Philadelphia. By the 1990s, these stadiums had fallen out of favor, particularly with baseball fans, because the rounded stands put them too far from the action. By 2008, Shea was the fifth-oldest stadium in baseball behind Fenway Park (1912), Wrigley Field (1914), Yankee Stadium (1923) and Dodger Stadium (1962). Yankee Stadium was extensively renovated between 1973 and 1976.

A revolution in baseball stadium design began in 1992 with the opening of Camden Yards in Baltimore. The so-called "retro" ballparks soon followed from coast to coast, and the once-resplendent multi-purpose stadiums like Shea were going the way of the dinosaur.

A new ballpark for the Mets was in the planning stages as early as 1998. The initial designs placed it adjacent to Shea with stands holding 45,000, a retractable dome and a grass field on a platform that could be rolled out into the parking lot to receive sunshine and moisture. By the time the Mets' new home was built, the capacity was reduced to 42,000, and the plans for the dome and movable field were scrapped.

Shortly before leaving office in December 2001, New York City Mayor Rudy Giuliani announced "tentative agreements" for new ballparks for both the Mets and Yankees. But Michael Bloomberg, Giuliani's successor, said the city couldn't afford to build new stadiums for the ball clubs. By 2006, however, agreements were in place for the new

facilities, and ground was broken on the future sites of Citi Field and the new Yankee Stadium.

Fred Wilpon, a Brooklyn native, wanted his new ballpark to be evocative of Ebbets Field, home of the Dodgers from 1913 through 1957. The exterior facade of Citi Field is reminiscent of Ebbets Field as well as the rotunda behind the main entrance. Named the Jackie Robinson Rotunda, it had a 160-foot diameter floor, with many features celebrating the life of the man who broke baseball's color barrier in 1947.

Many fans complained that Citi Field had an overemphasis on the history of the Brooklyn Dodgers at the expense of the Mets' legacy. In response to the criticism, the team installed photographic imagery of famous players and historic moments in Mets history on the field and promenade levels. More Mets colors, banners and logos were added. There were also problems with obstructed views from many of the promenade seats. In addition, visiting players had an obstructed view of the field from their bullpen. This was resolved prior to the 2010 season by turning the bullpens 90 degrees, with the pitchers throwing toward the field instead of across it.

Early indications are that Citi Field will be a pitcher's park, perhaps an extreme one. During the first season at the ballpark, the Mets led the league in batting average (.270) but were least in home runs (95). In 2010, the club was 13th in both batting average and homers. During those two seasons, there were 1,309 runs scored by the Mets and their opposition in 162 games at Citi Field. On the road, there were 1,427 runs scored in 162 contests involving the Mets. Using those figures, the new ballpark reduced scoring output by 8.3 percent.

The dimensions at the opening of Citi Field were 335 feet down the left-field line, 330 in right and 408 in dead center, with fence heights ranging from eight feet to 18. In 2010, the height of the center-field fence was reduced from 16 feet to eight.

With both the team and the economy in turmoil, ticket prices were slashed in August 2009, with more cuts forthcoming during the following offseason. Attendance dropped from 3,168,571 in 2009 to 2,559,738 in 2010.

MAY 6	The Mets collect only two hits, but beat the Phillies 1–0 at Citi Field. Johan Santana (seven innings), Pedro Feliciano (one inning) and Francisco Rodriguez (one inning) combined on a three-hitter.

Feliciano led the NL in games pitched three seasons in a row with 86 in 2008, 88 in 2009 and 92 in 2010. Those are also the three highest figures by a pitcher in a single season in Mets history. Through the end of the 2010 season, Feliciano's 459 games pitched ranked second to John Franco's 695.

MAY 13	Fernando Tatis hits a grand slam off Buddy Carlisle in the fourth inning, but the Mets lose 8–7 to the Braves in ten innings at Citi Field.

The Mets peaked on May 16 with a 21–15 record and a 1½-game lead in the NL East. An unbelievable string of injuries led to the collapse, which resulted in a 49–77 record the rest of the way. Nearly every regular and starting pitcher missed a significant period of time on the disabled list. Angel Pagan led the Mets in games played in the outfield with 84. Gary Sheffield wound up leading the Mets in games played in left field with 46.

MAY 23	A two-out, two-run homer in the ninth inning by Omir Santos off Jonathan Papelbon beats the Red Sox 3–2 in Boston.
JUNE 9	The Mets make their first pick in the amateur draft with the selection of pitcher Steven Matz from Ward Melville High School in East Setauket, New York. Matz was chosen in the second round. The club lost its first round pick for signing Francisco Rodriguez as a free agent.
JUNE 12	In the first Mets-Yankees game at the new Yankee Stadium, second baseman Luis Castillo drops a pop-up, which results in a 9–8 loss. The Mets led 8–7 with two out in the ninth inning with Derek Jeter on second base and Mark Teixeira on first. Alex Rodriguez lifted a routine pop-up, which Castillo fumbled, allowing Jeter and Teixeira to race across the plate.
JUNE 14	The Yankees score nine runs in the fourth inning for a 13–0 lead and clobber the Mets 15–0 at Yankee Stadium.
JUNE 24	The Mets crush the Cardinals 11–0 at Citi Field. Fernando Nieve (six innings), Brian Stokes (one inning), Pat Misch (one inning) and Bobby Parnell (one inning) combined on the shutout.
JUNE 26	In the first Mets-Yankees matchup at Citi Field, the Mets lose 9–1.

JULY 1   Mike Pelfrey ($7^2/_3$ innings), Sean Green (one-third of an inning) and Francisco Rodriguez (one inning) combine to defeat the Brewers 1–0 in Milwaukee. A double by Luis Castillo and a single from Ryan Church in the sixth inning produced the lone run.

JULY 10   The Mets trade Jeff Francoeur to the Braves for Ryan Church.

JULY 14   Francisco Rodriguez retires all three batters he faces in the ninth inning, but the National League loses 4–3 in the All-Star Game at Busch Stadium in St. Louis.

JULY 27   Fernando Tatis hits a pinch-hit grand slam off Franklin Morales in the eighth inning, which breaks a 3–3 tie and results in a 7–3 defeat of the Rockies at Citi Field.

> *On the same day, the Mets fired vice-president of player development, Tony Bernazard. Several transgressions led to the dismissal of Bernazard. In one instance, he removed his shirt and challenged several members of the Class AA Binghampton Mets to a fight. In another, Bernazard went into a tirade in the Citi Field stands over the seating assignment for his scouts and those of the Arizona Diamondbacks. He also got into an angry confrontation with Francisco Rodriguez on the team bus.*

AUGUST 1   Angel Pagan hits a grand slam in the eighth inning off Clay Zavada, breaking a 5–5 tie and resulting in a 9–6 triumph over the Diamondbacks at Citi Field.

AUGUST 7   The Padres score five runs in the ninth inning off Francisco Rodriguez and beat the Mets 6–2 at Petco Park. A walk and a double led to the first run. Two more walks, one of them intentional, loaded the bases prior to a walk-off grand slam by Everth Cabrera.

AUGUST 23   The Mets lose an event-filled 9–7 decision to the Phillies at Citi Field. Philadelphia scored six runs in the top of the first inning before Angel Pagan led off the bottom half with an inside-the-park homer. The ball was briefly lodged under the padding of the center-field wall. Phils center fielder Shane Victorino lifted his arms hoping for a ground rule double, but second base umpire Rob Drake let play continue. In the ninth, the Mets had Dan Murphy on first base and Luis Castillo on second with no one out. With Jeff Francoeur at bat and a 2–2 count, Murphy and Castillo took off on an attempted double steal. Francoeur lined the pitch to second baseman Eric Bruntlett, who stepped on second base to force Castillo and tagged Murphy for an unassisted triple. It was only the 15th unassisted triple play in major league history, and just the second to end a game. It was the first involving the Mets.

AUGUST 25   The Mets trade Billy Wagner to the Red Sox for Chris Carter and Eddie Lora.

SEPTEMBER 12   The Mets score three runs in the eighth inning and two in the ninth to beat the Phillies 10–9 in Philadelphia. The tallies in the ninth scored on a two-out, two-run homer by David Wright.

> *Wright led the Mets in nearly every offensive category in 2009, but had an off year with a .307 batting average and ten homers.*

SEPTEMBER 25   A two-run single by pinch-hitter Cory Sullivan in the ninth inning beats the Marlins 6–5 in Miami.

OCTOBER 4   At 35, Nelson Figueroa records the first complete game shutout of his career with a 4–0 win over the Astros at Citi Field. Angel Pagan contributed a triple, two doubles and a single in four at-bats.

DECEMBER 1   Brian Schneider signs with the Phillies as a free agent.

DECEMBER 29   The Mets sign Jason Bay, most recently with the Red Sox, as a free agent.

     The Best of The Mets

The following is a 25-man roster of the best players ever to don a Mets uniform. Only the years spent with the franchise are taken into consideration.

Pitchers
Tom Seaver, p
Jerry Koosman, p
Dwight Gooden, p
John Matlack, p
Sid Fernandez, p
Al Leiter, p
David Cone, p
John Franco, rp
Tug McGraw, rp
Jesse Orosco. rp

Starting lineup
Mike Piazza, c
Keith Hernandez, 1b
Edgardo Alfonso, 2b
David Wright, 3b
Jose Reyes, ss
Cleon Jones, lf
Carlos Beltran, cf
Darryl Strawberry, rf

Bench
John Stearns, c
John Olerud, 1b
Howard Johnson, 3b

Bud Harrelson, ss
Kevin McReynolds, of
Mookie Wilson, of
Lenny Dykstra, of
    Choosing the catcher to "back up" Piazza was a tough call as Gary Carter is a member of the Hall of Fame and twice drove in over 100 runs with the Mets, but played with the club for only five years. Ultimately, the spot went to Stearns, who played with the franchise for ten seasons. Alfonso is the best second baseman in Mets history, although he played almost as many games at third as a Met, with 524 at second and 515 at the hot corner. Other than Alfonso, the Mets have had few solid players at second. Wally Backman is the franchise career leader in games played at the position with 680. The Mets fielded a string of mediocrities at third over the first 25 seasons of franchise history, but the club has had All-Stars at the position for most the last 25, including Johnson, Alfonso and Wright. Beltran is one of three 2010 Mets to make the "starting lineup" along with Wright and Reyes. Other prominent Mets players include Dave Magadan, Wayne Garrett, Jerry Grote, Lee Mazzilli, Tommie Agee, Ed Kranepool, Ron Darling, Rick Reed, Johan Santana and Craig Swan.

2010

Season in a Sentence

The Mets suffer through a second straight losing season, resulting in the firing of Omar Minaya and Jerry Manuel.

Finish • Won • Lost • Pct • GB

Fourth   79   83   .488   18.0

In the wild-card race, the Mets finished in seventh place, 11 games behind.

Stats

	Mets	AL	Rank
Batting Avg:	.249	.255	13
On-Base Pct:	.314	.324	14
Slugging Pct:	.383	.399	12
Home Runs:	128	13	
Stolen Bases:	130	1	
ERA:	3.73	4.02	6
Errors:	87	5	
Runs Scored:	656	13	
Runs Allowed:	652	6	

Club Leaders

Batting Avg:	Angel Pagan	.290
On-Base Pct:	David Wright	.354
Slugging Pct:	David Wright	.503
Home Runs:	David Wright	29
RBI:	David Wright	103
Runs:	David Wright	87
Stolen Bases:	Angel Pagan	37
Wins:	Mike Pelfrey	15
Strikeouts:	Jonathan Niese	148
ERA:	R. A. Dickey	2.84
Saves:	Francisco Rodriguez	25

Attendance

2,559,738 (8th in NL)

Starting Lineup

Rod Barajas, c
Ike Davis, 1b
Luis Castillo, 2b
David Wright, 3b
Jose Reyes, ss
Jason Bay, lf
Angel Pagan, cf
Jeff Francoeur, rf
Ruben Tejada, 2b-ss
Carlos Beltran, cf

Pitchers

Mike Pelfrey, sp
Johan Santana, sp
R. A. Dickey, sp
Jonathon Niese, sp
Francisco Rodriguez, rp
Hisanori Takahashi, rp
Pedro Feliciano, rp
Elmer Dessens, rp

JANUARY 5   The Mets sign R. A. Dickey, most recently with the Twins, as a free agent.

Dickey was a nice surprise in 2010. Entering the season, he was 35 with a lifetime 22–28 record and a 5.43 earned run average. He began the 2010 campaign at Triple AAA Buffalo before being called up on May 19. With the Mets in 2010, Dickey was 11–9 with an ERA of 2.84.

JANUARY 22   The Mets trade Brian Stokes to the Angels for Gary Matthews.

FEBRUARY 11   The Mets sign Hisanori Takahashi, most recently with the Yomiyuri Giants of the Japanese Pacific League, as a free agent.

APRIL 5   The Mets open the season with a 7–1 victory over the Marlins before 41,245 at Citi Field. Johan Santana pitched six innings and allowed only one run. David Wright smacked a two-run homer in the first.

The Mets lost the first eight Opening Days in franchise history from 1962 through 1969, but from 1970 through 2010, the club was 32–9 in the first game of the season.

APRIL 17   The Mets outlast the Cardinals 2–1 in 20 innings at Busch Stadium. There was no scoring through the first 18 innings. The Cardinals left the bases loaded in the 10th, 13th and 14th innings and stranded 22 runners. Mets pitchers over the first 18 innings were Johan Santana (seven innings), Ryoto Igarashi (1^{1}/$_{3}$ innings), Pedro Feliciano (1^{1}/$_{3}$ innings), Fernando Nieve (2^{1}/$_{3}$ innings), Hisanori Takahashi (two innings), Jenrry Mejia (two innings) and Raul Valdes (two innings). The Mets were held hitless by Jaime Garcia until Angel Pagan singled in the sixth. That was the lone New York hit through the first 11 innings off Garcia and three relievers. In the top of the 18th, Tony LaRussa moved Felipe Lopez from third base to pitch and inserted Kyle Lohse, normally a starting pitcher, in left field. Lopez, who was the ninth St. Louis pitcher, got out of the inning without allowing a run. In the 19th, Lopez went back to third, and Joe Mather pitched. Mather entered the game as a pinch-hitter in the tenth and played center field and third base before taking the mound. The Mets loaded the bases on a walk, a sacrifice bunt, an intentional walk and a hit batsman before Jeff Francoeur delivered a sacrifice fly for a 1–0 lead. But Francisco Rodriguez blew a save in the bottom half, and the Cards tied the contest 1–1. In the 20th, with Mather still pitching, Pagan singled, moved to third on a single by Mike Jacobs and crossed the plate on a sacrifice fly from Jose Reyes. Mike Pelfrey pitched the 20th for the Mets and nailed down the save. It was his first relief appearance since 2007, his only one of the 2010 season, and his first career save. The Mets used 24 players in the game, while the Cards utilized 22. The Mets used nine pitchers; the Cardinals used ten. The game lasted six hours and 53 minutes.

The game was the fourth-longest in Mets history, by innings, following those of 25 innings (see September 11, 1974), 24 innings (see April 15, 1968) and 23 innings (see May 31, 1964). The Mets lost the previous three games of 20 innings or more.

APRIL 30   Ten days after an oil platform explodes in the Gulf of Mexico, killing 11 workers and sparking the worst oil spill in U.S. history, the Mets extend their winning streak to eight games with a 9–1 decision over the Phillies in Philadelphia.

The win gave the Mets a 14–9 record and a one-game lead in the NL East.

MAY 7   Rod Barajas wallops a two-run, walk-off homer in the ninth inning to down the Giants 6–4 at Citi Field. It was his second home run of the game.

MAY 8   A Mets catcher hits a walk-off homer for the second game in a row as Henry Blanco connects in the 11th inning to beat the Giants 5–4 at Citi Field.

MAY 11   Trailing 6–2, the Mets erupt for six runs in the eighth inning to beat the Nationals 8–6 at Citi Field. Five different players drove in runs during the big inning. A two-run double by Rod Barajas brought the Mets within a run. Angel Pagan tied the contest with a run-scoring single. Pinch-hitter Chris Carter broke the deadlock by delivering an RBI-double.

The double came in Carter's first plate appearance with the Mets and was his first career double. He previously played 13 games with the Red Sox in 2008 and 2009.

MAY 19   Angel Pagan hits an inside-the-park homer and starts a triple play, but the Mets lose 5–3 to the Nationals in Washington. Pagan collected the inside-the-park home run in the fourth inning. The triple play occurred in the fifth. The base runners were Nyger Morgan on first and Livan Hernandez on second. Christian Guzman hit a line drive to Pagan in center field, which he nabbed with a shoestring catch. Both runners, expecting the ball to drop, kept moving. Pagan overthrew second base, but catcher Henry Blanco caught the ball and tossed it to shortstop Jose Reyes, who stepped on second to retire Hernandez. Morgan was out on a throw from Reyes to first baseman Ike Davis.

The Mets were the first major league team with an inside-the-park homer and a triple play in the same game since the Phillies accomplished the feat on September 25, 1955. In that contest, shortstop Ted Kazanski, like Pagan, hit the inside-the-park homer and started the triple play.

MAY 25   R. A. Dickey (six innings) and Raul Valdes (three innings) combine to shut out the Phillies 8–0 at Citi Field.

MAY 26   Hisanori Takahashi (six innings), Jenrry Mejia (one inning), Ryoto Igarashi (one inning) and Fernando Nieve (one inning) combine on a 5–0 defeat of the Phillies at Citi Field.

MAY 27   The Mets shut out the Phillies at Citi Field for the third game in a row and win 3–0. Mike Pelfrey (seven innings), Pedro Feliciano (one inning) and Francisco Rodriguez (one inning) combined on the shutout.

MAY 28   The Mets' bid for a fourth straight shutout ends with a 2–0 loss to the Brewers at Miller Park. The game was scoreless until the bottom of the ninth, and the Mets had completed 35 consecutive innings without allowing a run. Johan Santana pitched the first eight innings and gave way to Pedro Feliciano, who retired the first batter in the ninth. Ryoto Igarashi relieved Feliciano and surrendered a single to Ryan Braun and a two-run walk-off homer to Corey Hart.

JUNE 2   Adrian Gonzalez hits a walkoff grand slam off Raul Valdes in the 11th inning to beat the Mets 5–1 at Petco Park. San Diego tied the score 1–1 with a run with two out in the ninth.

Mets batters failed to hit a single grand slam in 2010, while the pitching staff surrendered 12 of them. The 12-figure gap between grand slams hit and grand slams allowed is the largest in major league history.

JUNE 7   With their first pick in the amateur draft, the Mets select pitcher Matt Harvey from the University of North Carolina.

JUNE 8   A pair of solo homers beats the Padres 2–1 in 11 innings at Citi Field. Jose Reyes hit a drive in the seventh that struck the wall just above the orange line on the left-field fence and bounced back onto the field. Third base umpire Mike DiMuro ruled the ball in play, but the decision was reversed by instant replay, and Reyes was credited with a home run. Ike Davis struck a walk-off blast in the 11th.

JUNE 10   Jonathon Niese retires the last 21 batters to face him and spins a one-hitter to beat the Padres 3–0 in the second game of a day-night double-header at Citi Field. The only San Diego hit was a double by Chris Denorfia leading off the third inning. The Padres won the opener 4–2.

Pop star Lady Gaga created a sensation during the first game. Sitting in a luxury box owned by Jerry Seinfeld, Lady Gaga stripped to her bra and bikini bottom and repeatedly flipped off fans and photographers with her middle finger.

JUNE 13   Jason Bay collects four hits, including a double and a homer, in four at-bats and scores four runs during an 11–4 trouncing of the Orioles in Baltimore.

JUNE 16   The Mets tie a record for a National League team with four consecutive doubles in the third inning of an 8–4 triumph over the Indians in Cleveland. The doubles were by Angel Pagan, David Wright, Ike Davis and Jason Bay, each off Mitch Talbot.

JUNE 18   The Mets extend their winning streak to eight games with a 4–0 decision over the Yankees at Yankee Stadium. Hisanori Takahashi (six innings), Pedro Feliciano (two innings), Raul Valdes (one-third of an inning) and Francisco Rodriguez (two-thirds of an inning) combined on the shutout.

The victory gave the Mets a 39–28 record and put the club one-half game behind the first-place Phillies. The Mets were 40–55 the rest of the way, however.

JUNE 22   The Mets score eight runs in the third inning for a 10–0 lead and rout the Tigers 14–6 at Citi Field.

JUNE 28   The Mets play the first game of a three-game series against the Marlins at Hiram Bithorn Stadium in San Juan, Puerto Rico, and lose 10–3.

JULY 6   Johan Santana pitches a complete game shutout and hits his first career home run during a 3–0 defeat of the Reds in Cincinnati. The homer was struck in a 12-pitch at-bat against Matt Maloney in the third inning. Santana fouled off nine pitches in a row. He was the first Mets pitcher to homer in a shutout since Pete Falcone did it in 1981.

JULY 28   David Wright hits two homers and drives in five runs, but the Mets lose 9–6 to the Diamondbacks at Citi Field.

Wright hit 29 homers, drove in 103 runs and batted .283 in 2010. Jose Reyes had a .282 batting average and 11 homers.

AUGUST 7   A home run by Jeff Francoeur off Cole Hamels in the seventh inning accounts for the lone run of a 1–0 win over the Phillies in Philadelphia. Johan Santana (7²/₃ innings) and Francisco Rodriguez (1¹/₃ innings) combined on the shutout.

The Mets were 9–9 against the Phillies in 2010, but five of the victories were shutouts.

AUGUST 10 Mike Pelfrey (seven innings), Hisanori Takahashi (one inning) and Francisco Rodriguez (one inning) combine to defeat the Rockies 1–0 at Citi Field. Jose Reyes drove in the lone run with a sacrifice fly in the seventh inning.

AUGUST 11 Francisco Rodriguez is arrested following a 6–2 loss to the Rockies at Citi Field.

Rodriguez was accused of assaulting Carlos Pena, the father of his girlfriend Daian Pena. Rodriguez was reportedly upset over remarks Carlos made about *his mother. Rodriguez was released without bail on August 12 and ordered by a judge to stay away from his girlfriend and her father. Rodriguez was suspended for two games by the Mets and pitched on August 14, but was placed on the disqualified list after that appearance with a torn ligament in his right thumb, possibly stemming from the altercation with Pena. The injury required season-ending surgery, and by placing him on the disqualified list, the Mets did not have to pay their closer until he was physically able to perform. Rodriguez was back in court on September 22 for sending text messages to the Penas in violation of the court order. The judge imposed a bond of $7,500, which Rodriguez posted.*

AUGUST 13   R. A. Dickey pitches a one-hitter to defeat the Phillies 1–0 at Citi Field. The only Philadelphia hit was a single by opposing pitcher Cole Hamels in the sixth inning. Carlos Beltran drove in the lone run with a double in the bottom of the sixth.

The one-hitter was the 33rd in Mets history of nine innings or more. There have been two other rain-shortened one-hitters. Through 2010, no Mets pitcher had ever thrown a no-hitter. Among the 33 one-hitters of at least nine innings, there have been 25 complete game one-hitters and eight by two or more pitchers. The 25 complete game one-hitters are by Tom Seaver (five), Gary Gentry (three), Jon Matlack (two), David Cone (two), Steve Trachsel (two) and one each by Al Jackson, Jack Hamilton, Nolan Ryan, Terry Leach, Dwight Gooden, Pete Schourek, Bobby J. Jones (in the 2000 NLDS), Shawn Estes, Aaron Heilman, Tom Glavine, Jonathon Niese and R. A. Dickey. The only two one-hitters in which the lone hit was collected in the ninth inning were by Seaver on July 9, 1969 and July 4, 1972. Mets with no-hitters either before or after playing for the club include Ryan (who pitched seven of them), Seaver, Gooden, Hideo Nomo (who had two), Cone (a perfect game as a Yankee), Don Cardwell, Dock Ellis, John Candelaria and Mike Scott.

AUGUST 18   The Mets outlast the Astros 3–2 in 14 innings in Houston. Ike Davis drove in the winning run with a sacrifice fly.

AUGUST 22   The Mets sell Rod Barajas to the Dodgers.

AUGUST 31   The Mets trade Jeff Francoeur to the Rangers for Joaquin Arias.

SEPTEMBER 5   The Mets collect 21 hits and thrash the Cubs 18–5 at Wrigley Field. The Mets score exactly five runs in the fifth, eighth and ninth innings.

SEPTEMBER 7   Dillon Gee makes his major league debut and allows only a run and two hits during a 4–1 victory over the Nationals in Washington. Gee did not surrender a hit until Willie Harris homered leading off the sixth inning.

SEPTEMBER 13   The Mets edge the Pirates 1–0 in ten innings at Citi Field. The tenth-inning run was created with a double by Ruben Tejada and a walk-off single from pinch-hitter Nick Evans. Dillon Gee (six innings in his second major league game), Elmer Dessens (one inning), Pedro Feliciano (one inning) and Hisanori Takahashi (two innings) combined on the shutout.

SEPTEMBER 15   Trailing 5–0, the Mets score seven runs in the fourth inning and move on to defeat the Pirates 8–7 at Citi Field.

SEPTEMBER 25   The Mets end their six-game losing streak and the 11-game winning streak of the Phillies with a 5–2 triumph in Philadelphia.

SEPTEMBER 28   Ruben Tejada belts a one-out, two-run, walk-off double to defeat the Brewers 4–3 at Citi Field.

OCTOBER 2   The Mets start seven rookies and beat the Nationals 7–2 at Citi Field. The seven were pitcher Raul Valdes (in his first major league start after 37 relief appearances), catcher Josh Thole, first baseman Ike Davis, second baseman Joaquin Arias, shortstop Ruben Tejada, left fielder Lucas Duda and right fielder Jesus Feliciano. Rookies Ryoto Igarashi (p) and Chris Carter (ph) played later in the contest.

OCTOBER 3   In the last game of the season, the Mets lose 2–1 to the Nationals in 14 innings at Citi Field. The winning run crossed the plate when Oliver Perez hit a batter, and then walked three in a row.

OCTOBER 4   Only one day after the end of the season, the Mets fire general manager Omar Minaya and manager Jerry Manuel. Minaya was hired in 2004 and appeared to have the team back on track when it almost made the World Series in 2006. But many of his free agent signings, chief among them Oliver Perez and Luis Castillo, failed to pan out. Others, such as Carlos Beltran, Pedro Martinez and Carlos Delgado, were beset with injuries. Manuel was tabbed by Minaya to guide the team from the dugout in June 2008. He posted a record of 204–212 in 2½ seasons.

OCTOBER 29   The Mets announce the hiring of 62-year-old Sandy Alderson as general manager.

> *A 1976 graduate of Harvard Law School, Alderson got into baseball in 1981 when his father-in-law, Roy Eisenhardt, became a partner in the ownership of the Oakland Athletics. Alderson was the A's general counsel before being promoted to general manager in 1983. Under Alderson, Oakland reached the World Series in 1988, 1989 and 1990, and won the world championship in 1989. Alderson left the Athletics in 1997 to work for Bud Selig in the commissioner's office as executive vice-president for baseball operations, a position he held until 2005. He was also CEO of the Padres from 2005 through 2009. At the time he was hired by the Mets, Alderson was back in the commissioner's office addressing issues involving the sport and the Dominican Republic.*

NOVEMBER 4   The Mets suspend clubhouse manager Charlie Samuels for betting on baseball. He was hired by the Mets in 1976 and served as clubhouse manager for 27 years.

NOVEMBER 23   The Mets introduce 61-year-old Terry Collins as manager for the 2011 season. Collins served as minor league field coordinator during the 2010 campaign. He never reached the majors as a player but managed in the minors in the Dodgers and Pirates organizations from 1981 through 1991 and was a coach with the Pirates at the major league level in 1992 and 1993. He managed the Astros from 1994 through 1996 and the Angles from 1997 through 1998 to an overall record of 463–444. His clubs in Houston and Anaheim finished in second place five seasons from 1994 through 1998 but none reached the postseason. Collins also managed teams in Japan from 2006 through 2008 and the Chinese national team in the World Baseball Classic in 2009.

DECEMBER 3   Francisco Rodriguez pleads guilty to attempted assault to settle charges he attacked his girlfriend's father (see August 11, 2010). The deal spared him jail time, but sent him to additional anger management classes.